MARIE OF ROMANIA
The Intimate Life of a 20th-Century Queen

MARIE OF ROMANIA

The Intimate Life
of a Twentieth Century Queen

Terence Elsberry

Cassell · London

CASSELL & COMPANY LTD
35 Red Lion Square, London WC1R 4SG
Sydney, Auckland
Toronto, Johannesburg

First published in Great Britain 1973

I.S.B.N. 0 304 29240 0

F. 1172

TO JANET

Acknowledgments

Most of Queen Marie's correspondence and the diaries she kept with unflagging persistence from Romania's entry into World War I until shortly before her death are held by the Communists in Romania. Therefore, I have based the bulk of my research on the personal reminiscences and papers in the possession of two people: the Queen's youngest daughter, the Reverend Mother Alexandra, and George I. Duca, the son of former Romanian Prime Minister Jean Duca.

Over a period of four years, they have graciously submitted to many hours of taped interviews, put me in contact with numerous helpful people both in this country and in Europe, and given me free access to all the relevant correspondence, unpublished manuscripts and photographs in their possession. I owe them both an inestimable debt of thanks.

For additional memories of Queen Marie and the people in her life, I wish to thank: Her Majesty Queen Helen, the Queen Mother of Romania; H.R.H. Prince Paul of Yugoslavia; H.R.H. Princess Olga of Yugoslavia; The Hon. Mrs. Spender-Clay; Lady Rachel Bowes-Lyon; Miss Ida Marr; Mrs. Marjorie Bowles; Mme. Elise Cretzianu; Mme. Alice Cantacuzene Lepoiac; and Mme. Marya Constantinesco.

I also acknowledge the gracious permission of Her Majesty Queen Elizabeth II to reproduce extracts from copies in the possession of the Rev. Mother Alexandra of certain correspondence relating to Queen

Marie preserved in the Royal Archives at Windsor Castle. They are: the November 26, 1901, letter from Queen Marie to King George V (GEO. V, AA43–107), appearing on page 70; the January 5, 1926, letter from Queen Marie to King George V (GEO. V, AA43–235), on page 192; the fall, 1926, letter from Queen Marie to King George V (GEO. V, AA43–241), on page 213; the May 21, 1928, letter from Queen Marie to King George V (GEO. V, AA43–371), on page 221; the July 27, 1932, letter from King George V to Queen Marie (GEO. V, AA43–404), on page 242; the January 24, 1936, letter from Queen Marie to Queen Mary (GEO. V, CC45–1003), on page 264; and the December 19, 1936, letter from Queen Marie to Queen Mary (GEO. V, CC45–1064), on page 267.

I am grateful to the following for permission to quote from their books: Charles Scribner's Sons for Queen Marie's two volume autobiography, *The Story of My Life* and *Ordeal: The Story of My Life;* Alfred A. Knopf, Inc., for *Queen Mary* copyright 1959, by James Pope-Hennessey; Faber and Faber for *Helen, Queen of Rumania,* by Arthur Gould Lee; and Bobbs-Merrill Co., Inc., for *My Memoir*, by Edith Bolling Wilson.

Special thanks are due Hector Bolitho and Irving Stone, for early advice and encouragement; John T. Lawrence, George Rinehart and Helen Partridge of the Famous Writer's School, for help along the way; Mrs. Clark, of the Des Moines Public Library, for providing me with many out-of-print sources; Dean Keller, for providing help and access to the Marie of Romania collection at Kent State University; Deborah Merrill, for answering questions about Queen Marie's final illness; Brutus Coste, for checking the war chapter and Epilogue for historical accuracy; Mme. Irene Fournaraki, for her attempts to provide me with the diaries of her mother, Mme. Symky Lahovary; Frances Melrose, for providing material on Queen Marie's American visit; and my agent, Malcolm Reiss, and editor, Leslie Pockell—for patient help and advice. My thanks, too, to my parents, who taught me persistence.

From the beginning of this project, my wife Janet has contributed creative advice, including psychological insight into Queen Marie and the other major characters, and constant support and encouragement. She has participated in every interview and edited and typed every page. Now I owe her my deepest thanks.

Terence Elsberry

Contents

Queen Marie's Family Tree   x
Foreword by Mother Alexandra (formerly Princess Ileana)   xiii
Map of Romania   xiv

PART ONE

1   Princess Missy   3
2   Fool's Paradise   15
3   The Romanian Hohenzollerns   27
4   Marriage   41
5   The Vine and the Wall   55
6   The Young Lieutenant   63
7   Friends   69
8   The Black Prince   80
9   The Hope of the Country   92
10   1914   98

PART TWO

11   Regina Maria   111
12   To Embrace Death with a Pure Heart   122
13   Romania's Soldier Queen   133

14   A Family Tragedy   143
15   For a Greater Romania   152
16   Mother-in-law of the Balkans   164
17   "Say I've Drowned"   178
18   The Woman Who Was Waited For   193

PART THREE

19   Romance, Tragedy and a Boy King   213
20   Absalom Returns   227
21   The She Wolf   239
22   The World Behind   250
23   The Road to Damascus   260
24   Character Is Destiny   269
Epilogue   286
Bibliography   289
Index   294

MARIE OF ROMANIA'S FAMILY TREE (PARTIAL)

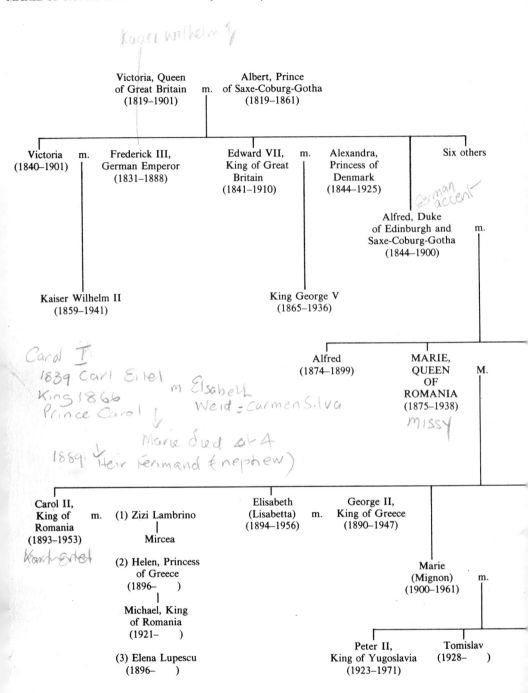

Kaiser Wilhelm I

Victoria, Queen
of Great Britain
(1819–1901)
m.
Albert, Prince
of Saxe-Coburg-Gotha
(1819–1861)

Victoria
(1840–1901)
m.
Frederick III,
German Emperor
(1831–1888)

Edward VII,
King of Great
Britain
(1841–1910)
m.
Alexandra,
Princess of
Denmark
(1844–1925)

Six others

German accent

Alfred, Duke
of Edinburgh and
Saxe-Coburg-Gotha
(1844–1900)
m.

Kaiser Wilhelm II
(1859–1941)

King George V
(1865–1936)

Alfred
(1874–1899)

MARIE,
QUEEN
OF
ROMANIA
(1875–1938)
M.

Missy

Carol I
1839 Carl Eitel
King 1866
Prince Carol
m Elsabeth
Weid = Carmen Silva
Marie died at 4
1889 Heir Ferdinand (nephew)

Carol II,
King of
Romania
(1893–1953)
m.
(1) Zizi Lambrino
|
Mircea

Karl Eitel

(2) Helen, Princess
of Greece
(1896–   )
|
Michael, King
of Romania
(1921–   )

(3) Elena Lupescu
(1896–   )

Elisabeth
(Lisabetta)
(1894–1956)
m.
George II,
King of Greece
(1890–1947)

Marie
(Mignon)
(1900–1961)
m.

Peter II,
King of Yugoslavia
(1923–1971)

Tomislav
(1928–   )

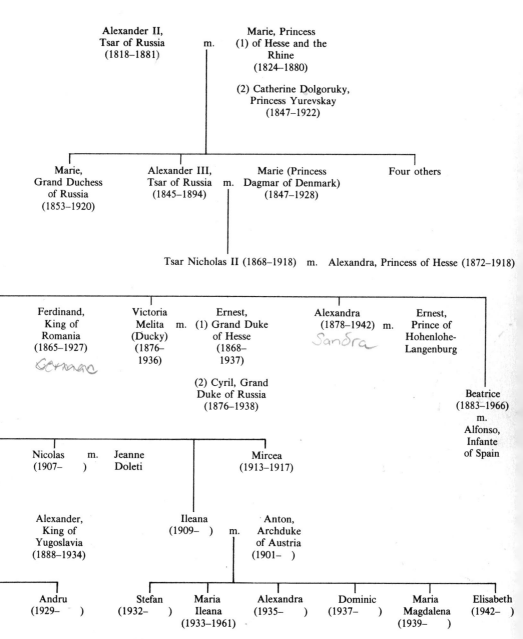

Alexander II, Tsar of Russia (1818–1881) m. Marie, Princess (1) of Hesse and the Rhine (1824–1880)

(2) Catherine Dolgoruky, Princess Yurevskay (1847–1922)

Marie, Grand Duchess of Russia (1853–1920)

Alexander III, Tsar of Russia (1845–1894) m. Marie (Princess Dagmar of Denmark) (1847–1928)

Four others

Tsar Nicholas II (1868–1918) m. Alexandra, Princess of Hesse (1872–1918)

Ferdinand, King of Romania (1865–1927) *German*

Victoria Melita (Ducky) (1876–1936) m. (1) Grand Duke of Hesse (1868–1937)

(2) Cyril, Grand Duke of Russia (1876–1938)

Alexandra (1878–1942) *Sandra* m. Ernest, Prince of Hohenlohe-Langenburg

Beatrice (1883–1966) m. Alfonso, Infante of Spain

Nicolas (1907–) m. Jeanne Doleti

Mircea (1913–1917)

Alexander, King of Yugoslavia (1888–1934)

Ileana (1909–) m. Anton, Archduke of Austria (1901–)

Andru (1929–)

Stefan (1932–)

Maria Ileana (1933–1961)

Alexandra (1935–)

Dominic (1937–)

Maria Magdalena (1939–)

Elisabeth (1942–)

Illustrations

All of the illustrations listed here appear on the pages immediately following Part One.

The Duchess of Edinburgh and her children.

The Edinburgh Princesses in 1902.

Carmen Sylva's Salon.

Crown Princess Marie in a photograph by Princess Nadeje Stirbey.

Prince Barbu Stirbey.
King Ferdinand and Queen Marie during World War I.
Waldorf, Pauline and John Astor mug for Marie's camera.
Waldorf Astor.

Family group in 1909.

The Romanian Royal family with their guests the Russian Imperial family at Constantza in 1914.

American newspaper cartoon at the time of Romania's armistice with the Central Powers in World War I.
Contemporary artist's conception of Marie nursing the wounded.

Queen Marie in 1923, "The Sun Queen."
Crown Prince Carol and Princess Helen at the time of their engagement in 1921.

Lisabetta, Queen of Greece.
Mignon, Queen of Yugoslavia.

Princess Ileana.
Michael, the boy king, rides to his accession, July 1927.

Marie at 60, from a painting by Sir Philip de Laszlo

Elena Lupescu in 1928 *(Wide World Photos)*

Queen Marie in 1936

Foreword

*by Mother Alexandra (formerly Princess Ileana),
daughter of Queen Marie of Romania*

Although the pattern of my life has been so different from that of my mother, I find myself more and more thinking back upon her advice and precepts to guide my way through life.

Born into Victorian England, severely educated by her Russian mother, a daughter of the Tsar, she came as a young, naive and strangely unprepared young woman to a land unknown and often incomprehensible to her Anglo-Saxon upbringing. Confronted by endless difficulties and trying situations, she fought her way through them by the force of her own completely honest personality.

Mama succeeded in breaking through the restricting shell of her upbringing and royal taboos without loss of dignity, and thus became the first truly modern queen, bridging the old and new order of things by her outgoing spirit and love of humanity.

In spite of all the sorrows of much of her life, and the sadness of her last years, she saw herself as a winner. As she herself said, "One must face life, for life loves the brave." And indeed she faced up to life and went down with colors flying, a beloved mother, a true and generous friend, a great and heroic Queen!

ROMANIA AND ITS NEIGHBORS, 1925

PART ONE

1

Princess Missy

Marie Alexandra Victoria, Princess of Great Britain and Ireland, was
born on October 29, 1875, at her parents' country house, Eastwell Park
in Kent. Her father was Queen Victoria's second son, Alfred, Duke of
Edinburgh. Her mother, the former Grand Duchess Marie Alexandrovna, was the only daughter of Russia's Tsar-Liberator, Alexander
II. Therefore "Missy," as her mother called the new little princess, was
born into an exalted position rare even for those lost days of empire.

Yet the memories haunting her at the end of her life were of homey
things, much like those we all remember from childhood. There was
Eastwell itself, a rambling gray mansion set in a vast English park, with
its marble-flagged front hall and terrifying back staircase overlooking
the Glory Hole, a sort of pantry little girls weren't allowed to explore.
There was the kitchen garden with its "perfume of violet leaves min-
gling with the mouldy smell of potatoes and old sacks"* stored in the
nearby tool house. And in the park, where magnificent old trees grew
well apart in "great stretches" of grass, herds of lowing highland cattle
grazed while deer scampered away into the woods.

In autumn, dead leaves filled the air with that heartbreaking intensity
of scent that would always recall Eastwell to her. And she and her

*Unless otherwise identified, quoted passages are from Marie's autobiography, *The
Story of My Life*. New York: Scribner's, 1934, or from unpublished correspondence.

3

sisters scuffled, as children will, through the fallen leaves while "wisps of mist, like smoke, played in the branches overhead." But best of all, even then, were the fairy tales she spun to herself, lying awake in the moon-washed nursery while her sisters slept in their neighboring cots.

Old photographs recalled her childhood too. There was one of Missy at seven with her sisters. Already she was the prettiest, her dainty features modestly downcast, her "great masses" of blonde hair cut in bangs, tied back with a bow and falling in shiny rivulets over the shoulders of her severe, dark-colored schoolroom dress. Another picture, of her alone at ten, showed her in a light-colored party dress (not white, because Mamma hated white for children) which left her shoulders partly uncovered. From a chain around her neck hung a tiny gold cross. It wasn't the cross of Mamma's mysterious Orthodox faith, but the familiar one of the church Missy and her sisters walked through the Eastwell woods to reach on Sunday mornings.

She loved having her picture taken, and she loved dressing up and having her hair brushed. When Nana Pitcathly had finished brushing, Missy would give her shoulders a little twist to catch a glimpse of the long mane her sisters called "yellow," but she preferred to think of as golden.

She was as delighted with all beauty as she was with her own: the beauty of the Eastwell primroses; of the lemon-scented magnolias and pink fan shells she found at Osborne beach on the Isle of Wight; of the ripple the black Orloff trotter's mane made when he pulled Mamma's carriage; of two aunts, Aunt Alix, the Princess of Wales, and Aunt Ella, *Elisabeth* the Grand Duchess Serge. All moved her to eye-stinging ecstasy. These *murdered* characteristics—uninhibited pleasure in her own good looks and sensual delight in beauty of every kind—remained with her to the end of her life.

Later she would discover what it meant to be a princess and a queen in the Europe of her day, that generations and centuries had gone into preparing her for her work, that she was expected to do great things and make noble sacrifices. But in her early childhood she was happily innocent of all this and innocent of the harsh realities of life. Spinner of this web of illusion and the most important person in Missy's life until she left as a bride for Romania was her mother.

After Missy's birth, she and her brother Alfred (born in November 1874) were joined in the nurseries at Eastwell and Clarence House, their parents' London home, by a succession of little sisters: Victoria Melita (1876), Alexandra Victoria (1878), and Beatrice (1883). Alfred, being a boy and already chosen to succeed one day to the dukedom of Saxe-Coburg-Gotha, was educated in Germany and therefore spent little time with his sisters. But the Duchess of Edinburgh, with a devotion rare in royal mothers of the day, lavished constant attention and chiding affection on her daughters.

For as far back as Missy could remember, it was Mamma who settled nursery disputes, calmed outbursts, comforted hurt feelings, took them for drives or walks, and at night tucked them into their cots. And because she was a happy child, Missy supposed her mother was happy too.

But Missy was wrong. Only much later, when she'd raised five children of her own in a foreign country far from home, did the Queen of Romania gain insight into her mother's personality. Then she realized, as she wrote in her autobiography, that her mother had "never been really happy or at peace with herself; many things tormented her, she did not take life easily."

When she left Russia for England, Marie Alexandrovna left "the wealthiest, the most bejeweled, the most ceremonious, and the most scandalous court in Europe." In flamboyant rococo palaces designed for eighteenth-century Romanovs by the theatrical Italian designer Rastrelli, she grew up in an atmosphere of incredible luxury. As the only daughter of the most powerful monarch in Europe, her position was extraordinary.

Her childhood hadn't been happy, however. For one thing, while she studied long hours by lamplight in marble and malachite salons overheated in defense against the endless Russian winters, she had to live with the thought that her adored father might be assassinated at any time. The tragic irony of Alexander II's life was that his early attempts at reforming the cruel and outdated autocracy had enraged the reactionary upper classes while paving the way for increased revolutionary activity.

During his daughter's youth, attempt after attempt was made on his life. After two had failed in a single month, he cried: "Am I a wild beast that they should hound me to death?"

As she grew older, Marie Alexandrovna's bluff joviality masked deep concern for her father's life. This stress, coming on top of a too-rigid religious and secular education, sent her into compensatory patterns of behavior that made her, as Missy kindly remembered many years later, "something of an original."

When she was about twenty, the Duke of Edinburgh came into Marie

Alexandrovna's life. The girl he met at her mother's old home in Darmstadt had inherited none of the Empress's finely-boned elegance. Instead, she had her father's features without his good looks. Her short nose snubbed a round Romanov face, and the medieval splendor of the Russian court dress ridiculed her stocky frame. Queen Victoria, in a rarely complimentary letter, wrote: "Dear Marie has a very friendly manner, a pleasant face, beautiful skin and fine bright eyes . . . there is something very fresh and attractive about her." Yet photographs of the time show that even then her chubby lips could purse in the expression of haughty disapproval that hid gnawing self-criticism from the world. As she grew older, it was this increasingly disdainful expression rather than a distinguished appearance that reminded others she was the daughter of a Tsar.

Queen Victoria's second son was as handsome as Marie was plain. Dressed in his captain's uniform and boasting a full dark beard and a "deeply tanned face in which his eyes shone extraordinarily, fascinatingly blue," Alfred looked like every young woman's idealized picture of an English sailor. And he spoke English with a strong German accent, as did most of his family, in a "soft voice with rather slurred r's" that could be charming.

Aside from a love of music, Missy's parents shared little. Marie Alexandrovna had a "rare intelligence," highly developed by her exceptional education. She spoke and wrote several languages fluently, declaring French the only language in which a beautiful letter could be written. Highly-cultured, she liked good conversation and preferred diplomats and politicians to soldiers, sailors and sportsmen. That she married Alfred of Edinburgh, who was both a "typical sailor" and a rabid sportsman, bears testimony to the irrationality of young love.

"Jovial and frank," Alfred was fond of wine, women, hunting and carousing with his older brother, the Prince of Wales. If we're to believe contemporary reports, he had his brother's shortcomings but very few of his good qualities. Even the Prince of Wales called him a "crashing boor," and Alfred's secretary said the Duke's mania for money "amounted to a disease." The story circulated that once in Paris he charged royalty-struck Americans and Englishmen who wanted to meet the Prince of Wales five *louis* for a presentation, fifty for a luncheon. He could be surly too. His rudeness to his mother's servants, especially her favorite, John Brown, was a constant source of irritation to Victoria.

When in 1869 Alfred took his older brother's suggestion and set his

cap for Marie Alexandrovna, one might have expected Victoria's relieved blessings on the match. Certainly the girl's blood was royal
enough, and her father, the Tsar, had been an early beau of Victoria's.
Back in 1839, she'd pronounced herself "a little in love" with the
youthful Tsarevitch.

But relations between Russia and England had greatly deteriorated
from the day when a Russian Grand Duke could squire the young
Queen of England. Now Russia posed a threat to British interests in
India, and the British public was angry with Russian advances in
Afghanistan.

Over this latest chapter in Affie's life, his mother's pen bit harder
than ever into black-bordered foolscap. She didn't desire the marriage,
she wrote, "on several quite serious grounds. Principally on account of
religion and politics, for these always seem to me precarious and un-
dependable in Russia." Visions of Greek Orthodox priests running in
and out of her son's Clarence House rose to taunt the Queen as she
wrote.

After a three-year courtship pushed forward by the politically-
minded Prince of Wales, the marriage negotiations lapsed due to the
Tsar's lack of interest.

Then in January 1873, word reached the Queen that the young
Grand Duchess had "compromised" herself with one Russian prince,
"if not others," and that her parents were ready to see her safely
married. Finally, news of the betrothal arrived.

Continuing to overreact, she wondered in her journal how a princess
with "*half Oriental* Russian notions" of self-indulgence could make the
kind of unassuming, hardworking wife she wanted for her sons. The
Romanovs themselves, she declared, were personally "false" and arrogant.

Victoria's wrath was ultimately dispelled by her first contact with the
bride. "On all sides I hear the highest praise of Marie, who knows all
the difficulties and sacrifices of her future position, yet does not shrink
from them. She has written me a very fine letter in English."

The marriage itself, solemnized in two magnificent ceremonies in St.
Petersburg, went off without the Queen's presence. An amusing figure
Victoria would have been, dumpy and disapproving in black, at the
lavish and wicked Russian court. But the Prince and Princess of Wales
were there, and Victoria sent the bride two sprigs of myrtle grown from
a piece of her oldest daughter's nosegay. "All the brides (I think) have
had a piece in succession," the Queen wrote.

In England the Queen stuck to her new-found satisfaction with the match. All Marie need do now to become a "treasure" was to learn English ways "good and fast." Her only concern was whether or not "Poor Affie" would make a good husband.

The lull was temporary. Victoria was naive to think a young woman raised as the second lady of Tsarist Russia would submit graciously to becoming a subservient fixture at her own rigid, monotonous court. Nor had she reckoned with Marie Alexandrovna's masterful and dominating personality. There would be no browbeating this new daughter-in-law as she was apt to do with her own children. The girl's likes and dislikes and pet aversions were as inflexible and as prejudiced as the Queen's. And from the first, Missy's mother hated England.

Marie Alexandrovna's early letters home to St. Petersburg were full of criticism. There was no court life in England. The food at the royal palaces was terrible. Worst of all was the weather; accustomed to clean Russian snows, she despised the English fogs. Once at Balmoral, when she'd had the courage to light a fire in her icy bedroom, the Queen had ordered it put out and a window opened. And when Marie had worn the dazzling tiara given her by her father as a going-away present, the Queen had glowered at it, "ruffling her feathers like an angry parrot," and implied that it was "too good" for a young princess.

Victoria wasn't alone in her anger. When Marie Alexandrovna discovered that not only the Princess of Wales but all her husband's sisters took precedence before her, she withdrew from court. The Tsar asked that his daughter continue to be called an Imperial rather than a Royal Highness, but agreed she couldn't take precedence over the heir's wife. Both father and daughter, however, held out for Marie's position ahead of the Queen's daughters. There was even tension over how her titles should read. Should Grand Duchess or Duchess of Edinburgh come first? Victoria's private secretary provided the only note of levity in the stressful proceedings. "Who comes first, a louse or a flea?" he asked his wife.

The British court reciprocated with snipes at the new Duchess. Victoria mentioned Marie's "bougouiserrie" [sic] in a letter to her oldest daughter. And Sir Henry Ponsonby called her the "most unpopular princess in England." The prim English ladies were shocked when she nursed her first baby herself, and the whole of society was horrified when she broke all precedent and smoked a cigarette in public. Years later, the Queen of Romania summed up the situation: "I do not think my mother always found it easy being Queen Victoria's daughter-in-law."

In her relationship with her children, the Duchess's peculiarities became even more apparent. She treated them with a strange combination of indulgence and spartan strictness. While loving them passionately, she never relaxed the barrier of the generations. When Marie of Romania was forty, her mother still treated her like a child, refusing to admit they might be equals. Though each of her daughters was gifted with either artistic or musical talent and Missy possessed an added gift for story telling, the Duchess was so disgusted that none showed promise of becoming a child prodigy that she gave them only the sketchiest of cultural educations. Hating the English language, she nonetheless spoke it with her children almost exclusively. "I have no wish to hear my beloved mother tongue mutilated by my own children!" she said.

Her list of dicta for the behavior of a princess was endless. A princess must at all times be punctual, a princess must never be ill (though when a princess *did* fall ill, Mamma swooped down like Tchaikovsky's Black Swan, castor oil and foul-tasting remedies in hand), a princess must never complain, never discuss digestion (even if digestion *was* a favorite British topic), and never refuse dishes put before her.

"But if they are not good, Mamma?"

"Then you must just behave as though they were good."

"But if they make you feel sick!"

"Then be sick, my dear, but wait till you get home. It would be most offensive to be sick then and there!"

Most important, a princess must be a good raconteuse, able to keep a whole table amused. To ensure facility, conversations were held with empty chairs. "Nothing is more hopeless than a princess who never opens her mouth." Missy learned her lessons well. Years later, when she became the queen of a difficult, far-off country, her punctuality, "Russian digestion" and ability to entertain a drawing room full of cynical Romanians were the cornerstones of her success.

Along with their schooling in royal decorum, the Duchess allowed her children a measure of freedom unusual for their station in life. "We were wild children," reminisced Queen Marie, "allowed to get dirty, wet, cold even . . . our lungs were allowed to expand, our faces to sunburn, our legs and arms to get bruised and scratched." "All Affie's girls are so strong," noticed Queen Victoria.

The Duchess's correspondence abounds with references to this

healthy attitude of hers. She reported to the Duchess of Teck on the
Teck children (among them the future Queen Mary of England): "They
are now romping with my children and making tremendous noise."
And from the Imperial Russian vacation home, Peterhof on the Baltic
Sea, she wrote to her friend Jennie Churchill in England: "My children
are very happy: ride about, bathe in the sea, and run wild nearly the
whole day." She closed on another favorite note: "London must be
detestable now. I quite pity you."

   Unlike their mother, the Edinburgh children loved England. All
their adult lives, though they lived far from home, Missy and her sisters
returned as often as royal duties and the precarious political situations
of their adopted lands allowed. Forty years later Missy experienced her
first English spring since childhood "like a convalescent breathing in
health and new life."
   Of her sisters, Missy was closest in age and affection to her sister
Victoria, called Ducky in the family. Ducky was a difficult child, som-
ber and passionate as Missy was gay and imaginative. Though a year
younger, she was taller than Missy, which caused people to think her
the older. "Ducky was our conscience," deferred to by her sisters,
though all but Sandra (Alexandra) were leaders in their own way.
Ducky also "loved jealously," a trait which would contribute to the
major, and ultimate, tragedy of her life.
   Her childish love for her sister Missy created no nursery problems,
however, because Missy returned Ducky's love in full. Hand in hand,
dark-haired Ducky and blonde Missy would explore the mysteries of
Eastwell woods or the Osborne beach. When they rode together in
Hyde Park, a characteristically fair plan always gave Ducky the larger
horse.
   At Eastwell the two of them, with sister Sandra running along behind
trying to catch up, played Robin Hood, Robinson Crusoe, Red Indians
and pirates. In a giant cedar tree in the front yard, they climbed among
the low boughs, each taking possession of her own private "room." In
winter they wobbled on skates over the Eastwell pond and, on the rare
occasions when snow fell and did not immediately melt, tobogganed
with Papa.
   The Duke of Edinburgh, though he'd grown taciturn with age, and
was given to an overfondness for alcohol, was popular with his children.
When he wasn't away from home commanding one or another of the

ships he was assigned to, he could turn his daughters' simplest outing into a stirring adventure.

The Duke's real forte, though, was Christmas. Excited as his children, he supervised the preparations that went on in every great English country house for weeks: the stirring of the plum pudding; the servants' party with gifts for each; the setting up of white-draped present tables for each family member; the selection and trimming of the tree. But the high point for father and children was Christmas Eve itself, when the library doors were at last thrown open. Then, advancing hand in hand as if into an Andersen fairy tale, the children would take possession of their gifts beneath the towering, candlelit tree. In later years when Missy had children of her own, she made their Christmases as nearly as possible like the Eastwell Christmases of her childhood.

The Edinburghs spent the summer "season" in Clarence House in London. Missy hated London. The "smuts" caused by London's great industries turned her fingers black whether she was indoors or out. And in London there were few places to explore. Instead, you took boring walks with an absent-minded governess in the hated Green Park. Only the balloon man made these outings bearable. The one respite from so much gloom were occasional forays into the Buckingham Palace gardens. Here birds of every kind swam in the lake, and Missy and her sisters covered themselves with mud sliding down the greasy back side of Queen Victoria's aviary hill.

Clarence House itself was a narrow mansion overlooking the Mall and separated from St. James's Palace by only a few "straggly" trees. Inside, the Duke of Edinburgh's huge hunting trophies and his collection of Oriental antiquities competed with his wife's Russian mementos; Japanese suits of armor, elephant tusks and Fabergé Easter eggs sat side by side. The whole mishmash was made tolerable for Missy by the Clarence House "odour," a scent comprised of fog, oakwood, cigarette smoke and the special Russian incense the Duchess burned in all the rooms.

This exotic setting provided the backdrop for the sisters' indoor games. Missy took the lead in these games, her naturally fertile imagination heightened by the Hans Christian Andersen stories the Duchess read to her daughters. Dressed as the Queen of Spain in a trailing curtain or tablecloth, Missy played the starring role.

For the children, the most important member of the Clarence House and Eastwell households, aside from their mother, was Nana Pitcathly.

A typical Scottish nanny, kind but severe, she ruled the nursery with a rod of iron. She even devised a special torture, the "strap," which consisted of a piece of leather cut in strips at the end and hung over the girls' beds as a warning to any calculated naughtiness. But for all her harshness, Missy was very fond of her Nana, and Nurse Pitcathly's death in 1883 when Missy was nine was the greatest grief of her childhood.

The other nursery tyrant was a French governess. "Mademoiselle" was Alsatian, a bony, long-nosed woman with drab hair and an ugly smile that "spread all over her face." Every afternoon, while they knitted stockings and then lay for an hour on the floor to improve their postures, Mademoiselle would read to her small charges. The books she read were mostly in French, a language Missy and her sisters hated because they considered it affected. But Missy loved these hours of being read to, a love that remained with her all her life.

The Edinburgh girls learned more from Mademoiselle's stories than from the educational program she devised. "Lessons did not weigh heavily in the plan of our lives," Marie of Romania remembered, due to the family's constant moving from place to place. The girls' brother Alfred didn't accompany the family on their yearly peregrinations between London, Malta, Osborne, Russia and Coburg. (Being the only son, his education was of paramount importance. He stayed home learning.) But Missy and her sisters moved with their parents among all these places, with visits in between to Queen Victoria at Windsor or Balmoral.

The prospect of a visit to Grandmamma Queen filled the girls with dread and excitement. At Windsor their nurses would herd them like "little geese" along endless, soft-carpeted corridors to the Queen's rooms. As the little group passed through door after door, the reverential hush surrounding the Queen would grow until even the nurses were whispering. "When finally the door was opened," remembered Queen Marie, "there sat Grandmamma not idol-like at all, not a bit frightening, smiling a kind little smile, almost as shy as us children, so that conversation was not very fluent on either side."

The bulk of these visits consisted of Victoria's inquiries into her granddaughters' morals and general behavior. "And I well remember," wrote Marie in her memoirs, "Grandmamma's shocked and yet amused little exclamations of horror when it was reported that one or the other of us had not been good."

Sentimental, narrow and naively optimistic, little Missy reflected her world. Yet even as a child she observed her environment with an outsider's eye for detail few of her contemporaries possessed.

On trips to Russia, where the Romanov myth was climaxing in an orgy of splendor, her camera eye worked overtime. After the sober sumptuousness of Victoria's court, life with the Romanovs filled her with ecstasy. It was like the Thousand and One Nights.

As she watched in awed delight, a phantasmagoria of incredible images danced before her eyes: huge palaces with endless glasslike floors and floodlit, fountain-studded parks; church services in golden cathedrals filled with sweet-smelling incense and rocked by thundering Russian chants; trotting horses with flying manes and tails and flanks so shiny they reflected your face. Even the Cossacks, though fierce and scary looking, were delightful, with their long red coats, high fur caps, and breasts barred with silver cartridges. As always, Missy was aware of the special smell of her surroundings. The Russian palaces reeked of "turpentine, Russian leather, cigarette smoke and scent."

Nor would she ever forget the sight of all her splendid Romanov relatives in court dress. Her handsome uncles and granduncles, "tall like trees" in their splendid uniforms, towered over her like figures out of a fairy tale. Each bent down in turn to kiss their small English nieces. And unlike the English uncles, the Grand Dukes never looked through you, never forgot about you in mid-conversation.

And wasn't it that giant, blue-eyed Lohengrin, Uncle Alexis, who'd paid her her first compliment? All her life, the memory of his greeting as she led a phalanx of cousins across the Peterhof lawn warmed her like sunshine: *"Ah! Voici la jolie petite!"* ("Here's the pretty little one!") he called. That night, she peered into a mirror at her sweet-lipped little rosebud of a face and knew she was pretty and could charm men. She was five.

Even more dazzling than the Romanov men were their women. The Grand Duchesses, arrayed in the Byzantine-like court dress, adorned themselves in the world's most stupendous jewels. When Aunt Ella floated by, carrying a few sprigs of lily-of-the-valley to contrast with her silver embroidered robe, Missy felt like kneeling in adoration.

Memories of "Grandpapa Emperor," her mother's father, were less intense. Alexander's love of his daughter had overlapped to include Missy; she was his favorite grandchild. But in later years Missy retained only three memories of her Russian grandfather. In one, he pretended to taste the sand cake she offered him on the Tsarskoe Selo terrace. In another, he bent to kiss her alone among the girls because she was the only one who hadn't caught measles. (The next night she too was among the unkissed. But the memory of triumph consoled.) The last memory of Grandpapa recalled Missy standing between his knees in a little carriage while he drove a shiny black Orloff trotter. Memories of Grandmamma Empress were even dimmer. She existed for her grandchildren only as a faintly-remembered figure with long waxen hands lying in a railroad car en route to some healing southern clime.

Clearer to Missy was the memory of coming into the Clarence House sitting room on a March day in 1881, when she was seven, and finding her mother in tears. "God has taken Grandpapa," the Duchess told her daughters. Alexander II had been blown to bits by a Nihilist's bomb because he'd stopped to help a man wounded minutes before by an earlier bomb intended for the Tsar.

The news of the assassination was followed by a hurried trip to St. Petersburg, where Missy and her sisters watched the funeral procession from a Winter Palace window.

As Missy grew older, she became increasingly aware of her Russian cousins, especially the boys. Though a natural leader and something of a tomboy, she was always "very much a little girl" in her feeling for boys and theirs for her. At home in England, Winston Churchill brazenly declared his intention of one day marrying her. "He and I had a sneaking liking for each other," reminisced Marie.

The Russian cousins were more subtle. With each trip she paid to Russia, they became increasingly aware of their gay and enchanting English cousin. Merciless teases, they "attracted and repulsed you in turns." Only Cousin Nicky, the future Tsar Nicholas II, never teased. Older than Missy, he caressed her with his gentle, sad eyes, but seemed "rather beyond our reach."

At any rate, there were enough boy cousins in both England and Russia that she could reasonably expect to marry one someday. Such safe, interfamily marriages, though deplored by many of her relatives, were common.

As it happened, the Duchess of Edinburgh had other plans for her daughter's future.

2

Fool's Paradise

In 1885, shortly before Missy's eleventh birthday, Queen Victoria hit on a way of removing the Edinburghs and the problems they caused from England. The Duke was assigned the command of Her Majesty's Mediterranean fleet based at Malta, that storied island, Homer's "navel of the sea," sleeping in the sun fifty miles south of Sicily and two hundred miles north of Tripoli. To show her pleasure at the new arrangement, Victoria shipped Marie Alexandrovna and the children off to join Alfred in the Queen's own yacht, the *Osborne*.

Relief was great on both sides. At Malta, where the fourteenth-century Knights of St. John had carved their bastion and defended the church founded by the ship-wrecked Apostle Paul, a beaming, sun-burned Duke of Edinburgh now took command of his fleet far from his mother's disapproving shadow. And the Duchess, happily enthroned in the fifteenth-century governor's palace of San Antonio four miles outside the little capital of Valetta, found herself a popular social leader of the ancient, inbred Maltese nobility.

Meanwhile young Missy embarked on a lifelong love affair with the sun-drenched beflowered island the Greeks called *Melita* (honey). Not since the summer spent with Grandmamma Queen at Balmoral in Scotland had she found a landscape as kindred to her spirit. Strangely enough, she was equally moved by both the misty moors and this setting which closely resembled the Holy Land. "I *feel* them both." And the

15

"glorious and blessed freedom" that from the first characterized the
family's Malta life had a lasting effect on the child, developing in her
a strain of independence that even the calculated rigidity of her later
environment couldn't destroy. These three years were the happiest of
her life.

For one thing, life was simpler at Malta. The Duchess, relieved at
being safely out of the despised England, relaxed much of her maternal
vigilance. "Mamma knew how to be severe and there was no pardon
for certain misdeeds," recalled Missy, "but she also knew how to give
us splendid liberty for harmless amusement."

And in the Malta days, as for much of her life, Missy's chief amusement was riding. No sooner had the family settled into San Antonio
than the Duchess, resigned to what she called her daughters' "insane
passion" for horses, presented the two oldest with horses of their own.
Ducky's was a bay she called Fearless, and Missy took gleeful possession of a high-spirited chestnut she named Ruby. Both horses were
wild-eyed, wiry little Barbary Arabs, a breed peculiar to the island.

On these adored mounts, Missy and Ducky (with Sandra bringing up
the rear on the old nursery pony, Tommy) would gallop at breakneck
speed through the little walled villages of pastel houses, scattering
children and squawking chickens. When they weren't terrorizing the
natives, they would fly along the narrow, walled roads past the old
houses, dodging fishermen in blue shirts and red-wheeled, mule-driven
carts. Or they'd run races at the Valetta race track in furious competition with young midshipmen from their father's crew. Missy usually led
these bouts—"I was fond of leading in those days"—her face sun-
burned and laughing, her long hair flying out behind her like a yellow
flag.

Like "little savages" the Empress of India's granddaughters took full
possession of the island praised by Scott, Thackeray and Disraeli for its
beauty. They scaled its highest trees with their pet monkeys and explored its terraced, flower-filled landscapes as they'd discovered the
Eastwell woods, the Osborne beach and the St. Petersburg drawing
rooms.

Malta's strange beauty was something Missy would carry with her
until she died. "Nothing that I have seen in later life has ever had
exactly that same charm," she wrote, remembering, "that strange feeling that something is hidden, not yet explored, worlds of beauty, gardens of enchantment you could stumble upon at any moment."

As if roaring good times, physical freedom and soul-nurturing beauty

weren't enough, the Malta years were further enriched by many colorful and delightful characters—from Tony, the local policeman, to
Beppo, the family's favorite servant, who trailed to Saturday picnics
with the tea basket and Russian samovar.

An exception to the rule of pleasant personalities was Mademoiselle.
This worthy dame, having come with the family from England, proceeded to turn the island's every delight into a personal discomfort. In
the fresh sea air loved by the plump Duchess and her daughters,
Mademoiselle sat skinny and shivering. Riding parties saw her misera-
bly hunched beneath a red parasol in some lurching local carriage while
she chaperoned her charges' noisy races with the young sailors. And
a fancy dress party meant Mademoiselle masquerading as the French
flag in a skimpy dress that showed too much of her bony legs, while
the Duke of Edinburgh glowered his disgust, the Duchess dissolved in
amusement, and Missy and Ducky went to bed furious because their
teacher hadn't dressed as Mary Queen of Scots or Cleopatra.

Closer to the children than girl friends, teachers or servants were the
sailors. The entire fleet was at their disposal, and they were continually
visiting one ship or another. Since their father's flagship, *H.M.S. Alexandra*, was their favorite, her midshipmen became their particular
chums.

Best of all the sailors was Captain Maurice Bourke, the first real love
of Missy's life. "Captain Dear" was Black Irish, sunburned, with pale
blue eyes and an irresistible, crooked smile. In short, he possessed every
quality necessary to make him the ideal of three high-spirited little girls
ripe for hero worship. And Missy brought to this first love the same
idealism she brought to all the loves of her life: "We would have gone
through fire and water for him."

They almost did. On occasions when even their mother despaired of
disciplining her tomboy daughters, Captain Bourke was dispatched to
talk to them. When the Duchess decreed their skirts should be lengthened the few inches in keeping with their growing limbs, only Bourke's
magnetism convinced his little friends to adopt the new fashion and
take their first step toward young womanhood.

For Missy, the incident of the skirts was the first of many destiny-
shaping forces beginning to crowd around her.

If Maurice Bourke was her first love, Cousin George was her first real
romance. The Prince of Wales' younger son, Prince George—later
King George V—was also stationed at Malta on his uncle's ship. And

since even the Duchess had grown fond of this good-natured young man who so obviously missed his own affectionate family circle, she began inviting him to spend his leavetime with the Edinburghs at San Antonio.

Completely different in personality and appearance from his languid brother Albert Victor, Duke of Clarence, George more closely resembled in both looks and temperament his and Missy's mutual cousin Nicky of Russia. Both were fine-boned, stood little more than five-foot-six, wore Vandyke beards and parted their light brown hair near the middle. And both preferred rigorous outdoor activity to drawing room pursuits.

At this stage, according to one biographer, Prince George had "two all-absorbing passions in his life: shooting and his beautiful deaf mother." His mother was Alexandra, "Aunt Alix," whose exquisite beauty had always fascinated Missy. With her graceful little head, childlike ease of manner, crashing elegance and ever-present Pekingese, the Princess of Wales belongs in any gallery of Britain's best-loved royal figures.

Unfortunately, the psychological effect that she had on her children was considerably less charming than her appearance. A woman who herself remained incredibly childlike until her death at 81, the Princess was never able to fathom that her children had actually grown up. She strove, therefore, to prolong their childhood into full maturity. Even now, with George in his twenties, she was still writing of his "dear tear-stained little face."

Perhaps as a result of her unfulfilling marriage to the philandering Prince of Wales, perhaps because she had herself grown up in a rather smothering family atmosphere, the Princess compounded her maternal felonies by overwhelming George with a superabundance of mother love. Around the time of his Malta duty, she wrote him a letter detailing "the bond of love between us—that of Mother and child—which *nothing can* ever diminish or render less binding . . . and *nothing and nobody* can or shall ever come between me and my darling Georgie boy."

Fortunately for George, his basic personality was uncomplicated enough to withstand such assaults. The hard buffeting he received aboard a British man-o'-war helped. So did the warm relationship he enjoyed with his father. Missy remembered Uncle Bertie, as she called the Prince of Wales, dressed all in white and standing, "a genial figure of rippling good humor," on the deck of his superb racing yacht, the *Britannia*. With his nieces he was royally condescending. But with his second son the hard-living and sophisticated Prince was affectionate and understanding. When his father died twenty-five years later, George wrote, "I have lost my best friend and the best of fathers."

Whatever the reason, when George arrived at Malta in 1886 he was neither dissipated and backward like his older brother, Prince Eddy, nor pigeon-breasted and melancholy like his three sisters. In fact, according to one biographer, he was "independent-minded, candid, straightforward, and had a very high sense of duty." Wrote Grand-mamma Queen: "I think dear Georgie so nice, sensible and truly right-minded, and so anxious to improve himself." Surely a young man could receive no better character reference.

Though ten years older than Missy, George was immediately taken with his irrepressible little cousin. If she'd undergone agonies of jeal-ousy when Maurice Bourke paid less attention to her than to one of her sisters, she now had nothing to fear. Dubbing her and her sisters "the dear three," George would ride beside them on his own glossy horse, Real Jam, or drive them in a high two-wheeled cart behind a steady brown cob. But Missy was the acknowledged favorite, "there was no doubt whatever about that." And she, in turn, was enchanted with this "dear chum" of a grown-up cousin who was everything she most ad-mired in men: uncomplicated, sporting, good-natured and handsome. He even wore a uniform!

If we're to believe one rather overblown account written in the twenties by an American journalist, Mabel Potter Daggett, George and Missy's Malta romance actually went as far as a kiss. And from that to a series of kisses, the most important supposedly occurring on the occasion of Missy's fourteenth birthday party. She was still "a flat little girl with golden hair hanging down her back." But for the party, she'd graduated into her first bustle and hung a string of pink coral around her neck. Catching sight of Missy alone in a San Antonio gallery, George is supposed to have said, "I say, Missy, my word but you're pretty," then "caught her in his arms and kissed her." There were more kisses to follow," continued Mrs. Daggett, "for it was first love that had occurred to both."

It has been confirmed that Prince George had indeed fallen for his young cousin. But that such overt romancing took place is difficult to believe, considering Missy's extreme immaturity. Nor does she mention it in her memoirs. In fact, she makes much of her adolescent innocence: "No unhealthy curiosity disturbed our peace of mind; there was as yet no desire towards the fruit of knowledge." She was, after all, only fourteen and, if anything, less mature than her contemporaries. "Our world was delusion and our mother was horrified if anyone dared to lift for us . . . the veil . . . of life."

Indeed, Marie appears to put an end to the kissing question in a later chapter in which she discusses her premarital romances: "None of my flirtations even went as far as a kiss."

But the two cousins had undeniably formed a warm and lasting relationship. And the kissing question is interesting in view of all that came later. For the results of this early romance were a spurned marriage proposal, a young man's broken dream, a royal family feud and a lost chance at the throne of England.

Whatever the nature of the young friendship, it had little time to blossom. In 1889, after three years on the "blessed island," the Edinburghs moved again. This time they took up more or less permanent residence in the little duchy of Coburg in Germany, which, along with neighboring Gotha, the Duke of Edinburgh would one day inherit.

The move to Coburg marked a tightening of the reins. The Duchess decided, so as to separate them less from their brother, that from now on the sisters should also study with German masters and even be confirmed in the Lutheran instead of the Anglican church. Their tutors filled the girls' days with lessons—geography, history, arithmetic, botany, literature, religion, natural history, painting, French, music and gymnastics.

Missy was neither a good nor an eager scholar, preferring all her other occupations to study. But she wrote a good hand, showed a real talent for composition (especially when allowed to invent her own subject) and learned from old Fräulein Helferich a solid basis in the principles of drawing, for which she remained forever grateful. She could never learn to spell correctly though, could remember historical tales but never the dates, and was prevented by squeamishness from enjoying Dr. Heim's natural history class.

To make matters worse, the new governess (a young German woman brought in to replace Mademoiselle) seemed to Missy an incredibly pernicious woman. The first of many deceitful women who pop with recurring regularity into Marie's story, Fräulein made the two older girls' teen years miserable. In league with her fiancé, brother Alfred's tutor, Fräulein managed to take over complete control of the children's education. Feeding on the Duchess of Edinburgh's dislike of England, she persuaded Marie Alexandrovna that Missy and Ducky must be forced to accept German manners, ideas and taste. Nor were they to continue living in the kind of super-refined English comfort and luxury they were used to. Realizing that both girls, especially Missy, loved pretty clothes, Fräulein forced them into coarse underthings that irritated their pampered skin and into the most humiliatingly ugly dresses she could find.

There's no way of judging whether Fräulein was really as destructive as Missy later pictured her. It's likely that the princesses, spoiled by years of overindulgence, overreacted to the strict Teutonic regimen. At any rate, it's a recorded fact that the governess ridiculed the girls before their mother and encouraged any small jealousies that sprang up between them. Fräulein also slyly led the girls to ask questions about the "hidden mysteries" of life, that aspect of creation the Duchess was most adamant about keeping from them, and then showed them up to their mother "as nasty little girls with unhealthy minds."

The tragedy of the situation is that while at the awkward, insecure stage when a girl most needs her mother's sympathy and understanding, Missy was denied these by Fräulein. The Duchess had been completely taken in by the couple and never dreamed they might be insincere or—far worse—cruel to her beloved children.

Had the two been anything but German, the Duchess might have been able to see through them. But at last Marie Alexandrovna and her mother-in-law had something in common: both adored Coburg, the hometown of Victoria's late lamented husband, the Prince Consort.

Coburg had a special charm, the cozy charm of a nineteenth-century German postcard or novel. Life here was simple and easy, characteristic of Germany in 1890. For although the War of 1866 had robbed the minor German kings, princes and grand dukes of any real political power, their principalities still made up the bulk of the German nation —tiny, prosperous courts, "little centers of importance that did much for the prosperity of Germany as a whole."

Here the Duchess of Edinburgh could live entirely as she wished. For the first time in her life, she could move through her days without a critical brace of disapproving educators or in-laws to criticize her every action.

A disturbing element for the Duchess, but a much-needed comic relief for her daughters was the reigning Duke, old Uncle Ernest. The complete opposite of his brother, the Prince Consort, in looks, morals and personality, Duke Ernest in this final stage of his life resembled nothing as much as an ogre in a frock coat. Known throughout Europe for his physical excesses, he now held court—which was hardly a court at all, but rather a collection of money-lenders, pimps, prostitutes and second-rate actresses—at his country Schloss Kalenburg. The Edinburghs, therefore, had initiated their own circle in town and carefully avoided any connection with the so-called real court.

Twice a year, however, the old Duke would appear at the Edinburgh *Palais* to pay the Duchess a duty call. For days in advance the girls would hover between paroxysms of dread and gleeful anticipation. And their first glimpse of the old rogue as he loomed in the drawing room door never ceased to horrify them delightedly.

For Missy, the great Coburg joy was the family's country castle, the Rosenau. A little schloss buried in the romantic Thuringian forest, its unpretentious atmosphere recalled the Malta days. The three older girls were allowed to sleep in a room at the top of the round tower. Here, in an atmosphere not unlike that in which Sleeping Beauty pricked her finger, they set up their camp beds brought from Russia, and each arranged one of the three deep window alcoves as her own private domain. Missy grew up arranging little corners to suit herself. Years later, when she was Queen of Romania and had access to a half-dozen palatial homes, she still set up her own little corner—with a piece of fabric, an earthenware jar, a curio and a few flowers—in every hotel, train, ship or house she visited.

The Duchess had most of the family's meals served outside under the big apple tree. And she would preside over enormous teas which followed the children's frenzied games of *Christenvervolgung*. This game, the result of their church history lessons, consisted of realistic forms of Christian martyrdom. This may well have been the greatest effort Missy ever exerted in the name of religion. All her life, she depended more on beautiful music or, more especially, a magnificent natural setting than on religious rites for communion with the Almighty.

The Duchess of Edinburgh had a theory that princesses must marry young. "When they are over twenty," she would say, "they begin to think too much and to have too many ideas of their own which complicate matters. Besides, an unmarried princess has no position at all. Princesses *must* marry."

To prepare Missy and Ducky for the royal marriage market, the Duchess now bent her efforts. In Missy, especially, she had an apt pupil. Despite the succession of governesses and tutors, the girl's education remained sketchy. But few princesses her age could better hold their own in society. She spoke several languages and knew how to make herself amusing and agreeable.

Missy had other advantages. At sixteen she was well on her way to becoming the most beautiful princess in Europe. She later wrote disparagingly of her adolescent appearance: "I was a thin, flat little maiden with very fair hair frizzled Queen Alexandra-wise on the forehead; my features were immature, my eyes blue, there was little dignity about me." But photographs of the time show evidence of her future remarkable beauty. Her nose ("Grandmamma's, but, thank God, improved upon!") already promises its ultimate grace, her eyes have the compelling gaze supposedly characteristic of those born under the astrological sign of Scorpio, and her lips are full and slightly pouting.

Her best qualities were spontaneity, a sparkling charm and an easygoing disposition. "She was happy and wanted everyone else to be happy around her," wrote a childhood friend. And another remembered young Missy as "a figure of wonderful charm, full of life and its joy, with a zest for all it might hold; triumphant in joy and beauty yet always with that added charm of consideration for others." More than anything, she wanted to love and be loved. With all the fervor of her romantic spirit, she delighted in young men's adoring looks "as well as whispered words that might have meant more than they actually said, and which I hugged to my soul, repeating them over and over again. They made my heart flutter, for all was romance in those days."

The Duchess suffered no illusions about her daughters' makeup. She knew both Missy and Ducky were too romantic to accept an obvious marriage of state. So although she began taking her oldest daughters about in society, introducing them to possible suitors and presenting them at various functions, she cleverly handled it in a manner subtle enough not to shatter the girls' romantic imaginings. Existing in a swirl of schoolgirl dreams, Missy thought of marriage, when she thought of it at all, as something remote and far off. She was thus able to enjoy the company of the young princes she met without worrying her head about their intentions.

Back home in England, a situation now developed that threatened the Duchess of Edinburgh's carefully laid plans. In January 1891, a few months before Prince George's twenty-sixth birthday, his grandmother Queen Victoria wrote to him, urging him to marry quickly. His older brother, Prince Eddy, had already been turned down by their beautiful cousin Alix of Hesse-Darmstadt and now seemed sidetracked on a hopeless romance with the lovely (but Catholic) Princess Helene of

Orleans. Therefore, asserted the Queen, it was up to George to insure the succession to the throne in the third generation. She had in mind either Missy or Ducky Edinburgh.

George was his mother's son. Time hadn't diminished his romantic infatuation with his golden-haired cousin. But he was still timid about marriage and felt himself too young for it.

Nevertheless, his proposal to Missy could now be only a matter of time. In preparation for the impending family struggle, the royal family took sides. Decidedly for the marriage of George and Missy were Queen Victoria, the Prince of Wales and the Duke of Edinburgh. The Duchess and the Princess of Wales were just as strongly opposed.

Fate now provided a lull before the storm. In Russia the young wife of Missy's youngest uncle, the gentle and handsome Grand Duke Paul, died in childbirth. Eager to comfort her favorite brother, the Duchess bustled off to the funeral, taking her daughters with her.

The Russian visit reinforced Missy's early love of her mother's home. She was drawn again by the magnetism of Tsarist Russia: "It had an extraordinary glamour for us . . . an enormous world of a thousand possibilities with a feeling of dark mystery as background."

Sensing Missy's mood, the Duchess of Edinburgh snatched her pubescent brood back to the uncompromising security of Germany. But not before another Cousin George, the Duchess's young cousin, Grand Duke George Mikhailovich, had fallen in love with Missy and proposed marriage. The Duchess loved her relatives, but her father's extramarital affairs had convinced her she wanted no Romanov son-in-law. Without telling Missy of young George's proposal, the Duchess turned it down. And to put a stop to any romantic thoughts on the girl's part, she told her: "Don't you know that the cousins who seemed so charming were also kissing the maid behind the parlor door?"

That same fall, wearing matching mauve dresses, Missy and Ducky "came out" at the pompous court of their thirty-four-year-old cousin, Kaiser Wilhelm II. The Duchess had laid her plans well: Missy's dinner partner that evening was a scholarly young German prince, Ferdinand, the heir to the Romanian throne. A good-looking young man with pale blue eyes and a hawk nose, he tried to cover his shyness by laughing, spoke no English and told Missy nothing about his adopted Romania. Nor did she ask him any questions about the far-off country, being rather vague about its geographical location.

On January 14, 1892, Prince Eddy died of influenza at the age of twenty-eight, leaving his brother George second in line to the English throne. George could no longer deny his responsibilities, the first of which entailed choosing a wife. That spring, he made a request to Missy's parents for her hand in marriage and was refused. In this first major turning point of her life, Missy had rejected a young man who loved her, of whom she was fond and who had asked her to share the throne of her beloved England.

Why?

To this lingering question, popular speculation has provided several answers: she didn't love him, she was too restless to settle in England, her governess forced her decision. None of these, however, stands up under close scrutiny of the characters involved. Nor does the even more popular theory—that the Duchess refused to allow her favorite daughter to marry, as had she, a younger son—hold water. Prince Eddy was already dead at the time of George's proposal.

There must, then, be another answer to the riddle of Missy's refusal, and her youngest daughter may provide it: "It was only because they were first cousins. And my grandmother disapproved terribly of cousins marrying."

"Did she want to marry him?"

"Yes, she did want to marry him. But she was only sixteen, after all. And I don't think my mother was aware of the proposal. In fact, I'm convinced she wasn't."

"And she *would* have wanted to marry him?"

"Yes. But it was her mother who made the decision."

The Duchess also handled the only direct communication Missy had with George around this time. Apart from the formal marriage request, which he made to her parents, the Prince wrote Missy a personal note. He had heard, he said, that George Mikhailovich had asked for her hand. What did this mean? Wasn't it all understood? "I had supposed that you belonged to me, and that some day we would be married."

Missy wrote her answer at the Rosenau, seated at the roll-top desk in the little upstairs sitting room decorated with floral wallpaper, rush matting and the odd assortment of pictures and furniture the Duchess liked. It was a warm afternoon for spring, and the shutters were closed. From outside came the sounds of splashing water from the fountain on the front terrace and the old garderner's rake scratching the garden paths. She wrote Prince George that he must not think there was anything definite in the friendship that had sprung up between them at Malta. However, she added, she would always think of him as a "beloved chum." It's not surprising that her words sounded mature for her sixteen years. Her mother dictated every word.

The Edinburgh refusal triggered a hot new round of hostilities between the Duchess and her in-laws. Queen Victoria, who'd felt sure "Missy will have Georgie," was stunned. The Prince of Wales, who considered the refusal a slight to his son, stopped speaking to both older Edinburghs.

Obdurately ignoring the fracas she'd caused, the Duchess now moved into the final phase of her operation for deciding Missy's future. Missy and the Romanian prince would meet again that spring in Munich. Once there, the Duchess threw the young pair together as much as possible. All three attended galleries, shops, exhibitions, the theater. Still excruciatingly shy, Ferdinand laughed more than ever to mask his timidity. Curiously, it was his timidity which attracted her most. It aroused, she said later, her motherly feelings. One evening, the two young people spent a few minutes alone at an open hotel window. Shyness prevented Ferdinand from saying much, but he offered Missy a bouquet of pink roses and pressed her hand in his as they watched a full moon rise slowly over the houses of Munich.

The pathetic side of this situation emerges when you consider that while it was Missy who put Ferdinand at ease, her own education up to now had been based on a "completely false concept of life . . . a sort of stupid happiness, but for all that it was cruel, a deliberate blinding against life as it truly is, so that with shut eyes and perfect confidence I would have advanced toward any fate."

Nothing remained but the proposal. On a lovely June evening in 1892, at the Kaiser's glittering *Neues Palais* at Potsdam, and with the encouragement of the Duchess of Edinburgh, the Kaiser, and Princess Charlotte of Saxe-Meiningen, Prince Ferdinand asked Missy to be his wife. In 1927 she wrote: "How he ever had the courage to propose is today still a mystery to me; but he *did* and I accepted—I just said 'Yes' as though it had been quite a natural and simple word to say. 'Yes,' and with that 'Yes' I sealed my fate."

3

The Romanian Hohenzollerns

"I have been expecting to get a telegram from you about Missy's engagement, which has us all by surprise," Queen Victoria wrote to her oldest daughter in the summer of 1892. "It seems to have come very rapidly to a climax. The country is very insecure and the Society—dreadful—and she is a mere Child, and quite inexperienced! Of course the marriage cannot take place till next year; Missy herself would *not* have Georgie. . . . It was the dream of Affie's life. I believe Ferdinand is *very* nice."

Victoria's opinion of Romania, shared by most western Europeans, was only partly accurate. To be sure, at the time of its heir's engagement to Princess Missy, the ruling dynasty was a mere twenty-seven years old. Romania's life as a nation was even shorter. Yet in these few years, the country had achieved a measure of political stability totally out of keeping with Romania's traditional role of fair game to the major powers—Turkey, Russia, and Austria-Hungary—surrounding it.

Romania's newfound strength, like Missy's future, depended on the personality of one man.

The man was King Carol of Romania, formerly Karl Eitel, Prince of Hohenzollern-Sigmaringen. As the second son of *Fürst* (Prince) Karl Anton, head of the south German (Catholic) branch of Prussia's ruling Hohenzollern clan, Karl Eitel had spent a relatively obscure childhood at his family's ancestral Schloss Sigmaringen, where he was born on April 20, 1839.

A medieval stronghold rising out of the green Swabian countryside midway between Württemberg and Baden, Schloss Sigmaringen in the 1840s was a haven of *gemütlichkeit*. Its cozy little town nestled about its walls like a flock of fat geese. And the Danube, here only a few miles from its source, reflected the old castle's peaked roofs and sharp towers in an untroubled surface. Inside, Karl Eitel's grandmother, a French Princess Murat, had invested the place with a little of her Gallic *joie de vivre*. But his grandfather, the reigning *Fürst* Karl of Hohenzollern-Sigmaringen, oppressed like an ancient Teuton chieftain the several generations living beneath his roof. He watched over every detail of household affairs, waiting to pounce on the first visible sign of imprudent spending. And he oversaw every phase of his grandchildren's education (Karl Eitel had three brothers and a sister) to insure that each was strictly invested with the Hohenzollern tenets of Catholicism, Germanism and moralism. Years later, when Karl Eitel was called to reign over one of Europe's most extravagant courts, he'd bring with him the same iron routine and rigid devotion to thrift, hard work and discipline he'd learned from his grandfather.

In 1849, when he was ten, Karl Eitel settled at Dresden to complete his education. He stayed for seven years. During this time, his character developed along with his body. Until now, both had been considered delicate. Perhaps because of his imagined delicacy, at Dresden he began displaying traits of remarkable persistency and determination. Karl Eitel learned slowly. But he retained what he learned. Already he could be seen pondering both sides of a question and, from available evidence, reaching an irrevocable decision.

Nor did Karl Eitel intend to spare his body. He wanted to become a Prussian soldier. Once his academic career ended, therefore, he was gazetted a Second Lieutenant in the Prussian Guard Artillery. Having trained at the Fortress of Julich, visited the Krupp munitions factory at Essen and endured a brief military indoctrination in Berlin, he was considered ready to join the swelling ranks of the Prussian military.

For the next ten years of his life, Karl Eitel enjoyed the gay existence of a Prussian military officer in Berlin. But he felt his life lacked something. A wife might have helped, but even more tantalizing to him than women were the shifting political patterns and intrigues of mid-nineteenth-century Europe. They caught his attention due to his father's recent appointment as First German Minister. In Dresden even the most academic foundations considered necessary for a political career had been ignored by a tutor preparing his charge for a Prussian military career. Yet Karl Eitel felt developing inside himself a passion for politics that denied his lack of training. Hard on the heels of this new awareness came the frustrating knowledge that in his present situation he couldn't hope to dabble, even lightly, in any phase of German political life.

Equally compelling to Karl Eitel was the inspiring sight of a newly-united Germany. Astride this increasingly powerful colossus sat his cousins, the ruling Hohenzollerns, with whom he'd formed a close and mutually-admiring relationship during these Berlin years. Partly the result of his exposure to these prestigious and powerful relatives, partly the result of early training from his grandfather, and due in part to something harsh and ambitious in himself, Karl Eitel was now seized by another fierce desire. His new compulsion, as intense and unbidden as his sudden flare for politics and far stronger than his wish for a military career, was to rule.

He hadn't long to wait. On Good Friday, 1866, the self-made Romanian strongman Ion Bratianu arrived at Karl Anton's Düsseldorf house and offered Karl Eitel the throne of Romania.

"Over thy creation of beauty there is a mist of tears." Thus in a few words does a Romanian poet distill his nation's sorrow-filled history. In 1866 Romania* as a country was less than five years old. Yet her history as a people dates from 101 A.D. Only twice in the intervening centuries after the fall of Rome did the proud and spirited Romanian people triumph over the foreign conquerors that trampled and exploited them.

In 1290, calling themselves Vlachs, they united behind *Voivode* (Prince) Radu Negru (Rudolf the Black), a Transylvanian chieftain. Rudolf won for them a brief, shining moment of freedom from the Hungarians and Turks. But the darkness soon closed over them again. Then in 1600 Michael the Brave united not only the mountain-dwelling Vlachs but the plains Romanians of Wallachia and Moldavia. For the first time since the ancient Dacian days, all the Romanians followed a single prince. Though Michael's reign over a united Romania lasted for less than a year (he was assassinated in 1601 by an imperial commi-

*The spelling of Romania is that currently accepted in common usage and preferred by the present government. Variants such as *Rumania* or *Roumania* represent contemporary styles.

sioner of the neighboring Hungarian government), the spirit of what
he'd accomplished lived on in his people. It lived in broken Romanian
hearts even while Turkish and Russian domination lay like chain mail
on bloodstained Romanian soil.

The clue to her tragedy lies in Romania's geographical position. The
Carpathians and the Transylvanian Alps, cutting the country in two in
a line curving from north to west, have always been more curse than
blessing. Hard to defend from the Romanian side, they're easily defended from the Hungarian. And Transylvania, ancestral heart of ancient Dacian culture and therefore traditional birthplace of Romania
itself, lies on the wrong side. Bessarabia, in the northeast corner, pro-
vides no natural defense against a Russia that has owned the little
province for most of its existence. And Romania's fat belly, the agricul-
turally rich and oil-drenched plains of Wallachia and Moldavia, lies
defenseless to any conqueror with a will to sail down the Danube or
cross the Dobrudja plain from the Black Sea coast. In one century
alone, from 1754 to 1854, the Romanians suffered no fewer than six
Russian occupations and as many reconquests by the Turks.

Still the spirit of Romanian nationalism refused to die. In the mid-
1840s, fed by the revolutionary fever spreading out of the west, it found
new life in the passionate rediscovery by young Romanian intellectuals
of their link with Latin culture. Centuries of Turkish, Greek and Russian influence fell away as young Liberals devoured the works of great
French Enlightenment writers. Had not Romania, like France, been
part of the Roman Empire? Had not the Latin language and culture
survived in the Transylvanian mountains even as the Slav and Magyar
barbarism swept across the Wallachian and Moldavian plains? Eyes
burning, hearts pounding, the new Romanian patriots resurrected and
refurbished the Romanian dream: "We are a Latin island in a sea of
Slavs."

Trajan's column in the Roman forum, with its bas-relief of the Roman conquest of Dacia, became the symbol of the new Romanian
nationalism. Its goal, denied since the time of Michael the Brave, also
resurfaced. It was the goal of a free and united Romania.

Incredibly, in 1856 the Romanian nationalists could welcome the
first step in their desired direction. The Crimean War had ended, leaving Romania's fate in the hands of the seven powers represented at the
Congress of Paris. As a result of the subsequent Treaty of Paris, the
Romanian provinces of Wallachia and Moldavia found themselves
freed of the Russian "protectorship" imposed on them since 1829. And

though they remained under Turkish suzerainty, they were no longer the Grand Porte's subject states.

Autonomy and union took longer. Admittedly, the Congress had raised the two provinces to the level of self-governing principalities. But to keep the Romanians from feeling like a country, the powers also decreed that Wallachia and Moldavia should remain politically separate from each other, should elect separate parliaments and reigning princes, and should entrust to a joint commission only those matters which concerned both. The Transylvanian Romanians, smarting under Hungarian despotism, were ignored by the Congress.

First things first. The Treaty, "intrinsically clumsy and grossly insulting to the national sentiment of the Romanians," collapsed in the face of Romanian ingenuity. Both Wallachia and Moldavia elected the same prince. On December 23, 1861, united behind the Moldavian Alexander Cuza, the principalities formed a united Romania and chose Wallachian Bucharest as their capital. After two thousand years of limbo, Romania was born at last.

It took more than a Romanian to weld together Romanians oppressed for so many years. Boyars, clergy and peasants had conflicting interests. In pleasing one group, Cuza alienated another. Besides, the strongest man in Romania was not Cuza but Ion Bratianu.

Bratianu was a man with a dream. He envisioned "the miracle of a Danubian France." But he knew his fantasy could never be realized as long as rival nations from without and quarreling factions from within competed for control of the new country.

The answer, as Bratianu saw it, was a foreign prince. Someone who enjoyed the support of even a few of the major powers, and who also had the personal strength to calm internal disorder and withstand foreign assault. Karl Eitel wasn't Bratianu's first choice. He first offered the Romanian crown to Philip of Flanders. But Russia and Turkey, determined to squelch further Romanian unification, were so opposed that Philip fled in terror. Next, Bratianu appealed to Napoleon III of France to support Bratianu's second choice, Napoleon's cousin, Karl Eitel. Napoleon, eager to see a relative so near Russia's back door, eagerly agreed.

Encouraged by German Chancellor Bismarck, Karl Eitel finally accepted Bratianu's offer. Donning a disguise to see him through hostile Austria and Hungary, he rode down the Danube on a steamer. He arrived in Bucharest on May 22, 1866. That afternoon, he took the oath of office as reigning Prince Carol of Romania. Karl Eitel was gone forever.

Prince Carol's first view from a Romanian window took in a run-down guardhouse, a camp of gypsies, and a flock of swine wallowing in the muddy gutter. He had to admit that his over-all view of Romania was little better.

Romania in 1866 was completely cut off from the rest of Europe. At least a century behind other European nations, its people were hungry, illiterate and ignorant. The army and police force, having only recently been freed of their Russian and Turkish masters, were hardly trustworthy. And Romanian officials, schooled for generations by corrupt Greek Phanariote concessionaires imposed on them by the Turks, were masters of graft and baksheesh. Carol never got over his horror of this Romanian trait. Thirty years later he was still writing of the "after-effects of Levantine misrule, which blunted the public conscience and confused all moral conceptions."

But there were some good points, too. Romania was rich in salt, gold, copper and wheat. The geographical position that made her so vulnerable to invasion could also, in the right hands, make her powerful. "Whoever dominates Romania controls the Danube," said Bismarck.

Carol and the new and struggling Romania now formed one of history's great teams. The country needed in a ruler everything that Carol's rather unlikable personality offered: abnormal energy, a conservative outlook, an iron will, unswerving ambition, abnormal self-control, patience, harshness when needed, unscrupulousness (if Romanian interests demanded) and deft political skill.

Even his appearance seemed to reflect his character. Short, with a "dark, impressive, rather austere" face and an aquiline nose, he wore a short black beard and planted his feet, in thick-soled boots, firmly on the ground. With his slight, symmetrical figure and clean-cut profile, he resembled his mother's family, the French Beauharnais, more than the Hohenzollerns. His eyes, pale-blue and bloodshot below strong black brows that met across his nose, roamed constantly from side to side. His movements, slow and deliberate, possessed a sort of "conscious majesty."

And when he spoke, it was often to air one or another of the axioms by which he lived. "Only those who have nothing to do say they have no time," he'd say. And in explaining his political impartiality: "A ruler must take up one and drop another as the interests of the country require." Nor was he swayed by popular opinion: "I am against press prosecution in Romania, for what the papers write is valueless."

Underlying all this was a marrow-deep pride. Call it Hohenzollern pride. Whatever it was, it didn't keep him from personally liking even lower class people, he said, as long as they led "useful lives and have raised themselves honestly by their own merit." It was his own *Sitten-reinkeit* (moral purity) that allowed him to condemn anyone who deviated morally. Usefulness. Honesty. Morality. Work. With bull-like persistency, he sledge-hammered these themes into the foundation of a new Romania and thereby achieved a success recalling the great founders—William the Conqueror, Clovis, Charlemagne—of powerful medieval dynasties.

His personal success came fast. While his cousin Napoleon's star sank in the west, and France and Germany drew nearer a major war, Carol managed to play the Austrians, Russians and Turks against each other to Romania's benefit. When the quarreling Romanian political parties, the Liberals and the Conservatives, threatened internal catastrophe and Carol's own position, he rode the storm. "A Hohenzollern," he crowed to Bismarck, "cannot be overthrown so easily as a parvenu prince!" He spent his thirtieth birthday inspecting the progress of his pet project, the Moldavian railroad. And thanks to Carol, a bridge stretching 550 yards across the Busen River now connected Wallachia and Moldavia even during floodtime. In 1869, hoping to cement his gains and ensure his dynasty's future, he left Romania in search of a bride.

In the course of his career Carol made two tactical errors. One was his pursuit of a pro-German policy in the face of the Romanians' obvious preference for France. The other lay in his choice of a wife.

August 15, 1869, found him strolling through a Cologne garden with Princess Elisabeth of Wied. "German princesses are so well brought up!" Cousin Napoleon had said. And Carol was inclined to agree, at least in this case. Besides, the Wied princess had other things to recommend her. Aside from possessing an active, intelligent mind, she was also a Lutheran. Carol had already risked papal fury by promising to raise his children in the Romanian Orthodoxy demanded by Romanian law. He could hardly ask a Catholic bride to make the same sacrifice. Also, since Elisabeth belonged to a non-reigning house, he could marry her without provoking Russian and Austrian jealousy.

Even on that first day they must have made a stunningly incongruous pair—Carol, short and self-important in uniform, his black beard bobbing as he discoursed on Romania; Elisabeth, apple-cheeked and buxom, floating beside him in trailing gauze and answering him in poetic cadence. Her high-flown way of talking should have warned him. That, or the tragedy in her bright blue eyes. But Carol, like everyone else meeting Elisabeth of Wied for the first time, was too dazzled by her magnificent white-toothed smile and sweet voice to see beyond them. So what if her mother was something of a royal witch, with her talk of faith healing, spiritualism and levitational phenomena? Elisabeth seemed sensible enough.

Three months later she said *ja* to his proposal. And four months to the day, on November 15, they were married in the presence of both families and Queen Augusta of Prussia. The text chosen was appropriate enough: "Whither thou goest, I will go." Yet seldom have two people been so disastrously ill-suited. Even their one common trait—no sense of humor—was hardly conducive to marital understanding.

Still, their first years together were happy enough. On September 8, 1870, at the height of the Franco-Prussian War, Elisabeth gave birth to a daughter, Marie. While the ecstatic parents watched and guns barked outside, the child was baptized in the chapel at Cotroceni, an old monastery outside Bucharest.

The next August, Carol took his little family and withdrew from the Romanian political fray into the woods. At Sinaia, the tiny vacation resort in the Carpathians, they put up in an old cloister. The arrangements were primitive. But the magnificent mountain scenery compensated for the lack of comfort.

Carol actually seemed to be softening beneath the warming influence of family life. "You ought to see my little daughter now," he wrote his parents in 1872. "You would certainly take as great a pleasure in her as we do. She already speaks three languages—Romanian, German, and, above all, English. She is very independent, runs about alone, calls everybody by his proper name, and on Sundays goes to the chapel of the Monastery, where she keeps quiet during the service."

Less than two years later, four-year-old Marie contracted scarlet fever. After a brief illness, lying in the lap of her English nurse while her horrified parents knelt beside her, the child died. The day before Good Friday, they buried her in the Cotroceni park.

Grief-stricken, Carol plunged deeper than ever into affairs of state, finding solace in his old passion: work. But his wife, though she attempted to distract her grief by translating Romanian legends and fairy tales, could not. Until her own death nearly forty years later, she wore white mourning. And her mind—always fanciful at best—took a paranoiac twist that drove a wedge between her and her husband. Both Carol and Elisabeth burrowed deeper into their own personal compensations, thus severing forever the fragile bond of their communication.

As his home life deteriorated, Carol's political successes compounded. In 1877, during the Russo-Turkish War, he led a Romanian and Russian contingent to victory over the Turks at Plevna. Though the resultant Congress of Berlin gave Romanian Bessarabia to Russia and in return ceded to Romania the unappetizing province of Dobruja on the Black Sea, it also recognized Romania's full independence from Turkey. In 1881, therefore, Carol declared Romania a fully independent kingdom and laid plans for his coronation. That May, in a twelve-day celebration in Bucharest, it took place. Holding high his crown, fashioned by his order from a Turkish gun captured at Plevna, he said, "I assume with pride this crown, wrought from a cannon sprinkled with the blood of our heroes, and consecrated by the Church. I accept it as a symbol of the independence and power of Romania." And he placed it on his head.

He spent the next ten years consolidating his gains. Then he surveyed his domain, noting as always "every shortcoming" of the Romanians themselves, but prophesying for them a bright future. Had they not, after all, a mighty, navigable river, access to a sea, and inexhaustible treasures of soil, coal and iron? Another raw material not to be discredited was his own ability to maintain a stable ship of state. He'd increased military efficiency, and by keeping Romania's "real interests" uppermost, he'd steered her closer and closer to the "great Teutonic powers" and finally, in 1883, into a secret treaty with Germany and Austria.

To symbolize his faith in Romania's and his own future, he'd built himself a monumental castle in the beautiful Peles Valley just up the mountain from Sinaia. Here, where streams ran beneath towering firs, flower-filled meadows beamed in the sunlight and peaks soared a mile into the clear blue sky, he indulged his own personal brand of Hohenzollern showmanship.

Flamboyance marked Castle Peles from start to finish. *Altdeutsch* Gothic in style, to remind him of Nuremberg and the Rhineland, it boasted an incredible array of towers, turrets, cupolas and spreading wings. Inside, the palace was furnished as Carol desired, with tooled Italian leather walls, fringed chairs, darkly ornate wallpaper, marble and red-carpeted floors. Everywhere on the walls, gilt-framed mirrors

and El Grecos mixed with cheaply sentimental German prints. Stained
glass windows shut out the sunlight, heavy doors shut out the sounds
of nature and the laughing streams, and carving everywhere there was
an inch for carving prevented the existence of a comfortable corner
anywhere. There was even an organ for Elisabeth. In short, Carol's
palace was exactly as he'd planned it.

As Carol approached fifty, the question of an heir dominated his
mind. Casting about the various limbs of his family tree, he finally
settled on his brother Leopold's oldest son, Wilhelm. But Wilhelm,
jovial, bland and rotund, possessed no Hohenzollern lust for ruling.
Neither did his younger brother, Ferdinand. But already strangely
overwhelmed by his uncle's stern personality, Ferdinand agreed to go
to Romania in Wilhelm's place. In 1889, despite Elisabeth's objections
to his naming anyone to the position that would have been her child's,
Carol proclaimed Ferdinand heir-presumptive to the Romanian throne.

Ferdinand was born, like his uncle, at Sigmaringen. But he grew up
not in the old schloss but in his parents' mansion, the elegant and
homelike Furstenbau, at the edge of town. The dominating influence of
his boyhood was his mother, the aristocratic *Fürstin* Antonia, born an
Infanta of Portugal. Young and lonely for home while carrying this
second child, she'd hoped for a daughter. When he was born, on August
24, 1865, she called him after her second name (Fernanda) and proceeded to make him her favorite.

From his father, the courtly *Fürst* Leopold (Carol's older brother,
the successor to their father's title), Ferdinand had inherited a gentle,
modest disposition. From his mother came his love of beauty, scholar-
ship and Catholicism and the major passions of his life: botany, biology
and natural history. A victim of the hothouse atmosphere in which she
lived, Antonia was a strange mixture of poise and childish futility. She
was also vain, self-centered and petty. But her devotion to this favorite
child lasted until her death. And in Ferdinand's study—the lifelong
retreat where he spent his happiest hours—the dominating decoration
was a watercolor of wildflowers painted for him by his mother.

Ferdinand's upbringing resembled Carol's in only one way: both
were brought up to obey. When Ferdinand arrived in Romania, his
devotion to duty proved his only asset. If Carol expected to find the
makings of another Iron King in his heir, he was sadly disappointed.
No two men could have been less alike. Before he was thirty, Carol had
wrested the reins of Romanian leadership from six centuries of turmoil

and intrigue and held them steady. At twenty-four, Ferdinand was unassuming and diffident, lonely for the friends he'd left at the Potsdam military academy and unsure of his own abilities. Carol's passions were work, politics and self-denial. Ferdinand's were botany, books and flowers. The Hero of Plevna was small, graceful and majestic and boasted a hearty Prussian constitution. His nephew was handsome and possessed one real physically beautiful feature: well-shaped hands. But he was also awkward and pale, shivered in chills and preferred riding in a carriage to getting wet on horseback.

Carol wasted no time on regrets. He knew what was best for the boy and for Romania. He'd mold Ferdinand into the successor he wanted. He'd teach him all he knew and therefore enable him to overcome his personality defects—softness, sentimentality, insecurity—and become a worthy successor of The Founder of the Country. For the remaining quarter-century of his life, the older man subjected the younger to a regime of all work and no play, keeping him in a position of demeaning, harrowing dependency. The effect this had on Ferdinand's personality is incalculable.

For one thing, his natural shyness increased. "I am certainly not exaggerating," wrote a Romanian princess, "in saying that for this modest man to pass before women, to walk ahead of old men, to be served before his guests were so many small but burning tortures. In consequence he never came into a salon, except sideways, as if his left shoulder was making excuses for what his right shoulder was obliged to do." Under the pressure of his uncle's regime, he also developed a series of nervous tics: twisting his mouth, blinking his eyes and giggling nervously.

Meanwhile the King continued Ferdinand's unending grind of work and study. The boy was to make no friends, meet no young women and never take a vacation. His only recreation consisted of a nightly game of billiards with Carol. As a result, the boy's personality went underground. Inwardly proud and sensitive, he despised *der Onkel* for the misery he caused him, regretted the Germany of his boyhood, and disliked the new role being forced upon him. But to the outside world, he presented the picture of a dutiful Crown Prince. "He listened to his uncle in all things, blindly following his lead, submitting to his every demand, never revolting." Except once.

Under the strain of her prolonged grief, Queen Elisabeth (who now preferred her pen name, Carmen Sylva, to her royal title) had given way completely to the latent eccentricity Carol might have detected when he married her. Not since mad Ludwig of Bavaria had the ranks of European royalty sprouted such a royal show-off. Her prematurely gray hair cut unfashionably short, a dowdy pince-nez detracting from the effect of her flowing white gowns and veils, the contrast she presented to her dry and ceremonious little lord and master was greater than ever. Like an overgrown school girl, she'd inflated an unfulfilled existence into a Wagnerian epic come to life, with herself as the central character. She saw herself as all things: muse, martyr, humanity's benefactor, the court's inspiration. With manic exuberance, she strode with violin in hand beneath the Sinaia firs, devised grandiose charitable schemes she hadn't money to support, and bled her soul into romantic writings and paintings and unrequited friendships.

Wrote the beautiful Empress Elisabeth of Austria: "Carmen Sylva has remained under her white hair and exotic crown, a German *backenfisch*." That was superficial of the Empress. Carmen Sylva was much more than that. She was, among other things, a matchmaker.

One symptom of the Queen's restlessness was the daily salon she staged in her rooms. Like a medieval chatelaine, she'd assemble a flock of young girls about her and declaim. Her monologue left nothing to the imagination. With equal ardor, she discussed everything from the arts and the current state of her soul to her and her relatives' physical and marital complications, complete with "intimate physical details."

Her naturally warm heart having overcome her initial jealousy of Ferdinand's position, Carmen Sylva soon began inviting him to attend these salons. When the boy could break free of his bruising schedule, he came. It was here that he first met one of his aunt's maids-of-honor, a young Romanian girl of aristocratic family, Helene Vacarescu. A short, plump, vivacious girl with dark eyes, a full bosom and a winning manner, Helene had impressed the intellectual Carmen Sylva with her "remarkable culture, unfailing memory and dazzling gift of expression." The two had become great friends. By 1890 Helene was the Queen's favorite lady. Carmen Sylva paid her the ultimate compliment: she believed her dead child's spirit lived again in Helene.

From the moment Ferdinand and Helene met, Carmen Sylva threw the two young people together as much as possible. The expected happened: they fell in love. Ferdinand hadn't forgotten Carol; *der Onkel's* shadow darkened his every happiness those days. But the

Queen engaged the whole force of her not inconsiderable personality into aiding the romance. She encouraged the lovers, stimulated them, idealized them, helped them to meet secretly. She even wrote a poem about them. Borne aloft on the Queen's enthusiasm and hardly able to believe his good fortune at capturing the witty and scholarly Helene, Ferdinand lived through months of alternating ecstasy and despair. Finally, in the spring of 1891, he mustered up the courage to tell Carol he planned to marry Helene.

The crash, long in coming, came now. Absorbed in the business of ruling, the King hadn't had an inkling of the romance blooming beneath his nose. He and Carmen Sylva, despite their politely distant relationship, worked in harness. He administered the nation, she led its charitable, artistic and social affairs. But they shared separate apartments, coming together only at mealtimes. Carol had neither the time nor the interest to pursue what went on in his wife's domain.

Now he exploded. For twenty-five years, he'd struggled to overcome the centuries-old internal conflicts that had torn Romania. Now this pale, wide-eared boy proposed to ruin all his efforts by marrying the daughter of one of Romania's first families. Furious, Carol called in the Prime Minister, Lascar Catargi. Haltingly, reluctantly, the little Romanian told Ferdinand: "As a private subject, Your Royal Highness could not make a better choice than Mademoiselle Vacarescu, and I couldn't more approve of it. But the Heir Presumptive of our throne must marry a foreign princess, equal in rank and birth, who can be future Queen. The Constitution is quite definite on that."

Carmen Sylva now entered the fray. "Helene is dark-eyed," the Queen argued, "hot-blooded, she'll make a glorious mate for our pale prince. She'll lead and inspire him, fill him with life, spirit, ambition. They will have healthy children. God will smile upon them."

Turmoil ensued. The Queen stood for love; Carol for law. Ferdinand wavered. Helene collapsed with grief. Public opinion blasted the Queen for trying to damage the country's future. Finally, in a voice that left no room for argument, Carol ordered Ferdinand to decide between Helene and the throne. Ferdinand, his one revolt in a shambles, gave in.

Carmen Sylva and Helene immediately left together for Venice, where the fashionable novelist Pierre Loti wrote a book about them, *L'Exilée,* which was banned in Romania. After a year in Venice, Carmen Sylva went home to her mother's house in Wied rather than risk the resentment still blazing against her in Romania. She couldn't resume her duties anyway, she announced, because her health had failed. Helene, her dream shattered, found herself as unwelcome in Romania as the Queen. Mustering her talents and character, she moved to Paris. There she remained a spinster, devoting the rest of her life to successful social, literary and political careers.

Ferdinand, in turn, was shipped off to Germany, where Carol hoped he'd forget his grief and find a suitable wife. When Ferdinand at last wired Bucharest the news of his engagement to Princess Missy, Carol was elated. Romania was stronger than when he'd married Elisabeth, and need no longer fear the jealousy of adjoining powers. The heir's marriage to a granddaughter of both Queen Victoria and the Tsar of Russia would give the nation a prestige it still sorely lacked. To show their approval, cheering Bucharest crowds filled the streets.

In England the word was greeted with considerably less enthusiasm. "Disgusted," wrote one royal lady-in-waiting, "to see the announcement of the marriage of poor pretty nice Princess Marie of Edinburgh to the *Prince of Romania!!!* It does seem too cruel a shame to cart that nice pretty girl off to semi-barbaric Romania and a man to the knowledge of all Europe desperately in love with another woman."

Queen Victoria had her own doubts about the match. Before sanctioning the engagement, she wrote to Carol, asking him point-blank if there had been a previous engagement. For the first time, Carol found his wife's romantic temperament useful. The whole affair, he implied, had been a figment of Elisabeth's imagination. Victoria treasured "delightful memories" of her "niece" Elisabeth, but she admitted herself incapable of understanding the younger woman. Unprepared to question Carol's word, Victoria approved the match.

Meanwhile, at her father's last naval post in Davenport, Princess Missy played out the final scenes of her childhood against a Reynolds-like backdrop. Her head filled with romantic illusions of Romania, she trembled on the edge of life like Thumbelina on the edge of her leaf. The fall, when it came, would be long and hard.

4

Marriage

For all her blind optimism, the seven months between Missy's engagement and her wedding were not entirely happy. A major source of conflict was her sister Ducky. A blue-eyed, moody-looking beauty, sixteen-year-old Ducky resented her sister's ready consent to marry a man she hardly knew. Even on the enchanted night of Missy's engagement, while the Kaiser and his court toasted her at a gala banquet on Potsdam's Island of Peacocks, the sisters had clutched hands beneath the table, already dreading their impending separation. Missy felt herself torn between Ducky and Ferdinand, both of whom wanted her full attention.

Her mother, however, was experiencing no such conflicts. Having brought her maneuverings to a successful conclusion, the Duchess of Edinburgh was ecstatic. Princess May of Teck, the girl who later married Prince George and reigned at his side for twenty-five years as Queen Mary, lunched with the Duchess on June 16, 1891, a few days after the engagement. Afterwards, May wrote in her diary: "Aunt M. was looking flourishing and seems delighted at Missy's engagement." Even so, the Duchess felt it necessary to ease the tension between her in-laws and herself by loudly declaring that she'd really wanted Missy to marry George.

Though she knew nothing of George's proposal or the resultant fracas, Missy dreaded facing her relatives. Her father hadn't been present at Potsdam, but she instinctively felt he'd had other plans for her future. When the Edinburgh women finally arrived home from Potsdam, the Duke greeted them glumly. Even worse, she feared, would be the formal inspection of her fiancé by Queen Victoria.

Before traveling to Windsor, it was decided Missy should visit Ferdinand's family stronghold at Sigmaringen. She was always intensely aware of her surroundings. But in these last days of her girlhood, when her uncommon perception told her time was fleeting and there could be no going back, the people and settings of her life took on a kind of fatal clarity. Beginning with the July afternoon of her arrival at Sigmaringen, the scenes of 1892 would follow one another in her memory like soldiers on review.

Waiting to greet the Duchess of Edinburgh and her four children as their train steamed into the station, were Ferdinand and his family. Foremost among them stood his father, the handsome and amiable *Fürst* Leopold. Missy's future father-in-law was one of the most charming men in Europe—thoughtful, well-read and deeply cultured. Predictably, the Duchess adored him.

But Ferdinand's mother was a disappointment. Considered one of the great beauties of her day, Antonia had posed for the painter Franz Winterhalter in sweeping, low-necked crinoline gowns that displayed her best features: a Grecian profile, sloping shoulders and delicate hands. To Missy, watching her future mother-in-law preside at a welcoming tea in the garden of one of the Hohenzollern's country homes, the older woman looked more grotesque than attractive. Tottering about on tiny feet, she was smartly dressed to her disadvantage in the current style of puffed sleeves, tightly-cinched waist and bell-shaped skirt. Without the concealing crinoline, the disproportion between her small bust and enormous hips "made you fell positively uncomfortable."

The tea, composed of every kind of small German cake, was a feast. Used to their mother's indulgent Coburg teas, the Edinburgh children fell to and stuffed themselves greedily. Ferdinand, or Nando as his family called him, took Missy up to meet old family servants and friends. Under their warming congratulations, he lost some of his shyness. "All the same I detected a certain underlying sadness," she later wrote. "I felt this through everything—a certain anxiety, with just a touch of dread."

His dread, the girl soon realized, had to do with Romania. What little she knew about her future home she'd picked up from Ferdinand's aide-de-camp, Colonel Coanda, at Potsdam on the night of her engagement. Courtly and effusive, Coanda had charmed his future Crown Princess with images of Romania as a beautiful country of romantic scenery and picturesque peasants over which she would one day rule as a great and loved queen. Now Ferdinand's halting descriptions of his adopted country dispelled some of Coanda's magic. At the end of every sentence sounded one name: *"der Onkel."*

Before Missy had a chance for alarm, King Carol arrived at Sigmaringen to inspect the bride for himself. On the morning of his arrival, Missy awoke to the sound of music and the clatter of hurrying boots on the cobblestones outside her window. Looking out, she saw for the first time the red, yellow and blue of the Romanian flag fluttering from turrets and draping villagers' houses.

None of the exitement could disguise Missy's frank disappointment at the King's appearance. Photographs she'd seen of The Hero of Plevna had led her to imagine him as tall and imposing. Instead, she found him short, with "incurved" knees and an eagle-like habit of moving his eyes without turning his head.

Having dispensed gifts to Missy and her sisters, the King sat down with the Duchess and *Fürst* Leopold to iron out the difficulties involved in the marriage itself. They were several. To begin with, the Pope refused to agree that any children born to the match should be christened in the Orthodoxy demanded by the Romanian Constitution. Placating deputies, therefore, were scurrying back and forth to Rome. Also, since both Catholic and Anglican ceremonies were to join the couple and since in England neither church would allow its service to follow the other, the original plan of holding the wedding at Windsor Castle had to be shelved. The other natural solution, for a Coburg wedding, was impossible due to old Duke Ernest's reprehensible court. The bride's extreme youth was another delaying factor; it would be best to wait at least until after her seventeenth birthday. Finally Missy's wedding plans, cut and dried as her courtship had been, were presented to her. She would marry Ferdinand here at Sigmaringen on January 10, 1893, in three ceremonies—a Civil, a Catholic and an Anglican.

Not that plans for an event which still seemed far away and dreamlike much concerned the young lovers. Sexually unaware and naively believing that all dreams come true, Missy imbued her future with adolescent idealism. "Nando and I were two loving companions advancing towards perfect bliss," she wrote years later. "We would sit together hand in hand in any corner where we could be alone, and the love I read in Nando's eyes meant nothing to me but a promise of perfect happiness."

At Windsor Queen Victoria received the pair in the Great Corridor. In this curving 550-foot-long hallway built during King George IV's period of reconstruction, the weight of Missy's English family hung heavier than anywhere else. In the early years of her reign, the young Queen Victoria had played shuttlecock and ball here with her ladies. In 1861 members of the Royal Household had kept vigil in the Corridor while the Prince Consort lay dying a few feet away. And Missy and her sisters, like their father before them, had played here as children— inspecting the busts, screens and gilt clocks that lined its walls.

Missy never forgot that first meeting of Victoria and her future husband: "One could hear the sound of Grandmamma's stick before she came around the corner, and also the rustle of her stiff silk gown. Tap, tap, and there she was—wee and smiling and rather shy, with teeth like . . . a mouse, and a deliciously modulated voice when she addressed the young German prince in his native tongue."

That evening the entire British Royal Family turned out to inspect Missy's choice. Dressed in her best, she hurried with Ferdinand and her parents back to the Corridor. As she walked, she felt sinkingly that she'd betrayed much she'd loved by consenting to marry this strange man from an unknown country. Once in the Corridor, she had eyes only for Cousin George. With a lump in her throat, feeling herself a traitor to their shared memories, she looked into the eyes of the man she might have married. George was sympathetic in the face of her obvious distress. The two avoided speaking of the Malta days. "I could not have stood it," she wrote.

Whatever had gone before, Queen Victoria was now kindness itself to her granddaughter's tongue-tied fiancé. At breakfast on the second day of his visit, Ferdinand broke his rolls German-style into his coffee. Noting his obvious embarrassment when no one else followed suit, the Queen said, "You must come and breakfast with me one day, Nando, in my private apartments, and then we will break our rolls into our coffee together in the good old German fashion."

The Windsor visit was climaxed by the ceremonial arrival of King Carol and a colorful Romanian retinue. Carol proudly received the Order of the Garter from Missy's grandmother, but balked at wearing the knee breeches prescribed for formal Windsor dinners. Hardly out of uniform since boyhood, he now declared to his heir that he must wear wool stockings under his silk hose or catch cold. Wildly amused, Ferdinand and Missy sought at dinner to discern a bulky outline beneath the royal hose.

From Windsor Carol went to London. Here he spent a few days visitng "important" people and viewing "useful and interesting" institutions. His opinion of the English character had never been high. Even so, he felt he could learn something from visiting the Bank of England, the mint and the London docks. He therefore set about planning eduational excursions for himself and his nephew.

For once Ferdinand ignored the King's wishes. "He never was in love himself," he told Missy, "so he doesn't understand. I'm here to be happy—not to be dragged around looking at State institutions."

Finally, after several weeks with his future bride, the time came for Ferdinand to return to Romania. Missy spent the rest of the summer at Devenport. Here, warmed by flower-scented breezes, she joyously engaged in all her favorite pastimes—swimming, boating and riding with her sisters and their friends. The prewedding excitement was mounting. From all over Europe, presents came pouring in. Former admirers let her know their hearts were a little broken. Dressed in the colorful Romanian peasant costumes King Carol had given them, the bride and her sisters presided at charades. During one such game, one of Missy's former suitors defined Romania as "that town in Hungary." Shocked, Missy realized this was even more insulting than her own view of her future country as "some place in the Near East."

The autumn passed quickly. As often as he could, Ferdinand broke away from his duties in Romania and hurried back to Germany. When he was away, Missy and her sisters spent many hours in awed inspection of her vast trousseau and the staggering array of wedding presents laid out on long tables.

One emotional scene marred the last days before her wedding. On a day in late December the Duke of Edinburgh suddenly called Missy into his room. There he took her into his arms and burst into tears. He told her he'd had another dream for her, one that would have differently shaped her future. He hoped Ferdinand was a good man, he said, but he hated to see her leave for such a far country. He mentioned the dowry he and her mother were giving her and made her promise never to forget that she was a British princess and a sailor's daughter. Shaken, Missy finally fled to her own room and wept.

Shortly before the wedding, Missy, Ducky and their mother journeyed to Neu Wied to visit Carmen Sylva, the exiled Queen of Romania. It was January, and the snow in Neu Wied was piled high beneath dense pine forests when the Edinburghs—pink-cheeked and bundled into a sledge—arrived at the Wied house. Carmen Sylva's mother greeted them at the door. An unusually ugly old woman with a high forehead "round and polished like a globe," the Princess of Wied was beset with problems. Clustering about her to greet the Tsar of Russia's daughter and Queen Victoria's granddaughters were a startling array of minor German royalty, all handicapped. Blind, deaf, dumb and lame, they'd come to benefit from the Princess's rumored powers of healing.

But Carmen Sylva, sighed the Princess, was her major difficulty. Unable to walk or stand, the Queen spent every day painting in her bed. She loved the woods, but refused to leave the house. "*Ach!* my Elisabeth is very fantastic," confessed her mother. "She was always like this, even as a child. The real poet temperament, inclined to be tragic always. But now, alas, there has been enough to be tragic about."

Then turning deep-set eyes toward Missy, the old woman added, "But she will be unable to resist you, my dear, you are like the blossoms of spring."

In her room, dressed all in white and lying in a sky-lit bed, from which she painted enormous, unbalanced still-lifes, Carmen Sylva waited. At the sight of Missy, she threw out her arms in elaborate gestures of welcome, clasped the girl to her generous bosom, murmuring "*Lieb Kindchen,* dear, dear child," and stroked her hair. She compared Missy to the classical bust of a forlorn-looking maiden placed on a table near the bed, and when the Duchess of Edinburgh attempted to bring the encounter back to earth, Carmen Sylva took off on yet another romantic tangent.

The Duchess was disgusted. But Missy was enchanted, if somewhat alarmed, by this melodramatic personage she would one day succeed as Queen of Romania. Only a faint note of tragic resignation in Carmen Sylva's manner hinted that Missy had not been her choice for Ferdinand's bride.

A few days later the Edinburghs boarded the train for Sigmaringen and the wedding. In her list of abnormal dislikes the Duchess included saloon carriages. So in weird contrast to the splendor of the approaching ceremonies, the family bundled into first-class compartments that were unheated and large enough for only two people each. To their delight, Missy and Ducky found they were sharing a compartment. Once inside, however, they discovered it contained only one narrow seat and no bed. That night the princesses took turns sleeping on the cold, dirty floor and in the morning washed in a pan of icy water.

At Sigmaringen the Kaiser and a huge suite of bombastic Lohengrins in blazing uniforms arrived to join the growing ranks of wedding guests. Uncle Arthur, the Duke of Connaught, represented Queen Victoria. The Tsar had sent Grand Duke Alexis, the Duchess of Edinburgh's lusty brother. Albert, the future King of Belgium, arrived with his forceful mother, the Countess of Flanders. To greet these luminaries as well as less important officials, constant processions shuttled back and forth between the Schloss and the station.

At the heart of receptions, formal dinners and family gatherings, Missy sat pale and overdressed. The constant changing from one elaborate costume to another reminded her of playing Queen of Spain as a child. But surrounded by aged Romanian officials who embarrassed her with their flattery in rapid-fire French, she felt awkward and lonely.

On the morning of January 10, while bells pealed outside her window, her maids dressed her in a white silk wedding dress with puffed sleeves and a bell skirt that spread out to form a train. On her head she wore a tulle veil, held in place by a diamond tiara, and a wreath of orange blossoms. She didn't much like her appearance; "I had more romantic ideas about how a bride ought to look." But the Duchess had decreed her daughter's wedding gown as she'd chosen the rest of her trousseau.

As if in a trance, the girl walked through the old castle's intricate passages to participate in her three weddings. The first ceremony, the Civil, took place in the registry office. Then the whole vast retinue proceeded to the church adjoining the Schloss for the Catholic service. The Anglican ceremony was performed in one of the Schloss drawing rooms by Mr. Lloyd, the Naval chaplain from the Duke of Edinburgh's flagship. A festive banquet, held in a glass and steel amphitheater built to hold the guests, celebrated the union of two royal houses. That night at nine, the young couple left the banquet for a flying sleigh ride across moonlit drifts to their honeymoon house, the nearby Schloss Krauchenweiss.

At the Krauchenweiss Ferdinand discreetly withdrew while a maid readied his bride for bed. Tucked in at last, Missy watched in amazement as her maid backed out the door, three times making the sign of the cross and three times repeating, "Your Royal Highness, I shall pray for you."

George Sand wrote of gently-reared young women: "We bring them up as saints, only to dispose of them as fillies." The Duchess of Edinburgh's goal had been to bring Missy to the altar totally innocent of sex. "And in this," her daughter ruefully wrote many years later, "she succeeded marvellously . . . A *risqué* book never reached our hands, we blushed when it was mentioned that someone was to have a baby, the classics were only allowed in small and well-weeded doses; as for the Bible, although we were well up in both Testaments, all the more revealing episodes had been carefully circumscribed."

On her wedding night the treasured fool's paradise of Missy's childhood shattered forever. She never forgot this moment, and it set her on a lifelong search for idealized romance as she'd once imagined it. Years later she wrote: "Nando was terribly, almost cruelly in love. In my immature way I tried to respond to his passion, but I hungered and thirsted for something more. . . . There was an empty feeling about it all; I still seemed to be waiting for something that did not come."

Irrevocably the time drew near for the couple's departure for Romania. They spent their last few days in Germany at Coburg, skating with Missy's old friends on the Rosenau lake, playing charades in the big Rosenau hall.

On the last evening a scene occurred that revealed a heart beneath the Duchess of Edinburgh's Spartan exterior and furnished Missy with a memory to cling to during her first desperate days in Romania. On this night, the Duchess had encouraged Missy to go to bed early in order to counteract the emotions involved with leaving. Her camp bed had already been removed from the row of three in the tower room and packed to accompany her to her new home. So it was to the guest apartment, where Missy and Ferdinand were spending their first Rosenau visit as a married couple, that the Duchess came to kiss her daughter good night. Both attempted bravery. Missy knew her mother disliked sentimental outbursts; "scenes" she called them. With a Herculean effort, the girl choked back the fear and sorrow she felt at leaving.

The Duchess tiptoed out. Lying in the dark, Missy could hear her mother whispering with Ferdinand in the next room. Then, after some time, she heard the Duchess say: "I must just have a last look at her." The door opened. Partially illuminated by a crack of light, the Duchess peered in at her daughter. Shocked, Missy saw there were actually tears running down her mother's face. The Duchess smiled. Mother and daughter nodded to each other, though neither spoke. With a stab of pain, Missy longed to throw her arms around her mother's neck, but the rigid repression of emotion the Duchess demanded both of herself and her child prevented either from giving way to her feelings. Every night for months afterward, Missy would cry into her pillow the grief and longing she now kept herself from expressing.

The next morning the family, old friends, and servants with hats in hand gathered at the station for leave-taking. After emotional good-bys, an order rang out, and the train slowly moved away from the station. Watching from the window, Missy saw Coburg and her family, waving from the snowy platform, grow smaller and smaller until they disappeared completely.

It was a long journey to Bucharest. As the train rolled across the frozen plains of central Europe, Missy felt lonely for the first time in her life. Though she longed to talk to Madame Gracianu, the motherly-looking woman who'd been appointed her lady-in-waiting, Ferdinand would have none of it. Since the Vacarescu fiasco, he'd lost his faith in people. He trusted no one, especially those connected with the Romanian court. So the two spent the long days isolated in their luxurious private carriage. As they drew near the Romanian border, Missy grew increasingly more anxious about what she'd find "down there," as she privately referred to Romania.

In Vienna the pair stopped to pay an official visit to the old Emperor Franz Joseph. Here Missy's usual delight in her surroundings was dulled by her current state of emotional trauma. A festive dinner at the Imperial Court swirled around her in a haze of sparkling gold plate, uniformed officers, beautiful women and lilting music. Shy and self-conscious, she was more aware of a grease spot on her pink dress than she was of Franz Joseph himself.

In the town of Predeal on the Romanian border, the train halted for an exuberant welcoming ceremony, complete with bands, flags, crowds of cheering peasants and speeches made by dark-eyed officials in top hats. During the rest of the trip, despite the bitter cold, they were stopped at every station by equally exuberant demonstrations.

Bucharest in 1893 was, according to one Romanian, "a charming, semi-Oriental capital, composed of low rambling houses set deep in spacious gardens, and of poorly paved narrow streets seething with

picturesque life, gaiety, and gossip." On the day that Missy and Ferdinand arrived, it was buried under mountains of snow. To Missy's relief,
the train was delayed several hours while whole army regiments cleared
drifts from the tracks.

From the moment the royal train slid slowly into the outskirts of
Bucharest, the entire city exploded with delight. From afar, then growing louder, came the sound of music, bands playing what Missy recognized as the national anthem, *"Traiasca Regele"* (Long Live the King).
As they drew near the center of town, the din—saluting cannons,
frantically cheering crowds and massed bands—grew deafening. Looking out, Missy saw rows of troops, swarthy little men with dark eyes
and very white teeth, lining the station platform and cheering lustily.
"They wore dark grey coats," she wrote, "and had queer-shaped hats
with long cocks' plumes hanging down one side."

On the platform, trembling with emotion, King Carol awaited the
young couple. He greeted Ferdinand warmly, then embraced Missy.
Also on the platform stood all the major Romanian officials and their
wives. In an instant, Missy was overwhelmed by her first Romanian
welcome. The mayor of Bucharest pushed forward to offer the traditional bread and salt. The officials' wives—fascinating painted creatures
with olive complexions and "slumbrous" eyes—buried her beneath
more bouquets than she could hold. Everything assaulted her—the
thunderous noise, the bouquets, the crush of people, the intense cold.
Yet underlying her stage fright and confusion lurked a glimmer of
relief. All this was somehow less frightening than she'd imagined it. The
Romanians conveyed an undeniable good humor that warmed her in
spite of herself.

A blue and silver coach drawn by four black Russian stallions waited
to carry the Royal Family to the Metropolitan Church for a *Te Deum.*
As Missy rode through the cheering crowds, her beauty worked its
magic on the Romanian people as it would a thousand times in the
future. The peasants especially were delighted at the sight of the white-
skinned girl dressed in a violet cloak with a huge fox collar and wearing
a small gold and amethyst toque in her curled blond hair. "The top of
the basket," they murmured, "the angel without wings." Equally fascinated, she stared back at them. The Romanian peasants were unlike
any people she'd ever seen; men and women muffled in brightly-
embroidered great-coats, the women wearing veils or colored handkerchiefs on their heads.

After the church service the family drove to the Palatul Regal (Royal

Palace). Used to Windsor and the glittering Russian palaces, Missy was unimpressed by the squat U-shaped building. Inside, King Carol conducted her up the palace's one noble construction, a grand staircase. Ferdinand followed nervously behind. White-dressed schoolgirls lined the stairs, singing songs and throwing flowers in the royal path. Finally the three reached the rooms prepared for the young couple. With a flourish, Carol threw open the doors of the apartment.

At the first sight of her new home, the loneliness and misery that had been welling up in Missy since her last night in Coburg finally burst. The apartment was a disaster. Carol had redecorated the rooms as he'd furnished the Peles Castle at Sinaia, in *Altdeutsch* and bad rococo. Heavy red plush drapes shut out the blazing January sunlight. A hideous German Gothic four-poster nearly filled the bedroom. Overcarved gilt furniture was forced by too many doors and windows into awkward arrangements. Old religious paintings studded the walls with portrayals of suffering and tragedy. There were no fireplace, no cozy corner and no flowers except a camellia plant with one red bud.

That night Bucharest glowed with light, rang with the music of many celebrations. But inside the palace, after the formal dinner had ended and the officials gone, Missy sat forlorn and lonely with her only consolation—the box of treasures she'd brought from home. They included a blue bead from Venice, a little ivory Buddha she'd found in Green Park, photographs of the Rosenau, photographs of the Malta picnic parties, a braid from Ruby's tail and a crystal clock. The clock's inscription, printed in gold, read: "From George to Darling Missy, Christmas, 1891."

The Palatul Regal without Carmen Sylva was a man's world. King Carol worked long and hard at his desk, a massive edifice resting on two carved lions in a room decorated with stained-glass windows depicting martyrs and crusaders. The corridors were filled with secretaries, servants, and offiicials—all whispering. No one was allowed to speak above a whisper anywhere in the palace unless addressed by the king.

Utterly disillusioned, Missy lived the first months of her life in Romania as a virtual prisoner in her unlovely rooms. What little she saw of Bucharest seemed inferior to London and St. Petersburg. She knew nothing of its madcap winter gaiety. Nor was she allowed to mix with the supremely sophisticated Romanian aristocracy. Her only companions by day were her two maids, both named Louise, and a pet bullfinch,

Bully, which one of the Louises soon stepped on by mistake. Another grief was the change that had come over Ferdinand. In his uncle's shadow he'd become nervous and tense, preoccupied with his military duties and with the difficult task of pleasing the king. Gone was the shyly humorous companion of Potsdam, Sigmaringen and Coburg. And he agreed with Uncle that she must have no friends in Romania. Evenings, she watched while her husband and the king played billiards and talked politics. Their cigar smoke burned her eyes, which were already red from crying.

Too late she realized that these Hohenzollerns had a totally different concept of how life should be lived than the one she'd learned from her mother. Fair play and honesty, fresh air and exercise had been the Duchess of Edinburgh's bywords. But in the Palatul Regal, every movement was cloaked in secrecy and buried beneath endless discussion. Even harder to bear was her enforced inactivity. Riding in such harsh weather, the king told her, was out of the question. And late afternoons, when she begged Ferdinand to take her out for a drive, he said there was no place to drive to.

Above all, she missed Ducky—missed the healthy daily contact with another teen-age girl with whom she could giggle and share romantic musings, missed the long exultant hours spent on horseback exploring the woods and gardens of Coburg and Davenport. The sheer magnitude of her loneliness was brought home to her the day she received Ducky's first letter. With typical lack of insight, the Duchess had ordered Ducky to avoid writing Missy how much she missed her. So Ducky, though equally heartbroken, had dutifully written cheery letters describing her first "season" at the Russian court. Along with the letter came a note from the Duchess, chiding Missy for writing such boring letters. Where were her descriptions of the gay Romanian court? Of Missy's new friends? Of the parties and entertainments she was attending?

A few weeks after her arrival she sustained the most crushing blow of all. When she complained to her lady-in-waiting that she was "not feeling well," the older woman pronounced her pregnant. Missy took the news of her first pregnancy tragically. She felt trapped, resentful. So this was what the Romanians had wanted her for; to give them an heir. Existing in a vacuum of boredom, loneliness and physical discomfort, she grew morbid and depressed. The weeks dragged toward spring. That Easter, at a Communion service in a Lutheran church, she fainted.

At this point King Carol finally yielded to the demands of those who understood adolescent psychology better than he. Other attempts to cheer his homesick niece—tea parties attended by officials' wives and a tour of the Bucharest fortresses—having failed, he now planned a visit to a monastery and a convent near Bucharest.

This outing on a spring day in 1893 was one of the great moments of her life. Riding in a carriage pulled by four apricot-colored Norwegian ponies, she and the king traveled first to Cernica, a monastery built on an island in swamps abloom with yellow iris. Her artistic nature responded to the old church, with its dim, frescoed sanctuary; to the monks themselves, with their silver beards and melancholy eyes; and to their thatched cottages set in bright flower beds.

At the Convent of Pasarea, the nuns ushered their royal guests into a large carpet-hung room scented with old apples and wood smoke. Here they offered the traditional Romanian jam and some unclear water the king told Missy not to drink. "The nuns were voluble in their praise of me," she remembered years later. "They hugged me and kissed me and kept throwing up their hands to the heavens, calling down a thousand blessings on my head. Of course I could not understand a word they said."

Driving home, they passed through small Wallachian villages composed of tiny huts like those she'd drawn as a child. It was her first sight of the wide Wallachian plain, of the gray oxen pulling farmers' carts, of the ancient stone crosses leaning beside pole wells. Picturesque hordes of gypsies moved past, followed by creaking carts filled with wild-eyed children. On this day she felt the first stirring of the love and understanding that was to grow up between her and Romania.

In June the royal family moved from Bucharest to Peles Castle at Sinaia. The bracing air, forested mountains and flower-starred meadows had a restorative effect on Missy. To complete her new-found happiness, Ducky finally arrived late that summer for a visit. In an ecstasy of renewed sharing, the girls took tea under the trees of the Sinaia monastery, rode out in a carriage pulled by the apricot-colored ponies, and picked flowers with Ferdinand beneath the benign Sinaia sun.

October brought the Duchess of Edinburgh to preside over the birth of Missy's baby. At once, endless controversies sprang up between the Duchess and King Carol as to how the birth should be handled. Equally strong-willed, they saw eye-to-eye on nothing—from doctors and nurses to which room should serve as a nursery. Finally Queen Victoria put an end to one part of the controversy by sending an English doctor to attend her granddaughter. "We want to be on the safe side," wrote the Queen. "So near the East you know . . . must uncertain."

On Sunday, October 15, 1893, at one in the morning, twenty-one years to the day after the birth of her brother Alfred, Missy presented Romania with an heir, Prince Carol. As she lay holding the baby, she listened to the cannons saluting her success while a tear trickled onto the baby's fuzzy head. In spite of her mother's entreaties, she could feel no joy. "I felt like turning my head to the wall," she wrote later, "unwilling to take up a life again in which such pain could exist." Nor did she care about the happiness of the Romanian people. "I had not yet discovered my people, they had been carefully kept from me."

The baby was christened at Sinaia with great ceremony on October 29. For the occasion, a triumphant Duchess of Edinburgh draped herself in festive ropes of pearls. Later, holding her baby at the maginificent reception attended by government officials and representatives of Romanian towns and provinces, Missy felt "proud and a little trembling . . . rather as though I had suddenly been given a living doll to play with."

It was her eighteenth birthday.

5

The Vine and the Wall

Missy and Ferdinand spent three years in the King's household. In those years and for nineteen more, Carol's influence was a smothering presence which dominated their every waking moment. Concerned with building a dynasty, the King regarded his Crown Prince and Princess as necessary, but potentially dangerous to his creation. He needed them—to carry on his work, to produce a third generation. But he was suspicious of the harm they might do if allowed free rein.

Consequently, they found themselves hemmed in and overcontrolled. The King chose their servants and the people who were to raise their child. Prince Carol, said the King, was national property. Such an important appointment as his nanny—or wet nurse or governess—should not be left to parents who were little more than children themselves. So, from the moment her son was born, Missy was surrounded by people who worked for the King and spied on her daily activities for him. Nor was she yet allowed to make friends, go to parties or visit the Romanian villages. The King even frowned on her riding. He feared it might interfere with her having children.

Ferdinand, though he despised his uncle's repression, had grown used to it. Missy could not. Like a dying woman gasping for oxygen, her craving for freedom grew with each new restriction. Before her marriage she had unconsciously based her happiness on the freedom to do as she pleased. Now that she saw this happiness threatened, it became her only reason for living. Anyone opposing her "rush toward that luminous goal," became her enemy. And how much more formidable the enemy was when embodied by a Teutonic self-made monarch who saw her as only a cog in the wheel of his dynasty. All she asked from life was freedom—to find herself, to live her life as she wished. But the King of Romania had just the opposite in mind.

Years later, when she had gained an illusory freedom, her answer to a routine question told the story.

"What does Your Majesty compare herself to?"

"To a vine which has grown through a stone wall."

It was a romantic allusion, but a frustrating third of her lifetime lay behind it.

Even visits to her family were suspect. Though Ferdinand in marrying Missy had managed a dynastic coup, the King refused to profit from it, denying the pair all but one or two trips a year outside Romania. He refused to let them attend Prince George's marriage to Princess May of Teck in May 1893. But in April 1894, he couldn't keep them from going to Darmstadt for her sister Ducky's wedding to their handsome, flighty first cousin Ernie, the Grand Duke of Hesse-Darmstadt. (Evidently her mother's aversion to cousins marrying had been modified somewhat.)

That summer Carmen Sylva returned to Romania from a three-year exile, taking possession of her rightful place with predictable melodrama. From the first, there existed between the Queen and Missy an in-law relationship with all its traditional problems. Deepening the strain was the fact that Missy had produced in nine months what the Queen had failed to deliver in twenty-seven years: an heir to the Romanian throne. When Missy's son was born, the Empress Frederick of Germany had written her mother, Queen Victoria: "I had not the heart to telegraph [Elisabeth] as I feel that the joy cannot be without bitterness for her." Forceful, impulsive, generous and absurd, the Queen lived from rapture to rapture. From the moment of her return, she took up her old life with a martyr's vengeance.

Commented Missy: "She made promises she could not keep, spent money she did not possess, appointed people to nonexistent posts; she wrote letters, gave recommendations, received odd people and believed perfectly sincerely that she was saving souls."

To the Queen, Missy was awkward and frivolous, undereducated and too English. But Carmen Sylva admired the girl's beauty and "animal spirits." Frenetically pacing her rooms, the Queen would drag Missy in her wake, enthralling her with poetic monologues. The Queen also resumed the salons that had brought Ferdinand and Helene Vacarescu together. "I was ready as ever to adore, to admire," wrote Missy. But at eighteen, the girl had an instinctive sense of the ridiculous. It didn't take her long to realize that while Carmen Sylva admitted to her circle some of the great minds and artists of the day, she gave equal attention to untalented painters and musicians, charlatans who profited from her naive confidence, and fawning satellites who laughed up their sleeves at the Queen's sentimental eloquence.

The Queen seemed unsure of her feelings for the girl who would succeed her, treating her now with effusive sweetness, now with veiled jealousy. To make matters worse, the Duchess of Edinburgh was unable to be with Missy for the birth of her second child. Instead, the Duchess hurried to the Crimea to see her ailing brother, Tsar Alexander III. But before she could reach Russia, the Tsar had died of nephritis and Cousin Nicky had become Tsar Nicholas II. At Sinaia Missy's first daughter, Elisabeth, was born on October 11, 1894, with a less than sympathetic Carmen Sylva in attendance. Surrounded by strange Romanian doctors and exhorted by the Queen to remember that child-birth was the most glorious moment of her life, Missy longed for her mother.

As in a Chekhov play, the strain caused by the two families inhabit-ing the same house mounted. Missy and the King were destined to clash. They couldn't even agree on language: Missy still spoke no Romanian; the King spoke no English. So their arguments, and they were many, were expressed in German. These conflicts consisted of stormy rebellion on her side, stubborn persistence on his. Once she wrote him a passionate letter begging him to give her back her youth before it was too late. Replied the King: "Only the frivolous consider youth the best part of life."

For all the domestic tension, Missy was unconsciously learning much from the poet Queen: amiability, perfect manners, unselfishness. The Queen was "always working for others, thinking of others"—traits that, more than beauty or decorum, lead to successful queenship. She also helped Missy uncover a latent love of music and develop her natural talent for painting.

But Missy was too self-involved at this point to appreciate the Queen's strong points. Sad, lonely and desperate, the girl often felt like running away. She had learned early that her husband was no bulwark against heartache. Actually, Ferdinand and Missy were as ill-matched as the King and Queen. Ferdinand was a conformist, while Missy's greatest charm as a Victorian princess lay in her lack of conformity. All her life she would retain an untamed, almost primitive spirit that chafed at restrictions and made her unable to impose them on others. "There is a chronic impatience in my blood," she wrote. Under the burden of restrictions, Ferdinand retreated. Missy could no more swallow Carol's repression without a fight than she could have kept from climbing the Malta trees. The couple shared two interests: photography, in a day when the Kodak was all the rage, and flowers. For a girl as life-hungry as Missy, it was not enough.

With the realization that her marriage was not a success, Missy began to depend on a vein of iron within herself. "Although I had no opinion of my intelligence," she wrote later, "I had a firm belief in my strength." She would need all the strength she possessed for the long struggle that lay ahead.

The only break in her dismal life was provided by occasional trips abroad. On August 22, 1893, wicked Uncle Ernest died, making Missy's father the reigning Duke of Saxe-Coburg-Gotha. Wrote the Empress Frederick: "Aunty Marie will love being Number One, and reigning Duchess, I am sure." Missy's parents still kept a base of operation in England, however, and she loved visiting her childhood home.

She especially enjoyed such high-spirited family gatherings as the one occasioned by Ascot Week, 1895. On that occasion, her joy at again being with her relatives was lengthened by a month-long holiday spent with Ducky at a house lent them by Queen Victoria on the Isle of Wight. The Queen, in residence at Osborne House, gave her grandaughters the run of the scented gardens, sunny woods and broad beaches they had haunted as children. They also drove about the island in a one-horse pony trap, swam races, collected shells and took the ferry to Cowes. Here they shopped for presents for the sailors who now idolized their children as the Malta sailors had once idolized Missy and Ducky.

Seated under a green-lined tent and surrounded by Indian servants, Highlanders and dogs, Victoria received the young women for breakfast.

In April 1896, Missy and Ferdinand attended her sister Sandra's marriage to Prince Ernest of Hohenlohe-Langenburg. Sandra's Ernie was a grandson of Queen Victoria's lovely half-sister, Princess Feodora of Leinengen. This couple was not as clever as Ducky and Ernie of

Hesse-Darmstadt, nor as handsome as Missy and Ferdinand. But their marriage was destined for greater happiness.

In May 1896, like butterflies freed from a cage, Missy and Ferdinand traveled to Moscow for Cousin Nicky's coronation as Tsar of Russia. The three weeks she spent in Russia were among the most perfect of her life. After three years in harness, after boredom and restrictions and hushed voices, she was actually back in Russia—at the world's gayest court to witness the most stupendous pageant of the century.

Everything was sheer delight: the gold-drenched coronation ceremony itself; the brilliant assemblage of *Belle Époque* royalty; and the overpowering charm of Moscow in gala array, with bells ringing from the domes of its sixteen hundred churches and crackling nighttime fireworks painting the sky above the Kremlin. It was good rediscovering her tolerant and admiring Russian relatives, and she enjoyed going to constant balls and feeling herself admired by an endless number of handsome men.

She and Ducky were surrounded by admirers. Everywhere they turned, men fell in love with them: their cousin Grand Duke Cyril with Ducky, his brother Boris with Missy. A charming and attractive young man with a husky voice and a lisp, Boris fervently declared himself Missy's cavalier for life and would thank her thirty years later for having "always remained a lovely dream." And droves of Russian military officers, captured by her blonde beauty and grace on the dance floor, threw themselves at her feet.

Party followed party. For Missy it was a time of giddy enjoyment, "few of us," she observed cryptically, "except Nando ever pausing to think." Even the Khodynka tragedy, in which five thousand Russian peasants were accidentally trampled to death at an open-air feast in their honor, cast only a temporary pall on the young set's enjoyment.

Predictably, her greatest triumph in Russia came on horseback. Day after day, she had ridden with young officers, astounding them with her horsemanship. There was not one race she hadn't won, a horse she hadn't conquered—except one. Prince Wittgenstein, a dashing Elinor Glyn type with a tall Cossack hat and a dagger stuck in his belt, owned a fierce Cossack horse he said could beat at a trot any other horse at a full gallop. On a dare, Missy agreed to race on Wittgenstein's horse.

She never forgot that ride. It remained "one of the most glorious moments of my youth. There was a thrill about it which I have never been able to forget. The moment I was on his back, that untamed horse and I understood each other absolutely, and I was ready to accept any wager. I was given a few hundred yards start and then off flew all the other riders in wild pursuit. What a race it was! . . . the pace we went brought tears to my eyes, but never once did that astonishing animal break from a trot to a gallop."

She beat the runner-up by two arm-lengths. At the finishing point, a low hilltop, she turned and faced her competitors. Panting and flushed, the morning sunshine gleaming on her hair, she looked at that moment what she was, a beautiful, healthy young creature alive with an unquenchable zest for life. In the admiring glances of the men streaming up the hillside, she read the admiration that would follow her for the rest of her life, giving rise to countless legends and setting her alongside the great romantic queens of history.

The trip to Russia was a turning point in her life. The "constant admiration . . . had slightly gone to my head. My suppressed youth and spirits were responding almost dangerously to all this spoiling and adulation. Russians catch fire easily . . . and Slav tongues are soft. Besides it was my first revelation of that power which is woman's . . . and the discovery was pleasant."

Returning to Romania from Russia was like stepping from blazing sunlight into a darkened room. To Missy, the Romanian court seemed more dull and cramped than ever. Even her babies, whom she loved passionately, had become little strangers. She temporarily absorbed herself that summer with planning and decorating her first real home in Romania at the Palace of Cotroceni.

Her only other outlet was riding. On her horses, Sulina and Zimber, she rode everywhere, through every kind of weather, madly and fiercely, for self-preservation.

At Sinaia she broke all precedent by riding astride. A Russian admirer had sent her an authentic Cossack uniform consisting of a dark blue caftan, braided with silver, over a scarlet underdress. "I wore it with the silver cartridge belt barring my chest, and round my then exceedingly slim waist the belt and silver inlaid dagger."

Dressed in this colorful attire, she rode a wild Cossack horse, Cerkess, given her by Cousin Boris. Long-maned and sturdy-legged, Cerkess could climb the mountain paths like a goat. Sometimes he even plunged her off the trail into the heart of the Carpathian forest. Feeling herself one with the trees, soil and sky, Missy exulted in the forest's every mood.

And under the spell of the countryside both loved, Missy and the King of Romania called a temporary truce. They would meet happily in the woods, Missy astride her wild pony, the King on foot, and call happy greetings to each other in German.

In 1897 Carol made her Honorary Chief of the 4th Rosiori (Red Hussars) cavalry regiment. Ever since the Buckingham Palace nurses had taken her to watch the changing of the guard, she had loved soldiers. In Romania, her love of horses and the hard outdoor life gave her a natural kinship with the army. And from Romanian soldiers she received the kind of flag-saluting loyalty she'd grown up expecting in England and Germany but found sorely missing in most Romanians' critical attitude toward their royal family. At her first parade as chief, she thrilled to the sight of her soldiers passing in review. "Her beautiful figure was never seen to better advantage than when she rode at the head of her regiment," noted the London *Times*. On spring mornings she breakfasted outdoors at Cotroceni so she could receive her regiment's cheers as they passed by on their way to the nearby training fields, and afternoons she ran wild races with the officers.

These races gave her the reputation with Carmen Sylva's circle of being "fast." It was also around this time that the rumor first spread that she rode her horses to death. Admittedly, Missy was a hard rider. She usually tore at a full gallop, sometimes for hours at a time, and often took jumps and trails a tamer rider wouldn't have considered. But her horsemanship and love of animals was too great to let her ever willingly harm a horse.

That winter her spirits received another lift when Ducky and Ernie arrived at Cotroceni for an extended visit. In Darmstadt Ducky had suffered none of the restrictions her sister found in Romania. Both Ernie's parents were dead, so they made their own rules. At their hunting lodge, Wolfsgarten, weekend parties excluding anyone over thirty made it the "in" vacation spot for royalty's young marrieds.

When she could break away, Missy came too. Then she and Ducky were "always painting and drawing when we were not on horseback or among the flowers." Strikingly dressed, they once drove four white Lippizaners to the Frankfurt races. As a result, the Empress Frederick fired off a condemning letter to their mother, whereupon the Duchess reproved her daughters for their "sinful love of dress" and their desire to look "different from other princesses."

Before long, Europe was buzzing with stories about Ducky. Always moody, she now plunged from giddy heights to deep melancholy. She

neglected the duties she was expected to perform as Grand Duchess—
forgetting to answer letters, postponing visits to older royalties and at
parties ignoring people who didn't amuse her. At the Kaiser's court in
Berlin, she was known as "the fighting Grand Duchess" and "the little
spitfire."

Such lack of restraint did not lead to marital harmony. Sensitive and
idealistic, Ernie was still aware of his duties as Grand Duke. When he
tried to remind Ducky of her responsibilities, she responded by drop-
ping a loaded tea tray or throwing china. Even the birth in 1895 of their
daughter Elizabeth didn't ease the growing breach.

Since the Moscow coronation, the rumor had been filtering out of
Darmstadt that Ducky and her cousin, the Grand Duke Cyril, were
lovers. She was harshly criticized for the affair, but what few people
knew was that Ernie was a homosexual. "No boy was safe," Ducky
later told a niece, "from the stable hands to the kitchen help. He slept
quite openly with them all." The young Grand Duchess might have
shirked her duties anyway. She might even have fallen in love with
Cyril. But her most criticized actions were the direct result of frustration and resentment in her marriage.

Ernie left Romania after a few weeks, but Ducky stayed on for four
months, until June 1897. Under the liberating influence of her younger
and equally unhappy sister, the hapless Crown Princess, long overwhelmed by King Carol's restrictions, began the subtle transition into
the free spirit who was to electrify Europe.

6

The Young Lieutenant

What do two high-spirited, unhappily married young women do for amusement? Missy had long hovered on the edge of Romanian high society—intrigued by what little of it she saw, but prevented by the King from joining the gay Bucharest whirl. From the first, she'd been both fascinated and repelled by the older society women, with their French manners and disturbing frankness. At a palace tea shortly after she discovered her first pregnancy she'd actually burst into tears when an overpowering dowager said, "Your Royal Highness, since your condition is no longer a mystery, may we felicitate you upon it?" But she unreservedly admired the striking beauty of the younger women.

Now the King finally allowed Missy and Ferdinand with their guests to attend some carefully-screened parties at private homes and to even make a few friends among the Romanian aristocracy. It was a heady experience.

The history of the Romanian nobility closely parallels their country's mercurial fortunes. During the thirteenth century the ancient reigning families produced courageous warriors to battle the persistent Turks. And after 1718, when the conquering Turkish Sultan overwhelmed them with Greek Phanariote rulers, they intermarried with the Greeks to form a cultured and influential Great Boyar class. In the early nineteenth century they rediscovered their Latin heritage and as a result

63

began sending their sons and daughters to Paris en masse for culture and education.

By 1897 the contrast between the Paris-imitated existence of the aristocratic upper class and the simple feudal ways of the villagers and peasants was one of the dominant facts of Romanian life. Highly polished and sophisticated, the great families divided the year between their ancestral estates, their town houses at Jassy or Bucharest, and trips to France. Both men and women were intensely cultured—usually speaking four or five languages fluently. It was common practice to engage English nurses and governesses, with the result that upper class Romanian babies often babbled English before they could speak a word of Romanian. By adulthood they were better educated and better read than their contemporaries anywhere else in Europe.

Along with their brilliance, Missy couldn't help noticing another characteristic of the Romanian upper class: their carefree morality. "If love is sin, then glory to him who created it. He made the sin exceedingly beautiful," wrote one Romanian writer. And another says, "Life was too rich in a free and easy-going country to breed rigid principles."

Upper-class Romanian women were strictly controlled and carefully educated before marriage. After marriage, according to one of their own number, they launched on a series of "passionate, violent, and usually short-lived affairs . . . so numerous and intricate that unless you live on the spot, it is difficult to keep track of the unending intrigues of one's friends." The church, which in most countries served as a deterrent to divorce, in Romania allowed a person to marry up to three times.

A few Romanian gentlemen squandered their fortunes in a life of ceaseless pleasure at Monte Carlo and Paris, and nearly all were as ardent adventurers as their women. But most combined their love lives with a higher sense of duty, immersing themselves in politics or in running their country estates. Enhancing an Italian-like appearance with eighteenth-century manners, they were among the most charming men in Europe.

The Bucharest season officially started when society returned from the country for the opening of Parliament on November 15. After Christmas the Ball Season began and lasted until spring. Some of the gayest balls were given at 17 Chaussé Kisseloff by the Theodore Vacarscu family. Vacarescu himself was a long-time friend of King Carol, his cousin Helene had been Ferdinand's first love and his son Radu was the handsomest man in Romania. Tall, dark and widowed young, Radu infected his parents' home with the wit, culture and superficial gaiety of the Romanian rake. Careening in and out of violent affairs and financial escapades, he lived a life alternating great luxury with sordid poverty.

With the King's permission, Missy and Ducky danced often at the Vacarescu house. They arrived early and were often the last to leave. "One more dance, Madame Vacarescu, please, I want to have a dance with Radu," Missy would plead at five in the morning, when Radu had already gone downstairs to order breakfast.

Missy learned much of life this winter, but she could not learn money management. To decorate her Cotroceni rooms in the neo-Byzantine style she liked and to entertain Ducky and Ernie with the first parties she'd given as a married woman, she far exceeded the conservative budget allotted her by the King. With Ferdinand bewailing her extravagance, she went directly to Carol, admitted what had happened and arranged to borrow enough money to see her little household through the year.

That spring, dressed in form-fitting riding habits, Missy and Ducky attended riding picnics similar to the Malta outings. Again the girls were surrounded by young men, "espicially the precious 4th Rosiori, of which all the officers, of course, became our very devoted slaves. We sisters let ourselves go . . . and each day invented something new."

Mornings were spent discovering tiny villages in the countryside around Bucharest. The Princesses viewed the picturesque hovels with the eyes of sheltered young romantics who have never wanted for any material thing. The more desolate the huts, the more they appealed to the girls, who knew nothing of what it meant for human beings to actually exist beneath the crumbling, maize-dotted roofs. Nor were they yet capable of grasping the harsh reality of an unfair feudal system which still bound eighty percent of Romania's population to soil they did not own. For Missy, a social conscience would come with time. On the sweet spring mornings of 1897, she preferred searching out the first flowers to charity work.

By summer Bucharest's dust and heat were unbearable, and the city water supply became so impure many people fell ill each year with typhoid fever. That June, Ferdinand was among them.

Three doctors, Missy and the King rushed to his bedside, and old Neumann, the body servant who'd come with the Crown Prince from

Sigmaringen, acted as nurse. Ferdinand's initial typhoid was complicated by double pneumonia, and for days he lay near death.

One night Ferdinand's fever soared drastically. Rushing to his bedside, Missy found her husband lying on his back. "He was so thin that his body seemed one with the sheet. His face was livid and he was breathing with difficulty. His eyes were wide open, glassy, but . . . when I sank on my knees beside his bed, instinctively his hand groped for mine. I closed my fingers over his, they were wet with perspiration. Perspiration was pouring from him, our hands lay in a small pool of water. I had often heard of the 'death sweat,' now I knew what it was."

After the crisis of that night, Ferdinand began to improve. Ducky left for Queen Victoria's Diamond Jubilee, to be held on June 20. Soon after, Missy, the children and Ferdinand—carried on board in a litter —took the train to Sinaia. Here they spent the rest of the summer in the Foisor, a small Swiss-style hunting lodge on the grounds of Castle Peles.

Ferdinand's recuperation was slow. For over six weeks, he lay in bed, pale and gaunt, and for many weeks more could sit up for only a few hours a day. In August the King and Queen left Romania for their yearly "cure" in Switzerland, and Missy's mother came to visit with Missy's youngest sister, Baby Bee (Beatrice). To amuse the patient, the Duchess played endless card games with him on the sunny Foisor balcony.

But during that summer of 1897 Missy was not able to focus her full attention on her husband's convalescence. Her spirits soaring after the long strain, she rode wildly with her sisters throught the Sinaia woods. They even rode in blinding rain, urged on by a mother who stated, "it is ridiculous to remain at home because it rains; people who allow their exercise to depend upon the weather never take any exercise at all."

That was also the summer she launched the first of the many affairs she's been credited with.

Army Lieutenant Zizi Cantacuzino had been acutely aware of the young Crown Princess from the day she arrived in Romania. Spellbound, he'd watched her step from the train, and in the intervening years his obvious adoration had brought them together and made them friends. "Very ugly, very intelligent, and very amusing," he had a wiry, graceful build and wore his uniform with distinction.

During Ferdinand's illness the King had decided to appoint an army aide for Missy—someone she could turn to in case of emergency. Aware of Cantacuzino's loyalty to the Crown Princess, Carol gave him the post. It was a good choice. With the sympathetic and intelligent Cantacuzino, Missy felt she could defy much of the bitter loneliness that had plagued her. "Everyone has people who care," she'd often thought, staring into throngs of cheering Romanians, "except me." Now, when she needed him most, she too had someone who cared. And Cantacuzino, overjoyed by the growing intimacy with the beautiful princess he'd worshiped from a distance, served as an effective buffer between Missy and a court that prophesied she would soon become a widow. This very intimacy, warming to each, was to prove their undoing.

Their attraction for each other grew during the summer of Ferdinand's recovery, but was arrested when Missy and Ferdinand moved, at doctor's orders, to Nice for the winter. The King hated to let the Crown Prince and his wife visit a country Carol considered as frivolous and decadent as Republican France. For protection, therefore, he sent with them "safe guardians" who were secretly instructed to send him daily reports on the couple's activities.

On her return to Romania in the spring of 1898, her relationship with Lieutenant Cantacuzino developed into a romance which lasted for nearly two years. Looking back on this episode in her youth, Marie of Romania wrote: "It never struck me that my high spirits might fill others with suspicion, nor that my actions would be misinterpreted, which they nearly always were." Later she added, "In fairness to all sides I must admit prudence was not my specialty."

Oblivious of how their actions might look to others, the two were always together—riding in the woods, waltzing together at parties, leading the quadrille at balls. Most of Romanian society was amused by their princess's little romance, but the women surrounding Carmen Sylva responded by blowing it into a full-scale scandal.

Whispers and rumors about the affair spread to Germany. "I fear she gets into scrapes," her aunt, the Empress Frederick, wrote of Missy. "Like a butterfly, instead of hovering over the flowers [she] burns her pretty wings by going rather near the fire."

Strongly seconding the Queen in her scandalmongering was Prince Carol's new governess. A grossly ugly British woman, she'd been hired by the King over Missy's objections because she had once worked for Carmen Sylva's cousin, Queen Emma of Holland. "Overbearing, interfering, and impertinent," the governess tried to turn five-year-old Carol against his mother and constantly fanned Carmen Sylva's jealousy of the Crown Princess.

In the summer of 1899 the King and Queen again left for Switzerland. Before leaving, Carmen Sylva wrote a letter to Missy, asking her to invite Lt. Cantacuzino's cousin, a teen-aged girl whose mother had recently died, to stay with her in Sinaia. Ever kindhearted, Missy happily complied. That summer, Missy, the Lieutenant and his young cousin made a carefree threesome. Meanwhile the governess kept the household stirred up by constantly asking, "Where has the Princess gone today?"

On her return, Carmen Sylva joined forces with the governess in accumulating the stories of Missy's indiscretions to bring before the King. Foremost among their criticisms was the Crown Princess's use of Cantacuzino's cousin as a go-between.

When the King accused Missy of this, she was bluntly frank: "But Aunty asked me to invite her." Carmen Sylva, in turn, denied any knowledge of the letter she had written. The tension at court suddenly became electric while the Crown Princess, pregnant with her third child, searched unsuccessfully for the letter. Her trust in people temporarily shattered, she turned for consolation to the one friend she knew she could count on—old Green, her children's Cockney nurse. And every night for weeks she cried herself to sleep.

Finally Carol summoned her again. "A Crown Princess must never compromise herself," he told her. "We of course all know that Nando may not be very entertaining. But that doesn't mean you may find your entertainment elsewhere."

From Carol's office Missy went straight to her husband. "Nando, it seems the whole court is talking. Soon they'll be talking to you. It's true what they'll say. Zizi loves me. He's told me so. And we have walked in the woods together. That much is true—but no more."

By now, honesty wasn't enough to stop a scandal that had spread as far as England. In dismay, Queen Victoria wrote Carol, begging him to smooth the situation over. Missy demanded the dismissal of the spying governess, but the King refused. Instead, he exiled Cantacuzino and agreed with Missy's mother that the girl should leave Romania for awhile. She packed her bags to return to Coburg.

On the day she left, as she sat waiting for a carriage to take her to the train station, she absent-mindedly reached into a corner of the chair and found the letter from Carmen Sylva. Only now it was too late. Her marriage along with all the bright dreams she'd brought to Romania had collapsed about her, and she had nothing to look forward to but exile, disgrace and another childbirth.

7

Friends

Missy stayed in Germany until April 1900. Surrounded by her sisters and comforted by her mother's fiercely protective presence, she was able to unwind and regain her perspective. Whether at Ducky's Wolfsgarten house or at their parents' homes in Coburg and Gotha, the four sisters spent happy hours engaged in then-fashionable wood-carving and wood-burning, and in painting and embroidery.

The winter before, the girls' brother Alfred had died of tuberculosis at twenty-four. His death was a "staggering blow" to his sisters. Never sick themselves, they found it impossible to believe that one of their number had died so young. Their heartbroken father, having named a nephew heir to the Saxe-Coburg-Gotha duchy, sought solace in champagne.

That November, six-year-old Prince Carol suddenly fell ill with typhoid. As soon as she received Ferdinand's frantic telegram, Missy boarded the Orient Express for Romania. She arrived in Sinaia tired and distraught and flew up the stairs only to find the nursery door barrred by the hated governess. Protruding eyes glaring and arms folded, the woman refused to move. "It would be extremely dangerous," she said, "to admit anyone to the baby's bedside. The doctor's instruction—" For once Ferdinand took charge. "Stand aside. The Crown Princess is the child's mother." Whatever tension had divided Missy and Ferdinand, it was now dissolved over their sick child's bed.

But after Carol was out of danger, she returned to Gotha, determined to stay there until the governess had left.

On the night of January 9, 1900, her second daughter was born at Gotha. Called "a child of two centuries" because according to the Romanian Orthodox calendar she'd been born in December 1899, the baby was beautiful, with blonde hair and a cupid's-bow mouth. Missy named her Marie after the three generations of Maries in her family, but called her Mignon after Ambroise Thomas's opera, which was then playing at the Gotha theater.

When she returned to Romania in April, she found an Irish governess in her enemy's place. Though vague and rheumy-eyed, Miss Folliet was acceptable to both the "old" and the "new" palaces. She "gave a very limp hand in greeting," wrote Missy, "but I liked her."

Missy could now see her her two oldest children without doing battle with their governess. As a result, she took them with her on early morning rides in the Cotroceni park and for afternoon drives. Since her return the rest of her days had settled into dreary monotony. Midmorning found her giving audiences to people concerned with the many charities Carmen Sylva involved her in. She also busied herself with designing and wood-burning furniture. But her evenings were deadly dull. Prince Ferdinand, as Inspector of the Cavalry, was often away on tours of duty. When home, he spent every evening closeted in his study with his stamp and botanical collections.

Nor was the Cantacuzino scandal dead. That spring Prince George wrote Missy a sympathetic note decrying the rumors still circulating in English society. Her response was filled with a sense of acute loneliness.

"Yes, I have been through hard moments," the Crown Princess wrote, "partly through my own fault I know, but also because many things have been very difficult, and above all because I have been dreadfully lonely. I know one must not expect too much of life, Georgie dear, but you see I began very early and all was so different from what I thought. For me life showed me directly the hard rides, and I very soon found out that down here one has to be very strong to stand the loneliness of it all, and I was not always strong, and expected too much and wanted to be happy. And of course I had to learn by bitter experience all that one cannot have, and may not expect."

She temporarily salved her loneliness and boredom by redecorating her Cotroceni rooms, and an American magazine lauded the results. "Room after room is a fairyland of rare tapestries, rich marbles, golden embroideries and white bearskins, the only rugs which she allows.

. . . Robed in a trailing garment spangled with costly gems, her arms weighted down with barbaric bracelets, the Princess sits in a golden room under a golden canopy surrounded by many other golden things, including a spinning wheel inlaid with precious stones."

Once she'd drained her decorating budget, she turned with renewed vigor to her old loves: painting and riding. "I am only happy on days when I have painted for two hours and been on horseback for two hours," she said. The restlessness she developed now to counteract the frustrating emptiness of her daily routine would last for the rest of her life—even when the cause had long since disappeared. For a young woman with her warm heart and bursting vitality, such crushing boredome was even more deadly than the conflict that had preceded it.

Missy returned to England sooner than she expected. At the beginning of the new century, Queen Victoria's family had been struck by a blight of deaths. Missy's father, the Duke of Saxe-Coburg-Gotha, died at fifty-six of cancer on July 30, 1900. Five months later, the eyes of the world were trained on Osborne House where Queen Victoria threw out her arms to the Prince of Wales—the child she'd loved least—and fell into a coma from which she never recovered. On August 5, 1901, the Queen's favorite child and Kaiser Wilhelm II's mother, the sixty-year-old Empress Frederick, died of cancer at her elegant Friedrichshof.

In the summer of 1902 the ranks of European royalty, along with Indian princes and Colonial representatives, gathered in London for Edward VII's coronation.

Ecstatic at being back in London, Missy found the city unchanged since her childhood. But without Victoria's restraining presence, court life had taken on a new and dashing air. The giddy Marlborough House set that had long surrounded the Prince of Wales now made up the King's circle. And the sixty-year-old Edward, as excited as a boy at the prospect of kingship, set about planning gala entertainments, purging the royal homes of his mother's gimcracks and taking possession of the authority which had been so long denied him.

Missy shared the King and his court's sense of release and relief, though for different reasons. For her, Coronation Summer meant a respite from her dreary Romanian life. After the problems and conflicts inherent in any new and struggling society, the smooth-running perfection of life among the British aristocracy was especially soothing.

Like the Moscow coronation, Edward's had its moment of darkness.

Early in June it was rumored the King was ill. He looked tired and had gained so much weight his abdomen measured the same as his chest: forty-eight inches. Finally his doctor diagnosed appendicitis, but the King refused to postpone the ceremony and on June 15 had the press informed that he was suffering from lumbago. Desperately ill and racked with pain, he finally submitted to a midnight appendectomy on June 23, three days before his coronation was scheduled to take place.

All London reacted with concern. At Westminster Abbey the Bishop of London turned the coronation dress rehearsal into an impromptu service of intercession. And from all over the Empire, supercharged expressions of loyalty poured in for the dapper playboy-statesman who'd waited forty years to become King. His near-tragedy and quick recovery, coming shortly after the successful conclusion of the Boer War, made Edward VII a national hero.

The coronation, meanwhile, had been postponed until August 9. The King and Queen embarked on July 15 for a convalescent cruise, and Missy and Ferdinand spent the next three weeks at Cliveden, the palatial country home of Missy's new friends, Waldorf Astor and his sister Pauline.

Marie of Romania was often unlucky in her friends. Her inability to see falseness or betrayal in people she liked led to some of the major embarrassments and tragedies of her life. But in Waldorf and Pauline Astor she found friends that were to last a lifetime.

Missy first charmed the young Astors and their irascible father, William Waldorf Astor, variously known as "wealthy Willie" and "walled-off Astor," at a Sunday luch at Cliveden. The older Astor was not easily charmed. A dynamic, paranoid man with bright blue eyes, a yellow beard and eighty million dollars, he had been one of the richest and least-liked men in America. He'd left the United States in 1890, declaring "America is not a fit place for a gentleman to live," and moved his family to Britain, where he proceeded to storm British society and campaign for a peerage. To achieve his goal he needed a house in the country and a place in the British establishment. Therefore he bought two fabulous country places—Cliveden, a tawny stone Italian-style villa near Madenhead outside London, and Anne Boleyn's ancestral home, Hever Castle—and founded a publishing empire. With his driving ambition, "wealthy Willie" had little time for his children.

There were four young Astors. Gwendolyn, at eight, was dying of a congenital heart ailment, and John was at Eton. The two oldest, Waldorf and Pauline—though born in America, great-great-grandchildren of John Jacob Astor and only British subjects since their father's naturalization in 1899—had in eleven years become idealized products of their upper-class British environment. Well-bred, tactful, witty and charming, they were also handsome with "large velvety brown eyes" and flashing smiles.

From the first, Missy recognized in these two the soul-mates she'd longed for since Zizi Cantacuzino's exile. Everything she needed in friends the young Astors offered. Waldorf loved horses and riding. Both shared her opinions, ideals, tastes and sense of humor. Most important, they needed her sympathetic friendship as much as she needed theirs. Her overwhelming reservoir of emotion and understanding, so long frustrated, now poured out on these two delightful young people.

An act of kindness early in the visit set the tone for her relationship with Pauline. At twenty-one Pauline was emotionally exhausted from nursing her invalid sister. Since their mother's death, she had devoted her life to the child, channeling all her emotion and energy into this one consuming responsibility. One afternoon when the rest of her party returned to London for a reception, Missy stayed at Cliveden to see how Gwen would come through an emergency throat operation. When Pauline finally left the child's room after the operation, she was amazed to find Missy walking up and down in the hall outside. Pauline said later, "I had no idea she was there. When I asked her why she'd stayed, she said she couldn't have left without knowing how the operation had gone. I was deeply moved at such sympathy from one we barely knew."

A year older than his sister, Waldorf was "tall and exceedingly slim" with a "certain shyness of manner which added to his charm." He'd recently taken a bad fall while playing polo and was forced to use a lady's saddle for the riding he loved. What is more intriguing to a romantic young woman than a supremely handsome man who, because of an injury, inspires sympathy? On one or another of his polo ponies, Missy rode with him through the glorious English countryside, both at Cliveden and in Windsor Great Park. On those long summer afternoon their friendship deepened. "It was *absolute* happiness," wrote Missy.

One day, taking Ferdinand with them, they visited Blenheim Palace, the Marlborough estate in Woodstock. The current Duchess, formerly Consuelo Vanderbilt, described Missy. "Remembering that she was Queen Victoria's grand-daughter, I was not prepared for the disconcerting bohemianism she affected; nor did her evident desire to charm successfully replace the dignity one expected. Accustomed to the restraint of the English royal family, I thought her eagerness indiscreet, and was conscious of a theatricality usually associated with a prima donna rather than with a bona fide princess. It seemed to me that she overacted the part." All through life Missy's extravagant charm would have this effect on some people, just as it captivated others.

As the Coronation approached, the Cliveden idyl came to an end. On August 9 King Edward VII was crowned in a glittering ceremony at Westminster Abbey and Missy returned to Romania.

That fall the death of Gwendolyn Astor further strengthened the bond between Missy and her new friends. Pauline and Waldorf were invited in October to join the royal family at Sinaia. While the Astors stayed in Romania, Missy was happier than she'd been since her marriage. The friends spent their days riding, taking photographs, carving and painting. Sitting in Missy's room after dinner, the women rested while Waldorf read aloud. On nights when Pauline couldn't sleep, she and Missy sat up till morning on the Princess's big sofa while Pauline poured her heart out to sympathetic "little Ma'am." Missy responded by talking out the unhappiness, loneliness and frustration she had only hinted at in the letter to her cousin George.

From those weeks at Sinaia sprang a friendship both Missy and the Astors relied on. Underloved and high-strung, Waldorf and Pauline found Missy's older-sister affection healing, while their courage and humor impressed her deeply. They could see the funny side of situations Missy had found depressing, and the sensitive and perceptive Waldorf helped her learn to love the country she had resented along with King Carol's regimen.

On horseback they rode into the countryside, discovering frescoed monasteries, hidden villages and gypsy camps. And for the first time, Missy established contact with the peasants. She was enchanted. Moved by their simple dignity and melancholy humor and thrilled by their heoric legends and colorful handicrafts, she began spending hours listening to their problems. The peasants, in turn, responded warmly to her blonde beauty and sympathetic nature. Her heavily-accented Romanian amused them (she was only beginning to learn the language, and was never to be completely comfortable speaking it). Born of their mutual delight in beauty and love for children, animals and the picturesque Romanian countryside, the bond of affection and love which now grew up between Missy and the peasants would last a lifetime.

With their tact and perfect manners, the Astors charmed both King Carol and Missy's interfering and pretentious lady-in-waiting. Even

Ferdinand emerged from his private cocoon to take part in some of the parties and outings the trio planned. Though younger than Missy, the Astors were less naive and impulsive. Their many griefs had given them a well of maturity she now partook of freely.

When her friends had returned to England Missy felt hopelessly alone. She wrote them almost daily and poured out all her hopes and fears along with the minute details of her daily life.

That November she discovered she was pregnant for the fourth time. She felt sick and out of sorts and longed for the solace she felt in the Astors's company. Even the charm of Christmas couldn't shake her growing malaise.

Predictably, Missy and Waldorf fell in love. It was a deep and tender love, highly romantic and rather naive. But it gave rise to vicious rumors in Romanian society. At a court where affairs sprouted constantly, many people couldn't comprehend a platonic love based on mutual trust and loneliness. Missy was "beautiful, clever and artistic," remembered a friend. "They couldn't understand why she didn't have a lover."

The cooling relationship between Missy and Ferdinand gave her bond with Waldorf added importance. Early in their marriage, she'd been shattered to discover that though her husband was uneasy with society women, he apparently "frequent[ed], without reluctance, less commendable ones." She found his indiscretions even harder to bear in view of the hermitlike existence he preferred when at home. A passionate lover of beauty, she found the deterioration of his looks disconcerting. After his long bout with typhoid, his hair had faded to a dull brown mixed with gray. With hollow cheeks, nervous gestures and an ambling gait, and with heavy hips supporting a too-short body, he made an unprepossessing picture.

While Missy developed professional social ease, Ferdinand added yet another personality quirk to his growing list. Though he possessed an ear for poetry and frequently translated Greek and Hebrew manuscripts, with strangers he began playing "the ignorant as others pretend to be clever. It was done so as not to offend others who were not equally erudite. The result was that in public he began to stammer, repeating whatever another said to him several times even, and with emphasis. He had simply given up expressing any of his thoughts . . . and as he had to say something, discovered that the only way not to displease people was to say the same things they did."

He came across no better with the man in the street. "I remember a review of the troops before King Carol," recalled a friend. "The regiments paraded in perfect order. The cavalry came last, Prince Ferdinand at the head. There was a flutter among the ladies . . . as the heir to the throne approached. When the moment came for his horse to break into a trot and to bring him up in salute before the King, this indifferent horseman miscalculated his speed and did not succeed in making this easy manoeuvre which all the generals had made before him. All four feet of his horse went out from under him on the sanded asphalt, bringing the rider to earth. The gendarmes jumped forward, the prefect of the police at their head, to rescue the horseman. Impassible . . . without even turning his head, King Carol continued to review the troops. There were one or two handclaps, worse than silence, when the Prince picked himself up, unhurt but . . . pale. In those days the crowd did not care for him or admire him. Every time he appeared in public he made a bad impression or made people laugh."

Marie of Romania summed up her early feelings for her husband years after his death. To an American friend she wrote, "My husband was difficult and trying as a young man; jealous, unundersstanding, tyrannical, without the proper strength to master." Among Ferdinand's greatest difficulties must have been marriage to one to the most desirable women in Europe.

Waldorf Astor, on the other hand, "with his curly hair and flashing smile . . . was as opposed to the Crown Prince as an Adonis." He was also secure enough to offer her the flattering attention she craved. From St. Moritz, where the Astors vacationed in January 1903, he sent her a horse, Ringlet, which later became one of her favorites. He also wrote suggesting that if his coming to Romania would cause talk, that spring he might send Pauline and Dr. Madge, a friend, to cheer her up.

The spring visit was successful, and in July Pauline and Dr. Madge returned to Sinaia for the birth of Missy's baby. King Carol had built for the Crown Prince and his family a large house near the Peles. Though constructed in the same German Gothic style, the Pelisor was less pretentious. Inside, a huge hall formed the core of the house, and the family's rooms ranged behind open balconies on two floors. Missy decorated the reception rooms with English comfort and her own with neo-Byzantine exoticism. In her gold-painted boudoir she dotted the floor with large copper and brass pots filled with flowers and left the windows open to catch the sound of the waterfall outside. With its forest setting and background music of running water, the Pelisor more than any other house would be home to her family for the next thirty years. Here she gathered about her friends and relatives who'd come to see her through her confinement.

Among them was sister Ducky, whom Missy thought looked ill and depressed—and with reason. Ducky had divorced Ernie on December 21, 1901, to marry Grand Duke Cyril, whom she'd loved since the Moscow coronation. But the couple hadn't reckoned with the storm of scandal the divorce caused. Even King Edward VII and the nephew he hated, the German Kaiser, were united in their indignation against Ducky. Ernie's irate sister, the Russian Empress, made her husband repeatedly refuse the permission Cyril needed to marry his divorced cousin.

On August 7, 1903, European royalty shifted its attention from Ducky's romantic snarl to the Pelisor, where Dr. Madge presided at the birth of Missy's second son. All the gossips had thought the baby was Waldorf's. But of all Missy's children, her fourth looked most like Ferdinand. Tsar Nicholas was asked by the Crown Prince and Princess to be a godfather, and they named the boy Nicolas. Missy hoped the gesture might soften the Tsar's position against her sister.

Matters were hardly improved when Ducky's daughter, on vacation with Ernie, died suddenly of typhoid on November 16.

Meanwhile, thanks to the Astors, Missy's star was rising. With Pauline and Waldorf at the Pelisor and a new chestnut called Airship awaiting her in the stable, she recovered quickly from the baby's birth. As soon as she was able, she reconquered the mountain paths atop Airship, who assiduously earned his name by completely leaving the ground at the start of every ride. And thanks to Pauline she assumed a new prominence with the King.

Over the course of her many visits to Romania, Pauline had made an appraisal of Missy's situation. She realized that though her friend had "a very generous mind" and was "one appreciative of things of the mind," she was still treated as a child by the King and most of the Court. This attitude, coupled with the constant gossip and criticism that dogged the Princess, infuriated Pauline. A "very nice" young Romanian noblewoman, Princess Nadèje Stirbey, told Pauline: "You know, you're the only ones who have never made any trouble for her. Most of her Romanian friends have always been a burden. I would like to be friends with her; I like her so much and admire her so much. But I'm afraid of starting some evil gossip."

Pauline couldn't stop the tongues from wagging, but she decided to do battle with a more tangible problem: the King's attitude. Missy was obviously the head of her household. It was her common sense, not Ferdinand's, which kept the two palaces filled with whole armies of retainers, gardeners and stable hands plus four children, a schoolroom and a nursery in order. Indeed, Ferdinand found it impossible to make the most insignificant decision without consulting his wife. On the morning after Prince Nicolas's birth, Pauline watched while Ferdinand tried to dismiss all the Ministers who had come up from Bucharest for the occasion. They had already stayed awake half the night and now stood first on one foot then the other while the Prince "made faces at the clock," unable to make the break. Finally someone suggested they might miss their train, and the Prince watched gratefully while the Romanian government bolted out the door.

Yet in true Hohenzollern fashion, Carol continued to ignore Missy on household matters, working directly with the Prince. Determined not to leave Romania without telling the King what she thought, but desperate as to how she should broach the subject, Pauline finally had an idea. Though "no artist," she painted a portrait of Missy and asked for permission to present it to the King. He received her graciously and listened while she told him Missy was the "real man" in the Crown Prince's house. Taken aback at her frankness, Carol thanked Pauline and dismissed her. After that, the King treated Missy with slightly more respect.

The "dear threesome" was broken up first by Pauline's engagement to Lieutenant Colonel Herbert Spender-Clay. A product of Eton and Sandhurst and a Boer War veteran, he was several years older than his bride and sported an impressive mustache. He was not the sensitive charmer Missy would have chosen for her friend. But when he visited Sinaia she could appreciate his obvious strength and maturity.

Though chilled by the thought of the coming marriage, set for Missy's birthday on October 29, the Crown Princess began illuminating a book as a wedding gift "For Pauline. From one who loves and understands you." The book, so heavy Pauline's children would name it "Plum Pudding," was a great treasure. It was bound in a thick silver embroidery iced with moonstones, and the end pieces were solid silver. On each page, Missy painted all-white flowers intermingled with her favorite verses printed in French, English and German. Well-dosed with late Victorian *Weltschmerz*, the verses were "more sentimental than philosophical."

In March Waldorf arrived in Romania on his way home from Egypt. Never very healthy, he had added tuberculosis to his list of ailments.

Missy cared for him like a mother. When they rode, she made him take Dervish, her gentlest horse, and saw to it that he stayed in the saddle a maximum of forty-five minutes. His brother John arrived to join the party, and the magic weeks slipped by as they relaxed at Sinaia. Missy's photograph album for May to October 1905 documents the visit better than any words. There are Waldorf and John dressed in gypsy dresses to amuse the children; all of them exploring the countryside in Ferdinand's first motorcar; Mignon in a little Eton coat and top hat Waldorf had bought her; Waldorf lying on a bear rug; Waldorf shaving outdoors on a camping expedition; Waldorf on horseback; Waldorf lounging on the steps of the Pelisor. Waldorf.

It was to be his last holiday in Romania. In 1906 Waldorf met Nancy Langhorn Shaw, an irrepressible red-haired divorcée from Virginia. They were married. When Nancy found that Missy wrote him every day, she put a stop to their correspondence. Missy and Nancy Astor ultimately became friends, but remained rivals. The two families paid occasional visits to each other over the years and kept in touch, but the intimate phase of their relationship had ended.

In a letter Missy had written to Pauline's fiancé before his marriage, she expressed a longing to have someone to lean upon. With her friends now removed by circumstances from her life, her longing was more acute than ever. She couldn't know that its fulfillment lay just around the corner.

8

The Black Prince

In 1906 she turned thirty-one. Like a soldier who has endured protracted training for active duty, she could look back on twelve years of the old King's tutelage. The conflict had strengthened her. "Poor Missy" was gone, and in her place stood the Crown Princess Marie, sure of her position as a leader of young Romanian society and aware of her power over both men and situations. Only events of the next few years would show her how immature she still was and how undeveloped was her self-image as the future Queen of Romania.

What sort of young woman was she? Most incredibly, after twelve years at the Romanian court, she had managed to retain her ingrained rashness. She still said what she felt, though moments of deep emotion found her speechless with reticence, just as she exaggerated her lighter emotions with profuse adjectives learned from her Russian relatives.

Guileless, she exerted warm affection on those around her, even when they least deserved it. When she stumbled into the pitfalls still being laid for her by the court women, she reacted by blaming herself rather than the culprits, for whom she made endless excuses. But what some called her "stupid" belief in humanity was really the result of her sheltered and carefully guarded life.

Better founded were claims that she was remarkably vain, though her vanity expressed itself in an endearing, almost childish delight in having her presence felt. In any case, her vivid good looks and sex appeal inspired much jealousy, a situation that was aggravated by the scores of men who fell in love with her wherever she went. The result was a blaze of rumors which first erupted with Zizi Cantacuzino and burned until her death nearly forty years later. Smoke from the fire still blurs the facts of her life and loves.

Much of the criticism she brought on herself. For all her innocence, she was a born coquette. From the age of five she loved the attention and flattery her looks inspired. "I rejoice in my beauty," she would say. "Men have taught me to."

It was a remark hardly calculated to dampen jealous rumors. Nor can it be denied that in the years after her marriage she fell in love with a number of men. And as we've seen, she naively made no attempt to hide her feelings for either Cantacuzino or Astor. In her *Cuibul Principesei* (Princess's Nest), the three-room tree house she had suspended high in several giant Sinaia firs, she received officers of her regiment. It was all very aboveboard, no doubt, but rumor-producing nonetheless. To gossip mongers, her penchant for galloping across the plains with young officers coupled with her obvious disenchantment with Ferdinand was equally damning.

Despite the criticism, by 1906 Marie's life was less mournful than before. To bolster her natural high spirits, she could now depend on a large group of aristocratic Romanian friends. At the rambling Palace of Cotroceni, set in its large park on the edge of Bucharest, a smart set of gay young couples and lively bachelors gathered. There was nothing formal about Maries receptions, which she held in her newly-redecorated boudoir—a large room "reminiscent of both a church and a Turkish bath."

One of her most loyal new friends was Princess Nadèje Stirbey. Tall, alluring and supremely aristocratic, Nadèje was neither as handsome nor as intelligent as Marie's other friends. But she radiated warmth and good humor, was a gay companion and an excellent hostess. She lived for her family—a handsome husband, Barbu, and four daughters—and was never bored, occupying herself with endless hobbies. Nadèje had, Marie later wrote, "the secret of putting from her all that could sadden and complicate her life." It was a quality Nadèje would need in the years to come.

Princess Stirbey's sister-in-law, Princess Marthe Bibesco, was the most internationally famous member of the Crown Princess's set. Feted for her beauty and literary talent, Marthe had long idolized Marie, who found in Marthe the first companion since Ducky who matched her delight in collecting old stones, planning exotic interiors and gardens and exploring old churches.

That summer of 1906, Marie and her set flung themselves into the heady atmosphere of Bucharest's International Exhibition. Produced with a mixture of Teutonic thoroughness and Romanian abandon, the Exhibition celebrated King Carol's thirtieth year on the throne and the country's "almost American" material success.

Watching the Crown Princess laugh away the giddy summer nights, many Romanians saw only a beautiful, silly young woman. But there were some in power who saw beneath her fun-loving facade. They realized that her strengths, though largely untapped, were sufficient to make her the real power when Ferdinand should come to the throne. What she needed, in theatrical terms, was a manager. Other great queens had had them. Where would Elizabeth I have been without Cecil? Or Anne without the Marlboroughs? Or Victoria without Melbourne, Albert and Disraeli?

As if on cue, the man for the job entered her life in the spring of 1907. He was never to leave it.

That same spring, the country was shocked from its complacency by a serious peasant uprising. To the rest of Europe, the revolt came as a "thunderbolt from a clear sky." Even the Romanian government was caught off guard. But to a discerning few it came as no surprise.

In Romania the feudal attitude that had evaporated in Western Europe over the centuries was still a fact of life. In his comprehensive *History of the Romanians,* Dr. R. W. Seton-Watson declared, "Romania was one of the most fertile agricultural countries in Europe, and yet . . . the peasant was sunk in misery and had no say in the government of a country of which he was the real backbone." King Carol, though he personally admired the peasants for their conservatism and frugality, saw no reason to give them either a share in political power or ownership of the land they'd worked for centuries.

Finally, on March 15, 1907, the peasants suddenly took matters into their own hands. Clamoring for the division of the great estates and for better field wages, they began looting and burning. Within days, a band of four thousand marched on the panic-stricken capital. Government leaders, unable to leave Bucharest, sent their families to Carpathian summer houses for protection. Among them were Marie and her children, dispatched to the deserted Pelisor.

During these hectic weeks, while isolated at Sinaia, the link between

Marie and Prince Barbu Stirbey was forged. Lonely and worried, she often drove the few miles to Posada, the Bibescos' mountain home, where Marthe sheltered Nadèje Stirbey and the Stirbey daughters. On weekends Nadèje's husband Barbu arrived, bringing reports from the besieged capital. It was only natural that he should bring messages for the Crown Princess too. By the first of May, with the uprising firmly quelled and the aristocracy ready to embark on summer vacations, the court buzzed with rumors of Marie and Stirbey's romance.

The uprising's outcome was predictable. Watered-down laws were passed for the peasants' so-called "protection." They were allowed to use the public grazing lands and buy land of their own. But no one could have known that during the brief course of the rebellion, Marie had embarked on the single most important relationship of her life.

Barbu Stirbey is often considered one of the most compelling and contradictory figures in modern European history. His influence on Marie and Ferdinand of Romania has been the subject of endless controversy. Western journalists of the 1920s and 30s called him, variously, the Rasputin of Romania, the Gray Eminence, the Spider and the Black Prince. He has been accused of endless political intrigues and of carving a financial empire for himself while Romanian peasants were starving. Yet his admirers call him "a great patriot and a great statesman, one of the greatest men of his generation."

In appearance Stirbey was admirably suited for the role fate gave him to play. When he walked into Marie's life, he was tall, handsome and athletic looking. Always immaculately turned out, "he had a special way of holding his head very high and his back very straight," remembered a friend, "which gave him the appearance of a great gentleman." Shiny black hair, a close-clipped black mustache and a high noble forehead further contributed to this aristocratic appearance. Though charming, he was aloof and had a strongly Oriental appeal that women found irresistible.

Emphasized by heavy black brows, his eyes have been called "enchanting" by his friends and "satanic" by his enemies. Princess Callimachi wrote that Stirbey was "extremely personable, elegant and dark without Oriental exaggeration. Some strange hypnotic quality lingered in his beautifully expressive eyes." This quality greatly contributed to his considerable power over others. "His manner was unassuming, yet full of charm; he spoke little, but a gift of persuasion and instinctive psychological insight made him rarely miss his aim whenever he set himself one." These strengths, concentrated in his remarkable eyes, were the basis for his future success at the Romanian court.

His family background also equipped him for the position of royal favorite. "Although in public he was unfailingly courteous, dignified and tactful [with Marie]," said one Romanian, "he was never obsequious. He treated her more as an equal. Of course long before the Hohenzollerns came his family ruled Romania."

Barbu and his wife Nadèje shared a family background which was tightly woven with Romanian history. Their grandfathers, both members of the Bibesco family, were reigning princes in the last hundred years before the arrival of Karl Eitel Hohenzollern.

Born November 4, 1873, Barbu was the oldest son and second child of seven children. He was always a quiet boy, who from earliest childhood could either charm people or make them feel uncomfortable by the compelling gaze of his deep-set eyes. In his teens, with his home education completed, he left for Paris. Here he studied at the *Lycée* and took law at the Sorbonne. With his impressive good looks and cool manner, he became a formidable lady-killer. But he was no libertine, and no scandal touched his name. After returning from Paris at the age of twenty-two, he married his second cousin, Nadèje Bibesco.

Shortly after his marriage, Barbu's father died and he took over the task of running Buftea, the family estate outside Bucharest. From this moment he began the transition from cool-eyed boy into one of the most powerful men in Eastern Europe. His first move was into the political world. Always politically-minded, at twenty-seven he ran for office as a Conservative and was elected Member of Parliament for the district of Craiova. But the development of a chronic stomach complaint which would force him to follow a strict diet for the rest of his life soon discouraged him from the rigors of Parliament. Moreover, he found himself at odds with the Conservative leaders. Unlike them, he recognized the urgent need for agrarian reform and unsuccessfully pressed for changes in the party platform. Withdrawing from active politics, he turned his full attention to Buftea.

Combining economic genius with the most advanced and progressive husbandry methods known, he began carving a financial empire out of his ancestral estate. When he told his friends he planned to enter business, they regarded him with horror. A gentleman in business? It was unheard of!

Criticism notwithstanding, Barbu Stirbey dived into the task of converting Buftea from an oversized farm into a commercial colossus. He planted vineyards which would produce the renowned Stirbey wine. He planted the cherry and apricot orchards which would feed the bees for his honey industry and bear fruit for his preserves and canned fruit. He ordered acre after acre dug up and planted with phlox and peonies for his commercial flower business. He bought sheep to provide milk for the excellent Stirbey cheese and wool for weaving. He planted fields of cotton to use in his cotton wool and bandage industries. He built more cottages to house extra workers, sheds to shelter the sheep and work oxen, and factories for the canning and processing. Tan-colored beehives sprouted like weeds. Were distances long and roads miserable in Wallachia? He would lay his own railway. Before long, a track from the public line ran straight through the Buftea park to the sheds and canneries. It ended practically at the castle's front door.

While the Romanian nobility glowered, he opened specialty shops next to the Palace Stirbey on Bucharest's main street, the Calea Victorei. From the store's shiny windows glittered jars of his choice fruit and honey, bottles of his wine and beer.

With his commercial and industrial fortune launched, Barbu cast about for investment ventures. Before long, he had joined the administrations of every important bank and heavy industry in the country.

As he gradually developed into one of the richest men in the Balkan peninsula, his peers added a wary respect for him to their criticism. "He was considered more foxy and able than really intelligent," wrote the son of one of Stirbey's life-long friends, "more refined than clear-minded. He wasn't really cultured, being more oriented toward finance. But he possessed much knowledge. Essentially a practical man, he weighed coldly the various problems which came his way. He played on the weakness of some, the personal interest of others. But he always reached his goal with subtlety and detachment."

Then he met Marie. Before 1907 the two had been social acquaintances, brought together by Marie's growing friendship with the good-natured Nadèje. But at Posada, caught in the stress of revolution, they became sharply aware of one another. Stirbey was concerned about Buftea, ransacked by the rioters, and Marie's sympathy brought him relief from anxiety. That the attraction went further soon became obvious to everyone at court. "Since he was reputedly a devoted husband and loving family man," wrote a Romanian noblewoman, "it took the public a long while to awaken to this budding affair. Anyhow, within a short span of time his feelings and attachment were so conspicuous that no doubt was possible for those who knew him. Marie's feelings were no less apparent."

Indeed, the relationship born of this love holds the key to her evolution as a woman and later much of her strength as a queen. In *The Story of My Life*, she wrote, "I had more than one reason for remembering that spring of 1907."

Despite his growing relationship with Princess Marie, Barbu Stirbey's marriage seemed happy. His wife stayed outwardly content. Always gay, always pleased, she entertained well and wore her magnificent jewels with distinction. "She had the very lovable quality," remembers a friend, "of always giving others the benefit of a doubt. Everyone loved her." Nadèje Stirbey knew her husband possessed both an intellect and a life she could not share. Yet she neither complained nor expressed jealousy. He gave her wealth, warm affection and unswerving devotion. In return she created a home life that for unruffled bliss was unmatched in aristocratic Romanian circles.

Although he held no political office, Stirbey was intensely concerned with Romanian politics, and he explained them to Marie. For the first time she became aware of the country's problems. Much that she'd overlooked through ignorance she now understood. Politics, made attractive by the man she loved, became one of her major interests along with painting, riding, decorating and her children. Now when Ferdinand and Carol talked politics, she listened.

The King was relieved at her blossoming relationship with the respectable Stirbey. And Stirbey, aware of the untapped depths of Marie's intelligence, saw clearly that she could become a governing force in the country when Ferdinand became King. With this in mind, Stirbey set out to convince Carol that the Crown Princess could be politically useful. "It's essential not to break her will," he told the King. "But if we can persuade her to take herself and her duties more seriously, her natural intelligence will do the rest."

They could and it did. But as in any evolution, Marie's metamorphosis was a slow one. First, she had to be persuaded to take herself more seriously. In this task Stirbey was backed by his older sister, Elise Bratianu. Elise, like her brother, had become dissatisfied with the Conservative Party and joined the Liberals. Married to the increasingly powerful oldest son and namesake of the great old Liberal leader Ion Bratianu, Elise was a brilliant woman. Politically concerned and domineering, she wore her culture and her intellectual refinement with an autocratic swagger that irritated her equally brilliant husband. Even after he became Prime Minister, they fought continually. Unconcerned about either clothes or grooming, Elise nevertheless radiated, like her brother, a powerful physical magnetism. Unlike Stirbey's, though, her methods were direct rather than circuitous.

Once when Marie protested she couldn't do a certain thing, "because I am not intelligent," Elise pierced her with eyes less magnetic but just as commanding as Stirbey's. Her irritation flashed: "You have no right to say such a thing. You are full of intelligence, but you're too lazy to use it. Just try and see the things you could do, if you gave up being lazy!"

Unwittingly, even Carmen Sylva contributed.

"I cannot get accustomed to taking myself seriously," said Marie.

"You do not take yourself seriously? *You*, the mother of several children? I took myself seriously at the age of three!"

While her romance with Astor had been youthfully idealistic, Marie's bond with Stirbey was tightened by their common interest in Romania. As her understanding of Romanian politics and problems grew, so did their partnership—dedicated to the good of Romania as they saw it. Cold, perceptive, dispassionate and very quiet, Stirbey's personality was the perfect foil for Marie's.

At official functions, they presented a powerful contrast: Marie, gay and blonde; Stirbey, dark and quietly dignified. Always bubbling over with enthusiasm and humor, she was less guarded than he. "Her English temperament was often more Latin than his," said one Romanian. He, on the other hand, always treated her with tactful courtesy, always called her "Ma'am," and was once overheard telling her the story of a man who had spoken familiarly to his mistress in public. "Imagine! He called her 'thou' in public!" Barbu Stirbey would never have been so indiscreet.

Marie's memoirs shed little light on the enigma of Stirbey's personality. "Of a somewhat shy and retiring disposition," she wrote, "[he] always preferred a family life to a public one, but he was a man of quiet and practical common sense and one who kept his own counsel. Modest, but at the same time somewhat haughty and of few words, he was not perhaps cut out for wider popularity. But those who really knew him had a high opinion of his character and intelligence." A frustrating, if understandably laconic postscript to one of the century's great loves.

They saw each other daily. Stirbey came to tea at Cotroceni, and she visited Buftea several times a week to ride with Stirbey or his daughters, to take tea or stay for dinner and the night.

Buftea was as much an expression of Barbu Stirbey's personality as it was a symbol of the world that had bred the peasant uprising. To his friends it was one of the most delightfully hospitable houses in Romania. To the scandal-mongers, it was a sinister fortress from which he "gorged himself with the blood of a whole population and remains lean, alert and thirsty for more."

Half an hour by car and fifteen minutes by train from Bucharest, the main Buftea estate sprawled over the flat Wallachian plain next to a large lake. Here three generations of Stirbey princes had created an isolated retreat only slightly less self-contained than a medieval castle. Outside the Buftea gates, guarded from vagrant gypsies by an aging couple in a poplar-shaded cottage, stretched the high road. Inside the gates, a broad formal drive ran through magnificent forests to the main house. Winding bridle paths, cut by Stirbey's grandfather through the trees, offered riders thirty miles of relief from the Wallachian sun.

Before long, Marie began stabling a thoroughbred at the Buftea stables so that in hot weather she could ride the paths daily with Stirbey. "I loved these woods," she later wrote, "with their carpet of flowers changing according to season, from the little yellow crocuses to the deep violet pea-flower of full summer, which spread its gorgeous clusters of color over the ground. When I close my eyes I can still smell the pungent odor of the scrub oaks, so particularly aromatic of an evening when they seemed to exhale their very souls into the cooling hours of dusk.

"With steaming horses and glowing cheeks we would return full of joie de vivre to the cozy old-fashioned house where Nadèje, fresh and radiant, would be awaiting us on the threshold inviting us in for a welcome meal, tea or supper according to the hour of the day.

"Nowhere were the strawberries and raspberries as large nor the cream as thick and butter as fresh as at the Buftea board, and how I enjoyed the exquisitely fresh little peas and homebaked bread, all those good things I had once known in English country houses. There was also that pleasant atmosphere of family life lived 'far from the madding crowd' and many a happy hour have I spent under the Stirbeys' hospitable roof, surrounded by faithful hearts in which I could trust."

Occasionally she spent the night, sleeping in a large canopy bed in an elegantly furnished room set aside for her use. Next door were two sitting rooms, a pink and a green. In the green sitting room, on the shelves of a big table set between two windows, were stacked albums filled with the postcards Marie sent Nadèje from her increasingly numerous trips around Europe. Over the years the pile grew, impressive testimony to the untarnished friendship of the two women.

Marie's visits to Buftea have been harshly criticized. As word of her relationship with Stirbey spread across Europe and finally throughout the world, it was whispered that Buftea was the scene of diabolical plottings, that Stirbey had cast some sort of satanic spell over her and that he had a direct telephone line and a secret door to her Cotroceni boudoir. All were lies.

Equally persistent were the rumors that her last two children, Ileana, born January 5, 1909, and Mircea, born January 3, 1913, were Stirbey's. But though she inherited the passionate nature running through both her Hanover and Romanov ancestors, Marie apparently needed "physical ardours" no more than her equally passionate grandmother, Victoria. Years later Marie wrote: "Because I am animated, alive, keen . . . they imagine that the 'animal' in me must play a big part. They cannot understand . . . 'high spirits' without an underground of something more lurid. It always astounds me the enormous importance people give to a certain part of life, they uglify and degrade everything by it. I suppose it plays a much larger part than I realize. My royal life has in that way isolated me from that form of brutal reality. It is only through books and through certain things that have been said of me that I realized that such immense importance was given to that one thing which has played little part in my life . . . 'sexual' excitement, if that is the right technical expression?"

Her daughter Ileana threw further light on the legend of her mother's many involvements: "Having known my mother very intimately, I should say that at heart she was a puritan. And that with all her glamour and with men falling at her feet, she really hated any physical contact. She had a horror of it, quite simply, because of the initial shock in her marriage."

Meanwhile the malicious stories grew, and a Romanian newspaper published a lascivious caricature of Stirbey titled "The Real Ruler of Romania." The scandal saddened and bewildered Marie. "After all those years of attacks," said a friend, "she still never really got used to it. She was so innocent that these things astonished her. She enjoyed the glamour and play-acting of romance. It was a little bit of a fairyland and when it produced scandal, it really was a very great hurt. And it came as a surprise each time."

Undeniably, Stirbey exerted a powerful influence over Marie. But it seems to have been psychological rather than physical, constructive rather than diabolical—and it was soon augmented by events.

On October 8, 1912, the first of two Balkan wars which prefigured World War I broke out when Montenegro declared war on weakened Turkey. Hungry for equal shares of the former empire's European possessions, Bulgaria, Serbia and Greece jumped on Turkey too. The Turks were defeated, but the Balkan allies immediately began quarreling over the spoils. The Serbs demanded Salonika and a major chunk of Macedonia from Bulgaria. The Greeks made their own demands. In attempting to retaliate, Bulgaria soon found herself in a position similar to Turkey's, as Montenegro, Romania and even Turkey joined the Serbs and the Greeks. The new coalition cut through the Bulgarian forces "like a knife through cheese," and a peace treaty was signed on August 6, 1913. But with their interest piqued by the two conflicts, the major European powers again viewed the Balkans with an eye to dominion.

Marie meanwhile had played her own part in the tangled conflcit. Before recalling his troops, King Carol paid a visit to the front, taking the Crown Princess with him to inspect the Red Cross hospitals scattered along the Danube. What she saw appalled her. In poorly-staffed and inadequately-equipped tents, men were dying like flies from cholera, which had first broken out on the Bulgarian side. Here, in a stricken, nearly deserted village, conditions were even worse. Romanian soldiers lay dying with hardly any medical care at all.

It was her first contact with large-scale suffering, and it affected her profoundly. "Something never before felt rose from the very core of my being," she wrote, "an immense urge towards service, a great wish to be of use, even to sacrifice myself if necessary. . . ." She made up her mind to transform Zimnicea, one of the principal points where Romanian troops were to cross the Danube on their way home, into an emergency cholera camp.

Impressed by her urgency, the King granted the necessary permission for her to organize and run the enterprise. She paid numerous calls on influential friends and authorities, turning up a tremendous amount of excellent provisions. Her two foremost helpers were her son Carol and Sister Pucci, an old Italian-born nun.

For two weeks, in intense heat broken only by tropical rainstorms, Marie worked steadily. She was not head nurse, but rather chief inspiration for the entire camp. Wearing heavy riding boots, she plodded through the muddy barracks, bringing cigarettes, flowers and cheer to men lying on straw pallets without mattresses and, in many cases, linen.

She gave orders, galvanized other workers to action by the force of her own determined optimism, took a turn at the dirtiest jobs, and even braved the barracks appropriately known as "Hell."

Her fortitude was as impressive as her endurance. She who had seldom been sick in her life and shared her mother's loathing of illness gritted her teeth and stayed by the bedside of soldiers in the throes of the cholera crisis. The Princess who had grown up dining at Windsor and Tsarskoe Selo now sat on an overturned box in a leaky camp tent nibbling a skinny chicken cooked by Sister Pucci. By the end of two weeks she had earned the wholehearted respect and admiration of every doctor, orderly, soldier, officer and sister of charity in camp.

She had always wanted her people's love. Now she discovered the fulfillment of earning it through selfless service. It was a turning point in her life.

That fall King Carol made Barbu Stirbey superintendent of the Crown estates. Forming a royal domain of over fifty thousand acres, these were Carol's greatest pride. Under the deft touch of an old Greek Jurist, Ion Kalinderu, they had become a model of scientifically-applied agriculture and had made Carol a millionaire. When Kalinderu died, Carol saw Stirbey as the only man in Romania with the shrewdness to handle this most important job in the Royal Household. His appointment to the post also meant that Stirbey and Marie could now meet on business, meant that he was now an official as well as a personal part of the Royal Family's daily life.

By 1914, thanks partly to the revelation of the cholera epidemic and partly to the sure, subtle, guiding hand of Stirbey, Marie was a self-contained woman with an unshakable will to win and a burning desire to serve. By helping make her aware of her potential as future Queen of Romania, Stirbey had jogged her latent intelligence into political acumen, channeled her restlessness into patriotism and helped uncover in her personality a gallant self-possession that would serve both her and Romania well in the desperate years ahead.

9

The Hope of the Country

While Marie's personal star rose, she watched her oldest child anxiously. From the first, Carol had been the focus of the conflict between the King and Queen and his parents. In his own inarticulate way, the stolid, blue-eyed towhead adored his mother for her beauty and charm and for the glow she emanated. But he was allowed little time alone with her. His first governess maliciously cut his mother's name from his evening prayer. When Marie left for Gotha, she was forced to leave him behind and was allowed to return only when he nearly died of typhoid. Nor was he close to his father. He spent more time with the King than with the suppressed Ferdinand. And for a time his only refuge from old Carol's flinty environment was in the cloying atmosphere of Carmen Sylva's circle.

Until she retired, his nanny provided the only real stability in his life. On a picture postcard of his father he wrote Mary Green what may have been his first letter. "Thank you so much, dear Nana, for the pretty little ink-bottle you sent me; it will be very useful. Love and kisses from Carol." In 1903, when he was nine, she left, and there was no one to take her place.

Overcontrolled by the King and overindulged by Carmen Sylva, he received no discipline at all during the brief intervals he spent uninterruptedly with his mother. Marie loved her children passionately, especially when they were small. "My children were the central interest of my life," she wrote later. But as they grew older and began developing distinctive personalities of their own, she found them harder to handle. She had "just grown" herself and therefore had no idea of how to train and channel a child's development. Besides, she was crippled all her life by a complete inability to scold. Her own craving for freedom made her loath to curtail her children's liberty even for their own good.

As he grew older, Carol's personality bent in accordance with his experiences. The merry, docile youngster grew into a willful, repressed and temperamental adolescent. Certain unpleasant characteristics that would plague him later were already apparent. Among them were instability, lack of discrimination in choosing friends and an inferiority complex which sometimes erupted in childish spitefulness. But his obvious intelligence, touching determination and undeniable charm still outweighed his bad traits. Then almost simultaneously, he was confronted with two conflicts more shattering than his precariously-balanced personality could handle.

One was his violent jealousy of Barbu Stirbey. Like the young Winston Churchill, Carol had carried his mother fixation far beyond the normal age, and his reasons were essentially the same. Deprived by harsh Edwardian upbringings of real relationships with their parents, both Churchill and Carol deified mothers who were spectacular by anyone's standards. To see the mother he adored suddenly strike up a close relationship with a man not his father came as a colossal blow to fourteen-year-old Carol. The younger children liked the stately, dark-haired personage who visited Cotroceni daily, took tea with their mother and spent hours discussing politics with her. Ileana was especially fond of Stirbey. "When I was a little child I called him 'Good Man,'" she recalled years later. "Oh, that's 'Good Man,' I used to say. And that's the name he got and kept to the end." But Prince Carol hated him.

Meanwhile, King Carol took full responsibility for the boy's upbringing—with disastrous results. From the first, state reasons obliterated personal considerations. Choosing a German instructor seemed so awesome a responsibility to the King that for years Prince Carol went untrained in his father's language. Even a gym teacher was chosen only after endless, ponderous debate. But the King's major task, as soon as Carol reached adolescence, was finding someone to fill the position occupied originally by the malicious first governess and more recently by the bland Miss Folliet. After much reflection, the King selected Herr Schmidt, an unprepossessing Swiss, as tutor. Old Carol was delighted

with his choice. To him, the Swiss were a model race. So what better
mentor for the Hope of the Country than this humble little man with
a passion for botany and nature?

It is to King Carol's credit that he really loved the boy he helped to
destroy. But if it's hard to forgive him his choice of a tutor, it's impossible to overlook his stubborn clinging to Schmidt in the face of medical
evidence that the man was both emotionally disturbed and homosexual.

Long before Schmidt arrived, Carol's days had been forced into a
monotonous scholastic routine, with every minute rigidly mapped out
far in advance. Characteristically, within the framework of these rigid
outlines, he had proven himself a keen student and especially enjoyed
history and politics. But now he flung himself into reading binges. He
would start a book in the evening and finish it that night before falling
into exhausted sleep. His parents were used to his devouring knowledge. It amused them that he was turning into a bluestocking, and his
sisters teased him about it. They were not, however, prepared for the
secrecy he now cast over his reading. Instead of discussing what he read
at meals, as before, he sat as withdrawn and moody as the tutor. In fact
the two became wet blankets at the often hilarious family lunches where
Marie encouraged her children to say whatever passed through their
minds.

Carol was normally healthy and vigorous, with a liking for outdoor
activity. He rode, shot, hunted and played tennis. For all his pendantry,
before Schmidt's arrival he'd been gay and fun-loving, sometimes giving
vent to sudden restless energy and often longing, as would any adolescent boy, to break away from his sober routine. Now he turned to
solitary pursuits, collecting stamps and plant specimens from the Sinaia
mountains, and spent long hours depressed or lost in thought.

There's no way of judging how much Schmidt's influence harmed
Carol of Romania. No evidence other than family suspicion confirms
that the tutor actually introduced his pupil to homosexual practices,
though he later admitted having been "torn with desire" at the sight
of Carol kneeling in bedtime prayer. Nor can we *intellectually* blame
Schmidt for causing Carol, as Marie says he did, to doubt the desirabil-
ity of being a soldier and a prince. Intellectual doubt, introduced under
healthy academic conditions for the sake of philosophical argument,
strengthens the mind. But Carol was unbalanced before Schmidt took
over. All his life, he'd been bounced like a polo ball from Uncle to Aunt
and from parents to governesses. The last thing he needed during his
teens was someone filling him with doubts about the role fate had cast

him for. And that is exactly what the tutor did. Carol's later socialist leanings, which for a time earned him the tag "Carol the Bolshie," stemmed from Schmidt's influence. And his later heterosexual excesses may well have been overreaction to guilt feelings resulting from experiences he had had during the tutor's stay.

In short, what Prince Carol needed in a tutor was a strong, compassionate, inordinately healthy influence to guide him toward self-acceptance and a sense of belonging to his world. What he got was a misanthropic homosexual who drove a wedge between him and his family while further riddling the already loose mesh of his character.

One of the levers Schmidt worked with greatest success in driving that wedge was Carol's animosity toward Stirbey. With the tutor's help, it became political as well as personal, lapping over to include Stirbey's brother-in-law and intimate, the Liberal Prime Minister Ion Bratianu.

For good or bad, the man most responsible for what Romania became in the first quarter of the twentieth century was the second Ion Bratianu. Though rooted in the *nouveau riche* middle class, he was also one of the most cultured and intellectually-refined Romanians of his generation. These gifts, combined with an eye for dynastic gain, had helped him win the brilliant and caustic Princess Elise Stirbey away from her first husband, the leading Conservative minister Alexander Marghiloman. To the Romanian premiership Bratianu brought youth, vigor and a political toughness that reminded older party leaders of his father, who had been King Carol's strongman premier. A passionate patriot, he lived for the day when a Greater Romania would rise from the ashes of Russian and Hungarian domination. But he was also too realistic to expect immediate action. In the meantime he based his internal policy on expanding the new middle class, while younger, more idealistic Liberals like his friend Jean Duca turned sympathetic attention to the agrarian problem. In foreign affairs he was determined to keep the balance of power. If there was any change, he expected Romania to extract ample compensation.

Bratianu was never really popular with the Romanian people. Tall, broad-chested and handsome, with "dark, velvety eyes" and a dark beard, the new Prime Minister was an imposing figure. But despite his lazy movements and the ironic twinkle in his eye, "he was not really pleasant looking," said a family friend. "You had the feeling that there was something unfathomable about him. He was courteous and amiable, but he didn't give of himself unless something amused him. I felt there was something about him you couldn't quite trust." He conveyed this quality right down to the man in the street. People admired and respected him, but they didn't like him. He was too autocratic, too ruthless, too unconcerned with public opinion. Still, his tremendous intellect and vivid sense of history made him a gifted politician. Had he lived in a more internationally important country, he could have been one of the greatest political leaders of his time. As it was, he contented himself with virtually running Romania.

With the passage of time King Carol had taken Marie more and more into his political confidence. Now he praised Bratianu, who, he told her, "follows up my ideas, quickly understands my desires and is not in eternal opposition." It was obvious that Uncle expected her to someday work closely with both Bratianu and Stirbey.

Bratianu, for his part, took a jaundiced view of his brother-in-law Stirbey's influence with Marie. He considered a gray eminence at court unhealthy, much preferring someone who worked in the open. Despite their differences, however, by 1913 these three—Bratianu, Stirbey and Marie—already promised a political triumvirate to be reckoned with.

Prince Carol never saw the pressures and differences of opinion that sometimes divided his mother and the Liberal leaders. Nor was he aware that her political leanings were strongly encouraged by the old King, whom he admired. Inspired by Schmidt's revolutionary teachings, he hated the Liberal party—for their spoils system method of enriching both Romania and themselves, for what he considered their opportunistic agrarian platform and for the Bratianu dictatorship. But mostly he hated the Liberals because his mother, through the great Liberal Barbu Stirbey, was closely aligned with them.

Despite his burning resentment of Stirbey and Bratianu, Carol kept still. But by 1913, when he was twenty, it was impossible not to notice that his tutor had a sick hold over the prince. For months Marie and Ferdinand had suggested that the King dismiss Schmidt. But to no avail. Opposition only increased the King's affection for his choice. Old Carol never saw Schmidt at his worst, and he treated Marie's complaints as irresponsible. Carmen Sylva had her own theory. Schmidt *must* be a good man, she argued, "because he knows the Bible by heart."

Later that year, Romalo and Mamulea, the court doctors, finally convinced the King that Schmidt must go. "I will not speak ill of the unfortunate;" Marie wrote in her memoirs, "the man has suffered and finally went to pieces with remorse, but not before having done much harm." Schmidt was sent away, "but too late."

In an attempt to salvage the remnants of her son's personality, Marie now begged the King to send Carol to Potsdam for military training. What he needed, she reasoned, was a complete change. Surely in that healthy masculine environment he might recover from some of the harm done him. His faith in his own judgment shaken at last, the old King finally agreed to his niece's pleas. Perhaps Missy was right. Let the boy go to Potsdam.

Marie was ecstatic. And during the summer of 1913, drawn together by their work in the cholera epidemic, she and Carol were closer than they'd ever been. She was proud of the "great personal energy and initiative" he showed in traveling from unit to unit, giving orders and observing conditions so he could report back to her. After torrential rains, he would wade for miles through ankle-deep mud, doggedly pursuing the course he'd set for himself.

Heartened by his work at the cholera camp and by his interest in the Romanian Boy Scout movement he'd founded that same year, Marie's heart swelled with renewed hope for her oldest son. She'd always been impressed by his intelligence. She could appreciate his impetuosity and independence, both inherited from her. The servants adored him, and she took his great love for four-year-old Ileana and baby Mircea, with whom he even walked the floor at night, as indications of a warm and benevolent nature. So for a time these strengths offset his weaknesses that had nagged her. Unaware of his hatred for her best friend and closest adviser, and seeing Carol as she wanted to see him, Marie at last felt he might prove himself a fitting descendant of Queen Victoria and one day make a competent, even a great, King of Romania.

10

1914

Early reports from Potsdam were good. Though homesick, Carol had made a good adjustment to his new life. He appreciated the passionate militarism of the *Erste Garderegiment* and had enthusiastically flung himself into the stringent routine. By day he enjoyed a growing friendship with his first cousin and fellow cadet, Friedel Hohenzollern. Evenings he returned to a happy household headed for him by his Romanian aide-de-camp, the aging General Perticari, and run by Perticari's much younger wife, the lovely red-haired Helene. Marie's longtime friend and companion, Helene now sealed her affection by providing Marie's son with a warm and cheerful home life based on her own exuberant, patriotic and altruistic personality. In February 1914, his parents visited Potsdam to view Carol's progress for themselves. From there they planned to take him with them to Russia, where a match between Carol and the Tsar's oldest daughter Olga had been proposed.

In Potsdam, once she'd convinced herself that Carol was in good hands with the Perticaris and "earnest little" Friedel, Marie turned her eye on the Kaiser's Germany.

Much of what she saw irritated her. Bombastic, swaggering and militaristic, Germans considered themselves the best educated, most powerful and most efficient nation on earth. All Germany lacked was world mastery. And even that lay in sight, if you believed General Bernhard's best-selling book, *Germany and the Next War*. To Marie, the German Establishment—comprised of the nobility, the military and the rich merchant class—was vulgar and *nouveau riche*. But she could appreciate its attendant military display and magnificent order and discipline for what it was—great theater.

The impresario, her cousin Kaiser Wilhelm II, still sat firmly astride the colossus Bismarck had established and Wilhelm himself had guided for twenty-six years. No longer the blazing-eyed young egotist who had practically shoved his dying father aside to take the throne at twenty-nine, Wilhelm had become with time almost a caricature of·himself. With his provocative pronouncements, fierce mustaches, golden-eagled helmets and blazing retinues of soldiers, he saw himself as the central player in history's greatest military pageant.

Marie could appreciate Wilhelm's rash spontaneity and fearless belief in his divine right to rule. She shared them herself; she felt some men were meant to rule and some to follow. But the Kaiser's personal chauvinism annoyed her. She could hold her own with him, but she didn't like sparring.

On this trip, however, she saw her cousin from a new angle. Perhaps his own brush six years before with the homosexual scandal involving his best friend and top Prussian military officers had softened his attitude toward her. Or perhaps the proposed Russian marriage reminded him of Romania's pivotal position in the Balkans. At any rate, he invited the Romanian Hohenzollerns to spend a few days with him in Berlin on their way to Russia. There he actually unbent and treated his relatives like real people. "He even went so far as to talk to me as though I really existed," wrote Marie, "which he had never done before." At dinner one night he impressed her with his knack for description, cannily recapturing the Tsar's four daughters as they'd looked on a recent Baltic cruise.

At the grand opening of a grandiose new Berlin library she stood in for the vacationing German Empress. The formal procession through the building was led by Wilhelm with Marie on his arm. He wore his white cuirassier uniform complete with clanking sword and jangling spurs. As they walked slowly through a double row of bright-uniformed soldiers, silver trumpets provided an overhead cacaphony that echoed and re-echoed off the library's stupendous dome. For Marie, used to the understated Romanian court, it was like "being on the stage"—and she enjoyed it. Fleetingly that day she sympathized with Wilhelm for the first time. He reminded her of Carol as a small boy: confident he could conquer the world by waving a toy sword. But such blandishments were less than endearing in a fifty-five-year-old Emperor who commanded the world's mightiest military machine—especially when that machine longed for war as an antidote to the world's ills.

The Tsar's court presented a powerful contrast to Wilhelm's. Isolated from society and their relatives by choice and by the tragedy of their little son's hemophilia, Nicholas and Alexandra lived a life outwardly as magnificent and glamorous as the one Marie remembered from her youth. The glittering palaces, colorful parades, golden-domed churches and Cossacks were still there. "But," she wrote, "all this ended at the front door. Stepping over the threshold you entered suddenly into a quiet family life, uniform, exclusive and rather dull."

Nicholas was the same gentle, almost timid cousin she'd always known. Kindness itself to "darling Missy," he once again charmed her with his "dreamy gray-brown" eyes and "caressing" voice. "But this change there *was* in him," she wrote later. "He was like one who is gradually falling asleep under some hypnotic influence."

The change in his wife was more pronounced. Since childhood, Alexandra had been painfully shy with everyone but her immediate circle. Now her shyness had hardened into a steely reserve which made Marie acutely uncomfortable. Though only three years older than her cousin, Alexandra treated Marie "as though I were not even grown up!" At tea in the Alexander Palace, the Tsarina sat stiff and silent, dressed in pastel silks and covered with ropes of pearls hanging nearly to her feet. With her regular features, dark gold hair and large gray eyes, she was still a beautiful woman. But her lips formed a forbidding line that had chilled Russian society and the Romanov family for twenty years.

To Marie's bubbling good humor Alexandra responded with a pinched, patronizing smile that produced two "unwilling" dimples and acted as a dead weight on any conversation. "When she talked, it was almost in a whisper and hardly moving her lips, as though it were too much trouble to pronounce a word aloud."

All her life, Alexandra's personality problems cut her off from potential friends and badly-needed champions. And Marie's impressions of her cousin were darkened by Alexandra's long-time feud with Marie's Ducky and by the Rasputin scandal then sweeping Russia. "I kept wondering," she wrote later, "if [Alexandra] had come straight from her strange and awful adviser; and I felt appalled at the shadows that lay so close behind her."

Carol and Olga got along little better than their mothers. To Carol, the eighteen-year-old Olga's blonde hair and blue eyes were not enough to counteract her broad, plain face and brusque manner. And his trim physique and mop of gold hair left Olga unimpressed.

The marriage suggestion had originated with Sazanov, the Russian Foreign Minister, who quipped: "It's not every day that an Orthodox Hohenzollern comes along." On a deeper level, Sazanov hoped to draw Romania away from Germany and Austria-Hungary and nearer an alliance with Russia. Despite their affection for Nicholas and his daughters and despite the obvious flattery contained in the proposal, Ferdinand and Marie were against the match. They were afraid Olga would bring hemophilia with her to Romania.

With relief, therefore, the Hohenzollerns finally left the Tsar's home for St. Petersburg. Here Marie visited her mother, who was staying with the Tsar's mother, the charming Dowager Empress Marie, at the Anichkoff Palace. And she spent long happy hours with Ducky in her elegant town house. Ducky and Cyril had only recently moved back to St. Petersburg, having lived in exile since their marriage. When Tsar Nicholas heard that Cyril had married the divorced Ducky against his wishes, he'd dismissed Cyril from the Imperial Navy and banished the couple from Russia. This action, coupled with the Tsar's isolation from his relatives, had seriously undermined Nicholas's power as titular head of the Romanovs. Alexandra's unpopularity and the monk Rasputin's power—real or imagined—had killed it. Now reinstated and the parents of two daughters, Cyril and Ducky joined Cyril's elegant, worldly and ambitious mother, Aunt Miechen, the widowed Grand Duchess Marie Pavlovna, in criticizing Alexandra and demanding Rasputin's removal. Numerous family indignation meetings took place in Aunt Miechen's St. Petersburg palace, where the cream of Russian society also gathered.

Appalled by Russia's rapidly deteriorating political situation and missing the old congenial Romanov family gatherings, Marie enjoyed this visit the least of any she'd made to her mother's country. Nevertheless, she enjoyed yet another triumph at the Russian court. Since childhood, she'd enchanted the Russians with her charm and beauty. Now she impressed them with her brains and political expertise. Back in Bucharest the Austrian ambassador, Count Ottokar Czernin, warily eyed her success. The Austrians, secure in King Carol's pro-German foreign policy, had long since adopted a cavalier approach to Romania. Now Czernin warned his government that Marie's "character and mentality is one of the most important reasons for putting relations with Romania on quite another basis."

That June the Tsar and his family paid a return visit to Romania. Despite the overwhelming difference in the size and power of the two countries, the visit was an event of major political importance to both. Since 1878, when Romania was stripped of its northeastern province of Bessarabia by Russia after helping the Russians defeat Turkey, relations between the two governments had been unfailingly bad. Disagreements over the Bessarabian frontier erupted frequently, and Russian fishing boats provoked Romania by penetrating her Danubian straits. In the 1913 Balkan Peace, however, Russia had unexpectedly supported Romania, with happy results for the smaller nation. Russia had ulterior motives in befriending Romania. An alliance between the two could give Russia direct access to Bulgaria and Serbia and provide her with an attack route to her old enemy, Austria-Hungary. But on the warm, sun-washed day of the Tsar's visit, each camp expressed only genial good wishes and the desire, carefully veiled, that Prince Carol and the young Grand Duchess should spark the relationship their last meeting had failed to ignite.

Nicholas was the first sovereign to visit Romania since Franz Joseph's visit eighteen years before, and King Carol planned a regal welcome. With typical thoroughness, he supervised every detail of the one-day visit, which would take place at Constantsa, the Romanian seaport. It would be essentially a family affair, centering on the Tsar, his wife and their five children and the three generations of Romanian Hohenzollerns.

The day was a success. The two families attended a solemn *Te Deum,* followed by a naval review. At Carmen Sylva's seaside villa, with the old Queen dressed in a flowing seafoam-white gown, they enjoyed a gay luncheon. Marie glowed with delight at having her cousins on Romanian soil. And even Alexandra made "brave efforts to be as gracious as possible, but it did not come easily to her and her face was very flushed."

While the ten-year-old Tsarevitch taught Prince Nicolas and Princess Ileana to spit grape seeds into a lemonade bowl, the busy schedule moved from a military parade to a formal tea. Meanwhile the Russian Sazanov and Prime Minister Bratianu talked politics on a motor trip through Transylvania. Little did they realize that the Grand Duchess Olga had already made their machinations unnecessary. She would not marry Carol. That very morning, aboard the Tsar's fabled yacht *Standardt,* she had discussed her proposed marriage with her tutor, Pierre Gilliard. "I don't want it to happen," she declared. "Papa has promised not to make me, and I don't want to leave Russia. I am a Russian and I mean to remain a Russian." With that decision, Olga sealed her fate and turned irrevocably down the path that would end in a bloody cellar in Ekaterinburg.

The visit concluded with a huge banquet in a snow-white hall especially built for the occasion. Marie had personally consulted with the architect to make sure no "gaudy gildings" should mar the building's fine Old Romanian proportions. By her order, only roses decorated the tables. Then, as a climax to twelve festive hours, fireworks were set off over the harbor, painting the sky in brilliant colors. At ten o'clock the Imperial family reboarded their yacht for the trip home.

Marie felt a lump rise in her throat when it came time to tell the Tsar goodby. Yet again it struck her "how very lovable he was with his low voice and gentle eyes." As the gangways went up on the Imperial yachts, she broke away from her place in the farewell line and ran down the pier. At the end she stopped. Overhead, stars lit the sky in a twinkling mosaic. A soft breeze cooled her face and ruffled her long white gown. The only sounds, after a day of tumult, were waves swishing against the pier and the faint call of bugles summoning soldiers back to their barracks. Through a mist of tears she watched the black hulls of the Russian boats slip into the night and disappear.

Marie spent the rest of June enjoying the magnificent summer weather. With all her family but Carol, who had returned to Potsdam, she moved to Sinaia. There she rode with the younger children, enjoyed her flowers and serenely planned her annual trip to her mother at her Tegernsee villa. But she would never visit Tegernsee again. On June 28 the Archduke Franz Ferdinand, heir to the Austro-Hungarian throne, was assassinated with his wife at the Bosnian capital of Sarajevo by a Serbian nationalist named Gavrilo Princip.

For a month the Romanian court existed in a frenzy of suppressed anxiety. To the political leaders, the Archduke's murder spelled the end of many dreams. For despite his enigmatic and unattractive personality, Franz Ferdinand had been a pragmatist. Unlike his uncle, the Emperor Franz Joseph, he'd realized that the Dual Empire's only hope for survival lay in reconciling its subject peoples. For years Romanians on both sides of the Carpathians had consoled themselves for Hungarian atrocities with the knowledge that Franz Ferdinand was their true friend. Now he was dead and with him their hopes for eventual Transylvanian liberation.

As one summer day blended into another and the tension grew across

Europe, the Romanian people and their politicians expressed distrust
and indecision. Bitterly hating Austria-Hungary on one side, they were
unready to form an alliance with the old enemy Russia on the other.
They loved France and respected England, but both lay too far away
to make effective allies. By the end of July, Romania stood ready to wait
it out. Better to avoid diplomatic entanglements until war actually
started, and you could tell which side offered the best chance of success.

Unknown to the Romanian people and to all but a handful of political leaders, for thirty-one years Romania had been joined by a secret
treaty with the Triple Alliance—Germany, Italy and Austria-Hungary.
Responding to his fear of Russia and to his natural ties with Germany,
Carol had concluded the treaty on October 30, 1883. Since then, he'd
renewed it methodically every ten years, carefully shielding the
Romanians from their political ties with the hated Hungarians.

Now, near the end of his life, the grand old King faced his ugliest
dilemma. If war came, which way should Romania turn? Continued
loyalty to his cherished treaty would only strengthen Hungary's grip
on the Transylvanian Romanians. Alignment with the Triple Entente
—Russia, France and England—would put Romania in the untenable
position of acting as Russia's buffer. Even neutrality had its pitfalls: the
loss of powerful friends and postwar isolation.

His agony struck Carol at a bad time. Physically, the Hero of Plevna
had deteriorated rapidly in the past five years. A complicated liver
complaint caused him intense pain, though it seldom kept him in bed.
Weakened from a severe diet, he kept at his duties with characteristic
stoicism. But his springy step was gone forever. White-haired now, he
walked gingerly—as if a sudden movement would cause pain to shoot
through him—and stooped from the shoulders. Too frail for long walks
in his beloved forest, that whole tense month he spent hours shuffling
along the Peles terraces and garden paths.

"I vividly remember the anxious expression of his emaciated face,"
wrote Marie later, "which had taken on the color of old wax . . . almost
hour from hour he followed the development of events and how careworn he looked when he realized the hope of a peaceful solution
. . . became less and less."

On July 28 Austria-Hungary declared war on Serbia after presenting
her with an impossible ultimatum. Germany and France opened hositli-
ties on August 1, and the next day Tsar Nicholas issued a formal
declaration of war on the Triple Alliance. England, having hesitated as
long as possible, finally declared war on Germany on August 4. The

First World War had begun, a holocaust which would kill more than 8.5 million soldiers, wound countless others and destroy forever the world Marie knew and loved.

With war, emotions long suppressed erupted around the royal dinner table. Carmen Sylva, who had almost forgotten her nationality, now declared herself a *Rheintochter* (daughter of the Rhine). Over and over, she repeated such phrases as *Deutschland über Alles* and *Gott mit uns,* and told Marie: "But my darling Missy, you must be prepared to accept England's downfall. It's Germany's day, the beginning of the Teuton era. Germans must became lords of the world for the good of humanity. Besides, my dear Missy, England has to fall—her women have become immoral!"

Marie bit her tongue at this, but refused to argue. More upsetting was the gap between her and Uncle. Through the long years of open conflict, they'd forged a mutual respect which only recently had flowered into real friendship. Now, with their homelands locked in mortal combat, they were separated again. "Not violently or with unfriendly words; we were both careful not to hurt each other's feelings. But when we talked and he propounded his opinions, he felt I was no longer with him."

By August 1 daily telegrams to Sinaia from Berlin and Vienna insisted Carol declare war on the Entente. The pressure became unbearable. On August 3 he took his impassioned plea for Romania to enter the war on the German side to his Crown Council.

All that long afternoon, while Carol fought for his political life, Carmen Sylva paced up and down the red-carpeted Peles corridors with Marie in tow. Though never compatible, the old royal couple had resurrected their ancient affection for each other. And now the Queen declared her heart was fairly bursting with worry for her ailing husband and fear that the council might reject the Germans. Marie was afraid, too—that they might accept German pressure and declare war on England.

Aunty's worst fears were realized. All but one council member, Uncle's old political enemy Peter Carp, voted for Romanian neutrality. In one last heartbroken entreaty, Carol cried, "Gentlemen, you cannot imagine how bitter it is to find oneself isolated in a country of which one is not a native." Back burned the reply: "In peacetime it was possible for Your Majesty to follow a policy contrary to the sentiment of the country. But to make war in defiance of that sentiment is impossible."

Marie, like the rest of the country, realized the neutrality decision reflected more than rejection of the Central Powers. It also symbolized a universal sympathy with the Allies. Suddenly the Crown Princess, with her blood ties with England and Russia, reflected the country's current opinions just as King Carol now represented a past that had died forever.

Gripped with emotion, Marie longed to show the people she realized and shared their feelings. But she dared not. Her only outlet was a book she wrote by night, a passionate personal testament she called *From My Heart to Theirs* and never published. By day she was forced to remain silent, to endure endless tense hours sitting with Ferdinand and the King and Queen. Carmen Sylva waxed dramatic about Uncle's rejection by his people, while the others gloomily discussed the spreading war and tactfully kept their divided sympathies from erupting into open strife. Oblivious, the Queen declared Carol should "shake the dust of this ungrateful country from his feet and go rest in peace far from all conflict."

Writhing under her onslaught, the King sank deeper into misery. He considered the German army invincible. And as a Hohenzollern he felt he'd betrayed both homeland and family by refusing to fight on the side of the Central Powers. As the storm of war grew, all Europe reflected his pain. The novelist Sir Arthur Conan Doyle called that month "the most terrible August in the history of the world. One thought that God's curse hung heavy over a degenerate world." Marie wrote Pauline Spender-Clay, "The old world is changed and something terrible has been put in its place . . . One cannot know where or how we shall all be when this horrible nightmare is ended."

By September Carmen Sylva's rantings began to prove horribly prophetic. The rumor swept Romania that Carol meant to abdicate, that the entire royal family would leave the country. Soon the nation's anxiety penetrated Sinaia, and people began begging Marie for news. But she had no answers for their questions. Neither Carol nor Ferdinand had mentioned abdication to her. In this atmosphere, as nerve-racking as watching a short fuse burn, her own anxiety grew. She hated prying wives, but "this was not a political question, it meant our very existence. What understanding had the King and the Crown Prince which I was not to know?" After her long, bitter apprenticeship was she to leave Romania when her people really needed her? She did not know, and Ferdinand wouldn't tell her.

Nearly bursting with frustration, she called for her ten-year-old son Nicolas. On horseback they pounded together over the high Sinaia meadows, across hay fields mowed by white-shirted peasants and through shady fir groves. Finally she reigned in her horse on the edge of a clearing and watched Nicky wheel his pony around and around while the little animal's tail swept the grass like a "puff of smoke." And as she watched, her frustration was replaced by a new emotion.

Like a breath of cold night air, she suddenly knew what she had to do. She had borne this son with the thought that he, like the others, belonged to Romania and Romania to him. Over the last twenty years she had come to know and love this strange, beautiful land. She had ridden its roads in every season—in winter, when snow piled four feet deep from the Carpathians to the Danube; in green-clad spring; in breathless summer, when glowing sunflower fields spread over endless acres; in dreamy autumn, when the corn hung heavy and stars fell across a cloudless sky. She had visited villages unchanged since Michael the Brave's time, villages where illegitimate children were called "children of the flowers" and where on long winter evenings groups met for *shezatoare*—long parleys in which ancient legends were wound into a people's heritage. She had come to love the frescoed Moldavian monasteries, the tumble-down cottages, the gypsy caravans, the ancient crosses marking holy spots along the road, the flowers that were cultivated in other countries but grow like weeds in Romania, the fir-forested Carpathians, the baked and dusty Wallachian plain, the Eden-like Danube Delta. And she had formed an unbreakable bond with Romania's peasants.

At that moment she knew "with a rock-like certainty, that even if others could be persuaded to leave, I for one would cling to this soil with my children, and to tear us from it would be to tear the hearts from our bodies."

The Battle of the Marne, which dealt Germay its first major defeat of the war, gave Carol of Hohenzollern his last blow as a German. But as an old soldier, he could watch the battle patterns as objectively as an onlooker at a chess match.

One day at lunch late in September, Carmen Sylva announced that the whole family should leave the world's miseries: "Let us all die and go up to Heaven together."

"*Das ist Unsinn* (That is nonsense), Elisabeth," growled the King. "Nonsense. I have no desire to leave this earth. At present I am far too interested as to the outcome of the war. I want to see the end." Turning to Marie, he added, "With this new development things have taken, I am afraid we cannot hope for peace before Christmas."

In October Ferdinand and Marie left Sinaia for a few days in Bucharest. The King had decided it would be good publicity for them to show themselves at the autumn races, thereby reassuring the people that their royal family had not deserted them. Marie accepted an invitation to spend the night of October 9 at Mogosaia, Marthe Bibesco's country house outside Bucharest. Ferdinand would sleep at Cotroceni. In the morning they would take the train back to Sinaia together.

Mogosaia, a sixteenth-century palace built by the Brancovan family, stood reflected in a large lake and surrounded by 150 acres of park land. A long drive wound through heavy woods, past a small church and a large brick gatehouse to the main entrance. The palace, which Marthe had reconstructed from near ruins, was a large pale-red brick building with carved, cream stone pillars and a magnificently carved stone staircase which led up to a typical Old Romanian second-floor loggia. Formal English-style terraces spilled flowering petunias edged with clipped privet down to the lake's edge.

Before dinner that evening Marie and Marthe paddled in a small boat through the lake's high reeds. As the sunset burned sky and water bright orange, Marthe's soft voice evoked "a thousand dreams and also a thousand illusions."

Early the next morning Marie received a telephone call. Barbu Stirbey's familiar voice told her that her uncle had died during the night. Ferdinand was King, and she was Queen of Romania.

The Duchess of Edinburgh and her children. L. to R., Princess Alexandra (Sandra); the Duchess; Princess Beatrice (Baby Bee); Prince Alfred; Princess Marie (Missy); and Princess Victoria Melita (Ducky).

The Edinburgh Princesses in 1902. L. to R., Ducky, Missy, Sandra and Baby Bee.

Carmen Sylva's Salon.

Crown Princess Marie in a photograph by Princess Nadeje Stirbey.

Top left, Prince Barbu Stirbey. Top right, King Ferdinand and Queen Marie during World War I. Bottom left, Waldorf, Pauline and John Astor mug for Marie's camera. Bottom right, Waldorf Astor.

Family group in 1909. L. to R. back, Crown Prince Ferdinand, Prussian A.D.C., Crown Prince Wilhelm of Germany. Front, Prince Nicholas, Crown Princess Marie holding Princess Ileana, Princess Mignon, Princess Lisabetta, Prince Carol.

The Romanian Royal family with their guests the Russian Imperial family at Constantza in 1914. Back: King Carol I, Grand Duchess Anastasia, Princess Mignon, Prince Carol, Princess Ileana, Crown Prince Ferdinand, Queen Carmen Sylva. Middle: Grand Duchess Marie, Empress Alexandra, Grand Duchess Tatiana, Crown Princess Marie, Emperor Nicholas II, Grand Duchess Olga, holding Prince Mircea. Front: the Tsarevitch, Alexis and Prince Nicholas.

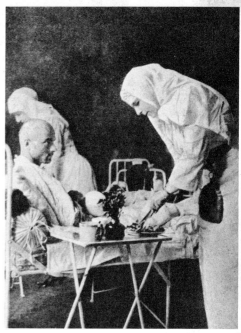

Left, American newspaper cartoon at the time of Romania's armistice with the Central Powers in World War I. Right, contemporary artist's conception of Marie nursing the wounded.

Left, Queen Marie in 1923, "The Sun Queen." Right, Crown Prince Carol and Princess Helen at the time of their engagement in 1921.

Left, Lisabetta, Queen of Greece. Right, Mignon, Queen of Yugoslavia.

Left, Princess Ileana. Right, Michael, the boy king, rides to his accession, July 1927.

Marie at 60, from a painting by Sir Philip de Laszlo

Ilena Lupescu in 1928 *(Wide World Photos)*

Queen Marie in 1936

PART TWO

11

Regina Maria

Queen at last. And with that realization came satisfaction of both the old craving for freedom and the more recent longing to serve her people. Years later she described that morning: "I drove quickly from Bucharest [to Sinaia]. I was Queen. I felt wholly capable of being a Queen when the moment came."

At Sinaia the new sovereigns found chaos. King Carol still lay on his deathbed. Draped in black and surrounded by her weeping ladies, Carmen Sylva sat by his side. Stunned, she described the death scene over and over: how she'd heard his smothered cry, "Oh! What is this?" before he'd fallen into her arms, dead of a heart attack; how she'd groped in the dark, unable to find the light switch.

Now Ferdinand and the children clustered around the stricken old Queen, holding her hand, murmuring comforting phrases. But Marie dropped to her knees at the bedside. Uncle's face, she thought sadly, was scarcely paler in death than it had been during these last troubled weeks. He had undoubtedly been a great king; certainly his era had been the most prosperous, peaceful and politically stable in Romanian history. But after forty years of glory, he'd died three months too late. His pro-German sympathies had sent his popularity plunging. A recent cartoon had pictured the ex-hero weighted down by a shoulder bag marked "200 Million Lei," while a balloon read, "You fools can do whatever you please. I'm going to enjoy my money in Germany." Now he was dead, and there were few enough in those uncertain times to mourn him. In a whisper, Marie promised the noble old warrior she would carry on for the kingdom he'd built and loved.

Then she walked up the hill to the Pelisor. With the shades drawn, she lay on her bed, fighting grief and gathering her forces. At last the children's old nurse Nini came, calling her "Your Majesty," to rub her aching forehead and tell her it was time to leave for Bucharest.

Ferdinand was proclaimed King in Parliament before the combined Senate and Chamber of Deputies. It was a profoundly emotional moment. The war was spreading closer, and no one watching the new king take the Oath of Office knew where he stood politically. Like his uncle, he was German-bred. But he'd also been a Catholic and had borne excommunication to raise his children in the Romanian Orthodox faith. That day some of the Liberal politicians whispered he'd already promised to follow the war wishes of his people, whatever they might be. And none in that crowded chamber questioned which way the majority of Romanians would vote if given the decision of fighting the Hungarians. After all, beyond the Carpathians lay Transylvania, the ancestral land. Victory over the Magyars would realize the ancient dream and national goal.

Only Marie knew what it would cost Ferdinand to declare war on Germany. Standing heavily veiled in black a few feet away with the children, she heard him begin the Oath: "I, Ferdinand, by the Grace of God, and the will of the Romanian people . . ." Emotion showed in his shaking hands. Marthe Bibesco, crammed in with the general crowd behind the delegates, reported that his voice broke as he spoke, that she heard him sob. The emotion in the hall mounted as he read the stirring lines. Marie's heart beat so loudly that it seemed to her to dull the sound of her husband's voice, but finally she heard him finish with the promise to be "a good Romanian." At that, a thunderous ovation shook the hall. Then she heard another salvo of applause and, for the first time, frantic cries of "Regina Maria!" Pulling the veil from her face to show her appreciation, she stood facing them, tears running down her cheeks. As the cheers mounted, "that was *my* hour—mine," she wrote later. "And at that hour I knew that I had won . . . that the girl . . . from over the seas was a stranger no more!" The Romanians might question the sympathies of their new king. They had no doubts about his wife.

As she stood shivering in the waves of their applause, an exhilarating strength surged through her, overpowering the day's grief and emotion.

It was the lucky strength, based on optimism and self-confidence, that would help her bear her new burdens and responsibilities.

But as she watched Ferdinand descend from the podium "on unsteady feet, his eyes red, his fingers clutched about the guard of his sword," she knew he would need her help in the battles that lay ahead. Timid, lacking will power and crippled by indecisiveness, he was badly cast for a wartime king. She would have to be strong enough for both. A few days later she gave him a golden bowl inscribed, "Tomorrow may be thine if thy hand be strong enough to grasp it." And on November 1, as he signed the guest book at a Mogosaia tea party, she told him, "Now you are a king, you must dot your i's."

If King Carol had lived his last months in an atmosphere of "general indifference," he was buried with all the pomp due the Founder of the Country. For three days his body lay in an open coffin in the central hall of the Peles. On the fourth, the coffin was closed, draped with the tricolor Romanian flag, topped with the austere steel crown he had earned on the battlefield of Plevna and transferred to a gun carriage. As its creator was carried away from the Peles, rain fell from a lowering sky and dripped mournfully from the black fir trees lining the road.

In Bucharest he lay in state at the Metropolitan Church for three days. Thousands of people passed before the reopened coffin for a last look at the first King of Romania. The funeral was doubly impressive, as both the Orthodox and Catholic churches claimed the right of burying the old sovereign. To Marie the prayers seemed endlessly long. Finally the coffin was placed on a train for the trip to the burial church, Curtea de Arges, in the southwestern hills of the Carpathians.

After the funeral Marie got down to the hard business of being a Queen. From the first, she found herself too busy to get along with only one lady-in-waiting, so she chose three more. Another appointment made Colonel Ballif her aide-de-camp. It was safer, while traveling about in these "war-like times," to have her own. An austere and unbending though kindly cavalry officer, Ballif was an "entirely competent and reliable" choice.

His first mission was escorting the Queen and her daughters on short trips around the country to distribute money to the poor. Eager as always for closer contact with her people, Marie particularly enjoyed the trips for the contrast they provided with the tense Bucharest atmosphere. In those days of neutrality, "all things were emotional," as Romanians waited for the plunge, which they knew would come sooner or later, into waters too deep to measure. Encouraged by the passionate welcome she received everywhere, Marie already felt like "the mother of an enormous family." She saw the links formed on these visits as comforting insurance against the struggles ahead.

Ferdinand, on the other hand, had no like opportunity for stepping gingerly into his new role. Foreign affairs filled his days and plagued his nights. There was no escaping war. For him the only questions were how long Romania could stay neutral and on which side she should fight. He alone could sign the declaration of war. So from the moment King Carol died, his nephew shouldered the old man's awesome burden.

Ferdinand was by no means totally unequipped for kingship. Like Carol, he was hard-working and honest, a virtual slave to duty. He was also better read, more versatile, more compassionate and a better judge of character than his uncle had been. But his indecisiveness and timidity, which irritated Marie, often overshadowed his good points in times of stress.

Now, however, while war burned in next-door Galicia, he stanchly clung to his temporary decision to remain neutral, conserve the country's resources and study the alternatives. All were laced with uncertainty. Both the Central Powers and the Allies wanted Romania—for her strategic seat in the Balkans, for her glut of grain and incredibly rich natural resources. Therefore both sides alternately wooed and threatened Bratianu's government. But Russian promises were suspect, and even Marie had to agree that England had always favored the old enemy Bulgaria over Romania. "Why on earth," she moaned, "is England sentimental about Bulgaria?" On the other side, proposed Hungarian concessions to the Transylvanian Romanians were so meager even the Magyars' German allies begged them to offer more. Above all, Ferdinand had to wait for Italy's decision. On September 23 the two Latin underdogs had wisely signed a pact to make any martial move together. But the Italian foreign minister's death, a week after King Carol's, had postponed Italian action indefinitely and handed Ferdinand a welcome breather.

Meanwhile, on November 2 Russia declared war on Turkey. This brought the war onto a third Romanian front, battles having already been fought in both Serbia and Transylvania. It also upped the stakes for both Romania and neighboring Bulgaria. Now honeyed German and Allied promises rained from the skies over Bucharest and Bulgaria's capital, Sofia, as Bratianu slapped an embargo on war materials from the Central Powers to Turkey, and Bulgaria took the same line on Russian supplies headed for Serbia.

By mid-November Marie estimated that "nine-tenths" of the country longed to join the Allies. A group of young nationalists at the University of Bucharest howled for immediate action. Their hot-eyed leader, a former Conservative Minister of War, Nicu Filipescu, had threatened to "break King Carol's windows" in defiance of the old king's pro-German sympathies. Now he transferred his hostility intact to his party leader, Conservative Chief Alexander Marghiloman, who along with Peter Carp led the country's small but dedicated group of Germanophiles.

That winter both rival Romanian groups bought or founded Bucharest newspapers to serve as mouthpieces for their political opinions. "Calumny and rumors celebrated veritable orgies" in their papers. Meanwhile the enemy European powers deluged the city with speculators who outspent each other on Romanian grain and maize and greased the streets with "corrupting baksheesh."

The new year began on a tense note. The city was still victim of the hysteria created by shrill political quarrels and the presence of bargaining Allied and German ministers. Full-blown rumors and shady dealings chased each other down Bucharest's slushy Calea Victoriei, and spies were everywhere.

Each camp had its hangout. Prussian officers, with monocles and inside jokes, strode into the enameled and gilded Athénée Palace Hotel. The French gravitated to the "faintly Bohemian" atmosphere of the Moderne, and "two or three lean and easy English colonized the Caspa Restaurant." According to one onlooker, the hostile representatives were no more segregated on the battle line than "here, in this neutral capital which is the political storm center of the Balkans." One night, the good-natured, bearlike United States Minister to Romania, Bulgaria and Serbia, Charles J. Volpicka, managed the unmanageable. He gave a tea party and dance for his daughter at the American legation, receiving guests from every embassy in town.

The result, noted a guest, "was somewhat stiff and formal." But the hostile guests actually went so far as to acknowledge one another's existence "as human beings, and to leave each other's throats alone. It was in the nature of a small miracle. Bucharest, which has watched them for months, saw it with amazement."

At the heart of the storm sat Marie. Secrecy and diplomacy didn't come naturally to her, and she hated neutrality. "It was like walking on eggs." The word itself was foreign to her nature. And she found it nearly impossible to adhere to the necessary "pretence and shilly-shallying." Yet circumstances forced her daily into tests which would have tried the nerves of a master statesman.

She has been harshly criticized for dominating her husband during this period. Some journalists have stated that she was the real ruler of Romania. The actual situation was much more complicated and subtle than that. And it involved not only the King and Queen but Ion Bratianu and Barbu Stirbey as well.

The real Romanian ruler, during the long years of his premiership, was Bratianu. Thanks to rigged elections and virtual control of the banks, his regime, according to one political observer, was "a dictatorship thinly masked by constitutional forms." One of these forms, the King's power, sometimes stood in Bratianu's way. For though a constitutional monarch, the Romanian King had considerably more power than the British monarch, for example. He could nominate and dismiss ministers, dissolve and adjourn Parliament. He had the right of absolute veto on legislation. He was the head of the Army and with the legislature's approval could conclude treaties with foreign countries. So to completely rule the country, Bratianu had to rule the King.

This he did, though the job was not always an easy one. Like many shy people, the King tended to echo the most recent opinion he'd heard. Therefore the last minister to see him during a political crisis was sure to carry the day. Bratianu, knowing his King, circumvented this problem in numerous ways. Whenever he wanted the King to bring home a certain point in an interview with the Opposition, he would say, "Please, sir, write down these special points that I want you to tell Marghiloman." And the King, who had a great, if diffident, respect for Bratianu, took the notes on his blotting paper. Here Ferdinand's incredible erudition proved convenient. He wrote the points in German, using the old Cyrillic alphabet, and spoke them in French or Romanian. To unsuspecting Conservative petitioners, the code which destroyed their arguments looked like so many ink stains.

This ruse, however, wouldn't solve every problem. For such overwhelming tasks as persuading Ferdinand to declare war on Germany, the Prime Minister needed more than a few blotting paper scribbles. He turned then to Marie. Though he had long criticized his brother-in-law's position as Gray Eminence to the Crown Prince and Princess, now that they were King and Queen he decided to put the triple friendship to use for Romania.

So, convincing Marie of her importance to the country, the two great Liberal leaders actually used her as a go-between to the King. They were sure Ferdinand would ultimately agree to anything she desired. For although he would deny open collaboration with his wife, Ferdinand constantly required her buoyant self-assurance to boost his flagging spirits. "He depended on me," she wrote. "I was the joyful companion, occasionally unruly, but one who would never let him down. Besides, our task as well as our goal were the same, and we both lived for the same goal—the good of the country." Besides, she knew the country's pulse. Weren't she and her people united in their desire to fight alongside the Allies for the birth of a united Romania? She must be Ferdinand's "soul doctor," she told herself, preserving his pride as she inched him away from Germany and toward the Allies. He was as inflexibly convinced as Uncle had been that Germany would win the war. Every one of his traditional loyalties and natural impulses drew him that way. Yet it was up to her to lead him another way. It would take all her love and understanding of his character and all the tact she could muster.

As usual, Stirbey's role was even more subtle than the Queen's. If Marie had the King's ear, she also needed strong and cogent arguments to bend it. These Stirbey provided—not only through Marie, but also in long personal conversations with the King. He also acted as the Queen's eyes and ears, informing her daily of shifting public opinion and every move the pro-German party made.

Years after her death, Prince Stirbey himself evaluated the situation. "Her Majesty was a forceful character, with great personal courage and great intelligence. Since the King was a weak character, it was more normal that we should go to her, and *ask* her to do this or that. But she never had the political influence she thought she had." Or, he might have added, "we let her believe she had." His love for her, apparently, did not preclude his using her, even through flattery.

The Central Powers, on the other hand, while not overestimating the Queen's power, saw her for what she was to them—the chief stumbling block between themselves and the King. The Germans had long anticipated this situation. When she married, Bismarck was reported to have muttered, "That little golden-haired girl is going to cook our goose in the Balkans." Commenting on her influence in 1915, the irate Kaiser called her a "meddlesome little flirt."

On January 15, in answer to threats of what would happen to a Hohenzollern prince who declared war on the Fatherland, Ferdinand wrote the Kaiser a long letter. He explained that he personally felt one way, but was torn another by his people, who clamored for the liberation of the Transylvanian Romanians. He pointed out that he was "bound by oath" to serve Romania "through every sacrifice." He also warned the All Highest that if Italy broke her neutrality toward Germany, Romania would be forced to follow suit. On February 6, as if underlining his words, Romania renewed the Latin pact for another four months.

Bratianu now saw another way the Queen could help. Her first cousins currently occupied the thrones of England, Russia, Germany, Norway, Greece and Spain. Unlike King Carol, the Prime Minister decided to take advantage of this genealogical quirk.

He planned to eventually join the Allies, but he wanted Romania to gain enough in postwar recompense to make the war effort worthwhile. So Marie was put to work explaining Romania's position to both Cousin George, whom she hadn't seen since his coronation as King George V in 1912, and the Tsar. The Queen in turn was glad to do her share. "I was considered a valuable asset."

Communication with these two favorite cousins was never difficult. Writing to "My Dear George" and "My Dear Nicky" and signing herself "Your loving cousin Missy," she nobly pleaded Romania's cause. Explaining that "no German success or victory shakes Romania's allegiance" to the Allies and that "we are well aware that the position of our country down here is of importance to both sides," she added: "We also know that whatever way we move we are staking our whole future, even perhaps our very existence." Then she detailed Romanian territorial requests. These included all of Transylvania plus "other parts of Austria-Hungary inhabited by Romanians," the whole of the Banat region over to the Serbian capital Belgrade itself, and Russian-held Bessarabia as far as the river Pruth. As she wrote, she must have smiled, remembering the "geography" games they'd played at Malta under her mother's critical scrutiny. European geography had never been George's strong point. Now she pictured him wrinkling his brow as he read her letter in his cluttered study on the Constitution Hill side of Buckingham Palace. So she ended with an apology: "Forgive the tiresome length of all this." She also felt compelled to explain her position as political spokesman. "When we came to the throne, my popularity was very great. This put me in a particularly delicate position. It is flattering, but I must not let it turn my head, for what is more odious than a woman who makes politics 'on her own hook'?"

King George replied warmly, promising no more than a British Constitutional monarch was able. But the Tsar answered her letter with affection for his cousin and a rebuff for Romania. "I must frankly own that we were deeply amazed by your country's *enormous* demands."

As summer came in, both warring sides redoubled their efforts to win Romania and Bulgaria. Of the two, Romania remained the harder to bag. She had already served the Allies well by letting Russian supplies through to Serbia and by stopping German supplies to Turkey, which lessened Turkey's chances of hanging onto the precious Dardanelles. As Marie put it, it would be "ungracious and misplaced" for the Allies "at this late hour to wrangle about our claims." Meanwhile Hungarian Prime Minister Tisza's stubborn refusal to make Transylvanian concessions snarled every German and Austrian lure. For all his political intractability, however, Bratianu was not above making several highly profitable oil and grain sales to the rival suitors.

Bulgaria was easier. Wild territorial promises sent her reeling toward the Central Powers, and on October 14 she fell. Almost immediately the German forces, led by General August von Mackensen, jumped across the Danube and landed heavily on Serbia. "Our brave little allies," as Tsar Nicholas called the Serbs, had routed the Austrians, but they couldn't defeat the Germans. With the fall of Serbia, Romania found herself more than half surrounded by armies of the Central Powers.

Wildly elated by their Balkan victories, the Central Powers tried a more arrogant approach with the Romanians. It got them nowhere. When Bratianu made a major corn deal with England, for which Romania received ten million pounds in advance, the Austrian ambassador, Count Czernin, exploded. He had already bought fifty thousand trucks of Romanian grain for starving Austrians, and it infuriated him that England, who didn't need it, should get the surplus. Czernin's German colleague, Herr Von dem Busche, informed King Ferdinand that Berlin could no longer trust Bratianu and would never deal with him again. For the Central Powers there remained in Bucharest but one alternative, and that was the Queen.

Von dem Busche tried first. He may have been an ambassador, but he was no diplomat. In a few minutes he managed to convey every

German characteristic she hated, none that she liked. Pompously he lectured her on several pedestrian subjects. Then he suddenly put his hand in his pocket and pulled out a packet of dumdums, the hollow-nosed Indian-made bullets that expanded on impact, inflicting a vicious wound.

"Would Your Majesty like to see the sort of bullets the English use against the Germans?"

She stood up and turned her back on him.

Czernin's interview was longer and more grueling. She had always liked this tall, blond, aristocratic-looking Austrian, with his charming if somewhat arrogant manners. On the winter afternoon he arrived for tea in her private sitting room, it was immediately obvious that today he had brought along his full battery of charm and none of his arrogance. He began his fateful interview with amusing chitchat, "eager to please a lady." Then as tactfully as possible, he brought up the question at hand.

He used every argument. He was her friend and admirer, he said, and had come to open her eyes before it was too late. The Central Powers were victorious everywhere. She—and she alone—held the fate of Romania in her hands. Therefore she must send Romania into war on the Central Powers side or hand it over to "everlasting perdition."

As a piece of amateur dramatics, it was a minor classic. "He made promises, dangled victory and triumph before my eyes. He played the advisor, the accuser, the tempter." But she could only shake her head. Finally his master assault shattered on the backbone of her unalterable stand: "I share Romania's great dream, and I believe that England always wins the last battle."

Czernin shivered all the way back to Bucharest. He'd already told Vienna that the King was completely under Bratianu's thumb and that Bratianu himself was "cowardly and false." Today he'd played his final hand and lost. When he reached town, he made an appointment to meet with the pro-German Marghiloman.

On March 3, 1916, Carmen Sylva died, and yet another cord was cut between Bucharest and the Germans. Following her husband's death, the old Queen had taken up residence at the Curtea de Arges bishop's palace "to be as near as possible" to his grave. Here, draped in yards of black crepe, she shared the winter fire with the equally "voluminous and imposing" old Bishop. Resembling two black owls, they sat the afternoons away, the Bishop nodding and dozing, Her Majesty tatting and talking about her latest direct communication with the Archangel Raphael.

Ferdinand and Marie had done everything possible to make the Poet-Queen's widowhood pleasant, as Carmen Sylva herself attested. "I am working hard," she wrote a friend, "and the young couple and I are leading a wonderful life together, in great harmony. Not only do they come to lunch every day, but in the morning I work for hours translating Missy's fairy tales and after lunch the King reads them, and copies them himself as a rest from state affairs. So we have that work in common, which brings deep joy every day."

On February 18 the Old Queen granted her last audience, to Volpicka, the American Ambassador. He came to thank her for a book of poems and received a blast of pro-Germanism. She expressed the novel opinion that Romanian hatred of Germany was inspired by Tsar Nicholas's mother, the Dowager Empress Marie, who had never set foot in Romania. She also told Volpicka that she understood the United States was making a hundred million dollars a year off the European war, and she ended with an attack on the English. "They are deteriorating as a nation."

Two weeks later, having caught pneumonia from her beloved fresh air, she died, one hand in Marie's, the other gripping the fingers of her old German maid. Her last words, painfully whispered, were to Marie: "You are supposed to say beautiful things, and you can't. . . ."

They buried her beside Uncle at Curtea de Arges, and her funeral wishes were followed down to the playing of Georges Enescu's orchestral transcription of her favorite Haydn quartet, *Mein letztes Quartette.* The funeral closely resembled the Kings's, though the ceremonial was less complicated. For this fairy queen, who had published countless Romanian fairy tales read by generations of European children, who was responsible for the renaissance in Romanian culture and folk art, and who lived immersed in high romanticism, remained all her life a stanch Lutheran.

12

To Embrace Death with a Pure Heart

That spring, Romania and the rest of Europe held their breath as Russia's mighty Southwest Army, led by General Aleksei Brusilov, massed for an attack on the Central Powers' two-hundred-mile-long eastern front. In April Brusilov's army crushed the enemy's entire defense and moved westward from the Romanian border. Austria's Fourth and Seventh Armies collapsed. By late June Brusilov had nearly reached the Carpathians. Then he had to stop for want of fresh men and supplies. Taking advantage of the breather, German Marshal Paul von Hindenburg, barely holding his own on the overlong western front, fired every German division he could spare off to the east. But it wasn't enough to stop the Russians. The Brusilov colossus, on its feet again by early August, kept advancing.

Bucharest was ecstatic and eager to join the Russians in Transylvania. Now was the time to declare war and liberate their kinsmen over the mountains. Marie and Stirbey held daily strategy meetings. The King, a harder nut to crack than either had imagined, still clung to neutrality. "Then let him abdicate!" shouted Filipescu's radicals. When the situation reached a breaking point, Marie met Filipescu on horseback one evening in the Buftea woods. While they rode, she convinced him to be patient, that she would convince the King he must go with the Allies.

Events kept the royal family in Bucharest that summer. On evenings when the August heat lay like a smothering blanket over the town, making sleep impossible, the Queen would suggest a drive into the country. With Ferdinand at the wheel of their open Rolls Royce and Marie beside him, they drove for miles over the dusty plains. Sometimes they dined on the open veranda of Copaceni, the old vacation house which she had admired in her youth and inherited from its aged owner. More often they drove aimlessly along back roads they hadn't visited since the golden days of their first touring car, when they had really discovered their country for the first time. They passed old churches and ruins, tiny villages squatting beside dry river beds. They crossed the undulating plain leading towards the Danube and rested at shady *luncas* (woods at a river's edge) where shepherds watched their flocks. They loved those treks, especially then "when we felt danger so near."

One of these evenings stayed in Marie's memory forever. It had been a hotter day than usual. No air stirred, and dust raised by their car parched their throats and obliterated the landscape. One after another, like phantoms, peasant carts groaning with harvest corn, wheat, hay or tomatoes emerged from the dust. Grinning, dust-caked children sat on the creaking shafts, brandishing whips. Beside them plodded sunburned men and women, as patient in their endless toil as the oxen pulling their carts.

The royal couple roamed farther than usual that night, driven by the demon of Ferdinand's indecision. As she watched him, wishing he could break down and talk through his agony, Marie's warm heart went out to her husband. She knew how it felt to love one country and sacrifice your life to another, and she groaned inwardly imagining the prospect of fighting England. The Hohenzollern motto, symbolized by the crested Prussian officer's sword he still carried, now took on a chilling meaning. The creed was "To embrace death with a pure heart."

Finally, like a scene from Dante, an enormous setting sun broke through the dust cloud directly over their heads. Overwhelmed, they stopped, watching as it bled fire across the whole horizon. Suddenly, so near that they jumped, a voice emerged from the dust. It was an old man, shaking a finger at the sun and speaking in the curiously poetic cadence of the Romanian peasant. He said, "It is a war sun, a bloody sun, a sun of battle."

On August 27, three days after his fifty-first birthday, framing his signature with the characteristic flourish Marthe Bibesco compared to "the background of a Japanese print," King Ferdinand signed the declaration of war on Austria. The decisive Crown Council debate had been heated. The King based his decision on the Austrian collapse, which, he said, now made a victory by the Central Powers impossible. Bratianu agreed, reminding the council that it was impossible to fight beside a Germany that was "encouraging Bulgaria to take our place in the East." Old Peter Carp became "excessively rude" and blurted out, "I wish you may be beaten, for your victory will be the ruin of the country." Whereupon Bratianu suggested Carp send his sons to fight with the German army. The more levelheaded Alexander Marghiloman told the King he couldn't sign the declaration. But it might be just as well, he added, to have an Opposition leader to fall back on in case Bratianu's government failed. "If things go badly, I shall be there to help." In retrospective view of the coming year's events, his words had a prophetic ring.

Although the declaration didn't include Germany, Berlin's reaction was swift and harsh. "The Latin traitors," shrieked German newspapers, "have proven their descent from ancient Rome's deported criminals." The "degenerate" Hohenzollern king was compared with the "frank and soldierly" Greek King Constantine, who leaned towards Germany. The Kaiser denounced Ferdinand, personally by telegram and symbolically by lifting his name from the House of Hohenzollern. At Sigmaringen his brothers went into mourning for him as if he were dead. The worst he had to bear were the tears of Neumann, his old German body servant.

"But, Sire," said Peter Carp, "it is not possible to vanquish the Hohenzollerns."

"You are mistaken, Monsieur Carp," answered the King. "I have already vanquished one."

The next day, Marie saw trainloads of young soldiers off to Transylvania. Heartsick at their pathetic gaiety, she flung flowers to them as they steamed away, crying from open windows: "We go to make you Empress of all the Romanians!"

The King and Crown Prince Carol left immediately for army Headquarters at Scroviste Peris. The Queen planned to keep the other children with her at Cotroceni, but within days her plans were violently upset. The Germans began bombing Bucharest. Their chief target, according to well-founded rumor, was the royal family. So at the Stirbeys' request, Marie moved her household to Buftea.

No matter that it was supposed to be an open city, or that Romania hadn't declared war on Germany. Almost daily, bombs rained over

Bucharest, killing people in their yards and gouging huge pits in the streets.

Terribly mutilated victims were carried into the hospitals. Already deeply involved in the war effort, Marie was soon prepared to meet them at her own hospital, hastily set up in the downtown Palatul Regal. Her days, after the frustrating inactivity which had preceded the declaration, were now wildly hectic. The move to Buftea may have protected the children; it profited Marie not at all. She spent every day in town, visiting her own and other hospitals, helping wealthy matrons organize new private hospitals, receiving deputations and giving teas for the Allied officers. She was elated that Romania was finally fighting with the Allies, and in "just a confidential letter from cousin to cousin" told King George so.

But from the first, she had a premonition that the general Romanian exultation was exaggerated.

Too soon, fate justified her fears. Instead of advancing into Transylvania, the Romanian armies should have dug in along their own border. As it was, their whole campaign depended on a phalanx of ifs. They could succeed in Transylvania if the German army stayed at Verdun and the Somme, if Italy ran interference on the Isonzo, if the Allies kept the Bulgarians busy in Salonika and—above all—if Brusilov held down the Austrians.

But Brusilov was finally exhausted for good. And the Germans, far from ignoring early Romanian successes in taking such Transylvanian passes as the Turnul-Rosu, the Timis and the Tulghes, had already dispatched offensive armies led by two of their top generals: Field Marshal August von Mackensen in the south and ex-War Minister Erich von Falkenhayn in the north. They were ready to crush the Romanian armies before the month was out.

In early September, with an army comprised of Turks, Bulgars and a few Germans, Mackensen began to march. He captured Turtucaia on the Danube, taking precious ammunition and 25,000 prisoners. With this single stroke he weakened the Romanian army's hold upon the Dobruja and dislocated its entire strategy. Instead of pursuing the Transylvanian offensive, the Romanians were forced to transfer vital forces to counteract Mackensen.

Breathless with horror, Marie watched the swift reversal. On September 12 she wrote King George: "The loss of Turtucaia was grievous; our people are so enthusiastic for the Transylvanian side they are inclined to overlook the great danger of the Bulgarians, who are good

soldiers and hate us with a deadly hate. I only hope Russia will keep
her promise and not leave us in the lurch."

That afternoon she spent three hours walking through the big military hospital. It was filling with wounded men brought by Red Cross
units from the front. The air reeked with the odors of singed and rotting
flesh. Gruesome sights were everywhere. Yet slowly, almost casually,
she moved through the rows of sufferers, distributing flowers, candy
and cigarettes. Touched by their stoic endurance, she tried to talk "a
little longer" to the worst cases. One, little more than a boy, lay on his
stomach, his back shattered by a dumdum bullet. She bent over him.

"You are suffering?" she asked.

"I am suffering, Mamma Regina. But never mind as long as you
become Empress of all the Romanians."

Everywhere the refrain was the same. Her eyes blinded with tears,
she went back to her rounds.

The Germans continued bombing Bucharest. On September 26, in
the diary she kept from the first day of war and would keep with
"unflagging persistency" for the rest of her life, she wrote: "Early into
town for hospital work. Hardly was I there than the aeroplane scare
began again. Once more the blue sky was full of bursting shells, once
more death streamed down upon us from the heavens. I saw something
like a snow-white bird high up in the air, something that with outspread
wings exactly resembled the classical symbol of the Holy Ghost, and
from that almost imperceptible speck of white in the shape of a dove
. . . murder and disaster were hurled down upon innocent inhabitants
peacefully walking in the streets!"

Bombs fell in the Cotroceni garden too, though none hit the palace.
"I was not there at the time, but later on, when driving to lunch, we
saw an unfortunate horse lying on the road with his legs blown off.

"It is very difficult to get any real military news. I can find out
nothing, but there is bad news from the North. On the line towards
Ramnic, German troops have managed to slip in behind our army and
cut off the railway; but I cannot discover how many troops, nor if this
is really serious news."

It was much more serious than she knew. Defeated by Falkenhayn
near Sibiu, the Romanians fell back across the Turnul-Rosu Pass they
had so recently won. Nothing remained but retreat.

The army backed up and entrenched around Brasov, the thirteenth-
century Transylvanian trade center of the Carpathians, and Falkenhayn opened fire. In Bucharest, people gripped hands and turned white

with fear. Brasov was less than thirty miles from Sinaia. Another defeat would mean German invasion.

Frantic with anxiety, Marie spent endless hours in the hospitals, serving meals to the wounded, clasping the hands of dying men, inspiring everyone around her. But her brain raced. What if they had to evacuate? Where could they go? How would they transport the wounded?

To relieve the anxiety, she took brief, mad rides through the Buftea woods on Grui, her favorite stallion. Evenings, she played with her children, then sat with Stirbey and Major Washburn, the perceptive and sympathetic little New York *Times* war correspondent. Till late at night they racked their brains for a way to save the situation. Finally from headquarters Ferdinand sent the Queen a message asking her to write Tsar Nicholas for help. On October 7 she wrote: "My Dear Nicky,

"If I write to you today, it is not as cousin but as Queen of a country I dearly love. We have bravely entered this war, well knowing what we were doing and that our resources are not beyond a certain limit. From all sides our Allies assured us that when we came in, such tremendous efforts would be made on all the fronts at once that we would not find ourselves fighting against forces quite beyond what we could cope with.

"Now we have come to the realization that we are facing tremendous and immediate danger, and that unless we are helped at once, it may be too late and we may have to experience all the horrors of invasion and destruction."

Cut off from the other Allies commanders, Romania's only hope lay with the Tsar. Where was the promised Russian help? Instead of 50,000 men, they had dispatched only 20,000 to defend the tottering Dobruja from Mackensen. The once-mighty Brusilov army lay shattered, ammunition gone and a million men dead. Those that lived, fighting with their bare hands, were ripe for revolution.

They hadn't long to wait. Unknown to Marie, Nicholas was facing the imminent disintegration of his government, his economy and his army. There would be no help from Russia.

Her greatest joy during those tense and exhausting days were her two youngest children. On October 7 she wrote: "In the evening Mircea and Ileana played in my room as in the days of peace; it did me good to hear their happy, innocent voices, to watch their games. What hard times these poor little things still have to see!" Almost as an afterthought she added, "Mircea is such a quaint little fellow, so intensely stubborn. We always speak Romanian together. Ileana is his slave, she adores him like a mother, and has an excellent influence over the unruly child."

Two days later, Ferdinand came to lunch with her at Buftea. He was horridly depressed. Mackensen now occupied the old Bulgarian border and was threatening what had been Uncle's great pride, the big bridge at Cernavoda. Brasov was weakening. She tried to boost his spirits, to spur him into more activity. After he left, she confided to her journal: "If I were King I would go everywhere, see everything myself and talk to the troops, be amongst them continually, till they would adore me and gladly go to battle for my sake." Then, in a burst of frustration: "Oh! sometimes I do mind being a woman."

Tragedy piled on tragedy. In late October Mackensen took Constantsa, the country's major seaport, and prepared to march on Bucharest. In the north exhausted Romanian troops streamed out of the Carpathians. In their wake came thousands of Transylvanian Romanian refugees fleeing Hungarian reprisals. And on October 23 an icy fear that had pricked Marie's spine for days became a reality: her three-year-old Mircea had typhoid fever.

In the first days of illness, before its diagnosis, he had been his old irascible self, loudly stating his likes and dislikes. When the doctors arrived, he would produce a special joke which he knew amused his mother. *"Pfui, docco!"* he would jeer. *"Pfui, docco!"*

Now he lay glassy-eyed in his little bed in the pink guest room at Buftea, his body thrashing with the fever that had almost killed both his father and his oldest brother. Day after day, Marie recorded the agony in her diary. He seemed to be sinking. Despite wet towels his temperature soared, and he kept calling for Ileana. On October 25 she wrote, "Three times my Mircea nearly slipped away." There was talk of evacuation too. But to where? And with a dying child?

Two nights later, her aide-de-camp woke her at half past twelve. Mircea was worse. She flew to his side. His pulse was nearly gone, and the doctors were trying to rouse him with artificial respiration and stimulants. "Finally they gave up," she wrote, "and laid him back on the bed. All white he lay there, his eyes half upturned in their sockets, his hands and feet were icy." But he still lived.

Numb with misery, she could neither move nor feel. Someone called a priest from the village. The priest came and gave the baby Holy Communion. A single candle lit the small face on the pillow and also illuminated some pink roses Prince Nicolas had brought for his brother. In the shadows behind her, people began gathering: "good portly"

Denize, Nicolas's tutor; Captain Georgescu, the officer of her regiment; Ferdinand and Carol, drenched from the mist that had made their drive from headquarters painfully slow. Somewhere in the back of the room a woman sobbed. The hours dragged on.

Morning came and Mircea still lived. His temperature had even dropped a few degrees. It could mean that he was better. "But it may also mean the beginning of the end," she wrote. Stiffly, she went through the motions of living. "My four ladies came to lunch, for I thought it unkind not to see them." But she couldn't talk. "I have nothing to say, all my strength must be used to suffer decently without upsetting others, without making a fuss."

Though he still lay in a stupor, staring with sightless eyes, Mircea had a few hours' improvement after that. So she took a day and dashed over bomb-riddled roads to a village on the Danube. There her regiment waited for her blessing before going into their first battle.

Then she tore back to Buftea, where she found Mircea "deadly pale —my heart stopped beating, but he opened his eyes and looked at me."

For six days the child hovered on the edge of death, kept alive by stimulants. His screams filled the house. Beside him sat Marie, alternating between wild hope, when his temperature dropped a degree, to total despair.

Sunday, October 29, 1916, was her forty-first birthday. Reassured that he would live a few hours more, she rushed into town. Like a sleepwalker, she moved through her hospital, delivering flowers to the soldiers. When she had used up all her flowers, someone filled her arms with more. She walked and smiled. But her lips were "too stiff" to talk. Every soldier whispered a prayer for "*Printul* Mircea's" recovery.

That night she couldn't force herself to go down to dinner. But she wanted as many people as possible to enjoy a treat on her birthday. So she ordered wine and good food sent to her regiment on the front, provided treats for the wounded in her hospital, sent money and flowers to the poorer hospitals in town and had cakes distributed to the Buftea village children.

By Thursday, November 2, Mircea was still alive. The Germans had taken Brasov, and both Mackensen and Falkenhayn were marching on Bucharest. Over the past several years her writing had provided an increasingly important emotional outlet. On this ghastly day she ran several times to write in her diary the agony she could neither verbally express nor let herself feel.

"He screams no more," she wrote that morning, "but for two days he has an incessant movement of the jaw, clacking and grinding his teeth. *Midday.* I think he is sinking. The doctors say nothing, but I think he is sinking . . . *Afternoon.* He is sinking, now I feel sure he is going . . . *Evening.* Mircea died at nine, his hand in mine."

She would never dance again. For weeks she couldn't bring herself to ride. Months later, Mircea—running from nurse Nini, bending over Ileana's dolls, coming towards her dressed as an American Indian and crying "Mircea is coming to Mamma!"— haunted her dreams. For the rest of her life she slept with his last shoes in an embroidered case under her pillow.

The next day, while a cold wind tore the last leaves from the court-yard trees, they buried him at the old Cotroceni church. Inside, white tapers glowed on banked white chrysanthemums, shone on Marie's white face as she knelt by the opening in the church floor, and picked out this inscription on a nearby tomb:

"In the prime of his life, in the flower of his youth, cruel death tore from the honors that were due him, the too young Constantine, fair offspring of Radu Hanai, Grand Spatan. He was twenty-two, and to his mother's great grief did he leave. Oh! Worthy indeed of tears is his loss. Having taken the root of immortality in the race of the Cantacuzenes, he has been here honorably interred so that his memory may remain unforgotten. It was in the year of Christ one thousand seven hundred and twenty-three. Many sighs did he leave to his relatives, but as to his mother, deep in her sorrow and her tears know no end."

As her eyes caught the familiar words, Marie realized that Mircea's death tied her to Romania as nothing else could. It bound her with the ancient queens who had lost sons defending their land against the Turks and with the Romanian mothers who were now sacrificing their boys to the Germans.

Unlike some people, she did not close up with her grief, but turned outward to others who suffered. For months she couldn't bear gay, frivolous people. But more than before she could help her dying sol-diers, having herself stared death in the face. "From that moment," said her daughter, Ileana, "she began that emptying of herself to feel the other person. It allowed her to reach the essence, the very soul of the country."

"I felt like a ghost, and all the faces looking at me were the faces of ghosts," wrote Marie after Mircea's funeral. But Oltenia and Dobruja had fallen. The Germans had reached Bucharest and were shattering the city's outer fortifications. Airplanes and Zeppelins rained death from the sky, slaughtering thousands of innocent people all over the country. Mircea's mother might be temporarily a ghost; the Queen of Romania had to keep on fighting.

Taking Nini, Colonel Ballif and a lady-in-waiting with her, she battled rough Moldavian roads and biting November winds in her open Mercedes to visit wounded in the villages of Romna, Bacau, Comanesti and Targul Ocna. They arrived at Targul Ocna minutes after a bombing raid. Seeing a peasant woman huddled over a child in the road, the Queen stopped the car. Getting out, she asked the woman what was wrong with the child.

"His leg has remained in the house," said the woman.

Similarly gruesome sights greeted her everywhere.

By the end of November three-fourths of the country lay in German hands, and the Bucharest defense was folding. The decision was made to move the government and the court to Jassy, the ancient Moldavian capital in the northeastern corner of the country. Marie galvanized her household, organizing their packing, and pushed through evacuation plans for her hospital.

On the evening of November 23 she drove alone to visit Marthe Bibesco at Mogosaia. The Princess lay in her red damask bed, surrounded by the collection of old icons and quaint objects which the Queen so admired. With her fine dark hair unbound and her big green eyes "appealingly pathetic," Marthe exuded the charm which had snared Proust and a host of other admirers. She told Marie she had decided to stay behind when the court evacuated, because she wanted "to taste every experience for the sake of literature, even occupation under the Germans." Before his reign was over, she would taste an affair with the King as well.

November 25 was a day of good-bys. Marie drove first to headquarters to say good-by to Ferdinand and Carol. Ferdinand showed her the letter he'd written to the French General Berthelot: "Tell the government, tell the whole of France, that I do not regret anything and that we shall fight to the last man."

Next she raced to her hospital, where a tidal wave of panic was rising. At Cotroceni she walked through the empty rooms she had occupied for twenty-three years, said a prayer at Mircea's grave and thrust a sealed letter at old Steinbach, the head of the household. Steinbach had come with her from Coburg as a footman. Now he would stay behind to guard her home from the enemy.

The letter read: "I do not know who will inhabit this house, a house that I have loved. The only prayer I ask is that they should not take away the flowers from the new little grave in the church."

It was evening when she returned to Buftea, to find her children, her possessions and her servants already packed into the train for Jassy. Ileana had included Mircea's little wooden horse and Foica, the doll he had loved.

Standing beside the train in a howling night wind, she said good-by to Stirbey, who was leaving for headquarters. In despair they gripped each other's hands, not knowing where or when they would meet again.

13

Romania's Soldier Queen

It was the worst winter in fifty years. The thermometer plunged to record lows, and freezing winds dropped crippling waist-high snows on crucial transport lines. At Jassy more than 300,000 refugees crowded into the normally sleepy little town of fifty thousand. Food was scarce and mostly spoiled. Even the royal family hardly knew from one meal to the next whether they'd eat again. One lady-in-waiting and her family lived for months on beans. Horses died from lack of fodder, and those sent to the countryside to carry hay either died on the way, their bloated up-turned bodies left to freeze solid on the roadside, or ate the provisions they had been sent for.

In unheated hospitals wounded soldiers transported from the occupied sector caught cold and died of pneumonia or developed infection from linen unwashed because there was no fuel to heat water.

Soon a typhoid epidemic raged through the town and far into the countryside. Patients were crammed two and three to a bed. Many people died in the streets. All day long, skeletal horses drew farm carts piled high with bodies through the streets to mass graves on the edge of town.

What remained of the Romanian army wintered in miserable little hillside towns outside Jassy. Driven back by the Germans, they'd been forced to abandon vital hospitals, depots and provisions along the way. By January the 600,000-man army had shrunk to 200,000, and a single railroad line served as the country's only evacuation, ammunition and refugee route.

When hordes of "earth-colored" Russian soldiers finally arrived to help re-form an offensive front, they devoured the land like locusts. Little realizing that money would soon be useless because there was nothing to buy, the Moldavian peasants sold everything they had in return for ready Russian rubles.

Unaccustomed to exerting effort, the Romanians met the demands of mass chaos with disorder, intrigue and interpolitical bickering. "At Jassy," one political correspondent reported, "they're all at drawn daggers. It's a wonder they don't knife each other." They almost did. Public blame for every misfortune suddenly shifted to Bratianu, who walked in daily terror of his life and fell a victim of neurasthenia. At night, his house was lighted by arc lamps to stave off surprise attack. Only one man found the seething situation exhilarating. That was the French Ambassador, Saint-Aulaire, who called it "the best year of my life." He was also so impressed by the Queen's strength under pressure that he flashed home the now famous line: "There's one man in Romania and that is the Queen."

In panic, everyone from the young mayor of Jassy to the humblest peasant turned to Marie for help. Still raw with grief, temporarily cut off from the King and Stirbey at headquarters and crammed with her household into inadequate housing, she nevertheless responded with impassioned pleas to those in command for better organization. Month after month, her diary resounds with a staggering list of uphill battles fought for simple efficiency.

Along with political battles, she also fought disease, death and starvation as head of the Red Cross, leader of the Refugees Workers, President of the War Invalids Society and voluntary inspector of all hospitals and camps. Day and night she worked, setting up hospitals, organizing relief and food crews, visiting the sick and wounded. Her Red Cross uniform, with its dramatic white wimple, became a symbol to the troops. Soldiers died with her photograph clutched in their hands, and the legend sprang up that others had been healed by her touch. When the typhus epidemic came, she visited the tents filled with dead and dying. Every night she stepped fully-dressed into a tub of boiling water, only her riding boots saving her from serious burns. Then she shed her clothes into the scalding liquid to kill the typhus-carrying lice that clung to them like a gray powder.

The doctors implored her to at least wear India-rubber gloves when visiting the worst typhus cases, but she refused. "I am told that I take too few precautions," she wrote, "and touch them all too much. I am aware that I am not really careful, but how show the slightest hesitation or aversion when they are suffering so cruelly? I must just trust God to allow me to pass through all this without catching the infection myself, as I begin to think that I can really be of some good to my country now, when it is important that every ounce of courage should be kept up."

Incredibly, Romania's military situation continued to worsen. On January 7 a successfully begun offensive against the Germans collapsed when the Russians inexplicably called retreat, an act which prefigured an overall Russian collapse. Three days later word reached Marie from her sister Ducky in Russia that Rasputin had been murdered and that their first cousin, Grand Duke Dmitry, was one of the murderers. On January 31 Ducky arrived at Jassy in a special train filled with presents for the royal family and "thousands and thousands" of provisions for her sister's soldiers and hospitals. She brought more chilling news about the Russian political situation, "which is very dangerous because of the prevailing hatred of the Empress, so that even the Emperor is looked on askance and there is actually talk of suppressing them one way or another. The Imperial couple keep sending people into banishment; no one is safe any more, and they make foolish and unjustified nominations."

On March 13 Prince Stirbey appeared with the alarming news that a revolution had broken out in St. Petersburg. "The troops are in full mutiny," Marie wrote in her diary. "It is even said that they are marching toward Tsarskoe and that divisions have been sent from the front to quell the revolt. It remains to be seen if these troops will be faithful or if the revolutionary ideas have spread through the rest of the army, which would of course be intensely serious. What would happen to us if things went wrong with Russia is not even to be contemplated. It would mean utter and complete disaster, it would mean the end of everything!"

Three days later Tsar Nicholas abdicated for himself and his son, designating his brother Michael as his successor. "I can hardly realize the whole thing," wrote Marie. "It seems so dreadful!" Torn with fear for Ducky and concerned about the fate of Nicholas and his family, Ferdinand and Marie sent the Tsar a sympathetic telegram. His answer, written in French, ended on a predictably largehearted note: "May God grant you final victory and the fulfillment of all your hopes."

Marie lay awake night after night wondering what would happen to her Russian family, and crept ghostlike through the days, longing for news. But what news she got was conflicting and came in scraps. Finally, to escape the suffocating sense of dread, she threw off her lethargy and turned with renewed energy to her work for the sick and wounded. From the depths of their suffering her people turned to her as their last hope. Inspired by their faith in her and tempered by prolonged grief and worry, she met their demands with a strength she would once have thought impossible. Forgetting her body and its limitations, she drove through the piercing cold in an open Daimler, stayed on her feet for twelve hours at a stretch and stared without flinching on grisly scenes of filth, desolation and death.

But one afternoon she came on a scene that shocked even her. At the train station a triage or clearinghouse had been set up to handle sick and wounded soldiers until they could be fit into Jassy hospitals. At her first sight of the triage Marie stopped, appalled. Lying shoulder to shoulder in dark, bare wooden barracks, hundreds of sick and dying men stretched in endless rows on the gritty floor. Swarms of typhus-carrying lice covered them like gray sand from head to toe. The stench was revolting. Groans and curses filled the air. Planting a smile on her lips and bracing herself, Marie began moving among them, stepping over corpses and men enduring the typhus death agony. As she walked, supplicating hands plucked at her skirt. Feverish voices croaked "Mamma Regina! Mamma Regina!" like a litany. One man who called her Mother was over seventy.

On the last day of March she finally had a letter from Ducky. They had lived through dangerous days, she wrote, with the St. Petersburg mob clamoring beneath their windows and shooting in the streets. Liberal-minded, Ducky and Cyril had long stood for a freer government. But now, "the people having taken the upper hand, and the new masters having to make concessions to the mob, we will probably be sacrificed for the sake of keeping momentary peace in the interior."

Spring with its snowdrops and mauve crocuses slipped in to revive a wretched Jassy, but that year it also brought unseasonable dryness and heat to choke the already decimated town. With the help of Jean Cantacuzene and her old friend from the 1913 cholera epidemic, Sister Pucci, Marie took the triage in hand and finally cleaned it up. But the typhus plague continued to spread. Together with Colonel Ballif, she organized a plan for sending Carol to the outlying districts with food and gifts. "I wish my son to be better known and better loved." And with the snow melting, she could finally get food, clothing and medicine to the troops holed up in the countryside. In every village she visited, soldiers greeted her with mad cries of *"Sa traiti Majestate!"* ("long live Your Majesty!") and flung carpets of wildflowers in her path.

Evenings she wrote a column for the little inspirational newspaper that kept morale high all over Romania. The column described scenes from occupied Romania. In a torrent of recollection they poured from her: Calugareni, the little village near the River Arges where Michael the Brave had won a major battle over the Turks; the convent Polovraci in the Oltenian hills, as she'd first glimpsed it through fairylike birch woods and masses of snowy, cheery blossoms; her friend Jean Duca's ancient country house, a tall building with low doors and an open gallery on top, built to withstand the Turks. When she came to Horez, her favorite Oltenian convent, her hand trembled. Horez! The serene, whitewashed building with its colonnades facing the inner courtyard, the frescoed church, the black-robed nuns greeting her with touching delight, the crumbling graveyard where weirdly-shaped crosses mingled with wild roses, tall waving grass and gnarled apple trees. One night, after a refreshing ride with her son Nicky in Bambino, his little sports car, she read him her chapter on Cotroceni. In it she described her garden, the old church and Mircea's death. "Suddenly he threw his arms around my neck, bursting into tears. I had no idea that these memories would stir him so much. We sat a long time hand in hand talking about Mircea and all that we have lost."

On April 5 she wrote an appeal to the American people. Published in several American magazines, it read: "In these days when the whole world is aflame, when those who struggle for an ideal see such terrible and inexplicable things, I, the Queen of a stricken country, raise my voice, and I make an appeal to those who are always ready to aid where disasters and sorrows have penetrated. Here in Romania there are disasters and suffering without end. Death in all forms has stricken the country: the sword, flame, invasion, famine and sickness. Our land has been taken away from us, our hope destroyed, our cities and villages devastated." Her plea was answered by the American Red Cross and by the Hoover organization after the war.

That spring the Russian revolution spread to the nearby Ukraine and bordering Bessarabia, and the peasants began appropriating land. Communist propaganda seeped into Moldavia. Bratianu had considered agrarian and electoral reform since 1914. Now there was no time to lose. Stirbey convinced the King that to avert a peasant revolt he must leave immediately for the front and address the troops.

On April 5 Ferdinand spoke to his gallant, dismembered little army: "Sons of peasants who, with your own hands, have defended the soil on which you were born, on which your lives have been passed, I, your King, tell you that besides the great recompense of victory which will assure for every one of you the nation's gratitude, you have earned the right of being masters, in a larger measure, of that soil upon which you fought. Land will be given you. I, your King, am the first to set the example, and you will also take a larger part in public affairs." Even before he'd finished, while his words still hung in the soft Moldavian air, Ferdinand had saved Romania from revolution and earned himself the lifelong title King of the Peasants.

Easter brought the first fruit blossoms, so that even the most wretched Jassy side streets took on a festive air. Marie spent the day taking food to outlying typhus-stricken villages. In one she encountered a scene that would live in her memory forever.

"On a low mound stood a wee church, and the bell was tinkling like a cracked voice. On the bank beneath the church all those who were not actually dying had been brought and laid out in the sunshine, a parade of skeletons. I passed in and out among them. It was very hot and there were hundreds of them and the sun was in my eyes. They all wanted me at once and kept crying for me from all corners at the same time, stretching out bony hands as though to grasp me and hold me fast. The sun was setting and they lay about like shadows, but the last rays of light seemed all to have converged upon my white dress, so as to light it up and make it shine like flame. I was loath to leave them, tears welled up into my eyes and I felt as I have often felt that something very strong, very real, almost holy, passed from my heart to theirs and from their hearts to mine."

The little Princess from Kent had come a long way.

The unnaturally dry spring melted into an unusually wet summer, and Marie, ever hungry for news from Russia, watched the Russian troops in Romania grow dissident and surly.

In St. Petersburg Ducky was faring less well with Kerensky's provisional government. Pregnant, imprisoned in her own home, her money and servants confiscated, she gave way to black despair. "What is left?" she wrote Marie in mid-May. "Neither pride, nor hope, nor money, nor future, and the dear past blotted out by the frightful present; nothing is left, nothing!" Cyril had been the first Romanov to break allegiance to the Tsar. Now even that claim paled in the face of violent popular demonstrations against the entire imperial family.

Though tortured with fear for her sister, Marie rose to new heights of energy and infectious optimism that summer. Her endurance was as superhuman as her courage. Like a soldier, she worked from eight or nine in the morning till seven-thirty, eight or even twelve at night. She constantly pushed her body to the limits of endurance and beyond. In one day alone, she visited fourteen different regiments in eight different villages, and in a single afternoon distributed one thousand cigarettes. She took any sign of fatigue as a personal affront. But on August 13, after a twelve-hour day in the hospitals, she had to confess: "It was pleasant to get out of my boots, to wash my face and hands, because I was what other people would call dead tired."

Two weeks later, for the first time since Romania's entry into the war a year before, she was too tired to sleep. "But next day I began early. I did not even go to breakfast, as I had to write my name on a few hundred post cards . . . At half past nine we began again visiting hospitals."

Meanwhile the head of the French mission, the fat and forthright General Berthelot, had pulled the Romanian army back into a standing position. Reorganized by Berthelot, re-equipped with French guns and gallantly led by Romanian Generals Averescu and Prezan, the Romanians successfully held their own against the combined German and Austro-Hungarian forces in the battle of Marasesti. It was the Romanian army's finest hour. While their Russian comrades turned revolutionary daily abandoned their posts by the thousands, the Romanian peasant soldiers fought from August 12 to 19—and so valiantly that even German Marshal Mackensen admitted himself impressed.

Marie saw herself as the harassed little army's shining symbol. She'd sustained them for months with her energy, encouraging them with her optimism. Looking into her eyes, the wounded had sworn to defend for her the last scrap of Romanian territory. Dying soldiers had whispered they were fighting for her. Thus this mighty battle was "for me, the mother of my people."

Early in September she moved for a while to a little balconied house her friend and co-worker Jean Chrissoveloni had built for her on a hilltop overlooking the military hospital at Cotofanesti. She had christened it "the little house where the four winds meet," because the wind whistling around its balconies sometimes woke her. But now she was awakened more often by guns firing on German bombers wheeling overhead.

Ostensibly, she'd come to Cotofanesti for a rest. But every morning, with Dana, her spoiled black cocker, at her heels, she descended to the hospital and there wandered about distributing cigarettes, feeding jam to stretcher cases or holding the hands of the dying. Constant exposure to death and suffering in every form had not hardened her heart or lessened her impotent rage at the folly of war.

With the Russian army in full flight, the Romanians were left in a harrowing position. Before long they had to give the ground they'd held at Marasesti. But their rugged resistance had kept Mackensen out of Moldavia and saved the eastern front.

Marie remained at Cotofanesti for three weeks. In the early morning hours she could hear the sound of cannons as the Germans battered nearby Targul Ocna. Day after day she worked in the hospital with her wounded. On September 9 she got word that her daughter Elizabeth, "Lisabetta," had jaundice, which was raging in an epidemic at Jassy. Mignon had come down with it while nursing at Ghidigeni. Carol, who was passing through on his way to head-quarters, was not feeling well either. And Nicky was looking "canary yellow and much quieter than he usually is." Of her children, only Ileana, who rode beside her on Tango for brief outings in the woods, seemed herself.

On September 12 she had a "great grief." She arrived at the hospital minutes too late to decorate a man she'd promised a medal. Many others in his ward had been decorated, and being left out had nearly broken his heart. He'd lost both legs and imagined that if he returned to his village with a decoration he would be considered a hero instead of a hopeless cripple. Now he was dead. "I pinned the much-coveted medal over his heart which beat no more, and I made the sign of the cross on his forehead as his mother might have done."

When she wasn't nursing and visiting the wounded, she traveled to the front. Here she visited the foxholes, smoking cigarettes with the soldiers in the mud and sharing mess with them in their tents. She prayed with them and bestowed their medals upon them and rode with their generals like a latter-day Joan of Arc.

Autumn heralded a long period of grueling uncertainty. On November 8 Stirbey sent a coded message to her at Cotofanesti, where she was again staying, telling her that Kerensky's government had fallen and the Leninists were in power. By the tenth she was back in Jassy, feverishly conferring with Ferdinand, Carol and Stirbey. Word had it that the Russians planned to make a separate peace with the Germans and had decided to arrest the entire Romanian government and the royal family. Bursting with anxiety, the Queen dashed out for a drive with Lisabetta and listened to Ileana's reading lesson.

A week later Nicky was desperately ill with what looked like typhoid, and Marie had decided the best alternative to a dishonorable peace would be for the family to cut with a small army through southern Russia to safety. On the eighteenth, Dr. Romalo came to tell her— "because you are a person who can stand being told anything"—that Nicky's typhoid tests were negative. He might have something much worse, galloping consumption.

On November 22, a "real royal day," Carol drove her and Colonel Ballif through blasting cold and wind in the open Daimler to visit the Mircea canteens she'd organized to feed the poorest, most isolated villages. They left at 11:30 A.M. and got back to Jassy after midnight.

On the twenty-ninth, a crisp springlike day with a brilliant sun, Prince Stirbey gave her a "beautiful" closed Cadillac on behalf of the military. When she demurred, he said, "Your Majesty goes about as much as any general. So why should you not occasionally have a closed auto, especially in winter?"

That afternoon, luxuriating in its warmth, she and Ballif drove the Cadillac to Roman to visit the American Red Cross unit and eat Thanksgiving dinner. "Of course it ended with a pumpkin pie, which it seems is the correct thing," she wrote.

By early December the disintegration of the Russian army was complete, and Jassy was in a state of panic. Word came that the Bolshevik rabble had taken *Stavka,* the Russian high command, and literally torn the Provisional General Dubonik to shreds. On the Moldavian front the Russian soldiers surrendered trenches to the Germans without warning the Romanians, who were left surrounded and completely helpless. Suddenly Bolshevik propaganda spread like wildfire through the Romanian ranks, and a Russian plot to murder Ferdinand and Marie was uncovered just in time. Yet the peasant soldiers stood firmly by their old loyalties, and Marie's pen burned the pages of her diary: "Above all we must show those Russian bullies that the much despised little Romanians are not afraid of their threats."

The situation grew steadily worse. Some politicians urged the King and Queen to flee; others argued they should beg the Germans for mercy before it was too late. King George wired Marie that she and the children were welcome in England "at any time." While those around her lost faith, Marie stood for "resistance at any cost." She remained unresigned to surrender, even though the army lay shattered at last, the "iron noose" enclosing them grew tighter and tighter, and the Russians began treating with the Germans.

Stirbey, who visited her daily, let her give vent to her feelings.

"Oh, God," she cried, "if only I were a man with a man's rights and the spirit I have in my woman's body! I would fire them to desperate, glorious resistance."

For hours he would sit quietly beside her, holding her hand, soothing her, helping her regain perspective.

Romania had no choice but surrender. On December 6, 1917, while Marie fought back tears and felt as though she were "slowly dying" with shame, the Russian and Romanian officers began armistice parleying with the enemy. Two days later she still had not accepted the inevitable. When the well-meaning English General Ballard came to convince her that further Romanian resistance was impossible, she exploded: "How dare you, an Englishman, come to me, an Englishwoman and a Queen, and tell her she must give up? If we're to die, let our Allies know we do not die like blind fools, but as conscious heroes. We know we've been sold and betrayed. If we're to face death, let us face it bravely."

Without saying a word, the General turned and fled. "For an Englishman he certainly is not inspiring," she sniffed in her diary.

That afternoon her old friend and a former officer of her regiment, Goe Odobescu, came to thank her for all she'd done for the country.

"Thank you for the way you have loved it, helped it, understood it and suffered with it," he said, near tears. "You too have been a soldier, we honor you as one of the bravest within our ranks." As he spoke, the bare walls of her little sitting room seemed to fall away, and she remembered long-ago springs when she'd ridden with her officers across the plain outside Bucharest and picnicked with them beneath flowering acacias.

When he left, she wept for the first time in months, "wept as small children weep, with great sobs, my head on the table."

14

A Family Tragedy

Desperate weeks followed. All through January the Central Powers negotiated peace with Russia at Brest Litovsk. In Romania militant Russian Bolsheviks marched on Jassy but were repelled. One day, while the royal family watched frozen, enlisted men rifle-butted their officers down the steps of the next-door Russian headquarters and lined them up against the brick wall separating the two gardens. The King's guard drew their swords and jumped over the wall in time to save the officers. But not all violence ended so happily. Famine and disease were rampant, and the Romanians uncovered more plots to kill their royal family.

Then came February 7. On that day, finished with the Russian armistice, the Central Powers addressed an ultimatum to the Romanian government: make peace or face annihilation. Bratianu resigned. At his suggestion the King named the army's idol, General Alexander Averescu, Prime Minister. On February 26 the King left for Bacau to meet with the Austrian Minister Czernin. Ferdinand, Marie and Stirbey sat up till after twelve the night before he left, working out "point for point" all the King would say to Czernin. "We pored over those points with the utmost care and anxiety."

On the fourteenth, Marie was torn from her immediate problems by long overdue news of Ducky. She was finally out of Russia. On foot, Cyril had carried his pregnant wife over the Russian border into Finland.

The next day, his face "ravaged by anxiety," Ferdinand returned from Bacau with Czernin's ultimatum in hand. Later it would form the basis for Romania's armistice. The terms, though preserving the dynasty, called for complete division of the country among Austria, Bulgaria, Germany and Turkey and total economic slavery for years to come. So much for their fine points. Ferdinand would have to agree to his country's dismemberment, Czernin had sneered, or the Central Powers could not guarantee the continuation of the dynasty or the royal family's safety.

On March 3, with mere hours separating her from the reality of Romania's surrender, Marie was still unresigned. When the King looked near capitulation, she fought him bitterly, stormed at him to abdicate rather than accept "a peace which is not a peace." When a telegram from the Germans demanded even more infamous conditions, Ferdinand wavered, declaring he couldn't reach a decision without a Crown Council meeting. He called one for the next morning.

Frantic, blindly ignoring undeniable facts, the Queen stayed awake all night forming a plan. Carol must carry her protest to the Crown Council. Before breakfast she called him to her, swore him to secrecy and gave him his orders. "Stand up in the middle of the sitting and protest in my name, and in the name of all the women of Romania, against the horror of peace in such a form." Carol did as he was told and then ran back to his mother, falling on her neck and thanking her for letting him express his own feelings in her words.

Despite Carol's entreaties, the government finally gave in to every German condition, and on the evening of March 8, the Queen assembled around her all those Allied friends who had upheld her during the war months. Foremost among them were courtly Colonel Anderson, the Virginia-bred head of the American Red Cross, chubby French General Berthelot and her newest champion, the "curiously fascinating" Canadian soldier of fortune, Joe Boyle.

"I threw myself into a corner of Lisabetta's large sofa," Marie recounted, "and asked Enescu to play us Lequeux's symphony. And there, surrounded by the friends who tomorrow are to leave us to our humiliation and despair, I listened with all my soul to that superhumanly exquisite music, and in its very notes I seemed to hear the agony of our dying country."

The Allies left Jassy after midnight the following day. She sat up waiting to see them off, pouring out her grief to Joe Boyle, who promised not to leave or "forsake me."

The next day, she wrote, was "a day of tears . . . I lay on my bed and did not accept my fate."

By March 15 it looked as though the Germans were confiscating both the telegraph and the mail services. While there was still time, she sent "a last cry of distress' to King George. "Rather would I have died with our army to the last man, than confess myself beaten, for have I not English blood in my veins?"

The next day Marie got up "bravely" to face the new state of affairs. But by evening she was "losing" herself. "I am sinking into darkness, like one who has lost too much blood. No one helps me, no one can help me. I am sinking down, and all my life and energy, my pride and courage are useless before this thing which is being done to my country . . . I am on the verge of madness. Sometimes I think that to slide over into complete madness would be infinite and wonderful relief."

On the eighteenth, Stirbey came to tea. "We sat contemplating a future we do not understand," she wrote. "Nor do we know how long we shall still be together."

For a while she considered leaving the country, then decided she shouldn't do anything rash that would cut her off from the people. But in those first furious, desperate hours of surrender, it would have been a relief to do something violent.

On Tuesday, March 19, 1918, the King received the new Prime Minister, Marghiloman, called to replace Averescu, who refused to sign the armistice. Despite her unsettling anxiety at this new development, the Queen's spirits had returned. That evening she wrote in her diary, "Now that I am calmer and that I feel less as though my mind were giving way, I know that I shall be ready to bear anything as long as I can keep the fire of our cause alive in the hearts of my people."

The month of April was a dark one. She mistrusted the new government, still could not accustom herself to the armistice. Feeling hatred for the first time in her life, she wrote: "I wish I could invent new words never yet used to express my loathing for those who are imposing upon us an abominable, mutilating, soul-stifling peace."

Word of her defiance reached beyond the Western Front. The London *Times* called her "the living centre of a Romania in exile under the shadow of defeat." In America, "Romanian Queen Defies Kaiser!" shouted the *Literary Digest* for June 8. "Declaring she would rather abdicate than rule over a country under German domination, Marie, Queen of Romania, beloved of her people, refused to recognize the peace treaty between the little country and Germany." She had become one of the war's major characters.

One day, she and the King attended a Requiem service for the Romanian dead. Standing by her throne at the front of the cathedral, Marie wept "as only a brokenhearted mother can weep." Then she returned to her house and fresh emotion. In her room stood a tub of magnificent flowers—"glorious" roses, peonies, irises and bluebells, the most beautiful flowers she'd seen since coming to Jassy. She stood dumbfounded, then glimpsed a card. It read, *"Gruss aus Cotroceni"* ("Greetings from Cotroceni"). Old Steinbach had arrived, dispatched by the conquering Germans. The flowers were from her own garden. "This quite broke me down and, turning to Helene Perticari, who was beside me, I fell into her arms and we both wept as though we should never cease."

By Easter Marie's stanch resistance was proving profoundly embarrassing to Marghiloman's government, which was trying to coexist with the Germans. Also she refused to go to church with the cabinet on Easter Sunday: "No prayers would have been possible for me in their presence." So she shook the city dust from her feet and fled with her daughters to her little house of the four winds. In the months ahead two things kept her from total despair: communion with the Romanian countryside and Joe Boyle.

Twenty years later Marie described their first meeting: "When Joe Boyle first entered my room as a stranger, as many entered in those days, it was as though a rock had miraculously appeared before me, a rock upon which I could lean." Later she added: "My heart becomes soft when I think of him, soft with a great wistfulness and with an aching longing."

Unlike the other men in her life, "Klondike" Boyle was not, according to any European court's definition, a gentleman. In 1918 he was nearly seventy, an outwardly uncouth, roughhewn giant of a man with rugged features, fierce blue eyes and a reassuring smile. Only his hands were "unexpectedly refined." A veteran of the Klondike gold rush, by the time he arrived in Romania with the Canadian Red Cross late in 1917, he'd made and lost several fortunes and packed more adventures into one life than a normal man could expect in ten. In Romania he soon added a whole series of daring feats to an already impressive record, not the least of which was capturing a queen's heart.

That first December, he returned from a romantic dash into Bolshevik Russia with part of the Romanian archives and crown jewels that had been sent to St. Petersburg for safekeeping in 1916. During the early 1918 upheavals he was credited with suppressing Red agitation and staving off a Romanian revolution. By the evening of Marie's farewell party for the Allied Mission leaders, his various successes had earned him Romania's two highest honors—the Grand Cross of the Order of Romania and the Grand Cross of the Star of Romania.

On March 25 the Queen decorated him with the insignia of her own order, the Cross of the Regina Maria, for singlehandedly saving a group of Romanian elective deputies imprisoned by the Bolsheviks in Odessa. In true Jack London fashion, Boyle had leapt, unarmed, aboard a Russian ship shuttling the deputies from Odessa to an unknown port. After two weeks spent putting from one Black Sea harbor to another, he'd finally convinced the Russian crew to put its frightened cargo off in Romania.

This latest enterprise made him the hero of the hour. Romanian government, army and court dignitaries met him and his precious cargo at Galatz with a special train. When they reached Jassy, cheering throngs jammed the streets. "It was a tremendous feat, an astonishing act of bravery and ruthless will power," enthused the Queen. "The series of miracles by which they were saved has passed into legend," gushed another admirer. The Romanian people, defeated and hungry for inspiration, called him "The Savior of Romania."

The court was less impressed. In that sophisticated, essentially Latin group, Boyle's rough-and-tumble manner made numerous enemies. Soon rumors spread about the Queen's latest "attachment." Behind their hands certain court ladies referred sarcastically to "colonel Lawrence of Romania." The gossip went international in late July when Boyle, having suffered a stroke while flying over Moldavia, moved into the Crown Estate house near Bicaz, where Marie and her daughters were spending the summer.

Ten-year-old Ileana was Boyle's greatest comfort during a long and inactive convalescence. In turn, "Uncle Joe" entertained the small princess with *Songs of a Sourdough* and *Ballads of a Cheechako*, both learned in his gold mining days. When he was able to leave the house, the unlikely twosome visited destitute villages, where Boyle's generosity to starving peasants laid the foundation for Ileana's later remarkable altruism.

Though greatly weakened, Boyle supported Marie more than ever that summer. Originally attracted by each other's strength they found that—in these days when each had reached a personal nadir—their relationship was deepening into a profoundly romantic love.

On July 22 the Tsar and his family were murdered at Ekaterinburg, and word of more Romanov murders leaked out of Russia. But Marie's greatest worry was Carol.

During the months of active battle, he'd served at the front with his Guards Regiment. He'd acquitted himself honorably if not notably and had won the army's good will. Now he had embarked on an affair with a young society girl, Jeanne Marie Valentine (or "Zizi") Lambrino. At first Marie was not alarmed. After all, Carol was twenty-five. He'd had a casual series of sexual flings since he was fifteen. She'd learned long ago to ignore his dalliances as she ignored Ferdinand's. Though Zizi was more attractive than most—with her dark, supple beauty, social accomplishments and flattering interest in Ileana—Carol knew the law: no member of the royal family might marry a Romanian. Certainly his father had come to grief enough for two over that rule.

When the "fling" stretched into weeks and word reached her from Jassy that Carol was declaring himself in love with Zizi, Marie decided to act. She had him transferred to the command of a regiment of chasseurs at Targul Neamtu, a little town near Bicaz. Relieved, she noticed his "new dignity" seemed to please him. But when he came to visit, she worried about his health. He was too thin, he coughed. Something was obviously preying on his mind.

Meanwhile excitement in Jassy mounted daily as Allied victories on the Western Front raised hopes. The Germans forced the King to arrest and begin trying Bratianu and his entire government for voting against siding with Germany. But Ferdinand, in secret contact with the former Prime Minister, had agreed to try him only after Bratianu's remark that the publicity would probably do him good when the Germans were defeated. Ferdinand was also secretly making remobilization plans with General Prezan. On August 14 Stirbey sent Marie the clipping of a Budapest newspaper article vilifying her for having fired the Transylvanian peasants with hope just before the Central Powers snapped them back. The accusation was true. She stuck the clipping into her diary, "because it will be most exceedingly flattering for me if our cause wins through."

On August 19 she and Mignon left for two days' tour of former battlefields with Carol and his officers. That night after a day spent watching her son in action, she wrote: "Carol is excessively precise and systematic, there is never any fluster or confusion. He organizes things according to his desires and convictions, very foreign to either of his parents, which occasionally, as his mother, makes me smile . . . Carol never doubts that he is right and entirely justified in all he is doing." Then the blow came. On September 15 the Crown Prince wrote his parents a letter stating that he'd decided to marry Zizi Lambrino and would renounce his rights to the throne. In all honesty Marie could write, "we were entirely unprepared." He wrote a similar letter to the head of the Romanian Socialist party.

Hours later the Queen heard to her agonizing disbelief that Carol had smuggled Zizi across the border into Odessa, now held by the Germans, and had married her in a ceremony arranged by Major Van Kessler, the German Chief of Staff. Celebrated by an Orthodox priest at the Church of the Intercession, the marriage was not morganatic but was fully legal in the eyes of the Church. However, in a single stroke he had defied the Constitution and deserted his regiment. By law the one act could cost him the throne; the other his life.

The King sent Joe Boyle to fetch his son. And since there was nothing to do but imprison him, Carol was confined to the Bistritza monastery near Bicaz. The first meeting between parents and son was terrible. Ferdinand branded him a traitor for marrying "under the bayonets of our enemies." Marie wept. He'd forsaken her, she said, "after having been my best friend, my fellow worker, my central hope." Of course continuing the marriage was out of the question. Before they left, Carol made one request. He wanted to see Ileana.

"At first my parents said they wouldn't take me," remembered Princess Ileana. "Then they changed their minds. I remember it was a coldish day when we went. Bistritza was a little monastery high up in the mountains, and when we arrived the bells were ringing. Papa and Mama were received officially by the abbot. Then we went inside for a *Te Deum*. Afterwards, Carol sort of slunk into the church, dressed in a baggy Russian blouse. We had lunch with him and he was very affectionate with me. He even gave me a book which he'd bought for me in Odessa. Then I was told to go for a walk and amuse myself outside while they had a conversation. I remember hearing awful shouts, and Carol screaming at my parents: 'She's my wife! I won't allow you to insult her.' "

All autumn, while Bessarabia broke away from Russia, Bulgaria fell and the Dual Monarchy crumpled, Marie's "wild ecstasy" at the thought of the inevitable victory was darkened by Carol's tragedy.

Though no one sincerely believed the Crown Prince should be executed for desertion, some ministers thought he should be disinherited. "At that hour," she wrote, "I knew the lioness feeling . . . of a mother creature defending its young. But it was a heart-rending struggle because the one I was fighting for had forsaken me."

Fighting to save Carol against himself—for he still insisted on renouncing his rights—she convinced the Crown Council that annulment was the only answer. "Which of you gentlemen," she asked, "is without fault in your relations to some woman?" Only Carol remained unconvinced. Finally Bratianu, in a long unrecorded conversation with the rebel at Bistritza, dissolved even this resistance.

October 29, her forty-third birthday, rolled around, providing relief from tension. "I'm getting old," she mused, "which is a pity, for I have still such a lot to do; a pity also because each year must inevitably take from me something of my good looks."

On November 3 Austria made her peace, and Hungary declared herself a republic. Events came in a rush. On November 6, able to again confer with both the French and the English, Ferdinand dismissed Marghiloman. Before leaving, Marghiloman remarked that a Bratianu government would be a "moral impossibility." But then Bratianu had stolen Marghiloman's wife.

Not Bratianu but the Queen's old friend, now General, Coanda, formed the new government. "It's almost too good to be true to have friends in power again," sang Marie. In his first act as Prime Minister, Coanda declared universal suffrage for all male voters over twenty-one.

On November 9 Romania again declared war on Germany. It was a token gesture, as there was no Germany to fight. That same evening the Kaiser with a retinue of thirty fled in his elaborate private train from a Germany in revolt to Holland. At eleven A.M. on the eleventh day of the eleventh month, 1918, the Great War ended.

Within the week, Juliu Maniu led the Transylvanian Romanian National Party in demanding "complete separation" from Hungary. Beaten, Hungary had no choice but to grant their request. After two thousand years the Carpathians again united rather than divided the Romanians.

On November 30 Bucharest welcomed their royal family and government home after two years' separation. Of all the autumn's mad victory celebrations, few were as justifiably intense as Romania's. Dressed in her military uniform, wearing a gray astrakhan bonnet strapped under her chin and perched on her huge stallion, Jumbo, Queen Marie rode with the King and French General Berthelot through a city half-crazed with joy. But her own greatest emotion came later, when she left the sobbing, shouting mobs behind and drove home to Cotroceni and Mircea's grave.

"It was still in the dear, dim church," she wrote. "I knelt down and burried my face in my hands."

15

For a Greater Romania

From Mircea's grave, still covered with the chrysanthemums she'd laid there two years before, Marie explored Cotroceni for damage. Amazingly enough, though the Germans had drunk all the wine in the cellars and dug up and eaten the bulbs in the garden, the palace had emerged from the occupation relatively unscathed.

"Yes, we are actually back in our dear old quarters, and not particularly upset either," she reported to Leila Milne, Lisabetta's former governess, who'd returned to England. On a deeper note, she breathed, "Dare I utter the great word—we have returned triumphant.

The rest of the country had fared less well. Not content with starving the peasants and completely despoiling their homes, the Germans had tried to destroy them psychologically by taking all their fine embroideries and preventing them from growing the flax from which they spun linen for their daily change of white clothes.

The Germans had also blown up what remained of the Ploesti oil wells and dug up the underground lines to the Black Sea. In retreat they and the Hungarians had stripped the railways, leaving only sixty-two live locomotives and a few thousand usable cars to serve nearly twenty million people.

"They even took away our beloved soil," cried a wild-eyed Elise Bratianu, returning from a trip to her country estate, Florica, "The very soil from our land!"

152

The servants brought Marie equally horrible tales of Russian atrocities. Of drunken Bolshevik soldiers ransacking Moldavian wine cellars, piercing huge wine barrels and rolling them downhill to lap up the wine as it trickled over the ground. Of Red troops chopping down whole forests for firewood. Of merciless raping, looting and killing.

But if "there was a taste of ashes about the hour of triumph," by February 1919, Marie was facing the problems at hand and had formed a daily routine that would last with little variation for as long as she remained Queen. Quiet and serious and based on hard work, it was a new concept of royal life. But it suited the perilous times all the Balkan counties were enduring.

No postwar queen loved her work more than Marie. Her sphere had been limited to Romania, but when a worried Ferdinand called her into his office one morning in February, the curtain rose on her career as an international celebrity.

At Versailles the Big Four had gathered around the green table to carve up the bleeding carcass of old Europe. Wilson, Lloyd George and Orlando arrived with chauvinistic ideas masked with impressive tributes to humanism and reason. Only France's wily old Georges Clemenceau, "the Tiger," openly admitted his goal of Germany's total and unequivocal destruction.

Bratianu, representing Romania, found the bickering Allied leaders agreed on but one point—keeping the ally who had signed a separate peace with the Germans from gaining equal representation at Versailles. Finally, after much wrangling and mutual abuse, perseverance and sharp Latin wit won out, and Bratianu won his seat. His problems, however, were just beginning. To a man, the Big Four rejected Romanian territorial demands.

"Does your claim go as far as Belgrade?" asked Wilson.

"It does," said Bratianu, basing his argument on the secret treaty of 1916, which the Allies had used to lure Romania into war. Far more important was the Allies' refusal to recognize territories that had already declared themselves Romanian.

"They've reached an impasse," Ferdinand told Marie. "So we wonder if you would have the courage to undertake an official mission to Paris and London? We think you're the only person for the job. Bratianu feels that your energy and feminine intuition might do more than all the politicians put together."

Paris! She felt like laughing and crying. To experience after five hellish years that city's bright lights and music and golden charm, to actually wear new clothes and go to the opera! And London—how she'd longed to breathe English air and see English faces. But to go as her country's chosen defender—that was too good to be true. Swaying in the grip of excitement, she closed her eyes to help regain her balance and had a fleeting vision of herself standing "very upright in glaring sunshine."

Taking her silence to mean doubt, the King rushed on. "You'd go unofficially, of course. I can't give you any specific directions. I leave it to your own intuition, which is at times keener than mine. Besides," he added shyly, "you have an easier flow of words." Only impending disaster could have forced that admission.

He ended by touching on her ultimate goal: to unofficially contact the Big Four and try and persuade them that Romania's new boundaries were just.

"When you go to England," he added, "plead our cause with George. He'll understand you better and have more sympathy."

She made one condition of her own—that he let her take their daughters with her.

As their train shook and rattled across Europe, Marie took a much-needed rest while Ileana nestled up against her, glowing with excitement. The trip was slow, due to coal shortages and the March thaw, and they never knew which country they were in, because the new boundaries hadn't been fixed. At Fiume a guard of honor gave them a military salute. Leaning far out her window to acknowledge the cheers, Marie inhaled the bright sea air, her lungs expanding "rapturously." A blue-washed sky outlined fruit trees decked with white and pale-pink blossoms.

Outside Paris, Colette came on board to interview the Queen, and presented her with a bunch of orchids. "Their exotic beauty burst on me like a revelation," wrote Marie, and she was equally enchanted with their giver.

Paris buried her under an effusive welcome. A dense and confusing station crowd included endless French dignitaries, generals, officers and personal friends. All plied her with flowers while bystanders cheered and photographers descended like a "swarm of mosquitoes."

Installed in the Romanian-flag-decked Ritz, she soon discovered the initial greeting was only the beginning of a social marathon that was to last without interruption for as long as she stayed in Paris. Into her suite poured old friends—artists, authors, dukes, politicians, deposed royalty—and when they could get in, journalists. "They buzz like swarms of bees, waylay me, dogging my every step. It's a modern conception of things I'm unaccustomed to." But one she would adapt to with remarkable alacrity.

To add to the confusion, vases and baskets of flowers arrived constantly along with perfumes and other gifts. Perplexed but delighted by the unexpected adulation, Marie relaxed and enjoyed herself. "I smilingly pass through the rush," she confided in her diary, "doing my best to remain calm and not lose my head."

Paris, after the drab war years, responded to Marie as to a nugget of gold in a slag pile. Her valiant war record had preceded her, but the French were unprepared for her vivid good looks and exuberant charm. Faced with these facts, they took her to their hearts and kept her there for the rest of her life. They gave her receptions and featured her smile on the cover of every magazine and newspaper in town. When she arrived at the opera, they rose as one and cheered when the orchestra played the *"Traiasca Regele."* When she went shopping, they mobbed her so that she had to retreat to her hotel, having only had time to buy books for Ferdinand and Carol and stare "like a country bumpkin" at the lavish window displays. Asked by a friendly throng why she'd come to Paris, she answered, "To give Romania a face. She needs a face, so I've come to give her mine."

The day after she arrived, Bratianu forced her into her first news conference. The experience haunted her dreams for years. "Just imagine," she wrote a friend, "a door opening upon forty real live newspapermen and I thrust into their midst as into a cage, all forty hanging over me, asking me every sort of question. I did my top best, looked them straight in the eye and spoke up bravely for my country. I hope I really kept my wits about me and that my French was not too English."

The press loved her too. Charles Merz, writing in *The New Republic,* reported that "Romania's claims, languishing all winter, picked up suddenly in the news." Another U. S. reporter dubbed her "the Business Queen of the Balkans" and said "her beauty enhances the charm of her forceful personality."

That same day the dressmakers mobbed her, displaying "shocking" dresses with "horrid" short, skimpy skirts and no sleeves or backs. "Preposterous frocks for a queen," she wrote. But her clothes were five years behind the times. And though the Romanians had arrived in Paris a little hungry, with Ileana dressed in clothes made from her mother's old coats, and the Queen wearing paste jewelry because the Russians

had kept most of her jewels, the least she could do was represent her
country dressed in at least a compromise of the current style. Besides,
tomorrow she had an appointment with Clemenceau.

Snowy mustaches bristling, he came running down the front steps of
the Quai d'Orsay and hurried her back upstairs for a tête-à-tête in his
private study.

She'd expected to like the fierce old Premier, and she did. But she
also found that he clung tenaciously to his anti-Romanian line.

"You treated with the Germans in 1918, before the armistice!"

"Yes, but we were encircled by the enemy and our Allies as well, who
went Bolshevist. We were tracked like game."

"Don't tell me those stories. You were for the resistance—you yourself."

She admitted that was true, adding, "But being a woman I had a
passionate point of view. Besides, I was too near events to see the
situation objectively. And I believed in the Allied victory, so I was
ready to hang on by the skin of my teeth. Others can judge if this was
wise. I'm not here to talk about myself but to modify your attitude
towards Romania. And this I mean to do as I've fought my battles
during our tragic war years."

She couldn't tell if she'd convinced him or not, but she was obviously
not boring him. When she half rose to leave, he impatiently waved her
back.

"I have plenty of time for you. You don't whine as some do. You
speak up. I like that."

They touched on the delicate subject of frontiers. Clemenceau
gripped his chair, knitted his bushy brows, bit his lip. "You think
Romania's requests are just. Others have equal claims—the Serbians,
for instance, who fought so valiantly at Monastio.

"But," said Marie, "we want to have the Danube as our natural
boundary."

Clemenceau exploded. "What? But that's the lion's share!"

"That's why I've come to see his first cousin, the Tiger," she parried,
and the interview dissolved on a burst of laughter.

She left him still laughing, with the "Marseillaise" playing in the
background and the air of Paris "filled with golden dust."

That evening the Romanian ambassador told her Clemenceau had
said, "We can only receive a Queen like yours with full military honors,
Marshal Foch in tow."

And the next day President Raymond Poincaré gave a luncheon for her at the Elyssée, telling her: "Clemenceau has much changed towards Romania since Your Majesty has given a new face to her country." After lunch Poincaré honored her as kings but not queen consorts are honored. He asked her to review the troops. Responding with her innate theatrical sense and inherent love of the military, she marched down the long ranks while bugles sounded, the Romanian legation wept and her own heart pounded with justifiable pride.

That afternoon M. Charles Vidor, president of the *Académie des Beaux Arts*, admitted her as the organization's only female member. Her war writings had paved her way into this august company, which included Henri Bergson, the renowned philosopher, and Francis Fleming.

At a luncheon given for her by Arthur Balfour, she met England's Prime Minister. It was a small party, and she had plenty of time to size up her second quarry. Lloyd George loved to talk. Thoroughly enjoying his own jokes, the colorful Welshman spewed wit like a firecracker shooting sparks. As he talked, one Queen Marie slipped happily into the old familiar patter of smooth, patrician British repartee; another reminded herself that this suave, absent-minded gentleman looked at Romania much as she had twenty-five years ago, and that it was her job to gracefully steer the conversation around to her little nation's needs and desires.

Whatever her success, in London she had to begin all over again. With Ileana and Mignon, she stepped off the crowded, storm-tossed boat to meet her aide-de-camp for the English trip, Sir Charles Cust. In choosing Cust, King George had made a sentimental gesture to their shared past. During the Malta years, Cust had served under the Duke of Edinburgh on *H.M.S. Alexandra*.

In a teaming, khaki-filled Victoria Station, King George and Queen Mary stood waiting for her with a crowd of officials and Joe Boyle.

Gripped with emotion, she rode through the dear familiar streets to Buckingham Palace. Waiting to greet them at the front door were Edward, Prince of Wales (or "David"), his younger brother Prince Albert ("Bertie," who was to become King George VI) and their sister Mary, the Princess Royal. Already cast in his postwar role as the Commonwealth's darling, Edward charmed Marie as he charmed millions of his father's subjects.

"At twenty-one," she wrote, "David is the most attractive boy I have ever seen. He is a real little beauty with still a child's face, an adorable short nose and hair the colour of ripe corn, and he is *so* nice and has an enchanting smile. To me he is irresistible."

The initial interchange between Marie and young Edward's parents was rockier. Conventional and strait-laced, George and Mary had restored Victorian propriety to the throne Edward VII had sat on so gaily. Content with their placid routine, they worked hard for their people though they remained separated from them by the British monarchy's traditional mystique and well-oiled ceremonial.

No two women could have been more different than George V's wife and the woman he almost married. United in their patriotism and devotion to duty, Queen Mary and Queen Marie were poles apart in their approaches to life. Hospital work was an example. Queen Mary had dutifully spent many hours visiting the wounded, but shyness and a rigid sense of royal decorum kept her from expressing her compassion.

"What a relief," she sighed to Marie as they left a London hospital filled with wounded veterans. "I never know what to say to them."

"Imagine," Marie told Ileana later, "not knowing what to say in your own language!"

Spared the reality that war had made Marie take for granted, her cousins were shocked by her outspokenness. Trying to tone herself down, she nevertheless felt them watching her, as if wondering what surprise she would spring next.

Her hosts may have had qualms about her. London didn't. Within days she was the toast of London society.

Meanwhile, to counter the maddeningly detached and smug way the British looked at Romania, she began hosting lavish breakfast parties in her suite at Buckingham Palace. These were attended by old and new British Establishment friends as well as political and business acquaintances who would help alleviate Romania's war-shattered condition. Buttressed by Waldorf Astor and Joe Boyle, she threw herself into the fray. "With never-flagging enthusiasm," she wrote later, "I demonstrated that our country needed immediate help, as we had our back to the wall."

Even that pompous and icily impressive Edwardian relic Lord Curzon gave an official dinner for her so she could plead her cause before the great of the realm. This she did, "with an eloquence I didn't know I possessed, sweeping my audience along with me, till each man promised to do what he could for my suffering country. Winston Churchill was one of those who listened with the most intelligent sympathy. I thought his wife perfectly beautiful."

Days later *Punch* came out with a cartoon representing England's ally Romania as a starving peasant woman who with hungry eyes watches British foodstuffs carted past her to the enemy.

As the Versailles talks moved around to Romanian claims and Lloyd George showed no sign of easing his hard line, Bratianu dashed over from France for a private chat with King George. The wily Romanian strongman and Britain's gruff and uncomplicated sailor king sat down to lunch with Marie between them to act as translator.

When she could, she made darting visits—to Nicky at Eton, looking longer, lankier and more mischievous than ever under his absurd top hat; to Carol's former nurse, Mary Green, at Villa Mignon, who, when confronted with her home's namesake, laughed, cried, blessed and scolded them all in a comic torrent of H-less words; to Queen Alexandra, who had finally aged since her husband's death and who clung to Marie as a link with the past. The high point of her trip was a visit to Cliveden, where she renewed her bantering relationship with Waldorf Astor's wife, Nancy.

Then, after an official luncheon given her by the Lord Mayor of London, she returned to Paris. Ileana, down with flu at the last minute, remained at Buckingham Palace, and Mignon wept to leave "Mamma's beloved England." But Marie fled happily to her second Parisian love feast.

It was the first of April, and they were waiting for her with spring bouquets. Her war-weary sister Beatrice arrived from Spain, where she had moved as the bride of the Infante Alfonso, and Bratianu told Marie that both Clemenceau and Lloyd George were proving more amenable. But her greatest joy was the unceasing enthusiasm of the Paris crowds.

Once, after an opera matinee, Marie reported "I found a huge crowd assembled at the entrance, and when I moved off, the crowd moved with me. At one moment my heavy closed car was actually lifted off the ground by the enthusiastic population, which was cheering, screaming and clapping. Indeed the crush became finally dangerous, so that I was in continual fear someone might get hurt. Letting my windows down, I smiled upon them to look out for their feet. My every word awoke fresh frantic cheers, and the moment I looked one way, impatient taps on the opposite side induced me to turn my head in the other direction. I did my best to deal out my smiles equally!"

The journalists, outdoing each other in opulent praise, tried to describe her charms: "Queen Marie has the subtlety, the fascination and the beauty which blend into a general impression of the Byzantine empresses who march through the pages of the famous history of the decline and fall of the Roman Empire by Gibbon, who alone could do justice to her paradoxical personality and her histrionic history."

In the *Revue Hebdomadaire*, Louis Barthou recalled "the grace of her smile, the caress of her voice, the seduction of her wit and the steady luminosity of her intelligence, all gleaming through features to which no photographer can do justice!"

Tougher spirits than Marie's have succumbed to less flagrant attention. "But how I am being flattered!" she wrote in her journal. "I am simply being lifted up to the skies. It's lucky I'm forty-three or I might really imagine I am 'irresistible.' Yet I begin to realize the degree of natural magnetism I exercise upon people, independent of age, especially as none like the French know how to appreciate a woman."

One night as the Queen was dressing to go out, she received a letter from her mother. It was their first communication in three years.

The grand old autocrat had lost everything. Nearly her entire family had been murdered by the Bolsheviks. Both her beloved Russia and adopted Germany had collapsed. Her own fortune was gone, and she was forced to live in a shabby hotel. "I dare not even look back and remember," she wrote, "for in remembrance lies the greatest agony of all."

As she moved mechanically through the reception, Marie's heart ached as she thought of her mother: weeping at the news of Grandpapa Tsar's assassination; urging her and her sisters to romp and gobble cakes on the seashore at Peterhof; entertaining Tegernsee parties with vigorous wit and gruff affection. She saw her mother's tearstreaked face on the night she left Coburg for Romania, and heard her say, "I must just have a last look at her."

Back in the world, she invited President Wilson to tea.

The peace conference, in one historian's words, had become "a victor's brawl over the spoils." Clemenceau and Wilson weren't speaking. "Talk to Wilson?" roared the Tiger. "How can I talk to a fellow who thinks himself the first man for two thousand years who has known anything about peace on earth?"

Marie also saw Wilson's messianic complex as symptomatic of the neurosis of the times. But she had to see him. Hoping to avoid her, the President answered that he was too busy to visit her after nine in the morning. Amused, she replied she'd gladly receive him and Mrs. Wilson at seven. Resigned at last, the Wilsons arrived at eight-thirty the morning of March 10.

Marie and Edith Bolling Wilson have left conflicting reports of what happened.

"The President was exactly like his picture," the Queen wrote in her diary, "tall, lean, with a very long face and benign smile, his whole appearance being very much that of a sleek and rather puritanical clergyman.

"I received him with my usual simplicity and directness, so that conversation never lagged, although our time was sadly limited. We talked about many things . . . touching upon the subject of Bolshevism, ever uppermost in my mind. I could give him a few savoury details about what the Bolsheviks really were, which he did not know. I also expounded upon the hopes of smaller countries for which he had set himself up as a defender. This led up to the League of Nations. He began by proclaiming the excellency of his pet idea, pointing out how it would be specially beneficial to the smaller countries. All in admiring the beauty of the thought, I could not however abstain from drawing his attention to the way great ideas were often marred by the future followers and partisans who usually corrupt the initial thought, finally making something quite different out of a noble ideal."

Mrs. Wilson, ignoring Marie's prophetic observation, wrote in *My Memoir* that the Queen had plunged without any introduction into Romania's claims, "insisting upon going into great details. She reviewed the new Russian laws concerning sexual relations, saying the proximity of Russia to her country made the menace very real. At first my husband listened courteously and attentively but presently he held up his hand and said: 'Permit me to assure Your Majesty that all this was conveyed to me through dispatches long before I left the United States, and it has been thoroughly considered by the Conference. Also your Prime Minister, Mr. Bratianu, has faithfully presented Romania's case. So it is useless for me to claim more of your time regarding it.'

"He rose to end the interview. She put her hand on his arm, trying to reseat him on the sofa beside her, and in dulcet tones said: 'Oh, Bratianu! He is not getting anywhere with such men as you.' When my husband did not yield the Queen tried another tack. Lifting from the mantelpiece a photograph of a dark-haired girl of ten or twelve years, she held it up to him, saying: 'This, Mr. President, is a picture of my youngest daughter, Ileana. My love child I call her. Is she not lovely? My other girls are blonde, like me; but she—oh, she is dark and passionate.' "*

The next afternoon temperatures mounted higher as Marie and her entourage arrived thirty-five minutes late for lunch with the Wilsons. "As the minutes flew by I could see all the provinces of Romania disappearing as the President fumed," wrote Mrs. Wilson's secretary.

Marie further annoyed Wilson by changing the seating arrangements: "My sister, the Infanta, not the Princess, must be on the President's left." According to Mrs. Wilson's biographer, during lunch the Queen "told tales of pillage and rape in such plain language that the President looked more and more the Presbyterian elder."

Marie recorded only one passage of arms. "He very sanctimoniously preached to me about how we should treat our minorities, demonstrating how very important this was. He spread himself out at great length upon this subject, treating me like a rather ignorant beginner who could profit from his advice.

"No doubt I could," she acknowledged, "but he struck me as being rather too fond of the sound of his own voice. So finally, when he paused for breath, I mildly suggested that he was evidently well acquainted with these difficulties because of the Negro and Japanese questions in the United States. Upon this he bared his rather long teeth in a polite smile, drew up his eyebrows and declared he was not aware there was a Japanese question in America."

Marie and Wilson never met again, but their mutual antagonism endured. Sixteen years later she had the last word: "In spite of my every desire to like him, I had the feeling he was a fraud, and that if put in the same situation as the clergyman in *Rain* he would probably have behaved in the same way."

Meanwhile Bolshevik aggression again threatened Romania from Hungary and Russia. In its weakened condition, the country couldn't hold out long without help. So, spurring her Red Cross friends to action, Marie filled railroad cars for her return trip with French military equipment and American and Canadian provisions.

Her visit ended with a dramatic farewell headed by President Poin-

*From *My Memoir,* copyright 1938, 1939, by Edith Bolling Wilson, reprinted by permission of the publisher, The Bobbs-Merrill Company, Inc.

caré and Marshal Foch. Standing at the train window, Marie waved to the cheering throngs while they fluttered their handkerchiefs and shouted *"Vive la Reine"* and even *"Vive notre Reine."* But tears filled her eyes at the sight of Mignon waving with the others. Both her older daughters had stayed behind—Mignon to attend an English school, Lisabetta to take drawing classes in Paris. That left only Ileana at her side. Accustomed to having her children all around her, Marie felt suddenly "very empty" as she watched Mignon's plump, tear-stained face disappear in the distance.

At home Marie plunged into the job of distributing provisions to the starving peasants. More trains full of provisions arrived from Paris constantly, and for help in the massive undertaking she depended almost entirely on the American Red Cross and the Hoover organization.

All was not well between Marie and Hoover, whom she felt was "prejudiced against Romania" in his food distribution. She paid him back with a 1200-word letter which burned its way across the Atlantic from Cotroceni to New York. But she liked the Americans.

That summer, while the Peace Conference gave Romania nearly all it desired, Marie and her American helpers traversed rural Romania, battling poverty, hunger and disease. "The name of the American Red Cross will forever be blessed in my country," Ferdinand wrote Washington headquarters. Even the peasants, though at first nonplused by American informality, ended up respecting and admiring their dedicated hard work.

For payment, the Americans shared in many touching Old World scenes as Marie, the Mother Queen, cemented the bond her war record had already formed with the adoring peasants. Confronted with Transylvania's beauty and the nationalistic frenzy which greeted their every appearance, Ferdinand and Marie temporarily forgot that Carol had shot himself in the leg to keep from accompanying them and that relations with Hungary were worsening daily.

16

Mother-in-law of the Balkans

"I am a lonely woman with an empty house," Marie wrote Leila Milne, having packed even Ileana off to France for a cure. And June found her at a low ebb. "Sometimes I get weary and long for green fields and long rides and not to hear about *tuberculeux* and orphans and *mutilés* and hospitals, but I don't see that I shall ever again get away from it all, even for a short while."

All the same, she fled to Sinaia before summer's end, hungrily gulping in the Alpine air and forest smells. But her real problem, and she knew it, was Carol.

Lately, he had alternated between profound despair and frenetic excitement. But if his moods changed, his loyalty to Zizi did not. Their marriage had been formally annulled in January, but he still firmly intended to elope with her again as soon as the Hungarian question resolved itself. To make matters worse, the girl was pregnant with his child.

"It's horrible," Mairie lamented to Leila Milne. "She has a fatal grip on him. She wants to tear him away from everything to feed upon him. If nothing happens to her, he is lost." And the joys and triumphs she experienced in those momentous postwar days were undercut by Carol's defection. Sometimes it was almost more than she could bear.

Later that month, word reached Sinaia that Hungary had invaded Transylvania. All summer, while Communists took over the Hungarian government and threatened retaliation for the loss of Transylvania, Versailles had ignored Romanian warnings. With this attack, Bratianu was forced to declare war for the third time in five years. Romanian forces soon repulsed the Hungarians and pushed on into Hungary, where they marched on Budapest.

During the centuries, while Hungary dominated Transylvania, the peasants had kept faith with a song ending: "O, poor strange land, How long have I kept watch with you?" Now, with the Romanian army occupying the Magyar capital, their painful underground guardianship was vindicated. Jubilant crowds thronged churches for thanksgiving services. In Bucharest Ferdinand and Marie received frenzied ovations every time they left the palace.

"Once," wrote Marie, "our motor was almost crushed to pieces by the crowd pressing upon us."

Popularity being one of monarchy's more elusive assets, this was no time to publicize a new royal scandal. So once again Carol's embarrassing behavior was hushed up. This time he refused to go with his regiment when it was called to fight the Hungarians. His excuse was that his duty to the pregnant girl the government had forced him to abandon was greater than his duty to the army.

With this act Carol canceled most of his mother's heartache. After his earlier misdeeds, she had wept for him and for herself, musing over the "tragic misunderstanding" that had built a barrier between them. Now she was furious.

Marie fired Carol an angry letter. "Is it possible that you could let your regiment go to the front without you? Is it possible that you could have lost to such a degree your sense of honor and duty, not to take up your command and go where your country calls you? Wouldn't it be better for you to die with a bullet in your head, and be buried in good Romanian ground, than to betray your country? One day you may understand the whole horror of what you are doing. Make one more effort. Be a man, go with your regiment, fight like a soldier, redeem your honor and show the world that you are the man I always thought you were."

Carol joined his regiment. But before leaving, he satisfied part of his resentment by slapping Ferdinand with another abdication letter. The rest of his rage, directed at Marie, was less easily assuaged. Written with typical passion and rashness, her letter had irretrievably poisoned his feelings for her.

The political situation remained unsettled. Bratianu resigned in pro-

test of the Treaty of Trianon's minorities clause, which called for
Romania's immediate withdrawal from Hungary. The new Prime Minister, Alexander Vaida-Voeved, was a Transylvanian. With Juliu Maniu
he had long headed Transylvania's National Popular Party. Now these
two redoubtable nationalists founded the National Peasant Party, based
on a truly liberal platform that would have been impossible before the
war. The old Conservative Party was gone forever, swept away by its
pro-German policy and the impoverishing land reforms. And more
than ever the Liberals represented the expanding business and professional classes.

When Vaida-Voeved signed the Versailles treaties, he signed into
existence *Romania Mare* (Greater Romania), a 122,282-square-mile
land mass, populated not only with Romanians, but with Hungarians,
Germans, Bulgars, Turks, Ruthenians, Russians and Jews. And though
she shuddered at the Treaty's harshness toward the former enemy,
Marie couldn't resist a crow of delight after helping Ferdinand open the
first Greater Romanian parliament: "For a short moment, those many
men forgot their own petty strife to hail the sovereigns who had realized
the age-long dream."

Her attention was drawn back to Carol at Christmas. To be with him,
the whole family entrained to Bistritza Năsăud, the little northeastern
town where his regiment was stationed. There the soldiers staged a
parade for the King and gave Ileana a piebald Russian pony she loved
on sight and named Bolshevik. But Ferdinand and Marie were horrified
to discover that Carol had thrown over Zizi only to involve himself with
another woman—a young dressmaker who was already pregnant with
his child.

On January 9, a year after their annulment, Zizi had Carol's son.
Naming him Mircea, she scurried the baby off to Paris with twenty
thousand dollars from the government and a renunciation letter from
Carol. "I had to surrender to pressure," he wrote her, "and obey the
call of my country. Besides, I'm convinced it's for your best interest.
What's happened is that in renouncing our union, to which my heart
will remain forever faithful, I've really sacrificed myself." He didn't
mention the dressmaker.

In February 1920, Ferdinand and Marie chose that age-old device for
curing princely broken hearts, the world tour. Carol set off with a
"suitable" escort on an eight-month cruise which took them from India
and Japan to Hawaii and the United States.

"My brain rejects him," Marie thought as his train puffed out of the Bucharest station, "but my heart is still a mother's heart."

Next Marie joined Ferdinand for an official tour of Bessarabia and Bucovina. Receptions were enthusiastic, but at Cernăuți in Bucovina, an overzealous patriot hit Marie so hard in the eye with a small bouquet that she had to undergo an immediate operation to save her sight.

The doctors sent her to Paris for special treatment. "There are moments in life when you are rewarded for all the dark hours you have undergone," she told a waiting crowd. "One of them is when France is welcoming you."

Delighted, Paris again went a little mad. "Her Majesty has all the brainpower of a man," said the Count de Saint-Aulaire at one reception, "and all the allurement of a woman."

When she left Paris this time, she left for Zurich and Lisabetta's engagement.

For nine years Crown Prince George of Greece had begged Lisabetta to marry him. Enchanted by her cold, stately beauty and refined intellect and taste, "Georgie" was too much in love with her to analyze their incompatability. He saw no further than the friend who told Lisabetta, "You can't escape your fate—your Grecian profile will ultimately take you to Athens."

In fact, few couples could have been less ideally matched. Mildly intelligent and mildly good-looking, the gossip-loving George would have happily left the Eastern European political arena forever to live the exquisite life of a landed English aristocrat. Described by a writer as "an amiable idiot, without any feelings for Greece, its people or for politics," he was nevertheless honest, articulate and manly—"one of nature's gentlemen," as a relative put it.

Lisabetta, on the other hand, had grown from a difficult child into a difficult young woman. Taught contempt for Marie by Carmen Sylva, she nevertheless envied her mother's closer relationship with the younger children, while her resentment kept her from forming close bonds with any of them. She had highly developed talents for singing, drawing and painting. But her natural indolence and self-indulgence kept her creative output low. It also allowed her to eat herself into obesity, so that her classically beautiful face sat incongruously atop an immense body. Marie worried about Lisabetta's weight and laziness. But the real problem ran deeper.

"Lisabetta wasn't simply immoral," said an acquaintance, "she was amoral. She just didn't have certain notions, either in business, love or relationships with others. She could be absolutely bewitching when setting out to capture someone. But she was basically a nasty person." Often sarcastic, she sometimes said certain things for their shock effect. "I've commited every vice but one," she once told a less flamboyant friend, "and I don't want to die until I've murdered." Whatever fierce passions existed behind her haughty exterior, Lisabetta needed a stronger man than George to bridle them.

But she was twenty-six, and everyone knew the quarter-century mark was a dangerous age for an unmarried princess. Besides, this time George pressed his suit with an intensity born of desperation.

He and his family were living in Lucerne as exiles. His father, King Constantine, married to the Kaiser's sister Sophie, had been falsely accused by the Allies of advocating a pro-German war policy. So after the 1916 French bombardment of Athens, the Allies joined forces with the pro-Allies Greek Prime Minister Venizelos and forced Constantine to abdicate and leave the country. Assuming dictatorial powers, Venizelos passed over George to appoint Prince Alexander, George's next oldest brother, as King. All contacts with his exiled family were denied the unhappy young king, who lived as a virtual prisoner in the Athens palace. And in Lucerne his impoverished, exiled family endured endless insults from former friends who believed the "anti-Tino" slander circulated by Venizelos and ill-informed Western journalists. For George, to whom congenial surroundings were all-important, marriage to Lisabetta looked like his one chance for happiness.

With the engagement announced, a delighted Marie invited the young couple to Sinaia for the official betrothal party. The fact that George's family were exiles didn't daunt her. She felt sorry for them. Nor did she share the general postwar feeling that Constantine had betrayed the Allies. To prove her faith, she invited George's sisters Helen and Irene to Sinaia too.

Princess Helen, at twenty-four, was tall and slender, dark-haired and gently humorous. To deep dimples, soft blue-gray eyes and a "sudden entrancing" smile accented by a dainty mole above her upper lip, she added the same superb elegance that would characterize her cousin Marina as Duchess of Kent. "She is a little shortsighted," wrote Princess Ileana, "which gives her a slight air of hesitation, and which has added to her natural shyness."

Reared by an English nanny and a decorous mother, Sitta, as Helen was called in her family, wasn't sure she wanted to visit the colorful Romanians. But to her father the invitation came as a gratifying compliment. "I would like you to go," he said, "so that it will be obvious to the world that my children are not treated like pariahs, even though I am."

Before they could leave for Romania, Carol arrived in Switzerland on the last leg of his tour. "He is tremendously changed, to his advantage," Marie enthused to a friend. "Much more manly, much more man of the world, intensely eager to work and be useful." Princess Helen was less impressed. "During the journey [to Romania]," she later wrote, "he seemed a retiring and not very affable character." And even at Sinaia he "showed not a vestige of interest in me."

It took a double family crisis to precipitate events. First the young Greeks received the shattering news from Athens that their brother Alexander had died suddenly of blood poisoning resulting from a monkey bite. Helen, especially, was heartbroken. Alexander had been her favorite brother and stanchest ally from earliest childhood. The next day, while touring Cernăuţi, Marie got word that her mother had died in Switzerland. Cernăuţi was where she'd been struck in the eye. It was beginning to look like her bad-luck town. Death having visited both royal families during official ceremonies announcing George and Lisabetta's marriage plans, Romanians shook their heads.

Taking Mignon and the stunned Greek princesses with her, Marie left Bucharest in a late October snow storm for Zurich. To her astonishment, Carol decided to go with them.

In Switzerland, Marie was jolted from grief to amazed jubilation when without warning Carol asked Helen to marry him, and she accepted.

"I was attracted to him," Helen admitted, "and felt that later I would come to love him. But what made me really decide to say yes was the thought of Alexander. To marry Carol and go to Romania and not have to live in the place that would constantly wound me with memories, seemed a kind of deliverance."

Though King Constantine approved the match, Queen Sophie fought long and hard against her daughter's marriage to the scandal-smeared Carol. But to no avail. The second royal Romanian engagement in a month was announced. "Carol is saved!" Marie trumpted to Leila Milne. And she applauded Helen to her ladies: "She is sweet and she is a lady. Besides, she's one of the family, since we're all descended from Grandmamma Queen."

Meanwhile Carol wrote secretly to Zizi Lambrino. "Yes, it is true that I am engaged to a princess. This is so much against all my principles that I myself am surprised. I haven't given up without a fight. I resisted to the last extremity and it was only when I was left alone that I declared myself beaten. I have found someone who can understand me and who, in her theories of life, has the same ideas as I. She has accepted to comfort a heart profoundly hurt. Yes, such is life."

On the Romanian New Year, January 14, 1921, Marie was pleased to note that her blessings centered on her children as never before. Ileana was doing well with Miss Ida Marr, her new English governess; Mignon was "well, happy and good"; Nicky had joined the British Navy; "and all goes well as far as the marriages are concerned," the happy mother wrote Lisabetta's former governess Leila Milne.

Meanwhile a Greek plebiscite unexpectedly returned the royal family to Athens and restored Constantine to his throne. To Princess Helen the longed-for return meant both heartache and joy—heartache because she must return to her brother's grave, joy because her adored father had regained his throne, and she could now marry Carol as an equal.

On February 27 Lisabetta and George were married in the Metropolitan Church in Bucharest. Predictably, the bride broke precedent by wearing a short skirt. But the traditional golden thread adorned her own ash-blond mane, and the crowds shouted themselves hoarse over her classic beauty.

A week later, thanks to a special dispensation required by the Orthodox Church before brother and sister could marry sister and brother, Carol and Helen were wed in Athens. The bride still lived in the shadow of her brother's death. "Never could anything be the same again," she mourned. But she still considered marriage her only way out, "especially as I was now beginning to feel that I did love Carol."

On May 7 the Crown Prince introduced his bride to her future subjects in a grand parade through Bucharest. Reminded of her friendlessness and lack of poise at her own grand entry, Marie whispered suggestions to the shy Helen.

From the first, despite protestations of affection on both sides, the differences between Queen Marie and her successor were obvious.

A friend described the new Crown Princess as "wonderfully polite and courteous, a great lady to her fingertips and one of the most harmonious women imaginable. The way she walked, her gestures, her clothes—all were sheer delight. Humorous, but not too; well-read, but not really intellectual, she had great charm and breeding. But she was always very distant. You had the impression that she only went up to a certain point in her relationships with others, and never beyond that point. She was one of those people who don't have much personality."

Marie, on the other hand, now that she at last lived free of all restrictions, had developed into one of the era's great personalities. Virtually a law unto herself, she ran her court and family with wit and charm. One of her greatest strengths was her tremendous self-assurance. Completely devoid of shyness, she would walk into a room of five hundred people, throw her arms out to them and call, "Oh, my dear people, come and talk to me!" According to her gardener friend, Mrs. Martineau: "There's a saying prevalent in Romania that if you want a thing done, you must go to Regina."

Basically a simple person, her keen dramatic sense often blurred the sincerity of her impulses. Take her annual Easter visits to the Moldavian front. She thought about them with humble sincerity, but once confronted with the situation's inherent drama, carried it off with theatrical flamboyance. Much has been written about her so-called common touch with strangers. Certainly she erased all royal haughtiness from her receptions. "Here I am," she would announce when opening an audience. And her journalist friend, Mabel Potter Daggett, describes her lying full-length on a sofa in her Pelisor boudoir, smoking cigarettes and chattering like a school-girl. Yet the boudoir was painted gold and stuffed with exotic furnishings and hundreds of lilies.

Her sense of humor was infallible. Having early discovered Helen's gift for mimicry, Marie would whisper to her at some public function, "Now watch carefully. You must do this." Later, watching her daughter-in-law imitate her large queenly gestures and blazing smile, she would laugh till she cried. Her humor came out in her own talents as a raconteuse. At Buftea she kept the Stirbeys and their mutual friend, the Liberal politician Jean Duca, entertained for hours with tales about Queen Victoria and the Russian court. "She never overdid it," remembered Duca's son George. "But by underlining her story with gestures and laughter she made it fascinating." Sometimes she went too far. "Please, Mamma, try not to be so funny," an embarrassed Mignon would groan. And once a new page was shocked when at lunch she recounted the story of an old American gentleman who had once fallen in love with her in Paris. Finding the Queen alone, the old rogue had fallen to his knees, grasped her hand and stirringly declared his passion.

When the moment passed, he discovered he couldn't get up, and Marie
wasn't strong enough to lift him. So she called next door to the King:
"Nando, this gentleman has just declared his love for me. Now will you
help us get him up?"

Sometimes her penchant for self-expression backfired. Like Carmen
Sylva before her, she succumbed to the flattery of cynical court women
who would draw her out on some favorite topic, then laugh behind their
hands at her rhapsodizing. Remembered one contemporary: "The
Queen surrounded herself with a bevy of young women who would hold
her hand and kiss it, and murmur, 'My Queen, my Queen,' and she'd
purr like a kitten."

Marie's theatrical sense reached a peak in her taste in clothes.
Though considerably heavier than before the war, she was as lushly
beautiful as ever. A young Englishwoman seeing her for the first time,
compared her to a full-blown carnation. But the Queen disliked the
scanty twenties fashions. So she devised her own garb—brightly embroidered peasant dress for touring the provinces, flowing pastel gowns with
long trains for tea. For formal evening occasions she added a blazing
diadem and a long veil that crossed under her chin. Wearing ropes of
pearls and masses of rings, surrounded by borzois and antique crosses,
she made a romantic picture.

Photographs fed the rapidly growing legend. Over the years two
female Transylvanian photographers immortalized her in thousands of
poses, nearly all theatrical in the extreme. With time, millions of copies,
printed on postcards, circulated throughout the world. Marie had definite opinions about which poses and lighting suited her best. During her
provincial progresses, when some village photographer attempted to
photograph her, she would take over, angling the poor man into position with a smooth-flowing dialogue that soon had him eating out of
her hand. By the time he could steady the camera, the Queen would
be ready—posed and smiling as Bernhardt on opening night.

Naive awareness of her own beauty and importance led to charges
that she was conceited. To call Marie of Romania vain is an oversim-
plification. Just as her lack of self-consciousness sometimes made her
do ridiculous things, so her self-objectivity often led to harsh criticism.
She talked freely about herself, both the weaknesses and her strengths,
"But she did it always either with so much humor or so much innocence," said a friend, "that you couldn't be angry with her."

Once a young relative came across these lines written by Marie and
left lying on a table: "Marie of Romania—one of the most wonderful

women in the world. A woman like that is born once in a century."
When teased about the remarks, she said, "But, my dear, I am like that.
And if I am, why shouldn't I say so?" And to sister Bee's husband she
once wrote: "Thank you for the photos. Some are excellent. I am quite
a fine woman in the one you had enlarged."

But to judge Marie by common standards would be a mistake. Neither her upbringing nor her life after marriage was commonplace.
Accustomed from childhood to accept public praise and attention, she
reveled in it with a child's delight.

"She was neither a lady nor not a lady," summed up a friend. "She
was quite out of this world. Glamorous from her head to her toes, she
was like a flame that went through life. She was a Sun Queen as Louis
XIV was the Sun King. She saw her actions as she *wanted* to see them,
and you couldn't criticize her; she was so full of bonhomie."

Whether bounding across the countryside on horseback or cradling
a dying peasant in her arms, Marie exerted a powerful charisma that
drew people to her like flies to honey. For despite her self-satisfaction,
she was humble too, seldom attributing to herself qualities she didn't
possess. A warm glow emanated from her. And whatever her faults or
absurdities, Marie of Romania's ultimate strength lay in her profound
sympathy for others.

Carol's marriage was off to a good start. At Sinaia he and Helen had
redecorated the rustic Foisor to suit Helen's refined taste, and she was
already pregnant. "They certainly did not lose any time," remarked
Marie. And though Helen had already begun to suspect that hers and
Carol's temperaments were less compatible than she'd hoped, only one
incident marred their happiness.

It happened when she noticed a battered alarm clock sitting on a shelf
in his study.

"Carol, what happened to that clock?"

Avoiding her eyes, he answered. "Oh, I once threw it at Zizi's head."

Shivering, Helen suddenly remembered the stories she'd heard about
him and the arguments her mother had used, hoping to keep her from
marrying him.

Having installed the young couple in their new home, Marie bustled
over the Carpathians to inspect one of the most impressive gifts she ever
received—a medieval Saxon fortress. Presented by the Transylvanian
city of Braşov, Castle Bran had stood empty since the crusades. Marie
was enchanted with its romantic setting, backed by the 8,000-foot

Brucegi mountain range, and decided to remodel it for a vacation home. The highly romantic result pleased her beyond her fondest dreams.

"Yes, it's very nice, my dear," remarked Greek Queen Sophie on her first Bran tour. "But at your age?"

"Yes, my dear, at my age," laughed Marie. "And I'm not finished yet!"

Marie was called back from a restful reunion with her sisters on the southern French coast by the premature birth of Carol and Helen's son. Born on October 25, 1921, he was named Michael after the great unifier.

That same fall, Alexander, the new King of the neighboring fledgling Kingdom of the Serbs, Croats and Slovenes asked for Mignon's hand in marriage.

The thirty-two-year-old monarch had succeeded his father, old King Peter, who had inherited the Serbian throne in 1903, thanks to the assassination of King Alexander Obrenovich. After the bloody and vicious reigns of several rival Obrenovich kings, Peter had restored badly-needed dignity to the Serbian throne. Before madness overtook him, he heroically led his country through the Balkan and European wars and, thanks to the Versailles treaty, added Croatia and Slovenia to the existing Serb kingdom.

Many of Peter's later successes were the result of his heir Alexander's undeniable abilities. A conscientious soldier and politician, young Alexander had proven his mettle during the wars. And as a popular regent during his father's illness, he'd provided the doughty Serbs with their first national hero in fifty years, while managing to soothe the ancient blood feud between those unlikely new compatriots, the Serbs and the Croats.

Ferdinand and Marie were surprised by Alexander's proposal. But they were pleased. The dynastic results of such a match could prove monumental. Both countries had already allied with Czechoslovakia to form the Little Entente, a pact all hoped would insure them against Bulgarian and Hungarian territorial drives.

The problem would be Mignon. Not the least romantically inclined, the plump, easygoing girl might need persuading. So Marie took matters into her own hands.

"A great and good man wants you for his wife," she told her daughter, "to make his home and bear his children. Moreover his country needs a queen. And there will be a great future for you in developing Serbia together. Of course, my dear, it's for you to decide."

Just before Christmas the Serbian King received a note from Marie inviting him to spend the holidays with her family at Sinaia. "The situation with Mignon is favorable enough," she added, "that we do not feel you'll be risking a refusal."

On an afternoon between Christmas and New Year's Day, Alexander took Mignon for a walk among the snow-decked Sinaia firs. Painted with frost that sparkled in the sunlight, the royal park glittered like a scene from a Hans Christian Andersen story. After three hours, leading her beau by the hand, Mignon trudged into the Pelisor to find her mother. "We have arranged it," she cried and burst into tears. It was her twenty-second birthday.

Bad news from Greece countered jubilation. The Greek army, led by an unwilling King Constantine, had attacked Turkey in the vainglorious hope of resurrecting a second Byzantine Empire from the ashes of old Turkey. An ancient Greek legend stated that when Constantine and Sophia once again sat upon the throne, Byzantium would rise again. But the Greek army deteriorated, while the Turkish troops gained ground under the masterful leadership of Kemal Ataturk.

Meanwhile Alexander returned to Romania in February for the official announcement of his engagement. Respectful Bucharest crowds ogled this man who had harnessed the diametrically-opposed Serbs and Croats to a single national dream. What they saw was a dark, narrow-shouldered, nearsighted man with a bright smile, a man *Time* magazine said looked like a small-town dentist. But John Gunther, in the first edition of his *Inside Europe,* said "he looked like what he was—a King. He was industrious, charming, capable of almost inexplicable sudden flights of worry, temperament, and fury, yet disciplined and shrewd— a complex character." And his nation, one of the most backward and ethnically untenable results of the Versailles Conference, was equally complex.

"Nevertheless, our Mignon is perfectly serene," Marie told Leila Milne, "and happy, contemplating her future life with hope and joy, although it will mean a great change in her life and none too easy position for such a young thing. Mignon, having never flirted in her life, thought it quite natural to accept the hand of a man who needed to build a home and uphold a country badly tortured during the many years of war. The glamour of it no doubt tempted her, but true to her nature she was especially tempted by the thought of making a happy home for a man who has never had any mother and no family life and none of what we call happiness. A love match it can hardly be called. But a bond of lovely friendship and mutual regard and sympathy it certainly can be called, and there is no anxiety and no apprehension in the dear child's heart."

For Marie the spring of 1922 was the most exhausting since 1918. First she visited Belgrade to inspect Mignon's future home. To her dismay, she discovered Alexander employed an all-male staff. "Not even the laundry is done by women!" She also noted that the separate bedrooms planned for Alexander and Mignon were separated by a reception room. And a sentry stood guard there day and night. "Not very conducive for producing an heir to the throne," laughed Marie.

She was still amusing herself with "Belgrade discoveries" when a cable called her to Lisabetta, ill with typhoid fever. She took the first boat to Athens, where she found her daughter improved but not out of danger. The Queen had hardly returned home at the start of the girl's convalescence when she received a telegram calling her back to Athens. Lisabetta had developed an acute case of pleurisy. Considering her greatly weakened condition, the doctors didn't expect her to live. This time Ferdinand accompanied Marie to Greece. They crossed the Black Sea in a man-o'-war that was nearly sunk by a violent spring storm. Throughout the ordeal Marie reminded herself that she was a sailor's daughter and that water was her favorite element. In fact, the romantic prospect of perishing at sea, battle guns and all, was rather appealing.

After ten harrowing days, Lisabetta climbed back a second time, and by June 1 Ferdinand and Marie were back in Bucharest to escort Mignon over the border to her wedding.

For Alexander's wedding the tough Serbs had produced a show unmatched in their violent history. Belgrade burst with thousands of gaily-dressed peasants come to present gifts to their new queen. Garlands, flags and bright carpets decorated every house. Multicolored bunting fluttered from boats chugging up the Danube and down the Sava rivers. Sirens screamed and cannons boomed deafeningly. "Really a sight for kings!" applauded Marie.

After an endless ceremony in the Belgrade cathedral, the overgrown girl with china blue eyes, flaxen hair and a penchant for wearing clothes greasy from repairing her own car, emerged from the church as Queen of the Serbs, Croats and Slovenes. The contrast between Mignon's preferred garb and the glittering emeralds, elaborate silver gown and fifteen-foot train she wore today was not lost on cynical observers. "She already has an air of grandeur," sniffed one. "How easily some people adopt the externals of their trade."

Elsewhere in the cathedral a more ominous note was struck. During the ceremony a Serbian officer turned to Marie's lady-in-waiting Simky Lahovary and hissed: "See that column, Madam? Well, that's where that other Alexander—Obrenovich—was butchered twenty years ago, and thrown out the window with his queen."

So there were still Serbs who remembered. And did some still believe the rumor that old Peter had planned the gory disposition of his rival? When Simky told her of the incident later, Marie dismissed it with a shrug of her shoulders and the old Arabian proverb, "Blood never sleeps."

The Belgrade festivities were barely over when the Turks defeated Greece. Again Constantine's ungrateful subjects made him the scapegoat for their misfortunes. Hounded into a second exile, he left his son George as King and Lisabetta as Queen of Greece.

With daughters occupying two Eastern European thrones and Carol someday to inherit a third, Marie was hailed as "The Mother-in-Law of the Balkans." The international press resounded with the rumor that she and Stirbey had engineered her children's marriages with the idea of forming a Balkan Empire on the lines of ancient Byzantium. Some writers even hinted that soon Ileana would be sacrificed as the bride of Tsar Boris of Bulgaria.

Frederick L. Collins, writing for the American *Woman's Home Companion,* called Marie "the most picturesque, perhaps the most powerful woman in the world. By a series of brilliant marriages between her children and the rulers of nearby nations, she has laid the foundations of a vast Balkan Empire . . . and achieved what many statesmen have tried for but none has ever approached, a basis for Balkan unity."

"I read these descriptions of myself with astonishment," said Marie, "because they certainly do not correspond with truth." Certainly she enjoyed power, but she wasn't an intriguer. She'd have loved presiding over a second Byzantium, though, and she adored the limelight of international prestige.

"I'm in very high spirits," she told the Minister of Foreign Affairs that winter. "It probably suits me well to be called the Mother-in-Law of the Balkans."

Then she turned her energy to planning her coronation as Queen of Greater Romania.

17

"Say I've Drowned"

"I'm a winner in life," Marie told her journalist friend Mabel Potter Daggett. "Somebody has to lose, but I believe I'm a winner."

No single event sealed her hard-won success as woman, Queen and mother as did Ferdinand's and her coronation. Held on October 15, 1922, it also consecrated Romanian unity and capped Ferdinand's popularity as "King of the Peasants"—an accolade he deserved more than ever now that the land reforms were law.

Unlike other European countries, Greater Romania possessed no coronation tradition. So King and court improvised. The ceremony was held at Alba Julia in Transylvania, the site of the fortress where Michael the Brave made his triumphant entry in 1599. A Byzantine church surrounded by columns and topped with a soaring entrance tower had been constructed for the occasion. But since neither Ferdinand nor Marie was Orthodox, it was decided to hold the religious service in the church and follow it with a crowning ceremony held outside in the public square.

Marie arrived at Alba Julia garbed in a picturesque costume she'd designed herself. Since no official Queen's crown existed, she'd had one copied from the crown worn by the legendary Princess Despina Doamna in the Curtea de Arges frescoes. Fashioned of yellow Transylvanian gold and studded with moonstones, amethysts and turquoises, it weighed four pounds and cost $5,000. She wore it Byzantine-style with a delicate gold mesh veil. Her train, embroidered with golden wheat stalks and the crests of all the Romanian provinces, was gold. And her gold tissue gown shimmered with an overlay of gold thread. Arrayed in her twinkling finery, she recalled Theodora and other Byzantine empresses—a comparison Marie was only too happy to endorse.

Colorful but not very well managed, her coronation compared modestly with the British and Russian productions Marie had seen. But Ferdinand crowning himself with Uncle's iron crown, then crowning her as she knelt before him, and embracing her in front of the 300,000 spectators—these were moments she would never forget.

That afternoon, mounted on a tall gray horse and dressed in the same uniform she'd worn for the 1918 entry into Bucharest, she rode with the King down endless rows of cheering troops, through streets jammed with shouting and weeping peasants. On the following morning they rode back into Bucharest at the head of the Romanian princes and a cavalcade of visiting dignitaries that included Marshal Foch and the Duke of York. The emotional peak for Marie came when she rode for the first time under the new Arch of Triumph, built on the Chaussée to commemorate Romania's war victory. For her, no matter what triumphs might follow, that moment was the symbolic crowning of her career both as a war and peacetime queen.

By publicly embracing his wife, Ferdinand had thanked her with uncharacteristic flair for her support as Queen Consort. But the gesture also signified a deeper, more personal emotion. After twenty-nine years, their marriage was a success.

Not that the original romance had flowered again. Seeing him in contrast with heady postwar pomp and circumstance, surrounded by their large and noisy family or amid the excitably gregarious Romanians, Marie found her husband as irritatingly shy and indecisive as ever. He, in turn, occasionally fumed at her, strutting with rage and barking "Maddy! Maddy! Maddy!" in his thick German accent—a display which always reduced her to fits of laughter. And she often treated him with less than total respect, referring to him as "the poor King," and once leaning down a banquet table to ask, "Nando, since when are we King?"

But since the war, maturity had dulled the conflicting edges of their personalities, allowing them to concentrate on their shared loves: Romania and the children. And differences that had once pushed them apart now served to balance their relationship. As he grew more candid in admitting her gift for handling people, she was better able to appreciate his talents as behind-the-scenes coordinator. She charmed foreign guests, but he told her the points to make. At Copaceni, her favorite weekend home, and at Scroviste, the shooting lodge she was remodeling for him, their complementary traits came to bear on the gardens both loved. With her artist's eye, she laid them out in sweeping acres of subtly shifting color. But his botanist's instinct told her which varieties to buy and what conditions of sun and shade best suited each flower.

"Nando, you are like good wine," she told him. "You sweeten with age."

And while Marie might tell old Mrs. Martineau, "You are the only woman I can trust the King with," neither Ferdinand nor Marie resented the other's relationships with other people. The King flirted with Marthe Bibesco and carried on a long-term affair with a Madame Disiscu. Time and distance had not severed Marie's warm relationship with Waldorf Astor. Joe Boyle still played a major part in her life, and Barbu Stirbey had never left it.

She and Stirbey continued to meet almost daily for tea or for long, unescorted walks or rides in the Buftea woods. With a sincerity that confounded the gossips, Ferdinand still depended on the Prince for advice in both political and family affairs. And Nadèje Stirbey continued treating Marie as one of her closest friends, which indeed she was. At Buftea Marie and both Stirbeys would spend long hours together, while Barbu read aloud or Marie read to them from her diary. One Christmas Nadèje hand-embroidered a tea gown for the Queen with thousands of pink rose petals.

Over the years Marie and Stirbey's love had ripened into a powerful personal and political alliance. This bond was seldom more strikingly portrayed than at a palace concert in the winter of 1922. An onlooker described the scene: "At intermission all the guests went to the buffet spread out in a long hall outside the throne room. I remember looking up from my plate to see Prince Stirbey standing with the Queen. She wore a very low-cut black velvet dress with a train and all her magnificent pearls. Her blond beauty had never been more striking. Dark and elegant in tails, Stirbey was her perfect masculine counterpart. They stood like that for some time, surrounded by the whirling crowd, yet isolated. What I remember most is that while talking together the whole time, they never once looked at each other."

That winter was the worst since the Jassy winter of 1916–1917. Marie diverted herself with daily riding and by planning major remodelings of all her gardens. "I have become a passionate gardener," she told a friend. "It is a joy I am preparing for my old age." But despite excellent health and her usual vigor, she was "a bit anxious about things in general." No sooner had the coronation festivities ended than her children's recurring problems surfaced again.

With George and Lisabetta occupying the shaky Greek throne, her mind strayed constantly to Athens. "The lot of my young ones down there is indeed hard," she wrote Leila Milne, "and our poor Lisabetta, who all her girlhood managed to be tragic and desperate in imagination, now plenty to be really tragic about!"

Then she added, "We were absolutely disgusted about the absurd and wicked inventions about Carol and Sitta's divorce. A happier, more united, contented couple it would be difficult to find. Absolute harmony reigns between them and she and I really love each other. She is *all* my heart desires."

But the facts already belied her brave words.

Though Helen married Carol for negative reasons, she later came to love him. His obvious adoration and touching dependency were impossible for a girl with her warm, open character to resist. And she found Sinaia and the cozy Foisor a welcome change from the tense, uprooted life she had lived since the war.

At first Carol also seemed content enough with their bucolic life far from the unsavory companions he often preferred. All who visited them that fall of 1921 while they awaited their baby's birth were struck by their happiness. But after the baby's birth, things began going wrong. For a variety of reasons, a difficult premature birth among them, Helen was unable to respond warmly to Carol's demanding advances.

Another mistake Helen unwittingly made was to spend the four months from December to April in Greece wth her family. Since her father's return from exile, she had watched his accumulating military and political difficulties anxiously. With her new house only partly furnished and Harrods of London unable to complete the job before spring, she saw that winter as the perfect time to support him with her presence. So after the christening, she and baby Michael set off on the three-day train trip across Bulgaria to Athens.

The Greek royal family had long depended on each other for a warmth and solidarity that saw them through their recurring crises. Thus they saw nothing strange in careworn Constantine's favorite daughter and new grandson cheering him with an extended visit. But Carol was not the sort of man a wife safely leaves to his own devices for four months.

At thirty, he was over six feet tall, broad-shouldered and slender. With his wavy, baby-fine dark blond hair, clipped mustache, bright "Windsor blue" eyes and appealing smile, he would have been strikingly handsome except for a weak chin which recalled Queen Victoria's family. One journalist, noting his "slightly puffed up face" and "stormy eyes," thought he looked more like his Russian relatives, especially his great-grandfather Tsar Alexander II.

Whatever his family resemblance, one of those relatives, his mother's cousin, Grand Duchess Marie, felt that in personality he was "a completely independent product, the product of his half-civilized, semi-Oriental, self-indulgent country."

Like a Renaissance prince, he was exceedingly intelligent, politically well-versed, an avid reader and a patron of all the arts. Politicians and intellectuals who despised him politically stood in awe of him intellectually. Hard-working and thorough, he had founded the Romanian Boy Scouts; the Romanian Federation of Sports, designed to foster athletic activity for men between eighteen and thirty; and the first Romanian Air Corps. He spent nearly every morning at No. 8 Strada Latina, the Bucharest office from which he ran his Cultural Foundation of Romania, a charitable organization founded to develop and extend Romanian culture and philosophy. More concerned than formerly with his country's internal problems, he had come to open conflict with Bratianu, who was back in power and again virtual dictator. Resenting Bratianu's and Stirbey's influence over his parents and the country more than ever, he served notice that when he became King they would both be exiled. Bratianu was no man to take such a threat lying down. Before long, another of Carol's Renaissance traits—his sexual overindulgence—would give the Prime Minister his chance to strike.

In Carol's defense it must be said that he made no conscious effort to replace Helen with a full-time mistress. Marriage had not stopped his casual sexual flings, and he saw no reason to form a permanent liaison now. Still, his curiously unfulfilled personality demanded something he got from neither the ladylike and sheltered Helen or from the numerous women who threw themselves at his head. What he needed was a woman who could hold him physically, dominate him emotionally and provide him with the mothering attention he'd craved since childhood. During Helen's four-month visit to Greece, he found that woman.

Unfortunately for Helen, her family's problems soon proved too overwhelming for her to give Carol and her marriage the attention they needed. When in September her parents had crept to Palermo, Sicily, and their second exile, she could hardly wait for the Romanian coronation to end before rushing to join them.

In Palermo she found her father crushed at last by events in Greece. On January 11 he died. All her life Helen had adored this brave, conscientious man, honoring him that much more as the world attacked him. Now he'd died on alien soil with a broken heart, while his enemies flourished in Athens.

When she left her father's temporary grave in Naples, Helen took her mother, Queen Sophie, to Romania with her. "Yesterday our poor Sitta returned at last, still horribly sad," wrote Marie on February 24. "The death of her father was a terrible and sudden shock, and her poor mother is a sad, penniless, homeless, country-less exile. Too sad." But as months passed and Helen was seldom without at least one female relative in attendance, even Marie joined the court in quipping: "Here come Carol and his wives."

Later, Helen's critics would point to the continued presence of her relatives as another reason why her marriage failed. In reality she made only one mistake that mattered—the mistake of treating Carol as though he were a mature and responsible adult. In interpersonal relationships he was neither. Just as his affections had danced unpredictably from Zizi to the dressmaker to Helen, now they blazed anew for Elena Lupescu. Married to an army officer named Tampeanu, whom she immediately divorced as a result of Carol's interest in her, Madame Lupescu was of the lower class, and was half Catholic, half Jewish. Her father was a pharmacist's assistant. After Helen's refined loveliness, Lupescu's voluptuous figure, horsy good looks, sensual gait and flaming red hair titillated Carol. Her sly intelligence, sexual prowess and commanding personality held him.

Marie, meanwhile, refused to accept the reality of so monumental a disaster. While supporting Helen with humorous affection, she threw herself into such ceremonial duties as the dedication of an Unknown Soldier's tomb in Bucharest's Carol Park and an official trip to Poland with Ferdinand.

In September 1923 King Alexander called her to Belgrade for the birth of Mignon's first child. The Serbs had ordained that it would be a son. "For the lovely newcoming little Crown Prince," said an enthusiastic Yugoslav peasant, stuffing a massive silver dagger into Mignon's hand. And they were not disappointed.

The baby, named Peter, was so dark that Marie dubbed him Black Peter, to go with his family name, Karageorgevitch, which means Black George. Hs godparents were Marie, Lisabetta and the Duke of York. Holding the baby in the center of a large family group, Marie beamed from innumerable photographs taken to immortalize the child's christening. "Cousin Missy as usual was in great form," the Duke of York wrote home to Buckingham Palace. And on the following day, magnificently dressed as a medieval Russian Boyarina, she stole the show at the marriage of King Alexander's cousin, Prince Paul, to the beautiful Princess Olga of Greece.

Buoyed by Mignon's happiness and still refusing to see Carol's affair with Elena Luspescu as a major threat, Marie wrote Carol's former nurse, Mary Green, "After many storms and much trouble, I am happy in my children. Pray God, Nana, to keep me so."

By winter her optimistic words echoed hollowly from a brighter past. King George had reigned barely a year in Greece when he and Lisabetta were forced by the Revolutionary Committee to leave the country. Lisabetta had failed at queenship, excusing herself on the grounds that Greece starved her mentally, that she hungered for the art, music and affection that had surrounded her in Bucharest. But she wept copiously on the day she left Athens. It was a fitting farewell; she never saw her husband's country again.

In Romania the exiled couple settled down in a wing of Cotroceni. After her brief unsuccessful bout with public duty, Lisabetta resumed her former selfish routine, painting occasionally and playing mahjong by the hour. Before long it was obvious that George interfered with her self-absorption. With few common interests and no shared work, goals or children to bind it together, their marriage began disintegrating. Years later, when he'd given up trying to make a life with Lisabetta, George would tell Marie: "When everything else crashed around me, you were the only one who made my situation bearable."

In March, to escape the knowledge that two of her children's marriages were failing, Marie sailed to Malta. She hadn't been back since leaving it thirty-three years before. After enduring a voyage that made her seasick for the first time in her life, she stepped ashore into a golden haze of nostalgia. Tearing herself away, she met Ferdinand for an official tour to renew ties with Allied leaders in Paris, Geneva, Brussels and London.

In London she rode the crest of her postwar popularity. The British press proclaimed "Queen Marie's smile" while their gravures showed her smiling at a Buckingham Palace ball for two thousand people, at the International Exhibition at Wembley, in the streets packed with cheering crowds.

Side by side, the woman who had been George V's first love and the wife who shared his throne as a loving and devoted helpmate moved through their ceremonial duties. The contrast between the two queens could hardly have been greater.

"She looks dull in the eternal photos we see of her in the many papers," Queen Marie wrote impishly of Queen Mary. "Always the same hat, the same cloak, the same parasol, the same smile, the same shoes. But she has a nice sense of humor. Only there is this, she told it to me herself: she does not like uncomfortable things. She likes prosperity, collecting, putting things in order. She likes wealth and position, jewels, dresses. She has little imagination, but she likes reading; history interests her, family trees. She likes to be amused, but decorously, though occasionally a risque little story can make her blush with the pleasure of having understood it.

"She has watchful but kindly eyes. She is always very smartly dressed, even in the early morning. Her clothes fit as though built for her. Her collars go right up under her ears. She wears what is politely called a 'transformation' so that there is never a hair out of place . . . She has endless diadems which she wears often as it is neither difficult nor painful to attach them to the 'transformation.' "

If Marie was amused by her mental image of the decorous Queen Mary attaching a tiara to her wig and then setting them both on her head like a mat, her biting little description ended with a sigh: "She passes smoothly through life—honored, guarded, appreciated, recognised."

A year later the good-will trail took Ferdinand and Marie back to England, France and to Italy. Joe Boyle had died, alone and penniless, at Hampstead Hill. Sick for a long time, he had refused to see Marie on her previous trip, begging her to remember him as he'd been.

"He was the grandest friend a woman ever had," she wrote Boyle's sister at his death. "In my heart he will never die. I bless his memory and keep holy the remembrance of every hour we spent together."

Now she brought an old Romanian stone cross from her collection to mark his grave. Before leaving for France, Marie saw the cross set over Boyle's grave. At his request, she had engraved it with the insignia of her Regina Maria order and words from his favorite *Songs of a Sourdough:*

> Joe W. Boyle
> A man with the heart of a Viking
> And the simple faith of a child

Years later she would write in the foreword to Boyle's biography, "He died alone, like an old lion in the desert, or an old eagle on a rock, who cannot bear man or beast to look upon his end. In our lives he left a gap nothing can ever fill."

By 1925 Marie had reached the pinnacle of her international prestige. Thanks to the mass media, her name was if anything better known in Western Europe and America than in the Balkans. Her war record, combined with her repeated London and Paris successes, had imbued her with a queenly glamor reminiscent of Catherine the Great, Elizabeth and Mary Queen of Scots.

Americans, especially, enjoyed reading about Marie. They knew she grew dahlias and favored Kipling, knew what color drapes decorated her private railway car, knew her opinion on royalty's place in the twentieth century and what progress she was attempting to achieve for the Romanian peasant. Now, as she began writing her own syndicated columns for Hearst and the North American Newspaper Alliance, they were given a still more intimate look at her mind's workings.

Contrary to popular belief, she was not the first royalty to put her writings to use for public relations purposes. Queen Victoria had salved public outrage against her long retirement by publishing *Leaves from the Journal of Our Life in the Highlands.* (Disraeli sometimes addressed her, "We authors, Mum.") But there was no royal precedent for Marie's choice of subjects. Over an eighteen-month span she wrote: "My Experiences with Men," "Clothes and the Woman," "Can a Woman Make Herself Beautiful?" "Dreams Do Come True," "Beauty in Woman," "Woman's Loss of Beauty," "What a Smile Can do," "Making Marriage Durable," and "How it Feels to be a Queen."

In a sharp-edged article for the *New Republic,* Charles Merz described the new royal phenomenon. "Here is no writing over people's heads, but an instinct as sure as Mr. Hearst's and a taste as catholic as Mr. Brisbane's. Here is sure-fire appeal for both the subway crowd and the farm-and-firesiders, served up by no less a personage than a reigning queen. Here is both the titillation of a bold idea and the profoundly moral overtone: for if Marie writes, under the head of 'My Experiences With Men,' that it is fun for beautful women to play with fire, one always discovers, before the essay ends, that the gentle reader is advised against it, if attractive, and patted on the back, if plain. Here, in a word, is journalism at its modern best: a 'news' subject, a dash of piquancy, but an anchor to windward, and a kind word for the also ran."

On October 29, 1925, she celebrated her fiftieth birthday at a party with all her children and most of the Greek royal family in attendance. "Since you tell me I'm already fifty," she laughed, "I won't make a liar of you. But it certainly will take a great amount of persuasion to make me feel that old!"

She marked the occasion with a syndicated piece called "Facing Fifty." After a few paragraphs advising women to combat age with a sense of humor, the article expressed her views on women's rights:

> I think the mistake the modern woman makes is that she wants to have it both ways. She adopts man's speech, his ways, his liberties, his looser morals. Yet when it suits her she will suddenly fall back on being a woman and want man to show her the deference to which she has really thrown away all right.
>
> Certainly modern life has liberated and is liberating woman from certain humiliations, from certain servitudes, and I am ungrudgingly with her in this. But she is going through a transient stage and she is not yet quite sure what foot she desires to stand on. She cannot be a man and must not try to be one, but she need no more be man's slave.

Marie wrote feverishly that fall. Yet try as she might, she couldn't obliterate the fact of Carol's growing affair with Madame Lupescu. As she rushed from pursuit to pursuit, gnawed by anxiety, she remembered Joe Boyle's words following Carol's annulment from Zizi Lambrino: "Your son has come around this time. But he'll stray again. He has a yellow streak that cannot be denied."

Meanwhile Helen watched helplessly as her marriage collapsed. Having won Carol without effort, she now had no idea of how to hold him. Raised by a mother whose concept of decorum and royal duty stretched back to Queen Victoria, Helen had been taught to live life by the rules. And according to royal code, when your husband strayed, you ignored it.

As the months passed, Helen, like Marie, took refuge in activity—adding Renaissance accessories to her Bucharest house, working to improve Romanian nursing techniques, playing with her baby son. And despite the criticism of members of the court, she leaned more than ever on her family. "What a relief it was to have my sister Irene staying with me," she wrote. "Suffering shared takes half the pain away. And a great comfort lay in the kindness and understanding shown by the people everywhere."

From Carol's parents to the man in the street, Romania stood behind Helen in her public embarrassment. Yet no Princess Party formed itself behind the wronged wife. Considering the country's relative political instability and the Romanians' penchant for taking sides, historians have wondered why. The answer lies with Helen herself. In this as in so many other critical decisions, she remained true to her parents. Her father had taught her that women should never mix in politics. And she never did.

By surrounding herself with powerful supporters, Helen might have assumed sufficient political strength to force Lupescu out of Carol's life. By asserting herself after Michael's birth, she might have charmed or bullied Carol into husbandly devotion before he strayed in the first place. But her character and training kept her from taking either course. As a result, nearly everyone felt sorry for her. And when she appeared dressed in her own regimental uniform and seated on horseback beside Marie at the May Tenth parade, the crowds gave her a rousing ovation. But no one stepped forward to help her. And she apparently did nothing to help herself.

There were even a few members of Bucharest society who took Carol's part. Citing his wife's fastidiousness, they spread rumors that she had rejected him physically.

By the fall of 1925 the tension at court had reached a fever pitch. With the Lupescu affair uppermost in her mind, Marie hoped desperately that a crisis could be averted. Finally, utilizing the same assault tactics she'd used to bring him around twice before, she confronted Carol. But the old methods no longer worked. She could no longer shame or inspire him to reform.

"My hand reached out to turn on the light," she wrote her "Faithful Four," American friends living in Constantinople. "But the contact was broken, the spark did not light. Aghast, I stood before the awful revelation—his mother's words reached him no more." The upward trend her life had taken for twelve years was unaccountably reversing.

In late October Carol and Helen appeared together for the last time. "It was at a flower show in Bucharest," recalled Marthe Bibesco. "They walked along looking at the huge chrysanthemums, the Princess as usual smiling graciously and finding a kind word for each of the exhibitors. Public opinion had been alarmed for some time by gossip about Carol. He was reported to have started some unworthy love affair. I could not believe this would be serious. The Crown Princess looked so lovely that autumn morning among the richly colored flowers. I still see the gentle courtesy with which she was handed into the carriage by her husband."

On November 20 the Dowager Queen Alexandra died at Sandringham. Relieved at this opportunity for a break in the tension, Ferdinand dispatched Carol to London and the funeral.

Aware that both Bratianu's government and the opposition party had lost patience with his latest affair, Carol at first refused to leave the country. When he finally gave in to pressure, however, his capitulation seemed complete. Queen Sophie traveled with him as far as Italy, and as their train rumbled westward, Carol played the dutiful son-in-law. A member of the suite cabled Helen in Bucharest that the Crown Prince was in a good mood and showed his mother-in-law "every politeness."

Twenty-four hours later, Elena Lupescu left Romania for Paris.

From November 27, the day of the funeral, until December 3, Carol's wife and parents heard nothing alarming from London. They were told that the Prince had acquitted himself with dignity at the state funeral. Admittedly, the British royal family treated him with marked coolness. But that was to be expected. Helen was a grandniece of Queen Alexandra, and the British King had always maintained affectionate ties with his Greek relatives. Also Carol's reputation had preceded him. The tabloids sandwiched news of the old Queen's death between lurid tales of Carol's liaison with the "Titian-haired Jewess."

Marie's first intimation that anything was wrong came from Ileana. Carol had visited her at Heathfield, where she was following Mignon at school, and promised to accompany her home for her Christmas holiday. But on the day he was to have stopped for her, Ileana heard he had inexplicably left for Paris.

Within hours, his family learned that Carol had moved to Elena

Lupescu's Paris hotel room. A week later the errant couple sailed for Milan.

The worst was yet to come. "All of a sudden, on the 21st of December," Marie wrote King George, "Sitta received a letter enclosing a letter for me, and two declarations to his father: one his demission from the army, the other a short and positive declaration that he does not mean to come back and an official renunciation as Crown Prince and member of the Royal Family, asking for a new name."

Ferdinand was furious, and in the frenzied hours that followed, he made a decision. Meanwhile Carol wavered in another letter to Helen. And spurred to action at last, she begged her father-in-law to send her to Milan. She hoped that by playing on his indecision she could convince him to return. Backed by Bratianu and Stirbey, the King refused.

"You are going through this for the first time," they told her. "For us it is the third time. He escaped the death sentence before only because of the Queen's intervention. Now, nobody must intervene."

"We can't afford a psychopath as our next ruler," declared Bratianu, "no matter what his intellectual accomplishments."

Nevertheless, emissaries, letters and wires followed Carol and Lupescu to Venice. Marie warned him of the consequences for himself and the country if he stayed away. The Court Marshal, General Angelescu, was dispatched with orders to bring the Prince back—without Lupescu.

Furious, Carol bellowed at the General: "I refuse both conditions."

"I must remind your Royal Highness that you hold a commission in the Romanian army and that I am your superior officer. I command you to come with me."

"I resign my commission as of this moment."

On December 28 Carol wrote a letter to Marie in which he renounced his rights to the throne.

"The decision is taken of my own free will. This I'm ready to swear on the Bible before God . . . I have thought a lot about what you told me and what you wrote me before leaving. I have often found life difficult to stand.

"I'm grieved by your sorrow, but will not change my mind. I'm young enough; I'll manage a life for myself. Hence, the best solution I can think of for avoiding a scandal is that one should find a way of declaring that I've been killed in a motor accident. Say I've drowned in the Lago Maggiore.

"As I'll be dead for many, let me be dead for everybody. I'll know how to disappear without leaving a trace." Without mentioning his father, his wife or his son, Carol ended with these words: "This renunciation is final."

Marie read the letter and collapsed with wild weeping. The court was at Sinaia, and she spent the whole day in her gold boudoir. She cried for the country, for Carol, for his wife and baby. But mostly she cried because she had reached a decision of her own. When she left her room at last, she agreed with Ferdinand: for the good of the country, they couldn't give him another chance.

Ferdinand called an emergency Crown Council, which accepted Carol's decision and approved a three-man regency to take over should Ferdinand die before Carol's four-year-old son Michael came of age. On December 31 a formal communiqué broke the news to the astonished Romanians.

Carol was gone. And by deciding not to fight for him, Marie had weakened the carefully nurtured popularity that had bound her to her people for nearly thirty years. Having anticipated Carol's desertion, the press tired of it the moment it became fact. Instead, headlines from Bucharest to Baltimore screamed that the Crown Prince was the helpless victim of a palace vendetta, that Marie had sacrificed her son to Stirbey's scheming, that Lupescu was in Bratianu's pay.

The royal family was horrified. To them, Carol's defection was so flagrant there could be no room for misinterpretation. But their very disgust and embarrassment, which had made them mask so many of his indiscretions in the past, now kept the man in the street from knowing the details. As a result, Marie especially was blamed for a drama she had been powerless to stop.

Bowed by the double tragedy of losing Carol and her people's confidence at once, she crawled through January 1926. But by February she felt emotionally healed enough to work through her feelings. They poured out in a letter to her "Faithful Four":

"The world, loving sensation and court scandal, invents . . . abominable stories of quarrel and intrigue. There have been no quarrels, ever, no political dissensions, no scenes, no hard words on either side— nothing. He has simply forsaken us because inside his flame had gone out, buried beneath the stifling evil of a woman with red hair who did but continue the destruction of her predecessor [Zizi Lambrino] . . .

"I have been hit almost beyond endurance, we all have, and by the hand that ought to have been our staff." Then with the optimism that had carried her through war, occupation and disaster, she added: "But my soul is invincible, that I feel by the way the inside of me has remained whole, unshaken even before the ugliest of accusations, broadcasted and sent to me to read in articles from the four corners of the earth: that I, the mother, had sacrificed my son to the intrigues of a favorite at court . . . .

"Nothing has been hidden from me. I know the ugliest tale, the foulest mud that has been thrown at me. And I feel like a deer when the hounds with flashing fangs gloat over what they consider his fall, perhaps even his end." For all that, she felt love couldn't die—neither hers for Carol nor her people's for her. "It is the spirit that counts, not the word. There may be more hate in the world than love. But love is strongest, and one day, even if I am not to live to see it, it must conquer."

18

The Woman Who Was Waited For

King Ferdinand was tired. Possessing neither Marie's resiliency nor Helen's youth, he took Carol's defection harder than either of them. His health, after a lifetime spent coping with a job he hated, was failing. A succession of minor ailments kept him in and out of bed until spring, and neither his annual Danube cruise nor a French cure in June restored his strength.

"Something is not quite right with Nando," Marie worried in family letters.

Fearful, as always, of causing a disturbance, he reassured her. "Nothing's wrong, my dear. Just a little weariness, that's all."

Both knew worry added to his health problems. Though the Queen waxed enthusiastic about the new heir, "tiny, sturdy" Michael, even she had to admit that "from sixty to four, the gap is very great."

In any case, she was emotionally incapable of brooding. Late summer found her and Ileana exploring monasteries and villages in Oltenia, Romania's mountainous western province. And in September she turned her mind to the one topic that could make her forget Ferdinand's illness and Carol's betrayal. It was that "great adventure," her trip to America.

Inspired by her war record, by the splash she'd made at the Peace Conference and by her recent column, thousands of Americans had written over the years inviting her to visit the United States. And she

longed to go. The country's size, comparative youth, physical beauty
and national character all attracted her. "Americans play a part in my
life," she wrote. "Their trusting simplicity fits in with my guileless-
ness."

On more than one occasion, especially in her friendships, her guile-
lessness proved her undoing. It's to her credit that more than any other
contemporary royal person she had hacked through stifling tradition,
etiquette and flattery to form relationships with commoners. "I must
confess Kings bore me," she wrote, turning the great force of her humor
and sympathy on a Pauline Astor, a Leila Milne, a Joe Boyle. But while
all three repaid her with long-term affection and support, many other
associations proved less fortunate. Indeed her childlike trust in others,
combined with an intensely loving and sympathetic nature, often
brought her to the verge of disaster. On her American tour, her idealism
and several friends' plans for advancing themselves at her expense
collided. And the collision didn't happen behind closed doors in a New
York hotel suite or even at a Long Island society affair. It took place
on a private train speeding over the frozen North American plain, and
20 million Americans read about it over their morning coffee.

Instrumental in getting Marie to America—and making innumerable
problems for her after she arrived—were her two oldest and closest
American friends, Loie Fuller and Sam Hill. A Syracuse, New York girl
who won international fame as an innovative theatrical dancer, Loie
first met Marie when her troup played Bucharest in 1902. She had
already enchanted Paris with her unconventional "Serpentine" and
"Butterfly" dances and her unique lighting techniques. Now, as the
young Marie had put it, she "rejoiced all my love of art."

Loie, seen backstage, bore no resemblance to the veil-fluttering on-
stage apparition or the whirling art nouveau creature adorning Orazi's
exquisite publicity posters. Madame Curie's daughter described her as
"an odd, badly dressed girl with a Kalmuck face innocent of makeup,
her eyes as blue as a baby's." But, like the Curies and Rodin before her,
Marie responded to the girl's waiflike quality and the obvious adoration
she brought to important personages.

When the two women became better acquainted, they discovered
they shared more than an emotional love of beauty. Both were sincere,
if idealistic, do-gooders. Bound by a prolific and intimate correspondence, their friendship grew over the years. When the war broke out
in 1914, Loie retired from her flagging career to inspire American

sympathy for the Allies. When Romania joined the war and the government retreated, she turned up at Jassy as a Red Cross nurse.

After the war Loie introduced Marie to another raving American eccentric, the Washington millionaire, globe-trotter, rancher, philanthropist and former gold miner, Sam Hill. A giant, aging sheepdog of a man with a cherubic face, a shock of white hair and a penchant for building ramshackle monuments to pipe dreams, Hill loved Marie on first sight. And, like Loie, he dramatically pledged his life to the Queen, a vow which brought her money for her charities, took him to Paris as her secretary in 1919 and inspired his Maryhill Museum of Fine Arts.

Hill had dedicated other monuments: to royalty, a Seattle palace for Belgian King Albert, which the King never saw; and to peace, a dilapidated stucco arch on the U.S.-Canadian border. But the Maryhill Museum, long in the planning and still unfinished, was dedicated to peace, Queen Marie and his dead wife Mary. He saw Marie's dedication of the building as the high point of his life. The Queen agreed to visit America for that purpose, and an ecstatic Loie whipped up a New York committee early in 1926 to help concoct an elaborate cross-country tour which would climax with the dedication.

In the face of train schedules, hotel rates and chamber of commerce demands, Loie's ideal trip soon evaporated. More realistic committee members took over. She pleaded, wept and threatened, but in vain. The Queen's visit would be an efficiently organized tour, declared men like railroad representative Colonel John Carroll.

While Marie watched sympathetically from Bucharest, her veil-fluttering friend collapsed in her Plaza Hotel suite, claiming illness, but pouring out her victimized feelings in twenty-page letters to Marie.

Meanwhile Romanians were puzzled by the Queen's enthusiasm for a trip that would transport her across the Atlantic when Ferdinand was obviously unwell. To be sure, the doctors had assured her he was in no danger. But he looked ghastly. Gossip also exaggerated "the dancer's influence" with Marie, an influence people considered undignified.

The political parties took opposing views. Bratianu's Liberals, temporarily out of power, were dead set against the trip. They feared exaggerated publicity and the Queen's "dangerous enthusiasms, which can be so easily misinterpreted."

But the People's Party leader, Prime Minister Alexander Averescu, agreed with Marie that her trip would mean good publicity for the country.

"She will put Romania on the map," announced Averescu.

"Yes, but how?" Bratianu snapped back.

While the politicians squabbled and Marie packed, the American press began searching for some ulterior motive in her visit. Some said she was going to obtain a badly-needed loan for Romania. Others thought Bratianu had an eye to making himself King, and that Marie was going to win powerful friends for the present dynasty.

Jealous that Marie had signed a contract to write her trip impressions for the North American Newspaper Alliance, rival syndicates began circulating even more damaging rumors: Marie would endorse commercial products for exorbitant prices; she was bringing Nicky and Ileana along to find millionaire mates; she and Loie planned to sell a movie they had coproduced.

One of the tragedies of Marie's life was that people constantly looked for underlying meanings in her simplest pronouncements. Invariably she said what she meant. In this case, she said she was visiting America to see the country, meet the people and put Romania on the map—and she meant it. That she was only partly successful in any of these goals was less her fault than the fault of those who exploited her for their own ends and of a press that enjoyed baiting her.

The United States in 1926 was a nation of innocents groping toward sophistication. As in the development of an individual, the country had reached the stage where self-realization temporarily depended on identifying with personalities who, for one reason of another, had risen above the mass. The result was a personality craze seldom matched in human experience.

Marie's October 13 departure from Cherbourg on the U.S. liner *Leviathan,* with Nicky and Ileana and a twenty-person retinue, followed the orgiastic ritual of Rudolph Valentino's funeral by a mere three months. The Prince of Wales had visited America two years before, leaving a string of broken hearts and society feuds in his wake. And Lindbergh's dramatic trans-Atlantic flight and attendant deification lay only seven months in the future. In other words, the time was right for Marie to receive her own share of the public adoration the American people were only too ready to shower her with.

The New York *World* analyzed her visit as extraordinary "because it brings together the world's first ultra-modern publicity machine and the world's first ultra-modern queen. When the modern publicity engine, which dotes on moving-picture-version queens, is actually confronted by a queen who, of her own accord, has become a moving-picture-version queen because she dotes on publics, the lid is off and almost anything can happen. Applesauce flows thick and fast."

In her NANA column Marie worried about her ability to handle American reporters. Charles Merz, in *The New Republic,* who had earlier written about Marie in Paris, worried about the reporters' ability to handle her.

Marie had begun her "Impressions" in Paris, where she stocked up on clothes for America. While there, she experienced the "terrible emotion" of a visit with Carol. After months spent openly indulging in Continental café society, he and Lupescu—whom the international press now insisted on calling Magda, after an Italian circus rider—had gone into seclusion in an unostentatious villa in the peaceful Paris suburb of Neuilly. There they lived surrounded by a motley assortment of opportunistic hangers-on who curried Carol's favor and further reduced his reputation.

On the *Leviathan* Marie prepared for America by refusing French soup and keeping her party "dry." She ate apple pie, baked beans, brown bread and corned beef hash. She described the Americans as "terribly sincere," "gloriously generous," and "marvellously efficient."

The *Leviathan* dropped anchor in New York harbor on Monday morning, October 18, and Manhattan exploded in the "most elaborate" reception in its history. Steamers in the harbor shrilled a welcome. Geysers erupted in the wake of bombarding fireboats. Guns bellowed a twenty-one-gun salute from Governors Island. Planes roared overhead. And Marie, dressed in a sable-trimmed maroon velvet coat and twinkling gold turban and carrying an armload of American Beauty roses, gave her first interview—to 150 rain-soaked reporters on the *Leviathan's* C deck.

Her answers, smoothly and quickly delivered, were punctuated with laughter. She hadn't seen much of New York, she said, and therefore couldn't judge it. No, the Jews were not mistreated in Romania. No, she would not star in a motion picture. Mostly, she hoped to see what the women of America were achieving. How many buckwheat cakes had she eaten for breakfast? One at a time, anyway.

As the tugboat *Macom*—crammed with a welcoming committee and more reporters and photographers—bore her toward the mist-shrouded Manhattan skyline, the Queen parried more questions. "Will you take Prince Carol back to Romania with you?"

"No," she shot back without changing expression, although this was the one question reporters had been asked to avoid. "I'm afraid not right away. He has made a great mistake in his life and must take his punishment like anyone else, prince or no prince. But I hope he will one day."

As the *Macom* drew nearer shore, individual skyscrapers began emerging from the fog. The sight elated Marie. She pronounced the effect "Egyptian," and "larger, darker, more imposing and sterner" than she had imagined. "But certainly not disappointing."

The rain held the street crowds to a smaller number than had turned out the previous August for Channel swimmer Gertrude Ederle. But bands played, 592 patrolmen held back thousands of cheering bystanders, and a cavalry brigade and thirty motorcycles with sirens screaming escorted Marie up Broadway through a ticker-tape blizzard to City Hall. "I was not prepared for the American custom of throwing papers of every size, shape and description," she told her readers. "The air seemed alive with fluttering wings, as though swarms of birds had been let loose in the streets."

But she loved it, and Manhattan apparently returned the sentiment.

On the front steps of City Hall, New York's handsome and youthful Irish mayor, James J. Walker, waited to offer her the key to the city. Marie and Walker hit it off immediately. During a brief indoor ceremony, he hesitated before pinning an honorary medal to her bodice.

"Proceed, Your Honor," said the Queen. "The risk is mine."

"And such a beautiful risk it is, Your Majesty," purred the Mayor.

While the enterprising crowd forced its way in at the windows for a glimpse of their Jimmie with the Queen, he officially welcomed her with such charm and sincerity that Marie's response "simply flowed from my heart."

Grover Whalen, official greeter for the city, pronounced her speech "a masterpiece. It was extemporaneous and I never heard anything better."

The praise for American women which ran through all Marie's public remarks appparently struck another responsive chord. No sooner had she left City Hall than hundreds of women who had heard her words blared outside over loudspeakers broke through the doors, filed into the reception hall and plumped themslves one after another into the thronelike chair she had occupied.

On the way to Penn Station, where the Romanians would entrain for Washington, D.C., the Queen's open car rolled past a half-finished skyscraper. "Hey, Jimmie," an ironworker bawled down to Walker, riding beside the Queen, "you made her yet?"

The Mayor turned scarlet, but Marie saved the day: "Tell him yes!" She fared less well with President Coolidge. Communication was part of the problem. The dour Vermonter's refusal to go out of his way for royalty was the rest of it.

Although the Romanians arrived in Washington at dusk Monday and were greeted by Secretary of State Frank Kellogg, blaring trumpets, popping flashbulbs and warm rush-hour crowds, Coolidge waited to receive the Queen and her children until Tuesday afternoon. By the time they finally arrived at the White House, the royal trio had crowded Arlington, Mount Vernon, the Washington Monument and the Lincoln Memorial into their trip's second day. And the air at 2700 Pennsylvania Avenue was already thick.

Coolidge's aides, it seemed, were piqued that Marie had acknowledged Grace Coolidge's welcoming flowers with a note written by her lady-in-waiting. Once at the White House, it was the Romanians' turn to boil. It was bad enough that Coolidge made the Queen first come to him, instead of attending her at her temporary residence at the Romanian Legation. Now they were thunderstruck to realize that the President wouldn't even greet her at the door. Instead, seven aides— "I never saw so many in my life," recalled Princess Ileana—escorted Marie to the Blue Room, where the Coolidges awaited her. Nicolas and Ileana were deposited in the Green Room: "We looked at each other in astonishment."

The scene in the Red Room, where the Coolidges took the Queen for a short conversation, resembled Marie's first meeting with the Wilsons. Again a President's entourage resented her breezy discarding of rigid protocol.

Marie told her side of what happened next: "According to the somewhat absurd custom, hardly were we back to our own legation, than the President and his wife drove up to the door to pay back our call. This visit, however, ended upon a humorous note. The never-to-be-avoided photographer—that tyrant against which neither King nor President can stand up—claimed his rights. The President, who had already put on his hat and coat, took them off again and patiently sat down with a resigned face between Mrs. Coolidge and myself and submitted to the camera."

The President may have been resigned. He was also furious. Much of the government's discomfort over the impending royal tour had originated with him. Worried to the point of paranoia that some of Marie's publicity might engulf him too, Coolidge had notified the

Romanian chargé d'affaires that he wanted no photographers recording his legation visit. As far as the legation was concerned, the effect of their Queen's stay would be diluted by half without photographs proving she had received the President. When Marie admitted a crowd of lurking photographers, Coolidge hid his rage, but exploded the next morning when photographs showing him seated beside Marie swept the country.

But by then it was too late for him to retaliate. The official reception had limped to its conclusion with Tuesday evening's White House banquet. Competition for invitations to this elaborate affair was so heated that the guest list wasn't printed until after the party. And the crowds jamming Pennsylvania Avenue were so huge that the White House gates were kept locked to all but the royal cars for fear of a major traffic tie-up.

At the White House Marie walked straight into what the Europeans considered another insult. Once again protocol did not allow the President to receive his guests at the front door, but had him enter the Blue Room after all the guests were assembled. At dinner Marie fought with the President's celebrated reserve—and lost.

After dinner and a stiff little gathering in the East Room, the royal party was hustled out the door at 9:45, exactly an hour and forty-five minutes after their arrival. When they arrived back at the legation, Marie's entourage exploded. The Coolidges had kept them waiting before dinner and rushed them out after.

Predictably, Marie was amused rather than offended. "No offense was meant. Why should I be offended? Besides, they just don't have the same kind of manners we have."

But the real problems were yet to come.

The Queen was up at six the morning after the banquet and out of the legation by nine. She left with relief. The official part of her trip was over. Ahead lay a two-month train tour that would carry her across Canada and the northern United States to Seattle and back through the Rockies and the midwestern and southern states to Florida. She would see the country's scenic delights and get to know its pleasant, open people. So went the dream.

Meanwhile incredible events crowded the five intervening days. An Annapolis review held in the rain soaked the cadets and worsened a head cold Marie had contracted, but Academy Commander Admiral Nultin believed it had been "worth the trouble." Baltimore gave her a "colossal" reception composed of yelling mobs, flower-scattering cherubs, an absurdly elaborate luncheon and an official welcome complete with endless speeches, baskets of flowers, gifts and scrolls of honor.

Wednesday night the prominent corporation lawyer William Nelson Cromwell, an aging admirer who had founded the Society of Friends of Romania in her honor, invited seven hundred prominent New Yorkers in to view Her Majesty at a Ritz-Carlton reception. It took thirteen motorcycle police to clear her way through the cheering throngs that crowded the streets between her hotel, the Ambassador, and the Ritz-Carlton. Another battalion held back the crowds at the door. Inside, she sat on a throne while all seven hundred guests filed past. Some knelt, some bowed, but all shook hands—an American custom she found "almost as fatiguing as I had been told it was." She enjoyed chatting with General Pershing, John Drew, the actor, and Edwin Markham, the poet.

In the morning, though her cold was so bad she could hardly talk, she left the Ambassador early for the New York Public Library. Here crowds scrambled over the lions for a peep at her, and later she sat down to lunch with the City's Chamber of Commerce. It was the first time a woman had been so honored in the Chamber's 158-year history. She ended her speech with the hope that they would let her tell Romania "how I have been able to make you love my country through me." At any rate, the Chamber assured her, the visit would lead to closer industrial and financial ties between the two countries.

Philadelphia claimed the afternoon and evening. She felt sick and weary on the train, but perked up at the sight of ten thousand cheering people crowding Reading Station and a mounted escort in Revolutionary costume waiting to conduct her to City Hall. The city's Romanian colony went mad at the sight of the "beloved Queen," and she upset the city's schedule and wrote headlines with her decision to slip away for a few moments of prayer in the little Orthodox church. She met Red Cross and YWCA representatives before dinner and Philadelphia social leaders after. She visited the city's "folly," the Sesquicentennial Exhibition, and watched Louie Fuller's dance pupils perform. She fell into bed exhausted at one A.M. and woke at seven to still more hoopla.

The Liberal Party's worst fears were being realized as a nation's attention riveted on the Ambassador Hotel, where Marie's party had taken over the entire fourth floor. In a welter of bouquets, presents, telegrams, jewels and clothes, the Queen wrote her column and kept her diary, signed photographs, answered letters, read petitions and wrote thank-you notes. (One, for a hat, was picked up by the manufacturer and run without her knowledge as an advertising endorsement.) The suite was crammed with people—policemen, detectives, diplomats, maids, ladies-in-waiting, delivery boys—all shouting over the loud barking of Marie's black cocker Craigi.

She loved the wild acclaim. But the extravagant publicity was getting out of hand. Though she loved Americans, she couldn't understand them. Never subtle, she failed to make the crucial observation that though they hounded their celebrities for every detail of their private lives, they perversely wanted the objects of their adoration to coyly retain an air of mystery. If a little public relations had served her well in Paris and London, she thought more publicity would serve her that much better in America. Her name became a household word as her "Impressions," signed with her bold black signature, appeared one after another, and she added radio speeches to the press's already major coverage of everything she wore, ate and said.

Even Prime Minister Averescu threw up his hands in horror when he learned she had given her readers this juicy morsel: "Often I have been obliged to put a screen before my bath, so as to be able to continue talking to people during my ablutions."

But the tour's real problems were created by people around her. Her value as a social prize had made her the center of petty intrigues long before she arrived. New York hostesses fought and bled over her presence at their parties. Nor was friend Loie Fuller above milking a nice profit from the royal visit. With her knack for placing faith where it didn't belong, the Queen had promised to sponsor Loie's dance troupe in several more performances. The one held at the Metropolitan Opera House on October 24 was to be the season's number one social event. Unknown to the Queen, exorbitant prices were to be charged: $1,000 to $5,000 per single box. While she staggered through New York crowds, interminable luncheons and opulent receptions, Loie published a list of wealthy and prominent patrons of the ballet without their consent. As a result, many of the so-called backers publicly withdrew their support, and the story assumed scandal proportions when word leaked out that Loie was to receive half the proceeds.

With rumor piling on rumor and late-night editions printing as truth the fable that Ferdinand had cabled her to return home immediately because of "scornful criticisms," Marie stepped on board her special train, the *Royal Romanian,* at half past midnight following the Met performance. After a restful night's sleep away from the Ambassador's mayhem, the party rolled out of New York at 7:50 A.M. on October 25. The cross-continent tour had begun.

What Marie needed at this point was a competent manager to guide her away from the exploiters and toward the real cream of American society. What she got was official host Colonel John H. Carroll and tour coordinator Ira Nelson Morris. Major Stanley Washburn would act as her spokesman and personal aide. A pompous, self-satisfied man, Carroll represented the nation's railroads and therefore symbolized the free passage the railroads were providing Marie "as a courtesy to a woman who placed her country on the side of the Allies long before America entered the war." Formerly United States Ambassador to Sweden, Morris was Romanian Consul General. Washburn, a former *Times* reporter and old war friend, had suffered shell shock, and some said he drank. Whatever their personal quirks, none of the three possessed the personality or the training necessary to effectively cope with the press, Marie's naïveté, and the eighty-five individuals who were crowded into the *Royal Romanian*'s sleek and luxurious cars for the ten-thousand-mile trip.

At least the good temporarily outweighed the bad as the train started north. West Point in a downpour reminded Marie of Windsor. Albany, Utica, Syracuse and Buffalo each turned out their ten thousand to cheer and give gifts. Niagara Falls offered a grisly choice: eat the elaborate Chamber of Commerce breakfast or see the falls. Beauty overcame moral obligation, as Marie grabbed a few bites and dashed to the observation platform.

Tension and adverse publicity were momentarily forgotten as the train moved into Canada. Here the trip adopted a sentimental tone. The Union Jack, which always filled the Queen with emotion, fluttered everywhere. Everyone mentioned Queen Victoria and seemed to love Marie for her grandmother's sake. Toronto. Talks with Joe Boyle's brother David and the brothers' good friend, Mr. Nesbit, eased the still-sharp pain for Joe's death. The French Canadians hailed her in Montreal. And dinner at Government House in Ottawa was served with such English order and precision that Marie and Ileana "allowed ourselves to be funny, a sort of moral relaxation between our good behavior." There was also a reception for seven hundred at Parliament Building, but no one shook hands. "A vast relief."

On October 29 she "awoke to the disagreeable truth that I was fifty-one. I thought of home and all those who generally celebrated this day with me. Husband, children, court and servants. Even the dogs are decorated with flaring ribbons and come to present their wishes."

The lump of homesickness grew as she read Ferdinand's cable: "Send you loving birthday wishes and greetings from Sinaia, which is white with snow. Have had some days perfect rest. Feeling so well that I am going downtown Sunday. We are extremely interested in the news from your journey, and I am utterly pleased at your success. I hope your cold is gone. Don't overtire yourself. Fondest love to all."

Papers printed the cable verbatim alongside headlines announcing his imminent demise. But Marie left all anxiety behind as the train rolled for two days through snow-covered plains dotted with frozen lakes, log trappers' cabins and Hudson Bay Company depots backed with distant pine forests. With Craigi a black ball asleep on the foot of her bed, she luxuriated in the unaccustomed solitude.

Meanwhile the pressure of eighty-five people boxed up together on one train, no matter how palatial, began erupting in petty bickering. Besides the Romanian suite and the American officials, the train carried reporters, photographers, hairdressers, trained nurses, railroad representatives, stewards, cooks and servants. All revolved around Marie, all vied constantly for her attention. But the major pressure involved the three Americans nearest the Queen—Carroll, Washburn and Morris. Three-way intrigues, jealousies and pent-up emotions contracted during the harrowing New York days exploded as each jealously guarded his own position and closeness to the Queen.

The pressure temporarily evaporated in the face of her undisputed personal success. As they traveled west, she proceeded from triumph to triumph like a conquering Roman general. Ten thousand Canadians of every age and station filed before her in Winnipeg's Parliament House. St. Paul and Minneapolis battled over whether gentlemen receiving her should wear top hats, but made up for it with a touchingly warm reception, a cozy private party at Sam Hill's brother's home and a delightful snowstorm.

North Dakota was better yet. Having expressed the desire to personally meet some farmers, Marie picked up two farm couples—complete with children and dogs—at Fargo, chatted with them until Valley City and there picked up two more. The guests changed at almost hourly intervals all the way to Medora. Dressed in colorful Romanian peasant attire, she received them on the icy rear platform while local townspeople gaped in amazement.

These visits were among the most meaningful of her entire trip. She talked crops, weather and machinery with the men, discussed jam-making and babies with their wives. Once she entered the car during a sharp turn and landed unceremoniously in the lap of a Bismarck farmer named Sperry. "That certainly was an informal reception!" laughed the Queen.

At Mandan a ceremonial Sioux Indian party greeted her with tom-toms and dancing. In a dramatic prairie setting framed with sage, arroyo and tumbleweed, Red Tomahawk, the aging Chief who had killed Sitting Bull, extended her the right hand of fellowship. In Sioux he explained that Queen Marie was a war woman because she stood at the head of a nation and because she had made sacrifices during the great war. He said her war work had endeared her to the people of the prairies, that they saw in her a comrade of the war trail. Therefore he was presenting her with the honorable badge of bravery, the headdress.

Then, wearing pearls that had belonged to Catherine the Great, she knelt on a white buffalo robe while the Chief placed a war bonnet on her head and the tribe adopted her as *Winyan Kipanki Wim* (The Woman Who Was Waited For). It was the high point of her trip. With tears in her eyes she turned to her son and whispered, "Nicky, never forget this, for it is so sincere and so wonderful."

The train finally reached Spokane on Monday, November 2, and Sam Hill and Loie Fuller came on board. They were inseparable, but a more incongruous pair could hardly be imagined. Her dance career a dim memory, Loie was now "little and dumpy," wrote reporter Harold Denney. "She shrouds herself in flowing draperies and her moist eyes look odd through horn-rimmed spectacles."

Hill, with his huge bulk, Santa Claus face, twinkling blue eyes and curiously soft voice, was in his own way equally melodramatic. He arrived at the formal Spokane reception dressed in a tweed suit and carrying a cowboy hat.

Reporters, who had blamed Marie for the ballet fiasco and challenged her acceptance of a free ride around the country, now sniggered openly at Hill's museum. Lying nine miles from a railroad or major highway and a hundred miles from a town of any size, the building stood unfinished and empty. There were no doors or windows, the stucco walls were cracking, and a road ran straight through the ground floor.

Reporters who had traveled with Marie from New York, knew her personally and liked her, had hoped something would happen to keep her away from the place. They agreed the dedication of such an atrocity could only make her tour look ridiculous and tarnish her personal image still further.

The scene at the ceremony was predictable: Marie sat on a draped platform in the barnlike hall, while local officials issued interminable speeches of incredible banality, and her friends cringed. Finally her turn came, and she stepped to the podium.

Marie of Romania's speeches were always effective, but now she gave one of the best of her life. In a few impassioned words she defended her loyalty to her two old friends—Samuel Hill and Loie Fuller—and her right to dedicate "this curious and interesting building." She said loyalty to friends had always been her code and that these two had stood by her and her country when both most needed friends. Asserting that "some have wondered at the friendship of a Queen for a woman whom some would call 'lowly,' " Marie added: "In this democracy there should be no gap between the high and the lowly."

In a voice ringing with sincerity, she said that Maryhill represented a great ideal both she and her friend Mr. Hill stood for: the ideal of beauty. She hoped that after she was gone, this ideal could live on, and that the finished project would bring joy to many. "Mr. Hill," she finished, extending her hand dramatically, "I would like very much to shake your hand."

She sat down to round after round of frantic applause, and there was hardly a dry eye in the hall. Wrote Harold Denney: "It is doubtful if any American public official could have the wit and courage to seize a disaster as she did and turn it into a triumph."

The triumph was short-lived. Back in Spokane, the unpredictable Mr. Hill took a sudden violent dislike to Major Washburn. Within hours Hill had threatened Washburn with a gun. At a Portland horse show, he shouted that if Washburn didn't stand aside and let him take over as the Queen's aide he would "crush" the younger man.

Tiny Washburn, cowering beside the Queen while the ferocious Hill loomed over him, took the threat seriously. He scurried back to the train and barricaded himself in his compartment.

By morning the quarrel was front-page news, and Colonel Carroll had come to Washburn's defense. The Colonel informed the press that the Queen's favor had obviously turned Hill's head and deprived him of his reason. Meanwhile Loie stoutly defended Hill. As the embattled train clattered toward Vancouver, officials there were kept waiting for confirmation of the Queen's arrival while the rival factions fought for control of Her Majesty's itinerary.

In Vancouver Washburn skittered off the train ahead of Hill and took the seat beside Marie in the open car provided for her. At that, Hill grabbed the Major by the collar and, while all Vancouver watched, lifted him out bodily and took the treasured seat himself.

Marie ignored the fracas as long as possible. "I simply did not see," she told Ileana later. But by the time the fractured party returned to Seattle, even the Queen knew that one side must quit the train. It couldn't be Carroll; his railroads were paying for the trip. And Washburn had fortuitously allied himwelf with the Colonel. Sadly, Marie informed Hill he must stay in Seattle rather than make the trip back east as planned.

Hill left the train, but all battles hadn't ended. As the party headed into the Rockies, the papers reported that Marie's Romanian aides had taken up where Hill had left off and were hotly contesting Washburn's position. Meanwhile Colonel Carroll attacked Loie Fuller's press agent for her "divisive intrigues" in a verbal fray which threw the woman into a "nervous collapse." The agent retired to her compartment under the care of Marie's nurse, and Loie, sensitive to her aide's distress and upset over Hill's expulsion, suffered a collapse of her own. Carroll announced he wasn't feeling so well himself, but added: "I'll get Her Majesty safely back to Washington if I have to throw a dozen people off this train."

"Maybe the train should be supplied with more exits," quipped a reporter.

Ahead lay Denver and peace. At Carroll's command, Loie and her agent left the train, following a dramatic farewell scene with the Queen in which both Marie and Loie wept copiously.

Denver gave Marie the warmest greeting of the trip. When she rose to speak at a reception, a crowd of thirteen thousand rose as one and cheered her to the rafters. The Romanian colors draped the streets, and the Governor announced that the state legislature had named a mountain after her.

The day was filled with amusing touches. At the auditorium a ninety-five-year-old woman took Marie's hand and told her she'd seen her and Ferdinand leave Schloss Sigmaringen on the day of their wedding. Outside, a six-year-old boy cried: "Hey, Queen! Where's the King?"

And at lunch Senator Henry Wolcott Toll agreed to edit the next fairy tale she published, and Craigi mistook the rear leg of the grand piano for a fire hydrant.

They moved east in a blaze of glory. Kansas City, St. Louis, Springfield, Chicago.

The blow fell in Indianapolis. She was already worried about Ileana, bed-ridden following a minor car accident, when word came from home. Ferdinand had cancer. The doctors gave him only a short time to live.

That night, at a festive banquet in her honor, she spoke to an unsuspecting group of Columbia Club members:

"It is with a heavy heart that I speak to you tonight. I have just received news that the King is not well, and I am extremely anxious. Duty often points to a different direction than pleasure, and I have duties that compel me to leave for Romania at once." Her voice broke. "It is difficult for me to say good-by, but I only hope that you will have kind and affectionate remembrances of me in America when I have gone from your shores."

The rest of the trip passed in a blur of anxiety. The press had a heyday inventing endless various reasons for why she was leaving early. And cutting the tour short meant foregoing the South, which she had most wanted to see. But she stuck to her decision. On November 24, after three hectic days in New York, the Romanian party sailed for France.

The adverse publicity persisted to the end. The day before she left, Marie broadcasted a farewell message to the American people. For the last time, she refuted the insinuation that she had come to collect money for Romania. Her words formed a wistful plea to the millions who, ignoring the papers, had opened their hearts to her.

"When I am gone," she said, "don't let anything tarnish that remembrance that you have of me. I did not come on business. I did not come for the sake of politics. I came for nothing but just to make friends with you."

Marie of Romania spent seven weeks and two days in America. She traveled 8,750 miles. Roughly six million Americans saw her in person, while millions more heard her voice on numerous broadcasts and followed her daily activities in the papers.

When she sailed home, she left behind piles of newspaper clippings to molder in public libraries all over the country. She left Robert Sherwood's thinly-disguised theatrical spoof of her trip, *The Queen's*

Husband. She left a commemorative plaque at Cartier's on Fifth Avenue, warm memories in thousands who still remember their first and last glimpse of a "real live" queen, and unfortunate tinges of ridicule and scandal which the American press had attached to her name then and would recall at every remaining crisis in her life.

PART THREE

19

Romance, Tragedy and a Boy King

America had seen her, Marie reflected sadly on the trip home, but she had not seen America. Even more disturbing were continued assaults by the press and news from England that King George in particular was disturbed by all the adverse publicity.

"I am sorry that my visit to America raised such unkind criticism," she wrote him. "I did what I thought right for my country. You in your beautiful old traditions cannot fairly judge. I have *had* to become a fighter. My life has been one long struggle. I had, so to say, to take my life in my hand and go forward as I thought best. I am not a conventional queen, I admit. I must often make your dear old royal blood curdle, but my heart is in the right place, Georgie dear. . . . Give me a kindly thought, I ask no more."

She arrived back in Paris to even more unsettling rumors. Ferdinand had only hours to live; he was already dead. He had abdicated and proclaimed Michael king; the National Peasant Party and the army were organizing a coup to restore Carol. Marie brushed these aside, but she couldn't ignore the Paris whisperings—that Carol planned to return and that Lupescu had promised to give him up if the government would reinstate him.

At Prime Minister Averescu's urging, Marie refused Carol's pleas to see him and rushed home. At Bucharest she and the children found Ferdinand alive but dying. The change that had occurred in him in less

214   MARIE OF ROMANIA

than two months was chilling. In constant pain from blood poisoning
resulting from a cancerous large intestine, the King maintained a cheerful front and insisted on attending family meals. But he looked old and
haggard. Dressed in a loose robe and slippers, he shuffled painfully
through the mountains of luggage crowding the Cotroceni halls.

Politically, truth was worse than rumor. Averescu's government was
verging on collapse. Russia on the east and Hungary on the west were
poised waiting for a political upheaval shattering enough to let them
snap back their lost territories. Faced with Ferdinand's approaching
death, certain factions urged Carol's return. An adult ruler, whatever
his character, they argued, was preferable to a boy king dominated by
a three-headed regency.

Panic-stricken, on December 14 Marie wrote her sister Bee's husband, the vacationing Infante Alfonso, begging him to talk to Carol in
Paris. Her penciled scrawl, covering eight large pages, aptly conveys
her agitation. Torn between her duty to the country and her "mother
love," she admitted Carol's return might work, but only if he could first
be rehabilitated. She wrote:

"There is not the smallest little hope for his coming back before he
has purged himself of all that atmosphere of sin and degradation he is
living in, and has showed us twice over this is the sort of world he *likes*
living in . . .

"I do not want to leave him without a shred of hope . . . Tell him
I send you to him because I am in utter despair about him and want
to help him at least to become a man again, someone who can enter a
clean house and look an honest man in the face.

"Perhaps later you will come here and tell us what you were able to
do with him. It needs a man of his own class to make him realise what
the world thinks of him. And because you are the dear clean creature
I know you are, you will perhaps be able to find something by which
he can be pulled out of the mire in which he is drowning."

Unknown to Marie, the Infante and Carol were engaged in a heated
discussion in Alfonso's hotel suite the very afternoon she wrote.
Though neither man raised his voice, both used "very plain and not
nice-sounding words," Alfonso later told Marie.

Handsome, witty, cultured and athletic, Alfonso was Marie's favorite
brother-in-law and her children's favorite uncle. Though morally irre-
proachable himself, he came from a family of rakes. Both his father and
his first cousin, Spanish King Alfonso XIII, were legendary rovers. And
his mother had dressed her children when small according to the na-

tionality of her current lover. Therefore he brought insight based on personal experience to his meeting with Carol—a meeting which he hoped, even without Marie's letter for inspiration, would set the Prince thinking about the obligations he'd so blatantly shirked.

Alfonso began by asking Carol if he had any desire to give up his present life and go back to Romania.

"Yes, I would like to go back," replied Carol. "I know, I feel I could do good work, even though when I went away I was fed up with everything. But I would only go back on certain conditions and if I felt these conditions would be kept."

"My dear Carol," cried the Infante, "I fear you completely misunderstand your position. It's not you who can ask for conditions, but your father and mother, your King and Queen, who will put forward conditions under which perhaps they might soften their hearts and let you return. Let me tell you this: there is not one person in a royal family, not one person who has monarchical principles who does not look with horror and sadness at the harm you have done monarchy in general, and who does not look upon your present life with anger and contempt."

Then he asked Carol about Lupescu. Was he sure what he felt for her was real love?

"Yes," answered Carol. "I have lived close to her long enough to know how good she is and how devoted to me. All these stories they invent about her renouncing her rights are inventions of the press. She has never mixed up in political things and has never tried to do what I'm accused of—forming a party to force my way back. I would never do anything political against Papa and Mamma, even though there are people around them who work against me."

Back home in Madrid, Alfonso repeated the conversation in a letter to Marie, adding: "I tried to see if he has any more tender feelings toward you and Nando or toward his child. He *has,* but he is so used to his present life he cannot see the connection between leaving it and affection for you, duty to his caste, faithfulness to his King or love of his country. He does not see it is frightfully wrong. He might be doing something unconventional such as wearing a soft hat with a frock coat."

Meanwhile Ferdinand's condition deteriorated. He had endured a series of intestinal operations in December which inserted a silver tube in his lower intestine and removed the blood poisoning. A respite from pain was followed by a flu attack around the first of April. His doctors gave him up for dead, and the Catholic Church, having finally forgiven him for raising his children Orthodox, administered the last rites on April 6. By May, however, he had recovered sufficiently to move to his whitewashed vacation villa at Scroviste.

Here, on a large covered veranda overlooking an iris-bordered lake, he played solitaire, listened to music and read the newspapers. With the same patient resignation that had bent his will to old Carol's and sent him to war against his homeland, he endured coughing fits and renewed pain.

Even when his condition again worsened, preventing him from sleeping or taking nourishment to bolster his ebbing strength, he never complained. He also never acknowledged that death might be near or once mentioned Carol's name. Characteristically, he put his faith in Marie. He knew that whatever happened, she would carry on. Usually restless and overbusy, she now spent every waking hour sitting quietly beside her husband, entertaining him and boosting his flagging morale with her own unquenchable zest.

"All is tragedy in my life," she wrote Loie Fuller, "but deep within me, my faith and hope are still green. There is an invincible something which I am built upon which cannot, will not despair."

The last great political upheaval of Ferdinand's turbulent reign occurred while he lay helpless at Scroviste. A fervent admirer of Mussolini, Premier Averescu tried to bluff the King into accepting a military dictatorship patterned after *Il Duce*'s. But Averescu had underestimated Ferdinand's flagging powers. When word reached Scroviste that regiments were already slipping into Bucharest, the king summarily dismissed Averescu and appointed Barbu Stirbey Premier.

Ferdinand had neatly side-stepped the peril. But his solution astonished the country and worried Marie. Whatever the ties that had bound her and Barbu for twenty years, she knew he was not cut out for militant politics. And by placing him in a public position, Ferdinand let the cap off every insidious rumor that had plagued them through the years. Still enduring her own first bout of unpopularity, she knew Stirbey's appointment would only further inflame Carol's supporters.

With more subtlety than she was feeling, she convinced Ferdinand that she knew he felt more secure with their old friend at the helm. "But," she added, "we need a stronger solution at this time of national emergency."

That solution, kept waiting in the wings those last sixteen months, was Ion Bratianu. Battle-scarred but game, the old dictator assumed his eleventh premiership with an international image tainted by the Liberal Party's reputation for corruption and exploitation. But at home he relied successfully on the always-popular Ferdinand's friendship and his own political stance as "guardian of the principles of Romanianism, defender of the national interest, and promoter of prosperity."

Bratianu was sixty-three. His heavy thatch of hair and elegant vandyke beard and mustache had turned white. But he remained trim and erect, moved quickly and purposefully, and sparred with his old antagonists, western journalists, with as much enthusiasm as he still gave his extramarital affairs. Asked to explain his political philosophy, he told a *Time* magazine reporter, "I try to put off until tomorrow the mistakes which people tell me I ought to make today."

A week after Bratianu's appointment, on July 18, Ferdinand died at Sinaia of pneumonia contracted from the mountain air. He had spent his last weeks sitting under a tent erected on the Pelisor's sweeping lawns, gazing at his beloved flowers, forest and mountains. When he could no longer leave his bed, he lay patiently, holding Marie's hand and listening to the rushing waterfall outside the open window.

Ferdinand died as unassumingly as he'd lived. "I am sure he must have been glad to strip off his suffering body," wrote Marie. " 'I am so tired,' were his last words, and when he lay so quiet in my arms about an hour later, I knew that I must thank God for him at least. This was rest indeed."

They moved him to Cotroceni, where he lay in state in Marie's dramatic new white drawing room. "As he rested there upon his pall of old crimson and gold velvet surrounded with red flowers which I laid beside him myself, he had a wonderful expression of peace and contentment. Never had he been so handsome. Now that he was quite still, his fine features stood out in statuesque repose, and all suffering was wiped from his face."

The morning after his grandfather's death, the new King, six-year-old Michael, was proclaimed in an impressive ceremony in Parliament. His black-veiled mother wept, but the boy watched solemnly while the three regents—his uncle Nicky, the Patriarch Miron Cristea and Chief Justice George Buzdugan—were sworn in. A sturdy, poker-faced child dressed in white shorts and shirt, he caught the international reporters' imagination. Their bulletins ascribed endless witticisms to the little King. "I knew he was only a typical little boy," his mother explained, "diverted as much by the plaster protecting a cut on his knee as by the ceremony, the plaudits of the crowds, or the explosions of the guns proclaiming his accession."

Closer to her husband during his last months than at any other time in their thirty-four years together, Marie was unprepared for the overwhelming loss she felt at his death. The day of the funeral, July 24, was agonizing. She nearly fainted after kissing him before the coffin was closed. And particularly heart-rending was the sight of Princess Helen lifting Michael so he could embrace his grandfather for the last time.

After a service in the Cotroceni chapel, the late King's body was carried on a horse-drawn gun carriage to Bucharest's North Station. On the coffin, covered by the Romanian colors, lay his Cavalry General's hat and sword, the steel cross and the royal scepter. Bratianu and other high political officials flanked the bier. Prince Nicolas, King Alexander of Yugoslavia and numerous male relatives walked behind the coffin, while King Michael and the royal ladies rode in carriages. Ferdinand's white charger, riderless and black-draped, the international ambassadors and Romanian political, civil and military officials completed the cortege. As the procession wound its way through the heart of Bucharest, thousands of mournful Romanians lined the streets in reverent homage. Every building was draped in flags, peasant rugs or black mourning. Great funeral urns, mounted high above the crowds, smoked incense. Church bells tolled, bands played the royal hymn and low-flying airplanes dropped flowers along the route.

Despite the pageantry, Romania mourned not a remote symbol but their beloved "emancipator" and friend, Ferdinand the Good, King of the Peasants. In the thousands, peasants crowded the 150-mile train route across the sunbaked Wallachian plain to Curtea de Arges. Some held torches, others threw flowers. All knelt as the train passed. At times whole groups fell prostrate, making the sign of the cross.

At Curtea de Arges, where a military escort waited to carry the King to his grave, the gun carriage moved through streets packed with delegations from all twelve thousand Romanian towns and villages. A thousand priests, their embroidered robes and swinging censers shining in the sunlight, marched behind the coffin. On the cathedral's front steps, their deep mourning slashed by the blue sash of the Order of the Crown, waited the three Queens—Marie, Lisabetta and Mignon—and Princesses Helen and Ileana. More peasants, many kneeling, surrounded the church on all sides.

After a short service on the steps, the military escort lifted the coffin and began carrying it into the cathedral. Suddenly Prince Nicolas, his face twisted with emotion, rushed forward and placed his shoulder under a corner of the coffin, helping lift it through the door. At that moment the embroidered mantle covering the bier slid off and covered him completely. The incident made an instant and ominous impression on the superstitious peasants. Row after row, back to the trees edging the cathedral clearing, they crossed themselves in a motion resembling autumn breezes dancing over a wheat field.

Within six months the portent bore virulent fruit. At three A.M. on November 24, a jangling telephone woke Marie to the news that Bratianu was dying. She rushed to his bedside along with the regents, the cabinet and Princess Helen. In a room warmed by a large tile stove, Bratianu was battling with a sudden throat infection that rendered him speechless and sent blood poisoning pounding through his body.

As Marie approached her old ally, she asked in French, "Do you feel better?"

Tears burning his eyes, Bratianu made a supreme effort. "Yes, Your Majesty," he whispered. "How good and gracious it is of you to come here at such an hour."

Bratianu died at 6:45 that morning, without resigning the Premiership. Five minutes later the Finance Minister, Bratianu's brother Vintila, presented the cabinet's resignation to the Regency, which immediately asked him to assume the Premiership. He accepted, and Romania had its third Bratianu Prime Minister. But Vintila, though more liberal than his dead brother, lacked the old tyrant's dominating personality. And the Liberal Party, with its traditional leader dead and its enemies growing hourly more venomous, needed stronger leadership than ever before.

Like his King before him, in death Ion Bratianu belonged to the peasants. Six white oxen drew his rough pine coffin on a peasant cart over the snow-covered hills of Florica, his country estate. Ten thousand peasants lined the way, clasping crosses, bottles filled with holy water and candles that flickered against scudding black clouds.

But the village priests who buried him buried an era in Romanian history and the only man strong enough to crush rising political and regional conflicts.

Marie was wise enough to realize this. "I am not ashamed of the tears I shed," she told an A.P. reporter at the funeral. "I feel it right to weep for him, as ever in the hours of gravest danger I never wavered from my belief of what he meant for Romania. The Almighty has called him away at an hour when we all needed him most. We can but bow our heads."

On May 6, 1928, fate dealt her an even sharper blow. Word arrived from England that Carol, who had been lying low since his father's death, had attempted a coup. Organized by British newspaper magnate Lord Rothermere and financed by a Romanian expatriate millionaire, Barbu Jonescu, the plot had been a simple one. Two planes would fly from Godstone airport in Surrey to a huge anti-Liberal political rally at Alba Julia, the Transylvanian town where Ferdinand and Marie were crowned. One plane was to shower the multitude with a stirring manifesto composed by Carol. Then, when the excitement peaked, the second plane was to deposit Carol at the rally, from which he would lead the peasants in a march on Bucharest.

Both planes were on the field and revved up, and the passengers had reached the gangways when they were stopped by Home Office officials. The British government, Carol was informed, could not allow an assault on a friendly government to originate from England. Carol retreated to Jonescu's plush estate, Oakhurst. Shortly after midnight on May 8, three Scotland Yard officers arrived at Oakhurst and presented him with an expulsion notice signed by the government.

Carol expressed surprised indignation and told a reporter he was sure the British government never would have done such a thing of its own accord, that they must have been activated by his enemies in Romania.

Meanwhile his enemies, the Liberal Party, were far too involved in their own problems to intrigue against Carol. The Great Depression sweeping Western Europe had reached Romania. Farmers couldn't sell their crops. Banks were closing. Foreign capital was unwilling to invest in the country. And the economic crisis intensified deeper problems: Greater Romania was united in name only. Since 1919 the Liberal Party had kept power centralized in Bucharest, ignoring the needs and demands of the dissatisfied minorities. Now, while the Prince sulked in Surrey, the National Peasant Party leader, Juliu Maniu, presented the Regency with an ultimatum demanding Vintila Bratianu's immediate dismissal. Confident that sooner or later the urban-supported Liberal oligarchy must fall before the rising tide of rural dissatisfaction, Maniu had even drawn up a new cabinet, listing himself as Premier.

Meanwhile, to prevent the peasant unrest from spreading, Vintila Bratianu stationed troops in every major town in Romania. In Transylvania, Maniu's home province, every town of any size was placed under martial control. Strict censorship was slapped on the newspapers, every telephone line leading out of the country was tapped, and foreign newspapers covering the attempted coup were confiscated.

On May 21, with tension still running high throughout the country, Marie wrote King George: "You can imagine how filled with grief I have been at Carol's behavior in England. . . . I thought the poor Prodigal had already caused me all the pain a child can inflict upon a mother, but the degree of suffering that these last events made me go through showed me we never go to the end of our sorrow.

"That a son of mine should have dared to go over to my old country, with such a degrading independence of feeling and dignity has been red-hot agony for me. . . ."

She ended on a personal note: "I have lived as bravely as I could. I have deeply loved my children and have given my life up for this country and am still doing all I can to help it over its bad hour. May God help me!"

Her words conveyed an unnerving and unexpected conflict. After living her first months of widowhood in "a sort of daze," she'd handled Ferdinand's death philosophically—"grief is also a step leading nearer truth"—and with memories of their good times together. But neither balm salved the bitterest pill of all: after thirteen years of influence unheard of for a twentieth-century queen consort, she was being pushed aside.

"Though not officially," she'd written an American friend in October 1927, "I am still the very heart of the country, so I must not let them feel forsaken. The father has gone, but the mother is still there for everybody. But I shall try slowly, slowly, to become a little freer."

But in reality she was lonely and at loose ends. She professed to having "steadily refused" a seat on the Regency: "The young should be given a chance." In fact she hadn't been asked. "I always stood behind the King," she wrote, "I can also stand behind the Regency. My steadying influence can be felt or looked for when necessary without shoving me to the fore, or giving me a special title."

Far from giving her a special title, both cabinet and Regency steadfastly ignored her. Her pride kept her from seeing that she'd been used in large part as a go-between before. But as the months passed and the government went through crisis after crisis without once consulting her, she realized that what power she'd enjoyed had died with the King.

Grief was replaced by what was for her a new emotion: bitterness. "It's inconceivable," she told a young Romanian friend, "that I, who have written my own page in Romanian history, should be ignored and put aside at this critical time. It's not that I'm ambitious, it's that I think I can help."

At fifty-two she had reached the height of her extraordinary vitality and political acumen only to be stopped short, like a race horse cut down in its prime. After thirteen years of intensely fulfilling personal and political involvement in the country's fortunes, she found herself frustrated by a situation nearly as stifling as old Carol's regime.

Added to her frustration was her unsatisfactory relationship with the little King and his mother. The rotogravures loved photographing the three together—handsome, manly-looking Michael flanked by his exquisite mother and still-beautiful grandmother, who was swathed in dramatic widow's weeds. But Helen, who had divorced Carol for obvious reasons, kept Michael from Marie. The implication was that she considered Marie a bad influence on the King. On the surface, Carol seemed no shining example of Marie's abilities as a mother. And Helen little realized that he'd been raised almost exclusively by old Carol, Carmen Sylva, and his Swiss tutor Schmidt.

In any case, Marie chafed at the sight of the little King spending his days in what she considered a hothouse, overprotective atmosphere. She remembered the freedom of her own childhood and longed to see Michael romping with boys his own age. "I itch to take that boy of hers out for a whole day with me into the country," wrote Marie, "and let him get dirty and wet, let him play with the gardener's child and risk his days climbing over the roof. . . . I don't in the least want to have my hand kissed by my grandson if he is not fond of me. I would rather he would tug me by my dress and say: 'Granny, come out and tumble on the grass.' "

Though outwardly affectionate, Marie and her daughter-in-law were never really intimate. Both were royal to their fingertips. But as in the case of England's Queen Mary and her mother-in-law Queen Alexandra, Queen Marie and Princess Helen found themselves poles apart in upbringing, outlook and personality. If Marie's breezy manner, informal court and personal involvement with her subjects were products of the twentieth century, her theatricality and monarchical principles harked back to the eighteenth. Helen, on the other hand, typified an understated brand of royalty that Queen Mary was making work so well in England and would bequeath to her successors.

Marie found it boring. "Outside things count too much with Helen," she wrote a friend. "A tidy house, a perfect dress, unruffled hair, punctuality, excessive politeness, good manners, form, precedence, and often I would like to pass my fingers through her too perfectly done hair."

Confronted with the fact of Helen's undeniable decorating ability, Marie had pronounced Helen "the *Hausfrau*" and herself "the woman of politics."

"But, Aunty-ma, are politics really so important?" asked the Princess.

"My dear, they are the only thing that matters," answered the Queen.

Whatever their differences, however, Marie had to admit that Helen's position—that of living alone in a foreign country torn with political intrigue, all the while entrusted with educating that country's future ruler—was gruesomely difficult for a young woman.

Besides, Marie had her compensations: her intensely fulfilling relationship with Barbu Stirbey and her daily work on the fairy tales and romantic novels she loved and sold with moderate success abroad. And late in 1927 she'd begun work on her memoirs.

"I've never been very learned," she confessed to Lavinia Small, a retired Colorado schoolteacher she'd never met but whom she wrote intimately. "I've a natural intelligence, not an intellectual one. I'm what the Germans would call *ein Naturkind,* a nature child. So my story will be a natural story about a natural person." And in August 1929, she told a New York *Times Sunday Magazine* reporter: "I have been criticized for being too expansive. Self-expression, self-revelation, require expansiveness. Of what good is an autobiography that conceals the heart and struggle of its writer? Mine will be a human document and in some respects a psychological study of some of the characters who have influenced my life." Alive with her wit, sense of wonder and dramatic flair, *The Story of My Life* was to provide her last great success.

Equally therapeutic were the ambitious decorating and gardening projects she carried out at her vacation homes, Castle Bran and her villa at Balcic on the Black Sea. Balcic, especially, provided an outlet for her creative energies. She was decorating it to remind her of the lost Malta days of her youth. She called the place Tenha-Juvah, which in Turkish means "Solitary Nest." And she visited here with increasing frequency as its developing beauty provided an antidote to her frustrating Bucharest life.

"A fairy house and gardens have arisen," she wrote an English friend, "perfectly in keeping with the Eastern aspect of the place. And each corner is a new enchantment, as terrace rises above terrace—not grand and monumental, but with an almost rustic haphazard appearance like simpler gardens found in Italy or Spain.

"The house has few rooms, but mine is huge, brick-floored and low-ceilinged with an enormous whitewashed Turkish hearth and a broad lone window. Through it, even from my low bed, I can see the sea, which has the color of turquoises and aquamarines melted together, for all that it has been called black."

To record her new life, she posed for photographers in her widow's weeds on a Balcic step with the cockers beside her and the sea behind. The sea and her beloved flowers provided the background for all her days at Tenha-Juvah. "The lilies last night in the moonlight were like a valley of ghost birds, incredibly wonderful," she wrote. "They had become quite mystical flowers, with strange souls."

But her greatest consolation lay in her close relationship with her youngest daughter, Ileana, "the creature on earth I am most closely and beautifully in sympathy with."

At twenty Ileana was a different physical type than her mother and sisters. Instead of their robust pink and gold beauty, she boasted a slender, supple figure (which the director of the National Physical Academy pronounced the "most perfect" in Romania), intense blue-gray eyes set beneath straight brows and dark hair shingled close to her shapely head. A talented artist and sculptor, Ileana was also good at sports. She rode, played tennis, drove her own roadster and led her National Girl Scouts of Romania in outdoor hikes, picnics, field maneuvers and the latest American gymnastic exercise. Dressed in a blue shirt, sombrero hat and kilt, she spent weeks at a time off camping with her scouts in the Carpathians.

Ileana was no frivolous princess. She'd learned royal duty and abnegation as a child while following her mother through hospital wards filled with dead and dying soldiers. Yet with her warm, exuberant personality and flashing smile which crinkled her eyes at the corners, Ileana was also, as even her mother admitted, "something of a flirt."

The American press called her "the most eligible princess in Europe" and linked her name with princes from Boris of Bulgaria to the Prince of Wales. But her one serious romance, with the Prince of Asturias, heir to the Spanish throne, had fizzled out, and she spent most of her time with her mother.

Sharing Marie's passion for the sea, Ileana also loved Balcic. Mother and daughter swam, sailed Ileana's yacht *Isprava,* rode, read and gardened together. "We are perfect companions," wrote Marie, "so much so that I cannot face the thought of her ultimate departure; it is a big grief to come."

It was partly an attempt to forestall that grief which landed her in her next crisis. At Sinaia in January 1930, she gave a fancy dress ball to celebrate Ileana's twenty-first birthday. One of the guests, the young son of Marie's old friend Princess Daisy of Pless, arrived from Germany too late to assemble an elaborate costume. So he appeared at the party dressed in ski clothes. Tall, slender, golden-haired, with blue eyes rimmed with black lashes and a blazing smile, Lexel of Pless might have stepped from a Wagnerian dream. After a few days' skiing together on the Sinaia slopes, he and Ileana fell in love. Lexel proposed, Ileana accepted, and Marie rejoiced because Pless promised that he and Ileana would live in Romania after their wedding. A June date was set.

Shortly after Lexel returned to Germany, Marie received an unexpected visitor from Berlin. Seeing her mother in tears after the stranger had gone, Ileana ran to Mignon, who was also staying at Sinaia, and asked her if she knew what was wrong.

Mignon burst into tears. "I can't tell you, it's too awful for Mamma. You mustn't make it worse for her. It's so terrible."

Finally, Ileana approached her mother. "But, Mamma," she begged, "we always share everything. Why can't we share this?"

Drying her eyes, Marie drew this favorite child to her, explaining that Lexel had been implicated in a homosexual charge in Germany several years before.

Despite Marie's efforts to suppress it, members of her household let the story leak out in Romania. Within days she was buried under a stream of invective, most of it in the press. Some papers declared the unfortunate situation was the Queen's fault, that she should have protected her daughter's interests more carefully. Others said that by trying to align her daughter with an undesirable husband, she was working against the government. The whole country demanded that the engagement be broken off immediately.

Marie hustled her heartbroken daughter off on an extended trip to Egypt, confessing to a friend: "There have been many griefs in my life, but this has been the most soul-searing, almost beyond the bearable. The truth is that against everything, we still believe in him. But of course no happiness could come of her marrying a man the country repudiated, especially as they want to live here."

She was occupied that winter with more than Ileana's problems. Vintila Bratianu's government had collapsed in December 1928, and free elections packed the Parliament with new Premier Juliu Maniu's National Peasant Party. But Maniu's much-touted reforms had allayed, not solved the country's problems. To make matters worse, the people had lost faith in the Regency, particularly since the death of its most capable member, George Buzdugan.

"The country has no leader," quipped Regent Miron Cristea. "Prince Nicolas passes his time smoking cigarettes. Saratzeanu, the new regent, passes his playing solitaire. And I, a priest, must confine myself to appeasing conflicts."

Steered by this politically inept trio, the dynasty seemed headed for collapse. Marie was actually relieved to hear the rumor that a coup was being planned to bring Carol back as King. Certainly the political situation couldn't be worse. Perhaps if Carol could overcome his weaknesses and turn himself into a capable ruler, the country would experience a much-needed renaissance.

She hinted at this possibility in a conversation with her old friend, Liberal politician Jean Duca:

"I frankly don't see how we're going to labor through another ten-and-a-half years of such an unnatural state of affairs," she told him. "No head, no one responsible, no confidence, no prestige, the dynasty falling to pieces. I, the only efficient member of it, put on one side, insulted, calumniated, denied and rejected so that I can't be of any help. We can't hold on like this. It's a hopeless task. We ought to look things more in the face and not slur over difficulties with formulas that are in fact nothing but painted lies."

"Ma'am," replied Duca, "I am more optimistic. We shall, we must hold the Regency together." Duca spoke the Liberal Party line. It was a line based on the salient fact that if Carol returned, the Liberal Party was as dead as Ion Bratianu.

Wild flowers sprang up as the snows melted, and tension continued to rise throughout Romania. Would the government collapse? Would Carol return? And if he came back would he make up with Helen or bring the hated Lupescu back with him? In June Marie accepted an invitation to attend the Oberammergau Passion play with her sisters and Mignon. She hated to leave the country at such an explosive moment. But the strain had become unbearable, and she needed a change.

20

Absalom Returns

Juliu Maniu was that rare creature in politics, a completely honest man. At fifty-seven he had a proud, aloof face, dark hair carefully plastered back from a high forehead, bushy brows separated by three vertical worry lines, and a sanctimonious mouth dominated by a dark mustache and a nose too large for his face.

Born in the Transylvanian mountains of peasant stock, Maniu was educated as a Jesuit—a life he later rejected for politics. But certain traits which he carried first into the Hungarian legislature before the War and later into the Greater Romania Parliament recalled his upbringing. He never married and showed no interest in money, women or personal power. Motivated by patriotism and a desire to better the peasants' lot, he effected the postwar coalition of the National and Peasant parties, thereby placing himself at the head of the single major political force opposing Bratianu and the Liberal Party.

But when the free elections of December 1928 packed the Parliament with National Peasant delegates and made him Prime Minister at last, he blinked with horror at an unexpected reality: Romanian political trends were so ingrained that only revolutionary measures could reverse them. And Maniu was no revolutionary. He bravely faced the problems of rising fascism, economic depression and ineffectual foreign policy. But he was too hamstrung by the corruption around him and by his own fundamentally conservative nature to solve them. God, he

227

realized now, had provided him with a personality better suited for opposing than for leading. From that moment, he began planning Carol's return.

Having committed his party to the idea of a restoration, Maniu sounded out the Regency. He could count on them, declared Prince Nicolas, an easygoing youth who preferred cars and naval duty to politics. And public opinion spoke for itself. Carlist plotters were constantly being apprehended, tried and enthusiastically acquitted.

The central problem, as Maniu saw it, was Lupescu. Therefore, before he would restore Carol he made the prince these conditions: shelve Lupescu, make up with Helen, return not as King but as Michael's regent.

When in May 1930, an emissary approached Carol with these demands, he balked. The way he saw it, there was no reason for him to leave Madame Lupescu behind. After all, she had no political interests. At that point Lupescu herself entered the room and swore she would not upset any restoration plans. "The day that His Royal Highness is restored to the throne," she announced, "I shall disappear forever."

Later that month Carol's devoted supporter, Major Vladimir Precup, visited Maniu and repeated Lupescu's promise. Convinced of Carol's good faith, Maniu moved secretly into the next stage of his plan. He obtained a forged passport for the Prince, chartered a plane to bring him from Paris, alerted accomplices in the government and army and communicated daily with Prince Nicolas. On June 5 Maniu sent his second-in-command, Deputy Mihalache, to the Chaussée Kisseleff house to prepare Carol's ex-wife for what was about to happen.

Princess Helen was thunderstruck. How could they expect her, she asked, to accept Carol back after all that had happened? Mihalache replied coolly that the government was confident that if Carol returned, he would return alone. And the people would expect her to forget the past "for the good of the country."

On June 6 at eight A.M., while Bucharest buzzed with rumors and Marie motored unsuspectingly through Germany, Carol landed quietly at Bucharest's Baneasa airport. His brother Nicolas and a formation of troops greeted him enthuasiastically and spirited him to the palace. That night a military deputy arrived at Helen's house and officially informed her that her ex-husband had returned. Distraught, she asked for details. What would happen to her and the little King?

The deputy stayed until midnight, trying to calm her fears. Then, echoing Mihalache, he said urgently: "The country needs Prince Carol. Now that he's here, he must be helped to succeed. If you take him back, if the divorce is annulled, it will re-establish him in the eyes of the people. It will give us unity and the determination to remedy past mistakes. It is Your Royal Highness's duty to think first of the country."

Tortured by reopened wounds she'd thought closed forever and by the terrifying fear that she might have to give up Michael to his father, the Princess paced her room till morning.

At five A.M. Carol summoned Maniu to the Palatul Regal and informed him that he wanted to be proclaimed King at once.

"Immediately?" asked Maniu.

"Immediately," said Carol softly. "And with the legal proviso that I have reigned since my father died in 1927."

"Then," retorted Maniu, "I must resign. For I have sworn allegiance to the son, not the father."

"Not yet, not yet," Carol replied, smiling.

Maniu was stunned. But he obediently relayed Carol's will to the cabinet, who put it to a vote. Five ministers voted for Carol's admission to the Regency. Six voted for proclaiming him King. Maniu voted with the minority, and was heartened when the cabinet said they would submit to his decision, whatever it might be. But during the meeting a large National Peasant delegation called on Maniu, begging him to proclaim Carol King. At that, something snapped the incorruptible old Prime Minister. Realizing he'd already lost control of the coup he'd so lovingly planned, he bowed his head to the people's will.

At four P.M. Carol and Nicolas drove to Parliament together in an open carriage, and Bucharest erupted in delirious thanksgiving. Bands thundered and hysterical crowds shouted *"Traiasca Regele!"* The man who had three times repudiated his country had returned as its savior.

That afternoon, Parliament, amid equally vociferous ovations, revoked the 1926 Act of Succession, which had removed Carol's rights to the throne. In a single stroke they returned Michael to the rank of Crown Prince and proclaimed his father King Carol II, whereupon Carol named Maniu his Prime Minister. The Liberal Party was crushed.

Down the street, Carol's son and ex-wife listened to his voice for the first time in five years as his acceptance speech trumpeted over the radio. Helen tried to explain the situation to eight-year-old Michael.

Papa had recovered from his "illness," she told him, and had come back in an airplane.

"Shall we see him?" asked the boy.

"Very soon, for a talk."

"Will he take me away?"

"No, he'll be too busy. He will be King."

"How can Papa be a King, when I am the King?"

Heartsick, she tried to explain. "Papa went away and left you in his place. But usually little boys aren't kings. They have to wait until they grow up."

Several hours later, dressed in a uniform blazing with decorations and accompanied by Nicolas and Lisabetta, Carol arrived at Helen's house. He looked, she thought, exactly as he had five years before.

Coming toward her, he said "Hello" casually, and they shook hands. But tension crackled in the air as minutes passed and nobody spoke. Finally Helen pulled herself together.

"The only thing for us to do is to be friends for Michael's sake," she said quietly.

"I quite agree," Carol answered quickly. "We will not talk of the past." After another pause he said he'd come to see Michael.

She went upstairs to get the boy. "I don't want Papa to take me away," he said, frightened.

"Of course, he won't," Helen tried to reassure him. "You're only going to have a little chat with him."

Back in the drawing room, Carol kissed Michael "emotionally" and told Helen he was taking him back to the Palace: "Public opinion demands it." At that Helen's visitors left the house, taking Michael with them.

"If after five years' absence," she thought, watching them go, "Carol can so casually walk off with our son, what can I possibly do if he ever wants to take him away from me entirely?"

Michael was back within the hour. But Carol sent for him every day after that, and each visit lasted longer. Meanwhile Helen faced the equally unnerving problem of a divorce annulment. Even Maniu came, begging her to say yes. It had been the cornerstone of his restoration plans, he told her, to cloak Carol in her popularity and respectability. "The nation wishes it, and King Carol knows they wish it. We cannot wait. Everyone wants a formal gesture now, and the only gesture that will mean anything is the annulment of the divorce." He added that since the new law stated Carol had reigned since 1927, she was now

Queen of Romania. Carol had even agreed to a September date for their coronation together at Alba Julia.

Emissaries ran daily between Helen and Carol, whose hatred of personal confrontation added to the situation's absurdity. Finally, overwhelmed by her sudden reversal from mother of one King to estranged wife of another and deluged by the country's and government's pleas, Helen agreed to have the divorce annulled.

Aglow with success, Maniu rushed with the news to Carol, who suddenly performed an amazing about-face. "Not just yet," he said. "First let her write a letter stating she's against the annulment. It's indispensable to my cause."

Maniu felt sick. Carol had obviously never had any intention of taking back his wife. By obtaining her signature on a document expressing her unwillingness to have their divorce annulled, he would have a major propaganda tool with which to destroy her popularity and martyrize himself.

But Helen refused to write the letter. She had given much in heartbreak and frustration to this prince and his people. She would keep her pride.

Marie's first impulse, when she heard the news of Carol's return, was to interrupt her German tour and rush back to Bucharest. No one knew better than she "how grievously he has sinned." But now that he'd come home and taken the reigns of government firmly in hand, she was elated: "My mother's heart shouts for joy!" She saw new hope for Romania led by a full-blooded king, a monarch who, though tainted, must justify the confidence twenty million people had placed in him. She also glimpsed herself working beside him in the future, giving freely of her love, vitality and experience.

When an urgent dispatch arrived from Bucharest asking her to postpone her return for two or three weeks, she was shocked and annoyed. Then her natural credulity took over. Of course it would be wiser to wait until the political situation had settled down. And she threw herself happily into rediscovering old friends and haunts of her Coburg youth.

She arrived home the last week in June. With the train still rolling into the station's great hall, she jumped out of her car and into Carol's arms. "Tremendously excited," and still clasping his hand, she bent down to kiss Michael, a forlorn, pudgy little figure standing beside his father on the red carpet.

Having greeted a phalanx of damp-eyed officials, the reunited family stepped outside into brilliant afternoon sunshine and the roar of massed thousands jamming the station's square. Wave after wave of applause swept over them as they drove through town in an open landau drawn by four black horses. Laughing and talking animatedly, Marie acknowledged the cheers with her characteristically flamboyant gestures.

Later, with the adrenaline still coursing, she turned vigorously to her favorite emotional outlet, her pen. "We are living history with a vengeance," she wrote Jean Duca's son George, "and you can imagine how I as mother and Queen look on with trembling anxiety. Of course I am with him with every fibre of my being, and all that I am is at his disposal to help him with all my might and perhaps to lead to him by slow degrees those who oppose him."

Overjoyed at the prospect of emerging from her enforced political seclusion, she even allowed herself a rare burst of acridity. "Joy and pain intermingled," she wrote Lavinia Small on June 28. "My joy and his ex-wife's pain. For her the day was dreadful. She had been everything, with that depressing hand of hers on the poor little King's shoulder, a picture I had lived with for nearly three years, wondering how it would be possible to live another ten years of it. And Nicky not caring for his work and not strong enough to give dignity and prestige to the Regency. And now suddenly it is *I* who am mother of the King!"

But charity prevailed as she took stock of Helen's humiliating situation. In a "heart-to-heart" talk, Marie tried convincing Carol to take Helen back, at least as his "official wife," even if they didn't "live together."

"*She* insisted on divorce," Carol shot back. "She hit me with it at a moment when I was being publicly humiliated. And when it was pronounced, she telegraphed to her mother 'at last liberated from this nightmare!' So why should I chain myself to a woman who loathes me and whom I detest? It would be immoral!"

And he continued pressing Helen to sign an annulment refusal. While she held out, he canceled the September coronation, allowed her to call herself "Majesty" but not "Queen," forbade her to receive official visitors and excluded her from official ceremonies.

Marie visited Helen before leaving town for Balcic. "You and Carol should never have met," she told the younger woman sadly. "Your characters are poles apart. I am sorry for you," she added, taking her in her arms. "Most people who meet with disaster in their lives are given a second chance, but you have not been free to build up your life again."

At Balcic the Queen reflected on an unexpected turn of events. After the first reunion, Carol had begun treating her evasively. He allowed her the interview concerning Helen and then announced he was too busy to see her privately. Except for a few carelessly-flung crumbs of affection, he ignored her.

"I am strictly keeping apart from all official life and honours," she wrote wistfully, "so that my son should in no way think I want to mix in politics and influence things."

Nevertheless, as the weeks passed, she began noticing a number of petty vexations directed at her household by the big palace. Some of her old friends and retainers were set aside, spied upon. Comments were made concerning her own income. Still filled with illusions, Marie refused to believe these affronts came directly from Carol. Instead she blamed them on his inexperienced young henchmen, like Puiu Dumi- trescu, a notorious lower-class playboy and procurer who had affixed himself to Carol during the Paris days.

Whatever her illusions, wariness had replaced elation. "Carol is a great sinner," she summed the situation up for Lavinia Small. "But he is a man, and the country was sighing for a master, for a real center around which to rally. I am not without anxiety, as I have not a big opinion of my first-born's character. But I know he is out of the way intelligent, that in spite of his desertion he loves and knows his country. I know that he is three-quarters good, with a quarter which at certain moments goes wrong. Perhaps now with all the responsibility on his shoulders and no more opposition, that quarter in him will be over- come."

Subsequent events proved she underestimated the bad. In July Carol took a revenge he'd planned for twenty years: he exiled Stirbey. Taking his wife with him, the Prince boarded the Orient Express for Paris. Bereft of her great love and stanchest ally, Marie was more than ever unprepared for the next thunderbolt.

In August a Berlin newspaper printed the rumor that Lupescu was back in Romania. Marie and the government refused to believe it, however, and Maniu even published a "contemptuous denial." But by September the foreign press stubbornly insisted she was living at Sinaia, where Carol had retreated for a rest. And rumors that Sinaia locals had glimpsed the King's mistress speeding by in a closed car began filtering back to Bucharest.

With sinking heart, Maniu ordered a discreet investigation and discovered the rumor was true. Lupescu had sneaked back into the country with a false passport. She was living in the Foisor.

"I often feel I must awake from some torturing dream," moaned Marie when she received the news. "I feel that this cannot be reality, that we are losing ourselves in some dark maze."

On October 4, pleading exhaustion, the battered Prime Minister sent Carol his resignation. "I am responsible for bringing Prince Carol back to Romania because I sincerely believed in him," he told his collaborators. "But since he has broken his solemn word twice—once about reconciling with the Princess, and once about leaving Madame Lupescu for good—I cannot accept to serve such a master."

The King received his Premier's resignation with "evident pleasure," and when he later expressed concern about losing Maniu, Madame Lupescu reportedly said, "There must be another somewhere who is equally good and doesn't dislike me."

With Maniu on the decline, the King's mistress cast an eye on another figure she could hardly consider friendly: the King's ex-wife. As Christmas approached, Carol dropped all pretense and began overtly persecuting the poor woman. While Helen was out of town, he had her wine cellar and several rugs and furnishings removed from her house. When she was in residence, he treated her like a political criminal, surrounding her with civil police. He deprived her of her position as Honorary Colonel of the Fourth Rosiori regiment. He had her visitors followed and refused her any contact with the nation's political element. Worst of all for Helen, he now kept Michael at the palace all day, allowing him to return only at night.

Marie took up her daughter-in-law's cause with a vengeance, but in vain. "The situation is profoundly tragic," wrote the Queen. "The only way I could gain Carol and his associates would be by entirely repudiating her. But it is not my way to abandon the fallen, never mind how they may have treated me in the day of their power. Therein lies our greatest conflict, and the child is being sacrificed to his spite against her . . . But certainly all would be different if he had a good, calm, conciliatory man beside him instead of having a pimp as closest friend."

Working through that friend, Carol sharpened his attacks on Marie too, humiliating her in every way he could. He didn't allow her to participate in official functions. He curtailed her social activities, and

Dumitrescu even outlined which of her charitable agencies she might continue supporting. He told her she must even start paying her own travel expenses, which the crown had formerly stood.

The money matter was particularly annoying. The Queen's annual civil list payment from the government amounted to twenty million lei ($182,000 in 1930s dollars). This covered her official expenses—entertaining and running her several residences—but little else. Foreseeing this, Ferdinand had attached a codicil to his will stating that though Michael was to inherit all the private royal estates at age twenty-one, the revenue from the properties would go to his grandmother during the intervening fifteen years. Ferdinand's plan would have given Marie a tidy retirement fund. Now Carol negated the codicil as he'd negated the Act of Succession and appropriated the money for himself.

Marie found these insults mortifying. But for a woman to whom independence meant everything, her son's next move was crushing. He infested her household with spies.

At first she couldn't believe it. But by February 1931, she was sorrowfully writing Lavinia Small that "no one feels happy, free nor safe. Never, even in wartime, have we lived in quite such an atmosphere. It makes us sad, anxious, depressed. It breaks our wings and weighs down our hearts. No one any more feels joyful and free, and each day hope becomes less. That your own nearest and dearest should have been able to bring this about seems incredible." Childish spite had become Machiavellian vengeance.

Deprived of freedom at home, Marie and Ileana left on the first of March for a trip through France and Germany with Ducky. They stopped at Mignon's on their way west. In Belgrade Marie discussed the Romanian situation with King Alexander, repeating what she'd already tried impressing on Carol: "It's a great mistake for a sovereign to allow the family feeling to fall to pieces. He is much stronger with the family than without. The moment he allows his family, through neglect or injustice on his side, to split up into parties or clans, the seeds of discord and sedition have been sown. And this is fatal in the hour of danger when he may find himself alone."

Far from heeding her advice, Carol seemed bent on pursuing the opposite course.

His traditional best friend in the royal family was Ileana. Since the Zizi Lambrino days, she had provided a link with his better nature. When he left the country for Lupescu, Ileana was the first relative to visit him. And when their father died, she alone had written him descriptions of the funeral. Though separated in age by sixteen years, brother and sister were sincerely attached to each other, and when he returned as King, both thought the old friendship would hold. But it didn't. For one thing, Carol counted on her support in his vendetta against Helen. Ileana, however—once she realized the full measure of his oppression—told him that what he was doing was "dishonorable and wrong." But communication between the two remained possible until Lupescu's return. Then like the Queen and Maniu, his little sister lost faith in Carol forever. When he began persecuting their mother, Ileana defended her fiercely, and the King responded by cursing them both at the top of his lungs.

Coincidental with Lupescu's return, Carol let his jealousy of Marie's popularity lap over to include Ileana's too. He forced her to resign the Junior YWCA presidency, give up her Girl Scouts and stop visiting her soldiers. Still not satisfied, he cast about for a more permanent solution to her annoying bond with the people.

He found it in Marie and Ileana's proposed visit to German relatives in March. Remembering that Ileana had struck up a friendship with the young Austrian Archduke Anton of Habsburg-Lothringen during a 1929 trip to Spain, Carol arranged to have Anton visit the Hohenzollerns at the same time Ileana would be there.

The plot worked. For the second time in two years, a handsome young man swept Ileana off her feet, proposed and was accepted. Carol heard the news with glee, but Marie was stunned.

She couldn't criticize Anton's family background. His father, the Archduke Leopold-Salvator, was a nephew of the late Emperor Franz Joseph. And his mother, a Spanish Bourbon, boasted blood as blue as any in Europe. But her personality exasperated Marie. "There were ten children," she wrote, "and the mother, a narrow-minded Catholic, thought more of the virtuous way she was answering the Church's behest than of what to do with the children afterwards. She never made a real home for them."

Anton was penniless, and Marie learned that he had pumped gas in Spain after the Austrian collapse. But she was no snob. What worried her far more than his lack of money was the fact that he also lacked the most rudimentary knowledge of art, literature and history—all interests Ileana loved. He was, however, an expert engineer and electrician and an accomplished pilot.

Her dreams for her intelligent and gifted favorite daughter faded before her eyes, and the Queen reflected that Ileana would have occupied a throne to better advantage than either of her other daughters who became queens. Not that she had necessarily wished Ileana married to a king. She loved the child too much to sacrifice her to a fleeting dream of superficial glamour. Still she had hoped, she had prayed that Ileana would find a position, either at home or abroad, which would utilize her resourceful personality.

Admittedly, Anton was attractive—broad-shouldered and muscular, with dark blond hair, bright blue eyes, and a mouthful of very white teeth. He was a man's man, not a quicksilver charmer as Lexel had been. "His appetite is so schoolboy-like," Marie wrote a friend, "that his way of biting into a goodly-sized slice of cake made me give him the name of Puma. So my young couple call themselves the Pumas now."

And Ileana was happy. She preferred a man she could help, and the challenge of filling the gaps in her Tony's education appealed to her. But Marie was wretched. "Yes, she is happy," she wrote, "and in her happiness I find, or try to find, mine. But something is breaking within me when I think of our parting. It feels like death."

Then suddenly Carol attacked again. He wrote Marie in Germany, commanding her to stay out of Romania for two more months. Wedding or no wedding, she and Ileana might not return until the first of June. He had also decided, he said, that the young couple should not settle down in Romania as they planned. It would be "politically inconvenient."

Marie reacted to this latest blow with a moan of despair: "I feel I'm losing all my battles."

With a month to kill, they decided to visit Italy. There Marie submerged her heartache in museums, palaces, churches and long drives through the romantic countryside. Mussolini entertained her with courtesy, high spirits and intellect.

"Did Your Majesty ever meet Eleonora Duse?" he asked.

"Yes, of course," reminisced the Queen. "And I must say that I never knew if I was more attracted by her sad, deep face, or by those wonderful hands of hers."

After lunch they attacked a matter which threatened Ileana's marriage. Anton was Catholic, and Ileana refused to give up Orthodoxy. Therefore the Vatican was trying to make Anton sign papers empowering him to dictate her religious practices after their marriage. Anton had refused, and the Vatican, in turn, refused to sanction the marriage.

Mussolini's realm was the state, not the church, he said with rare humility, and Marie admitted that she considered the whole affair a tempest in a teapot.

All the same, she and Ileana paid a courtesy call on Pope Pius XI. They admired the Vatican's endless halls, lit with flickering candles and lined with Swiss guards in their brilliant uniforms. But the Holy Father, a grizzled old gentleman who spoke atrocious French in a heavy Italian accent, was a disappointment. And the outcome was that whatever happened after, Ileana must marry in the Catholic church and raise her children as Catholics, or there could be no marriage.

The wedding itself, celebrated on July 27 at the Peles went off well enough. Carol celebrated the event by exiling Helen, but after three days of rain, the famed Sinaia sun smiled on the bridal couple as they rode up the hill in an open carriage, and peasants, crowded beneath the pines, threw flowers.

But Marie felt ill and exhausted. When Ileana somehow disappeared without saying good-bye to her mother, the Queen crept away from the family party to spend what she thought would be the most terrible night of her life alone. An hour later, Ileana burst in, crying apologies, and the two women embraced, joining their tears in an agony of weeping that had been stored up during all the bitter months.

21

The She Wolf

Marie collapsed after Ileana's wedding. "It all ended up in a sort of breakdown this summer," she confessed to a friend. "It was as if the Rolls Royce needed overhauling, a little garage and tinkering."

It wasn't her style to break down. But the shock of Carol's cruelty, combined with the crushing of all her hopes for what his restoration might mean for her and the country, had weakened her resistance. The wedding shattered it.

Her doctors, whom she hated on principle for their freedom-curbing restrictions, fussed around her for several days before prescribing complete rest. At Balcic, where the sea lapped against her terrace, she found it.

"Now I am calm, feel in a way purified, difficult to explain why. But my heart has learned a new strength. I am not resigned, resignation has in it a sound of defeat. There is no defeat in my attitude today, but the still deeper understanding of those who have neared the gates of despair."

She underscored her new outlook by dedicating the white stone church she'd built overlooking the Black Sea. She called it Stella Maris, "the smallest church in the land." It duplicated a tiny Byzantine church she'd seen in a Cypriote village, and she filled it with treasures culled from Constantinople flea markets. The church was Orthodox and she was Anglican, but she relished Byzantine architecture. Besides, though she possessed a deep and childike religious faith, she'd built her little church more for an emotional retreat than for organized religious observances.

Whatever her reasons, Carol approved her continuing projects at Cotroceni, Bran and Balcic. Since he couldn't relegate her to a convent as autocrats had done to inconvenient women in the past, he encouraged these nonpolitical labors. They were only partly fulfilling, however. She had worked actively at the nation's heart for too long to completely ignore the current political situation. And she didn't like what she saw.

"Ruling means abnegation, not a feast of power," she told Carol on her way to visit Anton and Ileana in their new home near Munich.

Irritated by his mother's outspokenness, Carol treated her more coldly than usual—which made her stay with the "Pumas" that much more healing.

"My life has entered a somewhat unfamiliar phase," she told Ileana. "I have become less active, less jubilant. They have put me in dry dock, and it needs little effort not to find it rather comfortable."

Life was teaching her new lessons in faith, acceptance and wisdom. But she found one lesson harder to accept than all the others: it was living alone, amid an antagonistic court and a divided family.

For many years Nicolas was Marie's favorite child. All her life she kept one of his glossy silver baby curls as a special treasure in a Fabergé box. And she often looked back with a smile on the irrepressibly naughty child he'd been. From the first, Nicolas combined Marie's eyes and coloring with Ferdinand's features. But his spritelike personality was his own, and it stole everyone's heart from old King Carol's down. By 1919, when he left home for Eton, it was obvious to his parents that their second son was no intellectual. But his easy charm and graceful manners paved his way through school and a term in the British Navy as they had freed him from nursery reprisals. When he was home on leave, he and Marie took off on exciting adventures, buoyed by their shared sense of fun and adventure. Then, when he was twenty, his father's death made him Regent.

By 1930 his relationship with his mother had tarnished slightly. She was disappointed in his political performance. And later, when Carol returned, it annoyed her that Nicolas hadn't kept her abreast of the restoration plans. Still she loved both her sons deeply and expected them to work closely together for the good of the country.

Shortly after the restoration, however, it became obvious that Carol's paranoia regarding his family included Nicolas too. Though he gave his brother titular control of all three branches of the military, the new King deprived him of any real authority, hoping Nicolas's diversions would land him in trouble.

While Marie was in Munich, they did. Like his father and brother before him, Nicolas fell in love with a young Romanian woman, Jeanne Luci Doletti, and decided to marry her. She was divorced, but that presented no problem in Orthodox Romania. The real difficulty, as in the Vacarescu and Lambrino affairs, resided with the Constitution's adamant stand against princes' marrying their subjects.

Marie found other objections.

"Now my poor, foolish Nicky believes he has found the wonder of wonders," she wrote in exasperation from Sinaia. "And she is merely a hardhearted, painted little hussy whose one idea is money and luxury in every form, and who is eating up his fortune so that soon he will have nothing but debts. But this I must say," she added, "it is touching the way he loves this quite ordinary, uninteresting woman from nowhere. He simply worships her and believes she has every virtue."

In motherly fashion, Marie blamed her sons' personal and political failures less on them or herself than on the "bad women" they loved. "I still declare they are good boys, led astray by women they believe to be angels, but who have only the most selfish motives and who destroy the family unity, perturbing a country that needs quiet."

What hurt Marie most about Nicky's romance was that Jeanne Doletti had begun alienating him from his mother, convincing him he'd always been misunderstood and slighted at home. Marie protested this absurdity with violence born of righteous indignation. "Ever since he was born," she cried, "his family made him the supreme favorite of everybody, and he always got what he wanted."

Meanwhile Nicolas confronted Carol with his decision to marry Jeanne. Carol studied the situation in light of his own interests. Perhaps if the country allowed his brother a morganatic marriage, he thought, then he might get away with marrying Lupescu on the same basis. On the other hand, if the uproar against Nicolas's marriage proved too great, he could always exile him.

With these consideration in mind, Carol turned to Nicolas with one of his rare dazzling smiles. "Put me in front of an accomplished fact," he said, "and we'll see what happens."

Heartbroken, Marie watched another of her children set off on a course potentially destructive for himself and unsettling for the country. What had gone wrong? she asked in a letter to Stirbey in Switzerland. Had she been too lax with her boys? Was it her inability to scold that had kept them from developing the moral sense and devotion to duty that guided her own days? Whatever its basis, their failure was the great tragedy of her life. "For I was a passionate mother and dreamed of fine things for our sons."

On October 28, 1931, in the little village of Tohan, Nicolas married his Jeanne without the government's consent. In less than two years, Marie had lost Barbu Stirbey and faith in both her sons. What remained was an aching void she was sure nothing and no one could fill.

The new year opened bleakly. Reflecting on Carol's actions, she wrote on January 13: "How much happier he would be if he could make *one* generous act that we could wholeheartedly thank him for. . . . If only he could be a son instead of a renegade, a brother instead of a selfish and suspicious tyrant. Am I never to see a single act over which I can fold my hands, thank God and say: It is good!"

Not in 1932. That February, Carol was having her correspondence opened before it left Romania. And in June he administered another blow. Ileana might not come home as planned to have her first baby.

"But why not?" asked Marie, her eyes burning with unshed tears of hurt and rage.

"For political reasons," answered Carol. "It's impossible for us to let a Habsburg come into the world on Romanian territory."

"A Habsburg baby endangering the security of twenty million good Romanians? Nonsense!"

But she had no choice. If Ileana couldn't come to her, she must go to Ileana. Therefore, early in July she left for the "Pumas' " new little villa at Mödling outside Vienna. With her went her entourage, Mignon, two Romanian doctors and a pot of earth to place under the bed so that Ileana could say her baby had been born on Romanian soil.

In a letter to her old friend King George V, the Queen expressed some of her grief at Carol's continuing harassment.

"What a terribly sad letter yours is," replied the King on July 27. "In reading it the tears came into my eyes as I fully realise all the misery you have gone through during the last two years. I have seen Sitta and George [of Greece], and they have both told me of the many insults and unkindnesses that have been heaped upon you. . . .

"I do hope that some day soon we may meet and then you will be able to pour your heart out to me and tell me all that you have gone through, as you know how deeply I sympathise with you in the impossible position in which you have been placed. I cannot help thinking that he is mad, certainly his actions lead one to think so and one wonders what he will do next."

On August 15, after a grueling labor which lasted nearly three days, Princess Ileana presented her husband with a son and her mother with her fifth grandchild. The baby was named Stefan, and the Viennese responded with unexpected rejoicing at this first archducal birth in Austria since the war.

Then, on the morning of August 29, while she was still at Mödling, Marie received a shock. The head of her household, the courtly Austrian General Zwiedineck, suddenly proclaimed his passionate love for her. She was nearly sixty. Three years before, she had entertained Lavinia Small with tales of the many men who had fought unsuccessfully to possess her over a span of thirty years.

"They were like sick children crying for what they could not have. But the suffering was real for all that. And I always hoped that by kindness on my part, things would get better, that I could make them understand that I was not virtuously offended by the sickness that had overtaken them, but that I could not cure them as they wanted to be cured." All the same, every man who ever loved her had remained her friend. It was a comforting thought for her old age.

And now this.

Zwiedineck was nearly twenty years her junior, tall, dark and magnificently erect with an elegant mustache, a booming laugh and a deep, expressive voice. "He looked exactly like a circus ringmaster," snapped one courtier. But then the favorite is always despised.

The General had led Austrian forces during the war, but his wife was a Transylvanian Saxon, and they lived with their daughter in Brasov, near Marie's Castle Bran. Thus when Romania annexed Transylvania, the couple became Romanian citizens. And when it was considered politic for the King to appoint court officials from among non-Romanian minorities, Ferdinand chose Zwiedinick as an aide-de-camp. Marie inherited him as aide-de-camp at Ferdinand's death, making him head of her household when Stirbey was exiled. She had always liked Zwiedineck for his good looks, Old World charm, managerial ability and tender heart. During Ileana's prolonged labor, "Zwiedy's big eyes were swimming in tears," noticed Marie.

But she had never considered him an intimate. Now, confronted with his unsuspected passion, which had "smouldered many years" beside her, she alternated between tickled vanity and dismay. But the romance of the situation charmed her beyond words.

"I am no more young enough to love, but one can still love the other's love," she confessed to Lavinia Small. "But is that enough? Above all, at our age one wants to play fair, absolutely and devastatingly fair. And yet that song of love has a warm sound. And the deep need of a soul which has burst through its reserve because the tide had mounted to overflow is fearful, and yet beautiful in its way, because it is no more purely a physical need, but a cry out of the deep."

Zwiedineck's declaration temporarily lifted her above smothering grief and frustration. Of course she explained to him that as a Queen she must "hold herself back—remain within certain bounds," thereby placing the relationship on the comforting level of romantic friendship. But she wasn't suprised that he should desire her physically. Her beauty and appeal, though altered, were incredible for a woman her age. And it was inexpressibly heartening that since she had lost so much after a vibrant and glorious life, she should have the sparkling strand of this last romance to cling to when she needed it most.

By an odd coincidence, Marie's oldest daughter Lisabetta, now thirty-eight, had also discovered a new love. She was still married to Princess Helen's brother, the exiled King George II of Greece, but their marriage had failed years before. Now this "late passion" for George's banker, the Russian-born Alexander Scalavi, had changed the selfish Lisabetta.

"As mother I should not approve," Marie wrote a friend. "But knowing how she had never developed, how she had never found anything real, I rejoice almost like a doctor that someone has appeared who makes her real right through."

Lisabetta's emotional awakening, the first in her life, had also made her appreciate her mother for the first time. "Suddenly she understands me. The barriers are down and she understands how I was always there, but could not bear her shams nor her petty infatuations. . . . I am glad we have come together. I know so much, I can help. Besides, I know how never to look either astonished or shocked."

The Queen's relationship with Carol showed no signs of improvement, however. By another New Year's, it was worse than ever. On January 11 she wrote: "I fought two years and a half against the horrible truth, but today I see it in all its naked sordidness: my son is a bad man."

It was 1933 and Carol was nearly forty. He had eloped with Zizi Lambrino in 1918. By her standards, his mother had kept faith in him fifteen years after he ceased deserving it.

What finally brought her to full sobering reality was her eleven-year-old grandson Michael's reaction to his father's regime. The boy lived entirely with Carol now, since Helen's exile. Carol loved his son and wanted Michael's education handled better than his had been. As a result, the boy spent long hours studying military science, government, history, mathematics, philosophy and languages. Carol brought boys selected from every class and district in Romania into the royal schoolroom so that Michael should know firsthand the people he would one day rule. But his emotional life was tormented by his mother's absence and by hatred of the corrupt, unscrupulous advisors his father surrounded himself with.

"The child is without women's care," wrote Marie, "and has adapted a sort of Chinese smile to the outside world which is his only shield. He as much as said this to me on Christmas day: 'I have learned not to say what I feel and to smile at those I most hate.' "

For years Marie had blamed Carol's associates for his transgressions. Now, for the first time, she began holding him responsible for his associates. "A man ought to be strong enough to hold his own council," she wrote, "and there ought to be enough straightness in him to stand out against the crookedness of others."

Though Carol's return slogan had been, "Not to divide but to unite," it should have been "Divide and control." For his paranoia had him playing off one party or politician against the other with Machiavellian gusto. His ultimate goal was to reduce every power in Romania except his own. As a sideline, he was busily amassing a personal fortune.

To realize these ends, he needed subordinates. He found them, in profiteering yes-men like Puiu Dumitrescu and the depraved Ernest Urdareanu, who in 1933 oiled his way from aide-de-camp to replace Dumitrescu as Carol's private secretary. The others were "as unscrupulous a bunch of toughs," wrote *Life* magazine correspondent John Phillips, "as ever swaggered down the Calea Victoriei, men of no background or importance, whose future depended on his."

And, Phillips might have added, Lupescu's as well. For many of the coterie's members were her friends or relatives. And the rest acknowledged her for what she was fast becoming: virtual ruler of Romania. While traditionalist Romanians like Queen Marie and Juliu Maniu watched in anguished helplessness, Lupescu's influence grew daily stronger and more malignant. Far from the nonpolitical figure Carol had pictured her before his restoration, she had a finger in every pie in the realm. As a result, graft and corruption, not unknown in Romanian political circles, reached an all-time high. Her cohorts occupied all the key jobs, and she employed her own secret police. Thanks to this efficient network, her personal fortune was growing along with the King's, and her power, based on his, was absolute. With Maniu and Princess Helen out of the way, the only person in Romania whose presence still bothered her was Queen Marie.

Carol often asked his mother to meet his mistress, but she refused. The Queen admitted Lupescu's existence only to close friends and family and seldom by name, usually referring to her as that "lady of light repute." Everything in Marie's code and personality was revolted by everything in Lupescu's.

Born in Hertza in Moldavia in 1896, Elena Lupescu was the daughter of a Jewish junk dealer named Wolff and a Viennese Jewish girl who'd embraced Catholicism. After Elena's birth, Wolff Latinized his name to Lupescu and deserted junk for pharmacy. His drug business thrived, enabling him to send his little Elenutza to Bucharest's German Catholic convent school, Pitar Mosi. At seventeen Elena emerged from six years at Pitar Mosi equipped with a fairly good education and the externals of ladylike charm. Underneath, she was vulgar, ruthless, shrewd, secretive and egocentric. Possessed of driving ambition, she had only one goal: power. After a youthful marriage, which ended in divorce, and ten years as Carol's mistress, she had it. And it bothered her not at all that in realizing her aims she'd severed Carol's ties with his family, broken his mother's heart and brought Romania to the verge of economic collapse.

Lupescu had also become the most hated woman in Romania. The politicians hated her because she usurped their power and because they suspected, rightly, that she fed Carol's suspicious nature. And though the "She Wolf," as they called her, lived unobtrusively at her two-story red-brick villa in Bucharest's outskirts, entertaining her cohorts at poker parties spiced only with off-color jokes, the Romanian people knew she existed and despised her—for lining her pockets at their expense and for being Jewish.

Anti-Semitism was embedded as deeply in the Romanian national character as in the German, Russian, Hungarian or Polish. Baiting the nation's two million Jews was a centuries-old political and local tradition. The peasants, especially, hated Jews because for generations the local representatives of the absentee landlords had been Jewish. When Lupescu's name became synonymous with vice and corruption, Romanian anti-Semitism increased proportionately and Carol's popularity plummeted.

Chief spokesman for the anti-Lupescu forces was Corneliu Zelea Codreanu, a lawyer of Polish and German extraction who had founded the Fascist Legion of the Archangel Michael after the war. El Capitanul, as his followers called him, was a darkly handsome youth with a radiant, childlike smile and a saintly expression. Wearing the white peasant costume and carrying a sword in one hand and an icon in the other, he rode a white horse into the villages, capturing the peasants with his strange, mystical aura.

Like most Fascist leaders, Codreanu's basic code was simple: nationalism, militant Orthodoxy, peasant's rights, anti-Communism and anti-Semitism. But clothed with his own personal magnetisim, it sounded to Romanian peasants, students and young priests like pronouncements from God. When Codreanu said he'd come to lead them down a better road and convert them into a nobler race, they believed him. Transfixed by the fanatical glow emanating from his dark eyes, they pledged to follow him to the death. Many of them would.

When Codreanu's influence began assuming alarming proportions, Carol tried compromising with him. "It's a dangerous game," Marie warned him. "You shouldn't encourage nationalistic demagogues who get their inspiration from foreign ideologies."

Circumstances soon proved her right. By 1933 the Legion, rechristened the Iron Guard and supported emotionally and financially by Hitler and Mussolini, had grown from a radical fringe group into a contending political force. Inflamed by the country's still desperate economic situation, Codreanu had opened vocal fire on Carol and Lupescu.

Marie couldn't ignore the crisis, but neither could she do anything about it. So she spent the spring and summer traveling to Morocco, to Norway and Scotland with the "Pumas"; to Mignon in Belgrade; and to Ducky in France, where she helped this favorite sister through a late-breaking marital crisis.

That fall, Carol tried diverting public attention from Codreanu's virulent attacks by staging a glittering pageant commemorating the fiftieth anniversary of Castle Peles's construction. Desperate, he even included his family in the ceremonies.

"The reunion was a good thing," commented Marie. "He could have had us all without great festivities, which were too great an expense for our actual situation. He might have had us for love, but all the same it was good to be all together. I loved having all my children—a handsome lot, but so troublesome!"

The celebration was only partially successful. While bands played and the military paraded in bizarre new uniforms Carol had designed himself, strikes broke out in all the major industrial centers, and the rumor circulated that Lupescu had been murdered.

Carol was beside himself. As a King, he was not all bad. He didn't spend all his time engaged in sexual diversion, psychopathic vendettas and personal enrichment. And his brilliant mind conceived one solution after another for the country's problems. But his erratic personality failed in their execution. Romania had glorified Maniu and Carol in turn, hailing them as potential saviors. Now both had failed. In the weeks following the Peles celebration, the people flocked by the thousands to Codreanu's banner.

Marie could appreciate Carol's dilemma. "He is the saddest man under God's sky," she wrote Lavinia Small, "a sulky, suspicious solitary with glassy eye and hanging lip. And it is this distress alone which still keeps alive in me a spark of motherly love. But there are also moments when I find myself shuddering before him with something almost akin to physical disgust!"

While the division between King and Guardists rent the country, Marie busied herself with finishing her memoirs and redoubling her social work. She shuddered as Carol tried first bribery and then physical threats to bring Codreanu to terms. When neither worked, he turned to the one man potentially strong enough to handle the situation, his mother's old friend Jean Duca.

A long-time Liberal Party leader and therefore Carol's traditional enemy, Duca had been the anachronism in Bratianu's fold: a liberal in the true sense of the word. He was also the only Romanian politician aside from Maniu who was completely honest. But the resemblance ended there. Aristocratic, excitable, charming, gifted and a brilliant public speaker, Duca possessed none of the Peasant leader's rugged impassivity. But he believed in Western democratic principles to the exclusion of any political compromise, especially with Fascists. The

Iron Guard, therefore, rightly counted him their foremost political enemy, and reacted to his appointment with general riots. The lid was off at last as Fascist brutality began spilling through the country.

For the first time in six years, a Prime Minister turned to Marie in his extremity. "I can't govern Romania," Duca told her, "with the Guardists out of hand and anarchy rampant. The law must be enforced." He'd decided to dissolve the Guard.

Carol disagreed.

"Then, Sir," announced Duca, "I'll sign the decree of dissolution myself and take the whole responsibility on my own shoulders."

The declaration was signed, and on December 9 Duca's forces searched houses and meeting places, arresting innumerable Guardists. Codreanu went into hiding. On the evening of December 29, while the Prime Minister stood on the Sinaia railway platform after an audience with the King, he was shot and killed by a Guardist terrorist.

The news reached Marie late that night at Mödling, where she'd gone to see Ileana through her second childbirth. Awakened from a sound sleep, the Queen and her daughter sat till dawn, discussing the possible consequences of this brutal act so alien to the Romanian character. But Marie's concern was more personal than political. In the night stillness she mourned the loss of a dear friend.

22

The World Behind

On her way home Marie stopped in Belgrade as usual. Mignon's happy household, like Ileana's in Austria, provided an antidote to her increasingly sorrowful life. Marie's placid second daughter loved spoiling her mother, saying she wanted to pay back a little of the long spoiling she'd received as a child. And King Alexander made a point of surrounding her with the attention and respect Carol deprived her of at home.

Alexander didn't really like his mother-in-law. She spoke French, their only common language, badly. Unable to catch the guileless sincerity underlying even her occasionally outrageous remarks, he found her superficial. But it's a testament to his kind heart and her trusting nature that Marie thought her son-in-law loved her as she loved him.

For if Zwiedineck provided her with much-needed emotional solace, Alexander gave her the intellectual support she craved. "Sandro is what my sons failed to be," she wrote, "brother, friend and upholder. I come to his house as to a safe haven when the seas at home grow too tempestuous. He has a big brain and in him I find some of my own uncalculating generosity. He's not an easy man. He has humours, and he's always in a hurry. But he's also an artist at soul and loves the same things as I: beautiful buildings, old churches and monasteries, nature, gardening. And, like me, he's a builder."

Dutiful son-in-law and artist were but two hats the Serbian King wore gracefully. He was also a pianist and a collector—of books (20,000 volumes), Packard automobiles (twenty-three) and wealth (an estimated $10,000,000). But the bulk of his personality was austere, politically brilliant and hard-working, traits that made him one of the most powerful kings in Europe.

It was this power that Hitler and Mussolini eyed jealously while their fascist militarism moved the world toward another war. Especially Mussolini, dedicated to restoring Italy to its ancient greatness, lusted after Yugoslav lands over the border. When his imperialistic policy butted up against Alexander's nationalism, *Il Duce* took advantage of internal Yugoslavian dissension by encouraging the Croatians in their traditional struggle for freedom from Serbian supremacy.

The conflict had already erupted twice during Alexander's thirteen-year reign. In 1921, within minutes after taking the oath of office, he was shot at by a Croatian separatist. And in 1928 a Serbian delegate to the *Skupshina* (Parliament) killed two and wounded three Croatian leaders for an imagined insult. Fear for the continuation of his hard-won kingdom had caused Alexander to abolish the old constitution, assume dictatorial powers and transform the Kingdom of the Serbs, Croats and Slovenes into modern Yugoslavia. Faced as he was with bloody strife and predatory neighbors, it's little wonder he had "humours."

But life had given him one consolation: a supremely happy home life. Possessing neither Lisabetta's distinction nor Ileana's energy and character, Mignon was nevertheless the perfect mate for the hard-driving king. Patient and unpretentious, she blindly followed his lead, admired him completely and eased his frustrations. Sometimes, when his problems overwhelmed him, he locked himself in his room. "He has one of his moods," Mignon would explain, folding her hands and lifting her eyebrows with a gentle smile. "We must just leave him to himself until he feels sociable again."

In their new white stone palace, gleaming atop a hill outside Belgrade, she brought civilized warmth and gaiety into what had formerly been a soldier's spartan existence. Rebecca West, in her classic *Black Lamb and Grey Falcon,* described this royal life: "It is as if the Karageorgevitches, usually immersed in the tide of their terrible and splendid experience, had for a moment come to the surface to breathe."

With Duca dead and Carol's tenuous grip on Romanian affairs growing weaker, Marie needed this "peaceful halfway house" more than ever. So much so, in fact, that after a flying trip home to help Carol receive Boris of Bulgaria, she returned to Belgrade the first of February.

On her return Marie admitted the existence of a problem in the happy Yugoslav household. Mignon had borne her king three healthy, dark-haired sons: Peter, the ten-year-old heir; Tomislav, born in 1928; and Andrei, born in 1929. The two younger boys were predictably carefree and riotous. But young Peter, Marie noticed with dismay, had inherited Ferdinand's overpowering shyness and insecurity. He even took refuge in the same awkward and unbecoming mannerisms. Worse than that, he was being poorly educated. Alexander's preoccupation with ruling and Mignon's easygoing disposition had let them keep Peter's English nanny, Miss Crowther, as his only instructor long after he should have been involved in a topflight educational program. As if that weren't enough, Miss Crowther was neither a governess nor even a professional-ly-trained teacher.

Marie couldn't stand the woman. "Crowdy has the word which drops poison, I have watched it," she wrote Ileana's retired governess, Ida Marr. "It is said with a lazy drawl—but it is *said*—and it goes into Mignon's mind to stay."

Deeply concerned, Marie convinced King Alexander that his heir must have a proper education. When she suggested an English school, he readily agreed and promised to make the necessary arrangements. The other unpleasant reality, that Mignon made an easy target for malicious intriguers, was less readily resolved.

Marie returned to Bucharest and political mayhem. Duca's assassins had been arrested, but Codreanu was still in hiding. Lupescu had fled the country in panic. And when the assassins got off with light sentences, angry Romanians openly accused Carol of bargaining for his mistress's life with his Prime Minister's killers.

Marie watched the mounting discontent anxiously. "I smell danger," she wrote Miss Marr. "But Carol seems unconscious, still hanging onto the influences and ways which have been gradually destroying him. Can I remain dumb on the edge of a precipice? Isn't it my duty to try and save him now that everthing is boiling? I don't know."

Doubling her pain was a growing sense of personal responsibility. "My fear of hurting," she wrote in April, "has been a shackle in my life. And much of the trouble I have today with my children is that I always respected overmuch their personalities and never wanted to tyrannize and oppress." She was right in feeling guilty; perhaps her greatest failure as a woman and as Queen was the failure to properly educate her children, either academically or morally. But it was a

reality she couldn't look at too often or too hard: "They did not understand my generosity. Nor do they pause to consider that if all things
are not well with them today as it was when their father lived, it is
because I am no longer at the helm . . . At his death, they all came into
their separate fortunes. They cut the string and each rolled into his own
little corner and did his or her worst, except Ileana and Mignon."

In May Carol's personal popularity touched rock bottom. The rumor
spread that an attempt would be made on his life during the national
independence day parade. Hoping to cloak himself in his mother's
popularity, he brought her out of mothballs for the occasion.

Whatever the reason behind it, Marie's last public appearance was
reminiscent of her great former triumphs. When she came in sight, as
she'd done every May Tenth in the past, on horseback and in uniform
at the head of her regiment, the crowds went mad with joy. No one
watching her ride by that morning ever forgot the enchanting mixture
of sovereign and still-beautiful woman.

Far from thanking his mother for saving the day, Carol exploded in
a jealous rage, stepping up the petty annoyances he used to plague her
daily life.

Since she was forced to endure such endless grievances, one wonders
why Marie didn't leave the country entirely, and build a house and a
life for herself near Ileana in Austria, with Ducky on the French coast,
or even in England, where her heart returned with increasing nostalgia
as life in her adopted country grew more painful.

The answer was twofold. Pride kept her from setting up residence
outside Romania, for by so doing she would have admitted her life was
a failure. Also, though permanently out of commission as a public
personality, she loved the country too much to desert it in its hour of
need, no matter the agonies she must endure in staying. Besides, her
royal code precluded surrender. With a tenacity that disturbed her
friends and astounded her enemies, she clung to one hope till death: that
Carol would change his attitude, take her back as mother and Queen,
and let her work once more for the people she loved and who, in her
view, desperately needed her.

In the meantime, like a person in pain who sees constant motion as
the only antidote, she moved constantly from place to place. Summers
were spent at Balcic, where she'd acquired a speedboat, built a small
stable and added new gardens and terraces on the upper level above the
house. Every September found her at Bran, wandering through a maze
of blooming dahlias. She returned to Cotroceni for the harsh winter

months, avoiding Sinaia almost entirely now, because Lupescu had installed herself in the remodeled Foisor.

Since Carol seldom allowed them to visit, she also had to constantly hop over the mountains to Mignon and Ileana. In late May of 1934 she visited Ileana and Anton in the third home they had occupied as a married couple.

The sixteenth-century Austrian castle of Sonnberg was a sturdy, foursquare little building built around a courtyard on an island surrounded by a medieval moat and a great park with many fine old trees. Marie loved the old schloss, and Ileana turned over one whole wing to her mother for use on her frequent visits.

To Marie, arriving at the "Pumas' " unconventional and affectionate menage was like plunging into restorative waters. Stays with them soothed her nerves and made her feel wanted and needed again. She still wished Ileana had done more with her life. But when she implied this, Ileana told her, "Mama, I'm climbing a staircase, and now I'm sitting on the landing. This is an interim period in my life; there's more to come." And Marie adored her grandchildren—toddler Stefan and the baby, Marie-Ileana, called Minola after a character in one of Marie's fairy tales.

She was loved in return. "My mother's presence radiated life and light," Ileana recalled years later in her book *I Live Again*. "Everyone loved her. Everything was nicer when she was there—even the village children's faces took on a new look, for she was always interested in each one. I remember that one year for Christmas she crocheted a little cap in bright colors for each child."

Marie never loved her grandchildren as she had her own children, but she delighted in their company. They, in turn, remembered her as a smiling, sweet-scented creature who moved through her flowers with dogs at her heels and told them wonderful fairy stories.

While at Sonnberg, Marie completed some unexpected plans for her will: "According to royal tradition, when I die I am supposed to be laid at rest in the beautiful church of Curtea de Arges where my husband lies. My place is at his side. But in my will, I ask that my heart should be taken from my body, put in a precious casket (which I leave), and buried in the little Stella Maris chapel at Balcic, the small rustic church overlooking the sea. In olden days the hearts of Kings or Queens were often taken from their bodies and brought either back to their former homes, or to some special sanctuary . . . I wish to have my heart buried in the wee church I built myself. All through life so many people came to my heart for love or understanding that I would like them to come also when I am gone. Walk up along the lily path, up to where my heart lies beneath the screened-in altar of the little Orthodox church built by a Protestant."

Sentimental? She herself admitted that it was. But she could no more stop romanticizing life, even its end, than she could stop living it to the fullest. As long as she was able to retain her ever-young capacity for enjoying beauty, she would find strength to withstand the ugliness. How long would it last? "As long as my health holds," she assured her friends, "for the spirit will not weaken."

On July 25 the assassination of Austrian Chancellor Dollfuss by the Nazis darkened her world with the growing shadow of European politics. Like so many others, the Queen still withheld judgment on Hitler. "What a curious figure he is," she said. "Mostly everybody's virulent against him abroad. And what Germany's real feelings for him are, it's difficult to perceive." But the blind chauvinism he represented disturbed her greatly.

Marie possessed less political acumen than she thought she had, but her prophetic sense seldom failed. Never pleased with the Versailles treaty, she viewed the extreme nationalism it bred as the major threat to peace, while envisioning a united Europe as the Continent's only chance for survival.

She saw not Germany but Russia as Romania's foremost political enemy. "Yes, Russia! It fills me with a feeling of horror," she wrote from Balcic when the Romanian government renewed diplomatic relations with the Soviets. The man responsible, Romania's celebrated Foreign Minister Titulescu, was a brilliant tactician and a long-time admirer of Marie's. But she wept the day she heard the news and could hardly shake hands when he came expecting congratulations. "We are so terribly near them," she fumed. "I think it is a huge and dangerous mistake. I certainly do not mean to receive in my house those who murdered all my mother's family!"

Having wistfully dubbed a new cloister well at Balcic *Suliman Leic,* the Waters of Peace, she summarized her feelings concerning the possibility of another war. "The cloud of uncertainty hanging over Europe is indeed a heavy weight, making all future outlook precarious. Even when I contemplate the work of my hands in the places I love, an anxiety steals into my heart, and I wonder what my ultimate fate will be. Will I also live to be uprooted and to become an exile one day, just at an age when one dreams of harvest and rest?"

A last triumph remained. In September 1934 she visisted England for the publication of her autobiography. Published in two volumes, *The Story of My Life* was an immediate critical and popular success. Beginning with her favorite Nietzsche quote, "Character is destiny," it covered her life from birth to accession. It was sentimental, witty, long and sometimes repetitious. After all, as she said herself, she knew nothing of the "rules of the game." But her book was so candid and sincere, breaking the traditional rule that memoirs of famous people are dull, that it blazed a trail for the long run of confessional autobiographies that followed.

She was praised high and low for her ability to shed a kind of magic over people and events, and one reviewer compared her to H. G. Wells. Even Virginia Woolf, in a wittily bitchy review, admitted, "Queen Marie can write."

She hadn't been in England for nine years. Since then, the happy and triumphant Regina Maria had become a lonely and persecuted woman. Too proud to accept pity, she had stayed away, enduring her humiliation without the support of her relatives and oldest friends. Now her book and its success paved her way back. And she stood basking in the praise and affection as in healing sunshine.

From London, where she visited the Astors and was enthusiastically toasted by society, she entrained for Balmoral. King George and Queen Mary greeted her with their usual restrained and decorous affection. "You can think, in contrast," Marie laughed to a friend, "impulsive, uncalculating, unconventional me. I am always astonished that they really like me, but they do."

Basking in the vacation castle she hadn't visited since Queen Victoria's day, Marie relaxed and unwound. King George had kept his special affection for her. "I stimulate him," she admitted. "My uncrushable vitality makes the blood course more quickly though his veins." And kindhearted Queen Mary liked her too. Besides, she was a good guest. "I have been so starved of certain things I can enjoy them with the intensity of a child."

Back in London, with two weeks of her trip remaining, she dived back into the heady whirl of parties and luncheons. Late on the afternoon of October 9, she visited a flower show featuring Michaelmas daisies, carnations and the dahlias she loved.

At five P.M. she left the exhibition hall for a cup of tea with her old friend Dr. Madge and his family. She was in the Madge sitting room, regaling her hosts with amusing anecdotes, when the phone rang. It was the Romanian ambassador telling her that King Alexander of Yugoslavia had been assassinated at Marseilles, while on an official trip to France. Mignon was a widow. Ten-year-old Peter was King.

Marie described her reaction: "I got up from my seat. I felt as though someone had given me a tremendous blow on my heart and I felt like crying out for mercy: 'No! No! Not that, do not let it be that! Do not ask me to accept this horror, this new, too great annihilating sorrow. Let this cup pass from me."

But it could not pass. Haunted by the realization she could no longer avoid, that her personal success story was ending in dire tragedy, she packed her bags and gathered up Peter at his new school.

Unable to directly break the news of his father's death to the skinny, wide-eyed boy, she finally said, "Peter, you know people will call you Majesty now."

"But I can't be King," he cried. "I'm much too small."

Marie learned the details of Alexander's murder on the trip to Paris. He had arrived at Marseilles on a man-o'-war, while Mignon, who suffered from a minor liver ailment, took the train at doctors' orders. Plans called for them to meet at Lyons the night of the tenth and travel together to Paris, where a reception with full military honors waited to conduct them down the Champs Élysées. After disembarking, the King had barely seated himself in an open carriage beside French Minister Louis Barthou when shots rang out, killing both Alexander and Barthou. The killer was a Macedonian terrorist named Vlada Georgin.

Now Alexander lay on a velvet sofa in Marseilles's little town hall, with the Serbian flag draping his body and a smile of greeting still covering his face. And without this self-made King at the helm, the Yugoslav nation automatically presented a weaker face to its enemies —both outside its borders and within.

Fearing another assassination, the French government had Marie and Peter's train stopped in the countryside outside Paris. Jacques Dumaine, Chief of Protocol at the Quai d' 'Orsay, waited in the rain-swept night with five cars to convey the boy King, his grandmother and their suites into Paris. A rickety wooden platform, hastily erected beside the track, and bricks laid through pools of water to the highway formed a makeshift welcome site illuminated by lanterns held high by men stationed on either side of the path.

The train roared into sight, stopping with a screech that woke the countryside. Marie stepped down, holding her grandson by the hand. Filled with grief though she was, she couldn't ignore the inherent drama the scene afforded.

"The grandmother found this opportunity to exercise her theatrical majesty," recalled Jacques Dumaine. "She did it magnificiently, stepping from stone to stone, never looking down, thanking us with a sad smile. As we reached the cars, Queen Marie turned to M. Flandin, who suggested that she enter a separate car: 'Do not separate the orphan from his grandmother.' "

Marie and Peter joined Mignon in Paris. Heartbroken but composed, the young Queen took the blow of her husband's death with impressive simplicity. Her consideration for French President Albert Lebrun's embarrassment won her the hearts of the French people. "She has become for us a national widow," a French politician told Marie. "The whole of France considers itself in her debt."

Alexander's funeral deified the national hero he'd been for the Serbians. Six million people filed past his bier, and weeping crowds knelt along the funeral route for miles outside Belgrade. "You had the sensation that the ground itself and all the buildings were shedding bitter tears," wrote Marie.

Her heart bled for Yugoslavia, so torn with internal dissension, and for Mignon, the most vulnerable of her children. "Now she is quite lost," wrote Marie, "and her helplessness hurts me. I know life. I do not wish to exaggerate anything, to dramatize or mourn or wail. But there is tragedy in our two fates. But hers has come too soon. She had, according to the laws of nature, the right to a longer happiness."

Marie felt strangely in touch with the dead King. "I understood him so well, so much better than most of them did," she mused with more sincerity than truth. "We were builders, and there is an inner loneliness about builders. We talk of him. We do not relegate him to his coffin. We let his spirit move among us."

That November she stayed in Belgrade. The days passed in a blur of sorrow contrasting strongly with the cozy domestic setting. Ida Marr, the family's beloved "Mimarr," read aloud, while a Yugoslav artist sketched Marie—badly. Zwiedineck looked pained. "That's not my Queen," he moaned. And Mignon held her head to one side, declaring, "Maica, Maica, you are a hopeless model." Marie wrote Ileana that the problem wasn't that she'd moved—"I sat like a statue"—but because her face was "baffling. Expression alone seems to make it what it is."

And grief, she might have added, for she had never felt more unhappy in her life.

Nicolas arrived on a flying visit. "He is leaving soon for the whole winter," Marie wrote. "I shall no more find him at Cotroceni when I return. The night he spent here, he sat till two in the morning talking to me. Nicky really yearns for a family life as long as it would include his Jeanne. All these events and complications weigh on my heart. They have all of them made such a mess of things, and the way they so unfeelingly destroyed all that used to be, has disabled me. I am no more *able* to stick together what they smashed. Nicky is talking with intense bitterness of Carol and his surroundings and he is detaching himself from everything in a way which fills me with apprehension. And Sandro the builder had to be torn away! How inexplicable it all is, how sad."

She spent Christmas "quite alone" at Cotroceni, after a "tremendously military" Christmas Eve at Sinaia with Carol and Michael; she had become great friends with her grandson. From Cotroceni she wrote: "My palace feels very large and empty. I am inclined to fold my hands in my lap, to sit quite still and to ponder over the strangeness of my fate."

In this melancholy mood, she slipped quietly into 1935. While the snow piled high beneath her windows, she sat alone for hours, drinking a cup of soup for dinner and writing letters. For the first time in her life, she looked backward rather than ahead.

"My world stands in the shadow behind me," she wrote, recalling herself at seventeen—"a little girl with confident eyes who believed in life and human hearts"—and wistfully remembering the happy, powerful years that had gone forever.

23

The Road to Damascus

Spring came and her spirits rose. Part of the reason for her good cheer was that her autobiography had been published in Romania and had become an immediate best-seller. The book completed the job that Carol's continual mistreatment had inadvertently begun—that of restoring her place in the people's affections. The peasants had never stopped loving her. But now even the fickle middle class and critical intellectuals closed ranks behind her, as an overwhelming nostalgia for the days when she had symbolized Greater Romania gripped Romanians to a man. Wherever she went, she was greeted with warmth and affection.

Indeed the book's success was her greatest consolation for the sorrow and grief that filled her life. Along with English, American and Romanian editions, it was being translated into German, French, Swedish, Danish, Polish, Czech, Italian and Hungarian. "They've even asked for it in Japanese!" laughed the Queen. "I feel like a hen who's hatched ducklings!"

Her ultimate triumph as a writer occurred in May. Coinciding with the appearance of her third volume, she was called before the prestigious Royal Literary Society in London as the first woman to receive their award. On a flying visit to England, she spoke "easily if not classically" at the Literary Society banquet, attended a literary luncheon in her honor and was asked by her publisher for a fourth volume, which she happily agreed to write.

Her trip also coincided with her cousin George's Silver Jubilee as King. In twenty-five years he'd evolved from a colorless unknown into the father of his people—a wise, benevolent, conservative symbol of all that was best in the English temperament and tradition. On May 6, with his equally popular Queen Mary at his side, he rode through cheering throngs to a moving service held at St. Paul's Cathedral. It was a soft, sunny day; the flowers bloomed in Green Park; and in those anxious, insecure times there was something reassuring about the celebration and the regal, gray-haired couple it honored.

Watching from her place in St. Paul's, Marie reflected that it might have been her riding through the brightly decorated streets. If her mother had so decreed, she might now be Queen of England and regal symbol of the far-flung British Empire.

Did she ever regret not marrying George and becoming Queen of England? It's safe to assume that occasionally she did, especially after she'd been publicly humiliated in Romania in a way that could never have happened in England. But she was wise enough to realize two things: for all their problems, she and the sensitive, scholarly Ferdinand had been happier than she could ever have been with brusque, rigid King George; and in England she could never have fulfilled her personality as she had in Romania. Still, she was first and foremost an Englishwoman. And her love for Romania never made her feel less proud of feeling English and loving England with all her heart.

After the Jubilee she paid a visit to her childhood home, Eastwell Park in Kent. Then she retreated for several days to Cliveden. Her affection for Waldorf Astor, and his for her, had never died. Even in the company of his wife Nancy, Britain's witty and acerbic first woman Member of Parliament, they were the warm and humorous companions they'd always been.

"Lord Astor is a born angel," Marie wrote an American friend, "and Nancy is wonderful, stimulating company, overbubbling with life, energy, wit, good advice and kindness. Her tongue's occasionally over-witty and outspoken. But she has a noble spirit and I love her."

Once again, Marie's self-delusion where others were concerned partially blurred the facts. Princess Ileana later said that Nancy Astor never got over her original jealousy of the Queen. And sometimes the wit she aimed at her husband's first love was cutting in the extreme.

"Marie, you're a moral prostitute," she exclaimed at one Cliveden dinner.

Aglow with renewed vitality, Marie turned up in Austria before the month ended to preside over the birth of her seventh grandchild and Ileana's second daughter, Alexandra. A "very Catholic" christening held in Sonnberg's big drawing room drew a large family reunion. Even sister Ducky arrived from France.

Marie spent the summer following the sun from Balcic to Castle Bran, exulting in her role of "gardener-Queen." In August she joined Mignon and sister Baby at Mignon's vacation home on the magnificent Dalmation coast.

Then came fall, bringing her sixtieth birthday.

Fearing another public demonstration, Carol canceled the Bucharest festivities that had been planned and staged a private party at Sinaia instead. Always a moral coward, he sent Zwiedineck to break the news to her.

She hadn't wanted a lot of money spent on her during this time of continuing economic crisis. But the birthday celebration had been organized by all the charitable organizations she'd founded through the years. And the thought of riding publicly through the streets of Bucharest for one last time had filled her with pleasurable excitement.

Confronted with this ultimate expression of Carol's ill will, she decided to have it out with him. Afer a family lunch at the Foisor, she drew him into his study and closed the door. No one ever knew what was said during that interview, but Marie came out, as Ileana remembered, with a "small gray face." And the Bucharest celebration was not held.

Carol was probably right—a public celebration would have turned into a love feast. For, having rediscovered her through her book, Romanians instinctively sensed that Regina Maria had attained a new maturity. It put her in a new light, and one they liked.

Her strength was still more of the heart than of the mind. She still loved looking at herself, still often spoke and wrote too candidly for her own good, still combined naive enthusiasms with childish vanities. She could still be disarmingly simple, though supremely royal. Despite heartache and disillusion, she remained a fighter. "All right, I'm supposed to be in dry dock today," she snapped, "but when the moment comes, I'll have it out." But the inherent humanism that had shown through her theatricality in the past now gave her what the French call "the intelligence of the heart." The term implies sensitivity, tolerance and compassion for human frailties. At sixty Marie possessed all three.

The problem for her was that these qualities also made her more vulnerable. She might bubble over with vitality and fun, maintain perfect health, look forty in a pink dress and announce: "I snap my fingers at my sixty years!" But something in her had died forever.

In what might have been her epitaph, she wrote: "I have lived my life with every fibre. There was never a way to Damascus in my life. Events which occurred were sometimes merry ones, but mostly tragic or painful, and that has modified my appreciation of many things."

Her appearance reflected her altered outlook. She called it her "Italian summer," this strange new beauty that had come to her so late. Her hair still shone dull gold, her profile flashed its patrician line, her skin remained unlined. But her ice-blue eyes, sunk more deeply than ever in their great sockets, burned with profound sadness. Along with excess weight, she'd also shed her spectacular costumes. And the streamlined hair and dress styles of the thirties suited her better than the ill-proportioned twenties garb ever had.

Marie observed her new look with characteristic vanity. "I can see it myself," she told a friend, "so when I am told about it, I know that it's true, not flattery. I feel a sort of vibration of appreciation shudder through a crowd when I appear, because my appearance is still a pride to them. I perceive this. But although it gives me a second's pleasure, it fills me also with sadness. I look down upon all the faces upturned towards me and tears come into my eyes. I would like to spread out my hands in a gesture of pity for myself and for them: 'Too late, my children, too late—*l'inutile beauté,* it is only a glimmer today of what was."

In January 1936, Carol commissioned the famed Hungarian portraitist Sir Philip de László to paint him, Lupescu and his mother. The Queen was involved with her settings, enjoying the froglike László's glib chatter about the many personalities his flattering brush had captured, when word came that King George had died in England.

Marie grieved for her first love and lifelong friend. His affectionate concern and Victorian mentality had made him a conscience from her childhood. And the further apart their lives and outlooks had grown, the more she'd valued their relationship. Now she made a great sacrifice. She let Carol attend the King's funeral in her place. She felt it was one moment when her son could take his place among other monarchs without being cold-shouldered. It would be good for him and for the country if he went. But she hated staying away.

On January 24 she wrote Queen Mary: "It is very hard to remain away from you all just now. But I considered I would only be in the way if I came, though all my instinct was to rush off to London so as to accompany the dear friend of my youth to his last resting place and to be able to tell you personally how I grieve for you. You were such wonderful companions, sharing faithfully all that life brought you, joy and sorrow.

"You will be very lonely now—and all changes are so harrowing, besides the great central grief. I follow your every feeling with almost painful understanding. May much be spared you which I had to endure. . . .

"I am horribly sad—so much goes to the grave with dear Georgie, so many happy memories! May you have the quiet strength you always have to bear all those sad ceremonies and the cruel loneliness which will follow—and may your children be a comfort to you as some of mine have been to me."

On February 19 Marie received word that her sister Ducky was dying in Germany. Ducky's life since the Russian Revolution had beeen unremittingly hard. She and Cyril had lost everything, counting themselves lucky to escape Russia with their lives. For the first three years after the Revolution, they'd barely subsisted with their children in a tiny house in Finland. With little food and firewood and no light at night, they'd spent the dark Finnish winters fearing Bolshevik attack. When they finally escaped to St. Briac, a small seaside resort in Brittany, Cyril had proclaimed himself Tsar of Russia, a pose which placed Ducky in many untenable and often embarrassing situations, though she backed him to the hilt.

Unbending, authoritative and domineering, Ducky was also proud, uncompromisingly honest and loyal. Her inability to compromise proved her undoing. During Marie's Brittany visit in 1933, Ducky had discovered that Cyril had been unfaithful to her since their marriage. For twenty-five years, while she'd worshiped and supported him to the exclusion of all else, he'd betrayed her. "After that," according to Marie, "she died by inches."

Now, felled by a sudden stroke, she lay in her daughter's modest house in Amorbach, Bavaria. The last meeting of the four sisters around her bedside was tragic and deeply moving. All but Sandra had been great beauties and born leaders. "I used gentleness and a deep understanding of the other's side of the question," explained Marie. "Ducky used strength and withering contempt when disappointed.

Sister Bee used and uses diplomacy." They had come a long way since the Coburg years. With marriage, each had adopted a foreign country and each had seen that country through political upheaval and bloodshed. Their nations had fought one another. But for all that, the sisters had remained close, forming an unbreakable bond of affection that the most intense national loyalty had never severed.

Marie had been Ducky's dearest friend and ally since earliest childhood; therefore her grief was strongest.

"When told by my sisters that I was there," the Queen wrote an American friend, "she immediately connected the thought of me with flowers and murmured something about lilies. We both loved our gardens. I also had the consolation to hear her say, when asked if she was pleased I had come, 'It makes all the difference.'

"She died at midnight. The next morning I went to her for a last time alone. We had wrapped her in a long soft white silk robe. We had few flowers at Amorbach, but I had some white lilies which I laid round her head and shoulders, and Sandra put a bunch of freesia in her hands. I had not many tears, but I talked to her. I told her how sad it was to see her go and how lonely it would be. We buried her at Coburg, beside Mama, Papa and brother Alfred. It was a cold day, half snow, half rain. I hate funerals. I am not one of those who like weeping on graves."

No death since Mircea's had struck her so deeply. Feeling lost and forsaken, she crept to Ileana at Sonnberg. But even in the Pumas' exuberant household she couldn't settle down. Deeply depressed, she seemed continually searching for something she'd lost.

László painted another picture of her in mourning veils to complement the original full regalia pose. The expression in the later likeness was sad and thoughtful. A friend who had seen the finished work told Marie it was "superb—at the same time dignified, simple and extremely royal."

"László realized by being with me," Marie answered sadly, "that if I had lost in brilliance, I had gained in depth. I had to be purified and to learn how much of my old life was vanity. It's not in vain that, on decline, so much is taken from us. It's to prepare us for the end. To sow the seed of longing for another life in our tired souls."

She moved to Balcic, where she busied herself planting a memory garden for Ducky and adding a white, domed sitting room to her pergola. She preferred solitude to company now. "Sometimes my wisdom seems to have become so deep that I have to hide it away not to become offensive. Because for most it is uncompromisingly strong."

Someone mailed her a copy of the *Illustrated London News* covering her wedding. "How quaint and pathetic it is," she mused, leafing through the yellowed pages. "How absurdly and yet touchingly old-fashioned. The Kaiser and all the rest! Such different times from today and so much fuss about small things, and all of us so well off and pompous." She smiled sadly.

Certainly times were different now. Mussolini was completing his conquest of Ethiopia. Hitler's troops had crossed the Rhineland to the French border. Spain teetered on the verge of civil war. Encouraged by these successes, the Iron Guard had made further inroads in Romania. Marie's fear of another war grew accordingly. "I don't believe in war," she wrote sadly, "but perhaps we are going towards a readjustment to which nothing in me agrees. Often I wonder what is to be my final fate."

For her at least, the handwriting was on the wall. If war came, Romania must choose between Germany and Russia. The prospect terrified her. "We could not stand another war. We could not live through it. It would be the end of everything."

In July she fled to England with Anton and Ileana. Even that haven was clouded by popular criticism of the Astors' so-called Cliveden set, which was reportedly advocating appeasement of Hitler, and by the approaching abdication crisis. But Marie ignored politics, settling into beautiful Cliveden with a sigh of pleasure.

And she'd always liked Britain's new King, Edward VIII. After a family lunch at Buckingham Palace, she wrote: "Certainly the young King is much more modern in all his conceptions than the old. Also they say he is very stubborn. Personally I think he is perfectly fascinating. Of course I should prefer having a Queen rather than a lady who already had a husband, and who, if she is thinking more of herself than of him, can do a lot of harm."

Privately, she hoped her English family's growing difficulties concerning the King's love for the twice-divorced American, Wallis Simpson, would give them a more sympathetic understanding of her similar torments.

Things on the home front were worsening. Carol's persecutions had grown apace with her personal grief to such an extent that she couldn't face Romania after England. She headed for Mignon instead.

"For the first time," she wrote from the Dalmatian coast, "I am obliged to make a mighty effort to preserve my optimism. I am continually hit in the back and subjected to ugly and unnecessary humiliations by those surrounding the master. They egg him on to maltreat me, because I will not bow down to what I consider wrong and harmful. Besides the cruel grief, there is also much danger. Sometimes I cannot even pray."

The situation had finally deprived her of all her "fine belief in others." And Marie recognized Lupescu as her foremost enemy: "I have reached the limit of my loyalty towards one who tortures me to please another who is as low-born as she is ambitious, a woman who is disastrous to the man who sacrifices honor, honesty, loyalty, duty to feed her ever-growing greed."

On December 11, in the "greatest news story," said H. L. Mencken, "since the Resurrection," King Edward VIII abdicated the throne in favor of his younger brother, the Duke of York, who became King George VI. That night Edward left England as Duke of Windsor to marry Mrs. Simpson.

Queen Marie had followed the events leading up to the abdication with concentrated interest. "I hardly dare wish you a happy Christmas," she wrote Edward's mother, Queen Mary, on December 19, "knowing all you have gone through. Perhaps no one can more completely understand your pain and grief than I, who have so suffered through my sons. It was even because of this that I have not written sooner. I knew too well what your sorrow must be. But my thoughts were with you in intense sympathy and with an understanding only possible to one who has been hit in the same way."

Queen Mary was only too aware of the similarities. "Really! This might be Romania!" she was reported to have said in the early days of the crisis.

Marie's attitude towards the ex-King was less sympathetic than her feelings for his mother. "Personally I am too royal," she wrote a friend, "not to look upon David as a deserter. Also I can work up no feelings for Mrs. Simpson. There is something . . . about her which does not make it a clean, fine love-romance. She has too much to do with cocktails and night clubs. She is an uninteresting heroine. I dislike her face, her name, her attitude, her style, the world she represents."

Meanwhile Marie's year was passing in a rising crescendo of grief. Death had claimed her favorite Balcic gardener, then her favorite aide-de-camp, a handsome, idealistic youth who'd loved her completely and stood up bravely to the "flood of iniquity" surging around her. Her favorite nephew, Beatrice's second son, Alonzo, was killed in the Spanish civil war. "He died heroically during his first battle," wrote Marie.

"His plane was shot down in flames." In December her favorite lady-in-waiting, Simky Lahovary, died of cancer. "We're all deserting her when she needs us most," Simky mourned before she died. And on Christmas Day Marie's old German maid, who had been with her for thirty years, died in Berlin.

But for all the empty places around her, somehow she minded Carol's failure most of all. "Sometimes I feel I must die so as not to have to look at such decadence," she told a friend. Then in tears, she asked pitifully, "Are all ends of life so sad?"

She spent Christmas at Sonnberg. Ileana felt her mother looked "awfully ill" and "terribly tired," but chalked it up to the many griefs accumulating around her. And though Marie herself noticed a minor physical irregularity about herself, she said nothing, preferring to lose herself in playing with her grandchildren and ice skating on the frozen Sonnberg moat.

What were her thoughts as she skimmed gracefully around the little schloss? Perhaps she searched the winter horizon for clues to what level of misery Carol's inferno held for her next.

Only one remained.

24

Character Is Destiny

Her resistance was low that winter, so low in fact that when she returned home she relaxed her proud reserve and with a cry of anguished
desperation wrote Carol a letter. Filling twenty pages, it covered twenty
grievances against her son and those of his henchmen who had harassed
her for six years.

"I want this to be a quiet talk between two friends," she began
calmly, "no accusations. But I've been silent for so long that the moment has come to talk."

Point by point, she took up the many griefs she'd endured. Then, in
spite of herself, she pleaded, "Consult me occasionally. I have links
with the rest of the world. Don't be so frightfully arbitrary, life becomes
too impossibly dull and restricted."

Her old fire returned in stormy conclusion: "I may be forced to
accept your rules and orders. But I do so under protest, and this protest
I shall not silence. I consider it an attack against my personal dignity.
Therefore, I ask, I even demand, as my right: give my house the
independence it had before. You can do it, I deserve this. I have been
patient and long-suffering. But do not tighten the bow too much, or it
will snap and there will be disaster."

Weary of the struggle, she made a final plea. "Give me your hand,
my son. Let us live in good peace and content. It *can* be done if you

leave my house alone, respecting my rights and treating me with all the respect you owe one who was a builder a long time before you."

Carol never answered the letter. It was found, years later, in the drawer of a table that had belonged to Lupescu.

As 1937 opened, Marie had few consolations against the tragedy that dogged her. Her flowers, riding, occasional visits with Ileana, her relationship with the thoughtful and charming Zwiedineck and her work on the fourth volume of her life story—these were the things that still made her happy.

Another consolation was the voluminous correspondence she carried on with a young American man she'd never met. Hearing of her World War I heroism, he'd written her a fan letter years ago. She'd replied. Now they corresponded frequently. Her "spirit talks," as she called them, with this "noble and good" youth were like a balm after the failure of her sons. Lonely and sad, she poured out her heart to this sympathetic listener. As she wrote, a wealth of wisdom and beauty flowed onto the paper. In a way this correspondence provided a summation of her life. In it she described her triumphs and tragedies, her hopes and fears. She discussed the men—and women—who'd adored her to smothering excess: "Ever again I had to put people out of my life." She described the personal magnetism that clung to her like a fading garland but would not die. "But within myself, I am aloof, too wise. I know too much, have seen and felt too much."

She admitted she'd never expected to be "anything but lovable," adding that "nobody ever understood that the kindness of my heart was the principle basis of all my nature—that and a sort of fundamental rashness, a desire to do as I desired, believing in my artless simplicity that people could understand me, which they did not."

She wrote of her "almost uncanny understanding of what others are feeling. Sometimes its torture and tears choke me." Then: "To me the hour of victory was always sad, because victory is always over someone, and I cannot bear to contemplate the beaten man even if he is my enemy. This weakness has all through life prevented my being a really strong woman."

Sadder, wiser, more reflective though she'd become, Marie of Romania still described how she *felt* in situations rather than attempting analysis of herself and others. She considered psychoanalysis "stuff and nonsense." Yet had she been able to observe Carol, for example, from a background of Freudian theory, it might have been a comfort. As it was, she could only ask "Why?"

As she wrote, another theme preyed on her mind: fear that she might live to see a second world war.

"If the instinct of destruction wins the upper hand," she wrote, "then Europe will go down and all the horror of Russia will sweep over everything that was beautiful and worthwhile living for. This thought is so frightful that my only prayer is not to have to live to see it."

As if in answer to her wish, she suddenly fell ill on March 11.

"It came to me as a great surprise," she wrote Prince Stirbey, "especially as all winter I had been feeling especially well, also looking my best. I had been very active and been a great deal to concerts, etc., doing my social work bravely, also giving many luncheons, receiving many people.

"Then I caught a slight grippe and having many engagements, I could not immediately look after myself. Then my stomach began to behave rather strangely and one night having to get up, I wanted to reach my bathroom, when suddenly I was taken by a queer faintness and my legs would not obey me. And instead of being able to turn into my bathroom, my silly legs carried me in another direction, and I finally fell over the screen standing near the door. The screen came down and I with it. I managed to pull myself together and finally reach my bathroom, where I collapsed on my couch. Luckily I could find the bell and my maids appeared.

"I was feeling awfully bad, so unlike my usual habits. I told them to telephone Dr. Mamulea and send him a motor. He came rather quickly and while talking to him, I was suddenly fearfully sick, before one was able to bring me a basin. And what I brought out looked awfully nasty and certainly like blood. He told me not to move but to keep quite still on my back—I think he had a good fright. I was still feeling very giddy, so was quite patient and did all I was told.

"They thought it must be a stomach ulcer, but after a radiograph they saw that my stomach was quite all right. But analysis proved there was a loss of blood from somewhere. I had no pain—it must have been a small vein which burst, or something. Of course absolute quiet was recommended and no food, except some cold liquid. I submitted with outward good grace, but inward revolt."

For over a month she lay in bed in her vaulted Cotroceni bedroom, severely weakened by recurring internal hemorrhages. Dr. Mamulea, the court doctor, and his associates, unable to diagnose her actual problem, said she might be suffering from cirrhosis of the liver and/or a breakdown of the artery walls in and around her liver. How this could be possible in a woman who never touched alcohol, Mamulea admitted he didn't know. In any case, what she needed was blood, live transfusions to replace the blood she'd lost. What Mamulea prescribed was complete immobility, cold food and drink. The central problem, her liver, he ignored completely.

Years before, Marie had written her invalid Colorado friend, Lavinia Small: "I do wish you could give me better news of your health. To be so bubblingly full of life and interest and to be chained by a body that will not 'play the game' is indeed a cruel fate."

Now that fate was hers. She'd hardly been sick a day in her life. Her favorite sixtieth birthday gift had been a milk-white stallion which she rode with the abandon of a woman half her age. Now she, the Regina Maria whose endurance had written legends, lay helpless and weak, her head throbbing from loss of blood, her soul burning with revolt.

On April 22 Carol suddenly turned on Nicolas and exiled him along with his wife Jeanne. The King pleaded the Romanian Constitution, which he said made it impossible for him to recognize his brother's marriage. Marie was aghast at such blatant hypocrisy. Nicolas had been married for six years. During those years, Carol had allowed him to dispense his official duties—both political and military—as though nothing had happened. Now he inexplicably stripped his brother of his title, his offices and his country. Before he left, however, Nicolas wrote his old professor and friend, the historian and former Prime Minister, Nicolas Jorga, telling him he'd never renounce his title or any rights provided him by the Constitution.

The result was a violent quarrel between the brothers, which gave rise to rumors that they'd fought in front of Marie at Cotroceni, and that a gun had gone off, wounding her in the stomach. Actually, they never fought in her presence. But Nicky's leaving, and the reasons behind it, nearly broke her heart.

"As to my Nicky," she wrote her young American friend, "I am afraid I have lost him forever, not *de coeur,* but he has been torn from me and about this I am inconsolable."

Her sister Bea and Mignon arrived to cheer the invalid. And, to her intense joy, Ileana came for a week. To these three who loved her, it was obvious that Marie needed more than bed rest and a cold diet. But

Carol seemed curiously detached from his mother's illness, declaring aloofly that Dr. Mamulea was sufficiently versed in modern medicine to handle the case.

In June Mamulea diagnosed her illness as "a weakening of the blood vessels" and sent her to Sinaia for the "air." Having personally driven her mother to the Pelisor, Mignon was able to observe her conditions first hand. Finally, Mignon put her foot down, telling Carol with rare spunk that since he saw fit to ignore the seriousness of their mother's condition, she would call in a liver specialist. Carol reluctantly acquiesced, and the famous Viennese Professor Hans Eppinger and a Roman doctor, Aldo Castellani, arrived for consultation.

When he heard Eppinger's name, Ileana's general practitioner, Dr. Alfred Fritsch, reacted negatively. "Eppinger's one of the greatest doctors in Vienna," Fritsch admitted, "but he's not a man who's really interested in his patients."

Nevertheless, Eppinger turned a clear eye on the situation. "But I can't give a proper diagnosis here," he snorted at Cotroceni. "She must be properly examined. One can't examine her properly in a palace."

Eppinger suggested the Queen be moved to a Vienna sanatorium, but Carol refused, demanding an on-the-spot diagnosis. Hastily given, the diagnosis agreed with Mamulea's original assessment: liver disease which certainly looked like cirrhosis, which also affected nearby blood vessels, thus provoking internal hemorrhages.

"All this is not particuarly cheerful," a drastically weakened Marie dictated on June 22, "especially since none of the doctors were able to fix any date when I should be up and about again. They did, however, one and all assure me that complete recovery was almost absolutely certain if I would only aid the situation by unrelenting patience and a firm will to overcome my state of actual weakness. Unfortunately, this means bed, bed, bed for an indefinite period, till my red globules eventually predominate again."

July was better. Sister Sandra, a sweet, gruff-voiced, absent-minded edition of her glamorous sisters, arrived to nurse the invalid. On the fourth, Marie was well enough to walk to the phone and discuss her new Habsburg grandson Dominic—already called Niki—with Anton. By the month's end, she was relearning to walk after four months of immobility and was writing: "At last I'm able to hold a pen again without feeling exhausted."

As anemia relaxed its grip, she wrote with characteristic willfulness: "Especially I would like to shake off what I consider my humiliating dependence on others who still have the right to rule my days for me and tell me what I may or may not do." But there wasn't much chance of emancipation as long as she felt so unsteady on her legs.

Then, as abruptly as they'd begun, the hemorrhages stopped completely. Much improved, Marie spent August at Bran. Still too weak to work in her gardens, she had her flowers brought in to her in great masses. She kept busy by working on her fourth volume and reading in four languages. At night, when she tired, General Zwiedineck read aloud to her in German, while rain beat on the roof and wind whistled around the ancient walls.

By the second week in September, she could write joyfully, "I think I'm almost well again!"

With renewed vigor came longing for her favorite child: "God only knows how much I'll be allowed to enjoy Ileana in this world."

In late September the Habsburgs came at last and escorted her down to Balcic, which she'd missed passionately all summer. Mignon arrived, bringing her youngest son. And for two weeks the little seaside house echoed with laughter, children's voices, barking dogs and the speedboat's roar. The Queen renewed her love affair with Stella Maris, with her hanging gardens ablaze with autumn roses, and—seated in the back seat of a Ford Nicolas had given her—with the village and its characters. She reveled in her grandchildren, especially Ileana's baby Niki, imagining that in that tiny bundle she'd recaptured her own Nicky. Always easily pleased, now she needed less than ever to make her happy.

In the middle of October, misfortune struck again. Ileana sat on an upper terrace basking in the sun after a morning spent romping with her children, when their nurse came running up the steps, carrying the baby.

"I don't want to give you a fright," panted the woman, "but I thought I'd better bring the baby with me. Your mother's had a hemorrhage."

Severely weakened again, Marie was forced back to Bucharest. They celebrated her sixty-second birthday very quietly at Cotroceni. And on November 2, the anniversary of Mircea's death, she felt strong enough to kneel at his grave for a few minutes' prayer. She even walked to the stables for a quick look at her beloved horses and received the Crown Prince of Sweden for lunch. "She was in high spirits," a lady-in-waiting wrote Marie's young American friend, "so much so that the Swedish guests were dazzled and fascinated. Unfortunately, she had a very bad night and feels so fatigued that she has asked me to send you a word."

All month she grew steadily worse. Ileana made the necessary plans to move her mother to Eppinger's sanatorium and was still battling Carol's refusal when the Queen was struck with a gastric hemorrhage so severe that specialists were flown in from Paris, Vienna and Zurich. Their recommendations proved useless. On December 29 she suffered another severe relapse and bled almost steadily until January 3. Fearing the worst, her family flew in more specialists. At last the doctors agreed to try what they considered a last resort—blood transfusions. Though crude and painful, the transfusions might be the only way of saving her life.

The country held its breath, while Western headlines screamed, "Queen Marie Sinking, Family Abandons Hope." Touching letters prescribing cures poured in from all over the world. Most were from people who had read her book.

Queen Marie endured three daily injections at three-day intervals, and at least the painful headaches and debilitating weakness subsided as they had before. On January 10 she felt well enough to receive a guest. Hector Bolitho, the young English biographer of her grandfather, Prince Albert, had come researching a book on Romania. All her life she'd been a warm, passionate woman who inspired great passions in men. That morning she made her final conquest.

Years later, in his *A Biographer's Notebook,* Bolitho recalled the scene: "A lady-in-waiting ushered me towards a pair of golden gates. These were opened, and I entered the Queen's bedroom. There must have been fifteen big vases of orchids and crimson lilies, forming a splendid fan of colour above and on either side of the bed. Queen Marie was sitting up, against a bank of lace cushions. . . . The Queen had the rare qualities and talent that stir men to immediate chivalry. To this day, I can visualize the oval of her face, the warming sympathy of her eyes, and a string of big, creamy pearls that lost themselves in a foam of shell-pink silk."

With heroic courage, Marie overcame weakness and pain to keep Bolitho amused, entertained, enchanted for over an hour. She darted spiritedly from subject to subject—Carol, Romania, the abdication, her own reign, Bolitho's book, her beloved old Rosenau at Coburg, where Bolitho had worked in the archives. Then back to Carol: "He sees himself as a seprate person, separate from me and separate from life. I am older now, and when one is older, one learns to fit into life—to realize that one is only part of the great pattern."

In February Dr. Mamulea sent her to the Sanatorium San Martino at Merano in the Italian Tyrol. But she needed more than mountain air. The transfusions had provided only a temporary solution. Renewed internal hemorrhages were literally bleeding her to death.

All through her illness, Marie had remained determinedly cheerful and optimistic. But on February 14 she confided in a letter to her young American friend: "I did not and do not *really* like nor believe in our court doctor who has been no consolation to me during my long sickness. He believes in his own superiority over all others and I think this belief is not justified. He turned up his nose at the advice of others and finally influenced my children so I was really subjugated by a doctor in whom I had no real faith.

"Why do I tell you all this? Perhaps because you are far away and not obliged to try and help me. I do not speak about these inner worries to those who are near me. It would only make them unhappy, and certain things must be endured dumbly when one knows that complaint would only make matters worse. I never complain, as I consider complaining an undignified weakness."

Perhaps if she'd complained in time to those who could have helped, her life might have been saved or at least prolonged. For growing doubts about Mamulea plagued her sisters and daughters, too.

As it was, Marie had long since come to accept human chicanery and cruelty as a fact of daily life. And as what she considered her humiliating dependence on others grew apace with her illness, she clung more desperately than ever to the one close-at-hand friend Carol would let her keep: General Zwiedineck.

Enchanted by his "dog-like" devotion, she imbued this tall, graying, chivalrous soldier with the glamour of a medieval knight. Had he not done everything in his power to guard her from persecution, thereby drawing the thunder down upon his own head? Had he not declared on numerous occasions that he believed in her as in a goddess, that he would have himself "chopped to little pieces" for her, that he would die for her if necessary? And there were his more practical gifts. A masterful organizer, he'd made her life more comfortable and better organized than it had ever been.

Of course she knew he wasn't perfect. He could never replace Stirbey in her life; for one thing, he was mentally inferior to Stirbey. And he sometimes stepped on toes. Sometimes he pouted, promising to leave, a threat which never failed to throw her into a panic, because without him she had no one in Romania she could trust. All the same, she wrote:

"I am very lucky to have found a man of his quality at a period when my life has become so lonely and difficult."

But was Zwiedineck's quality really as fine as the Queen thought? There's ample evidence that it was not, that he intrigued and even tried to thrust a wedge between her and Ileana. And it's hard to believe that if he'd been completely loyal to her—in other words, unfaithful to Carol —the King would have let him stay, since Carol had removed all her other stanch supporters.

At Merano Marie's sister Sandra, who'd again arrived from Germany, was shocked to discover the hold Zwiedineck had over the Queen. Every morning he forced her, weak as she was, to walk on the balcony outside her room. She needed the air, he announced, doctor's orders. Finally the Princess ran to the Romanian doctors, crying, "Please do something! He's going to kill her!" But nothing was done. And when Sandra suggested moving her to a Vienna sanatorium, Zwiedineck declared: "No, she's going to stay here for three weeks. I know exactly what I'm doing. She can't travel when the moon is like this."

She stayed at Merano for two months. Her flower-filled room, in an old fortress high in the mountains, overlooked magnificent vistas of vineyards and fruit orchards backed with snow-crowned Alps. She was able to take short motor drives, which provided a much-needed respite from her invalid's existence. She also received sympathetic visitors from numerous countries and social levels.

Two visits proved more emotional than the rest.

Nicolas came, bringing his wife Jeanne. Marie had never met this woman who had tried turning her favorite son against her and had caused his exile. But she'd bitterly opposed Jeanne's destructive influence. Now the Queen forgave her.

"I received her with open arms," she told Ileana in a telephone conversation. "You see, there is little left to me except to be kind."

Another "immense" emotion lay in receiving Princess Helen. Carol had kept them apart for seven years. Exiled and separated from her son, Helen had carved a beauty-filled, if lonely, existence for herself at Villa Sparta, a Renaisance house she'd bought outside Florence. Now Marie apologized for the times she'd taken Carol's side against Helen. "My dear child," she said, "I never realized how you'd been hurt until he hurt me."

Ileana came for a few days too, renewing her efforts to move her mother to a place where concrete measures could be taken to improve

her deteriorating condition. More than ever, the Princess had the feeling that something was abnormal about her mother's illness and about
the cavalier attitude Carol was taking towards its treatment. Before
Ileana's suspicions could be verified, however, she was called home.
Hitler was invading Austria.

She arrived home on March 13 to find her car covered with swastikas
and Sonnberg filled with Nazi storm troopers. When she telephoned her
mother that night to tell her she'd arrived safely, both received further
proof of what the *Anschluss* would mean for Austria. "I at first could
not understand what Ileana was saying," Marie told a friend later.
"Imagining that she was talking English, I could not grasp that she was
saying in German that we must talk in German. A fervent lover of
freedom, I felt my blood boiling, but was obliged to keep my emotions
to myself."

April was a good month, and the Queen felt strong enough to attend
a horse show, hoping it wouldn't tax her strength too much. It did.
"The next day, alas, there was a fresh hemorrhage, which this time was
a rather severe one and meant again bed and starvings upon a minimum
of cold drinks. After these bleedings absolute immobility has to be
observed, and I am not allowed the slightest movement."

The doctors prescribed peace of mind, as little worry as possible. But
how was that possible, she asked wearily, when Hitler devoured
Austria, tearing up Ileana's life by the roots, and in Romania Carol
dissolved the traditional political parties, abolished the old Constitution
and declared himself dictator? Another new grief was that in Yugoslavia Mignon had fallen under the emotional sway of a malicious
Englishwoman, a former schoolmate, who was turning the Yugoslav
Queen against Marie, and thereby destroying the warm relationship
that had meant so much to both mother and daughter.

But, as always, Carol was her source of greatest anguish. "I can't
believe he can be so blind and foolish," she wrote Stirbey concerning
Carol's latest political peccadilloes. "In spite of all his faults and mistakes he *does* work. He's always at it, and it's a cruel misfortune that
his vices destroy his virtues. With all my judgement of him, I must
recognize that he is somebody, a dominant personality. And why
should it have been thus?What could have twisted him so much? I
torture my brain asking myself that over and over." But she never
found the answer.

Except for the headaches and pain caused by transfusions, her illness
had caused her little physical discomfort. But by May 1 she'd lost so

much weight and blood that she was drastically weakened. Finally, Ferdinand's nephew, Friedrich of Hohenzollern-Sigmaringen, stepped in and demanded that she be transferred to the celebrated Weisser-Hirsch sanatorium outside Dresden.

Here brilliant young doctors made a diagnosis. She had, they said, esophageal varices (dilated blood vessels causing vomiting of blood) brought about by primary hypertension, which meant that Queen Marie's esophagus was almost completely eaten up. She also had fluid in her abdomen caused by cirrhosis of the liver that had spread to her pancreas.

"But it's not natural," Dr. Störmer told a deeply worried Ileana, "for a woman who has lived the kind of life the Queen has lived—no alcohol, fixed hours, daily riding, nutritious food—to have cirrhosis. Besides, as far as I know, esophageal varices results only from complications secondary to alcoholic poisoning of longstanding duration."

Störmer's colleague, Professor Warnerkrose was even more indignant. "Even if the illness itself had a natural beginning, which we don't know," he declared, "she has been neglected and mistreated all along in a way that's absolutely criminal. She's had this disease for years, and she's been given the wrong treatment from the beginning. I can only say that the doctor who did that had to have done it purposely. He can't have been that stupid." In any case, Störmer promised to do everything in his power to help the Queen.

The doctors worked overtime trying to build back her strength. But the long neglect had taken its toll. Even more blood transfusions failed to improve her condition.

"I am gradually crawling uphill after a very bad two months of complete exhaustion," she wrote on June 20. "I have undergone strenuous treatment, which left me no strength to hold a pen." Then, in a last anguished outbrust: "I do want to be my own independent self again. People are awfully kind, but I have to depend upon them and this is irksome, as I love being free."

Her inner craving for freedom and independence made her outward patience and cheerfulness that much more remarkable by comparison. As she grew worse, she seemed to transcend her own problems, and she concerned herself more and more with the problems of others. "Poor doctor!" she told Ileana when efforts proved useless. "I am so sorry for him. He's so disappointed."

By July Marie knew the end must be near. She wrote a last letter to Stirbey, ending with these words: "I want to get this off so I shall end it with so much unsaid which would lighten my heart to say—all my longing, my sadness, all the dear memories which flood back into my heart. The woods with the little yellow crocuses, the smell of the oaks when we rode through those same woods in early summer—and oh! so many, many things which are gone. God bless you and keep you safe." She asked to be taken home to die, but first Waldorf Astor paid her a last visit at Dresden. In a noble gesture to her old friend and rival, Nancy let him come alone.

On July 16, having been denied a plane by Carol, Marie boarded the train for Romania. Her car's lurching as it passed through the steep Carpathian passes brought on the dreaded bleeding, and oxygen was administered. On the afternoon of the second day, the train stopped in the little town of Cernăuţi in northern Romania. This was her bad-luck town. Here she'd received the word of her mother's death, and here she'd been wounded in the eye by a spinning bouquet. Now the train stopped so she could rest. All afternoon, the peasants brought branches soaked in water to cool her car against the blistering July heat.

The train started again. As her familiar blue and silver coach slid through the countryside, stationmasters bared their heads, villagers knotted at train stations and peasants knelt in the fields. Tearfully, people shook their heads, mumbling, "Regina is dying." It didn't seem possible.

When she arrived at Sinaia on the eighteenth, a crowd waited to see her for the last time. She refused to leave the train on a stretcher, so the officers of her regiment improvised a portable chair. Slowly, with infinite care, they carried her out into the afternoon sunshine and her last ovation.

In the old nursery at the Pelisor, she lay bleeding, surrounded by Carol, Lisabetta, Michael and the Patriarch Miron Cristea. She asked for the Lord's Prayer in English, but no one in the room knew it. So she received the last rites of the Orthodox Church. She asked over and over for Ileana and for Zwiedineck. Carol refused to admit Zwiedineck, and he phoned Ileana and Nicolas only when he was sure their mother was too far gone to see her favorite children again. But Marie didn't know that. She kept her eyes on the door, waiting for Ileana to walk through. Finally, in a barely audible whisper, she begged Carol to be a just and a strong King. They were her last words.

At five o'clock she lost consciousness. Thirty minutes later, the freedom she'd loved so passionately and known so briefly was hers forever.

Though the rumor persisted in the press of Romania and throughout the Western world that Marie had died of unnatural causes, no autopsy was performed. The story lives today, supported by liver specialists who agree with Doctor Störmer's comment that "esophageal varices results only from complications secondary to alcoholic poisoning of long-standing duration." And it's a fact that Marie hated the taste of alcohol and therefore never drank. Nor did she have cancer, as has often been surmised. Unfortunately, the poisoning question will probably never be resolved. The data that could have shed light on the puzzle—Störmer's and Warnerkrose's records at Dresden—were destroyed in the air raid of 1944.

Dressed in a simple white dress, Marie's body lay in state in her white Cotroceni drawing room, covered by the royal standard and surrounded with flowers and burning tapers. It was hot and the flies were numerous, so Ileana draped a white netting over her mother's face. Even in death, the Queen was beautiful. "I've never seen anything more beautiful in my life," recalled a relative. "Golden curls fell out and she looked sixteen."

For three days, four of her sorrowing officers stood on guard while Romanians by the thousands shuffled past for a last look at their beautiful Queen. On the evening of the third day, the palace gates were thrown open to admit factory workers who'd been unable to come during the day. Dressed in greasy work clothes, they formed an unbroken line that lasted till morning.

Carol gave his mother a magnificent funeral. Her coffin was closed the night before and taken downtown to the Palatul Regal. There it lay in Carol's opulent new throne room, covered with her standard and crown and attended by the last guard—two nephews and her sons.

On the following morning, after a moving service in the throne room, Marie was carried down the magnificent marble staircase she'd mounted so hesitantly as a bride of seventeen. As she descended, the Bucharest Symphony, massed in the dim hall below, played her favorite Wagner, music from the *Götterdämmerung*.

Outside, a glittering cortege waited to escort her through Bucharest to the train that would carry her to Curtea de Arges. "No one should wear black for me," she'd commanded, "but my favorite colour—mauve. All flowers placed on the coffin should be red." In keeping with her wish, the loyal Romanians had decorated the city in every conceivable shade of violet, lavender and purple. Mauve banners fluttered along the Chausée Kisseleff, and mauve touched the uniforms of her regiment. The effect was festive, commensurate with the Queen's gallant spirit. But the only audible sounds as the Wagner strains died inside the palace were the murmuring thousands massed for miles along the funeral route and her favorite stallion, saddled with her empty side saddle, pawing the cobblestones in the palace court.

Six officers of her regiment carried the coffin out beneath a mauve silk porte-cochere and placed it on a gun-carriage drawn by six black horses. The massed guard presented arms, the army band launched into the National Anthem and the procession began.

Calvary and foot soldiers in their brilliant uniforms were followed by state officials, marching in full formal dress. Next came the church officials and an endless stream of priests, their gold-embroidered robes and swinging censers providing a link with Romania's Byzantine heritage. The procession ended with Marie's own regiment, mounted on black horses, followed by high state officials dressed in their different uniforms and General Zwiedineck, carrying her crown on a purple cushion. Hushed silence broken only by muffled weeping greeted the Queen's mauve-draped coffin. With amazement people noticed the coffin looked very small. Imbued with her glorious legend, they had somehow thought of her as physically larger than life. Behind the coffin Carol walked alone, wearing the plumed helmet and flowing white cloak of his Michael the Brave uniform.

Carol had refused Prince Stirbey permission to return for the funeral. But he'd allowed Nicolas to come, providing he leave Jeanne behind. Therefore, Nicolas and fifteen-year-old Michael, a tall, boyish-faced figure in uniform, followed the King. Behind them walked King George V's youngest and handsomest son, the Duke of Kent; Alexander of Yugoslavia's first cousin, the Prince Regent Paul; the gold-braided diplomatic corps; and more troops.

The family conflicts that had torn Marie's last years lived on after her death. She had left Balcic to Carol, Copaceni to Lisabetta, jewels to be divided among her daughters and money to be divided among all her children. To Ileana, the only one of her children without a personal fortune, she'd left Castle Bran, a diamond and sapphire diadem and the quarter of her fortune the Romanian law allowed her to dispose of as she liked. On the way to the train station that morning, Ileana's sisters informed her that they and their brothers had decided to take the lion's share of the money from her. She might keep Bran; they would divide the money among themselves.

Meanwhile, as the cortege reached the Arch of Triumph, there was a slight hesitation. Marie and Ferdinand had ridden beneath the unfinished arch in 1922 on their triumphant return to Bucharest following their coronation. But upon the arch's completion in 1936, Carol had taken perverse joy in keeping his mother from attending the dedication ceremonies. Now he paused. At an almost imperceptible sign from him, the gun-carriage bearing his mother's body passed beneath the arch. But Carol walked around it.

From the station on the edge of Bucharest, the funeral train began the long journey across the Wallachian plain to Curtea de Arges. The trip normally took two hours. That day it took six. Peasants lined the entire route, kneeling in prayer. At every tiny train station along the way, more crowds waited to throw flowers on the open car bearing the coffin. So many flowers were thrown on board that the honor guard, riding with the coffin, were literally in danger of suffocating.

It was late afternoon when the train reached Curtea de Arges. As the cortege swept up the dusty road lined with soldiers bowed over their fixed bayonets and crowds of weeping peasants, twilight crept over the countryside. At the church Marie's coffin was taken from the gun-carriage and carried up the steps. From inside, glowing through the front door, a thousand lighted candles called her to rest.

She was greatly eulogized. Newspapers all over the world recalled her war work and her decisive appearance at the Versailles Conference. The New York *Herald Tribune* compared her to her grandmother, Queen Victoria, admitting that although superficially there could hardly be less resemblance, "both characters were extremely tenacious of their sovereign rights. . . . Both were stubborn, tremendous workers and eager to take a hand in the government of their respective kingdoms."

The *Saturday Review of Literature* remembered how many of her relatives had sat on European thrones at the beginning of World War I. "But the circumstances that withered the reputations of so many of her cousins, only served to enhance her courage and energy."

Marie may have penned her own best epitaph many years before. "Perhaps she was heroic," she had written of herself to Loie Fuller. "She certainly had quixotic courage for lost causes. And was she not herself a remnant of a class that was destined to pass away?"

But her greatest posthumous honor came from an unexpected source. Wrote *Time* magazine on August 1: "Citizens of Moscow gathered in little knots on the sidewalk near Bogoyavlenie Church, gaping in amazement last week as Orthodox dignitaries celebrated a Requiem High Mass for the late Romanian Dowager Queen Marie. This was accompanied by loud, priestly chanting clearly audible some distance from the church. So far as the press could learn, there has been no such honoring of royalty in Moscow since the revolution—yet last week the famed Communist Union of Militant Atheists took it lying down. The Secret Police kept hands off, evidently on instructions. In his youth, Joseph Stalin studied for the Orthodox priesthood, but that in 1938 priestly offices would be performed in the Soviet capital for a Queen of Orthodox Romania . . . is something few Reds ever expected."

A few days after her burial, Marie's people received two remnants of their great and beloved Queen: an open letter posted throughout the land, and her heart, cut from her body according to her wishes and placed in the little chapel at Balcic.

The letter was written in her candid yet romantic style. In it she summarized her great love for her adopted land and people and made this poignant last plea: "I confide my children to your hearts. Being mortal, they may err. But their souls are ardent, as was mine. Love them and be helpful one to the other."

But her heart, interred at Balcic and removed by General Zwiedineck to Castle Bran when Bulgaria annexed Balcic during World War II, became a lasting symbol for the Romanian people. After the war, when the Communist peril she'd feared for twenty years buried the country, the little shrine at Bran was boarded over. But even when it was most dangerous, the peasants brought flowers to her heart. For them she never died, but lived as the Romanian funeral service says, "in a place of light, in a place of greenness, in a place of rest."

And what of Carol? Did he ever regret breaking the heart of the mother he'd once loved so deeply? There's no recorded evidence that he did. And though observers reported that he looked "ravaged" the night of her death, the only personal note he added to the long funeral ceremonies was letting her coffin pass under the arch alone while he walked around it.

One thing is certain, however. The people who genuinely loved Marie never forgave Carol for the way he treated his mother. When he passed through Spain several years later, he stopped to visit his aunt, the Infanta Beatrice, Marie's beloved sister Baby.

King Carol was at the gate, a servant told the Infanta on that occasion, with a red-headed woman. "I'll receive the King," announced Beatrice, "but not the woman."

When Carol asked her why she refused to receive his mistress, the Infanta replied: "Why should you expect me to receive the woman who killed my sister?"

Then, according to witnesses, he wept.

Epilogue

After Marie's death, World War II drew nearer and the fate of both Romania and her king looked increasingly uncertain. Incensed by the 1938 assassination of their leader, Codreanu, the Romanian Iron Guard redoubled their attacks on Carol's dictatorship. Carol, in turn, had all key Guardists shot or imprisoned. Politically trapped as his parents had been in 1916—by Germany on one side and Russia on the other—he traveled to England, hoping for a promise of support. Receiving none, he visited Hitler, and signed a trade agreement with Germany.

When war came in September, Carol formally declared Romania's neutrality. But on June 28, 1940, Russia invaded Bessarabia and Hungary moved troops toward Transylvania.

Early in September, 1940, King Carol appointed General (later Marshal) Ion Antonescu as Prime Minister with full discretionary powers. By September sixth, Antonescu had forced his former leader into exile. Taking Lupescu with him, Carol fled the country, barely escaping assassination as his train sped toward the Yugoslav border.

Carol's eighteen-year-old son Michael succeeded his father as king. But Antonescu had proclaimed himself Leader of the State, thereby reducing Michael to a mere figurehead.

In August, 1944, Michael dismissed Antonescu and announced Romania's withdrawal from the War, which it had been fighting on the German side. Michael's new government invited German forces to withdraw peacefully from the country under safe conduct. Only when this arrangement was violated by Nazi bombing attacks against Bucharest and by an attempt to seize the capital, did the Romanian army turn against the German forces. Romania's new allies, the Russians, reacted little better than the Germans. At the announcement of Romanian withdrawal from fighting, Soviet Russia took more than one-hundred thousand Romanian officers and soldiers prisioner.

With Michael's accession, both his mother, whom he gave the title Queen Mother of Romania, and Barbu Stirbey were permitted to return to the country. Stirbey, for the first time in his life, publicly represented the Romanian government. In February, 1944, he acted as Michael's spokesman at Allied armistice talks in Cairo. That June, Romania accepted the terms issued from these negotiations. But the agreement was never formalized, because the Soviet representative never received authorization to sign. Moscow obviously preferred to enter Romanian territory without any restraining legal commitments.

The Red influx Marie had feared so long now swept over the country. On September 12, 1944, Stirbey was one of the delegates signing the Moscow armistice agreement with the Allied powers. This, too, was never formalized. In late February, 1945, Vyshinsky forced Michael to oust his cabinet. The king proposed a coalition government—including both Democrats and Communists—with Stirbey as head. Vyshinsky withheld approval, appointing his own cabinet. Thus, on November 6, 1945, Romania came under a thinly disguised Communist-controlled regime. From that moment, King Michael and the rest of the royal family were virtual prisoners of the Communists. The takeover broke Stirbey's heart and health. He died at Buftea in the spring of 1946.

In 1948, the Communists exiled King Michael and the entire royal family. On June 10, Michael married Princess Anne of Bourbon-Parma, whom he'd met at the wedding of Britain's Princess Elizabeth the year before. Anne and Michael settled in Switzerland, where they're raising five daughters (Michael works as a stockbroker). Queen Mother Helen, still lovely in her seventies, lives on at Villa Sparta, the Florentine estate she bought during her first exile from Romania.

Carol, the only royal Romanian to escape with money, ended up in Portugal. In 1947, when Lupescu was apparently seriously ill, he finally married his mistress in a civil ceremony performed at her bedside. The illness soon evaporated, however, and a religious ceremony held in the summer of 1949 united the couple a second time.

At this point, Michael severed all connections with his father. Meanwhile, Carol ignored the existence of his first wife, Zizi Lambrino, and their son Mircea. Zizi died on March 26, 1953, in the charity ward of a Paris hospital. And one week to the day later, on Good Friday, April 3, Carol died suddenly and unexpectedly of a heart attack at his Portuguese villa. He was fifty-nine. On April 7, he was buried beside the kings of Portugal in the crypt of the Monastery of Sao Vincente—a dispensation granted by the Portuguese government because Carol's grandmother, Ferdinand's mother Antonia, had been a Portuguese princess.

After Carol's death, Lupescu continued to live quietly but comfortably in the Portuguese villa he'd bought in her name. Rumor had it that she had retained Carol's fortune. But the ex-king died without leaving either a will or a trace of the millions he'd inherited from his father, vastly expanded during his ten-year tenure as king, and lovingly carried with him from Romania.

Lisabetta, the ex-queen of Greece, having divorced King George in 1935, lived luxuriously in Romania until 1948, when she escaped to Cannes. She died there, penniless, in 1954. Mignon, Queen Mother of Yugoslavia, who had left her adopted country at the outbreak of World War II, lived at Frogmore in Windsor Great Park until her death in 1961. During the war, her son the boy King Peter II was forced out of Yugoslavia by advancing German troops. He died of cirrhosis of the liver in 1971.

Prince Nicolas never returned to Romania to live. Today he resides with his second wife, a charming Brazilian, in Madrid. Queen Marie's last love, General Zwiedineck, fared less well. Imprisoned by the Communists, he was brutally tortured and finally released to die from his ordeal in 1949.

Princess Ileana was also exiled from Romania in 1948, having returned with her family after Carol's abdication. Her heroic war work, including the founding and running of a hospital near Castle Bran, recalled Queen Marie's record in World War I. Divorced from Archduke Anton, she raised her six children in Massachussetts by lecturing on Communism and selling her mother's diamond and sapphire tiara. Now an Orthodox nun, she has founded an Orthodox monastery in the Pennsylvania hill country north of Pittsburgh, and brings her mother's spirit to a new generation.

Bibliography
PRIMARY SOURCES

Unpublished:

Letters of Marie, Queen of Romania
—To her "American Friend," 1934–1938, (portions of which have appeared in Hector Bolitho's *A Biographer's Notebook*. London, Longmans, Green, 1950);
—To the "Friend in Fairyland," 1926–1938;
—To George I. Duca, son of the Romanian Prime Minister, 1929–1936;
—To Loie Fuller, 1927;
—To Leila Milne, the English Governess, 1907–1923;
—To H.M. King George V, 1901, 1926, 1928, and 1938;
—To H.M. Queen Mary, 1936;
—To Lavinia Small, 1927–1938.
Duca, George I. *Maria Regina.*

Published:

Balsan, Consuelo, *The Glitter and the Gold.* New York, Simon and Schuster, 1956.
Battiscombe, Georgina, *Queen Alexandra.* Boston, Houghton, Mifflin, 1969.
Beattie, Kim, *Brother, Here's A Man! The saga of Klondike Boyle.* New York, Macmillan, 1940.
Berkson, Seymour, *Their Majesties!* New York, Stackpole, 1938.
Bibesco, Marthe, "Ferdinand of Rumania: King and Martyr." *Saturday Evening Post,* Vol. 200: 6–7 (August 27, 1929).
Bibesco, Marthe, "The Madonna of Roumania." *North American,* Vol. 226: 438 (October, 1928).
Bibesco, Marthe, *Royal Portraits.* New York, Appleton, 1928.

Bolitho, Hector, *A Biographer's Notebook*. London, Longmans, Green, 1950.
Burgoyne, Elizabeth, *Carmen Sylva, Queen and Woman*. London, Thornton, 1940.
Callimachi, Princess Anne-Marie, *Yesterday Was Mine*. New York, Whittlesey House of McGraw Hill, 1949.
Carol I, King of Romania, *Reminiscences*. Edited by Sidney Whitman, New York, Harpers, 1899.
Collins, Frederick L., "Marrying an Empire." *Woman's Home Companion*, Vol. 50: 17–18 (May, 1923).
Cookridge, E. H., *From Battenburg to Mountbatten*. New York, John Day, 1968.
Cornwallis-West, Mrs. George, *The Reminiscences of Lady Randolph Churchill*. New York, Century, 1909.
Current Opinion, "The Queen Who Will Pay Us A Visit Soon," Vol. 67; 90–1 (August, 1919).
Denny, Harold Norman, "Mr. Babbit Draws A Queen," *Forum*, Vol. 77: 345–353 (March, 1927).
Dumaine, Jacques, *Quai D'Orsay*.
Ellis, William T., "Rumania's Soldier Queen," *The Century*, Vol. 96: 330 (July, 1918).
The Empress Frederick Writes to Sophie—Her Daughter, Crown Princess and Later Queen of the Helenes, Edited by Arthur Gould Lee, London, Faber and Faber, 1965.
Fleming, Thomas J. "The First of the Celebrity Mayors," *New York*, Vol. 2, No. 45: 41 (November 10, 1969).
Gernsheim, Helmut and Alison, *Victoria R*. New York, Putnam's, 1959.
Gilliard, Pierre, *Thirteen Years at the Russian Court*. New York, Doran, 1921.
Gunther, John, *Inside Europe*. New York, Harpers, 1938.
Ileana, Princess of Romania, Archduchess of Austria, *I Live Again*. New York, Rinehart, 1952.
Jullian, Philippe, *Edward and the Edwardians*. New York, Viking, 1967.
Lee, Arthur Gould, *Helen, Queen Mother of Runania*. London, Faber and Faber, 1948.
Letters of Queen Victoria: From the archives of the house of Brandenburg-Prussia, Edited by Hector Bolitho. New Haven, Yale University Press, 1938.
The Literary Digest, "A Queen's Among Us Taking Notes," Vol. 91: 34–40 (November 6, 1926).
The Literary Digest, "Why the Queen of Roumania is Here," Vol. 91: 19–11 (October 30, 1926).

Longford, Elizabeth, *Queen Victoria: Born to Succeed.* New York, Harper and Row, 1964.

Marie, Grand Duchess of Russia, *A Princess in Exile.* New York, Viking, 1932.

Marie, Queen of Romania, "Impressions of America," *North American Newspaper Alliance* (October and November, 1926).

Marie, Queen of Romania, "The Fallen Czar," *Woman's Home Companion,* Vol. 47: 7–8 (July, 1920).

Marie, Queen of Romania, *The Story of My Life.* New York, Scribner's, 1934.

Marie, Queen of Romania, *Ordeal: The Story of My Life.* New York, Scribner's, 1935.

Moats, Alice-Leone, *Lupescu.* New York, Holt, 1955.

Martineau, Mrs. Philip, *Roumania and Her Rulers.* Philadelphia, McKay, 1927.

Phillips, John, "King Carol of Rumania," *Life,* Vol. 8: 72–82 (February 19, 1940).

Pope-Hennessey, James, *Queen Mary: 1867–1953.* New York, Knopf, 1960.

Potter-Daggett, Mabel, *Marie of Roumania: The Intimate Story of the Radiant Queen.* New York, Doran, 1926.

Seton-Watson, R.W., *A History of the Roumanians.* Cambridge, University Press, 1934.

Sulzberger, C. L. *A Long Row of Candles: Memoirs and Diaries (1934–1954).* New York, Macmillan, 1969.

Time, "Rumania; Stalin and Marie," Vol. 32: 17 (August 1, 1938).

Tisdall, E.E.P., *Marie Feodorovna, Empress of Russia.* New York, Day, 1958.

Vopicka, Charles J., *Secrets of the Balkans.* Chicago, Rand, McNally, 1921.

Waldeck, R. G., *Athene Palace.* New York, National Travel Club, 1942.

West, Rebecca, *Black Lamb and Gray Falcon.* New York, Viking, 1941.

Whalen, Grover A., *Mr. New York.* New York, Putnam's, 1955.

Wheeler-Bennett, John W., *King George VI: His Life and Reign.* New York, St. Martin's, 1958.

Wilson, Edith Bolling, *My Memoir.* New York, Bobbs-Merrill, 1939.

SECONDARY SOURCES

Alexander, Grand Duke of Russia, *Once a Grand Duke.* New York, Garden City, 1932.

Alice, Princess of Great Britain and Ireland, *For My Grandchildren.* Cleveland, World, 1966.

Bent Silas, "The Passing of King Ferdinand of Rumania," *Current History,* Vol. 26: 974–80 (September, 1927).

Bolitho, Hector, *Roumania Under King Carol.* London, Eyre and Spottiswoode, 1939.

Buchanan, Sir George, *My Mission to Russia and Other Diplomatic Memories.* Boston, Little, Brown, 1923.

Clark, Charles Upson, *Greater Roumania.* New York, Dodd, Mead, 1922.

Daisy, Princess of Pless, *Better Left Unsaid.* New York, Dutton, 1931.

De Diesbach, Ghislain, *Secrets of the Gotha.* New York, Meredith, 1968.

Duff, David, *Hessian Tapestry.* London, Muller, 1967.

Easterman, A. L., *King Carol, Hitler and Lupescu.* London, Gollancz, 1942.

Gibbons, Herbert Adams, "Romance and Reality in Rumania," *The Century,* Vol. 115: 527–34 (March 1928).

Hoppe, E.O. *In Gypsy Camp and Royal Palace.* London, Methuen, 1924.

Lengyel, Emil, "The Situation That Made Carol King of Rumania," *Current History,* Vol. 32: 1085–1089 (September, 1930).

Patmore, Derek, *Invitation to Roumania.* London, Macmillan, 1939.

Literary Digest, "Romance, Tragedy and a Boy King," Vol. 94: 36–42 (August 6, 1927).

Marie, Queen of Romania, "How it Feels to be Queen," *Literary Digest,* Vol. 85: 50–4, (June 13, 1925).

Marie, Queen of Romania, *The Country That I Love.* London, Duckworth, 1925.

Marie, Queen of Romania, *My Country.* London, Hodder and Stoughton, 1916.

McCulloch, John, *Drums in the Balkan Night.* New York, Putnam's, 1936.

Morris, Constance Lily, *On Tour With Queen Marie.* New York, McBridge, 1927.

Nichols, Beverley, *The Sweet and Twenties.* New York, British Book Centre, 1958.

Nicolson, Harold, *King George the Fifth.* London, Constable, 1952.

Poincaré, Raymond, *Memoirs.* New York, Doubleday, 1929.

Pounds, Norman J. G., *Eastern Europe,* Chicago, Aldine, 1969.

Ross, Ishbel, *Grace Coolidge and Her Era,* New York, Dodd, Mead, 1962.

Schuman, Frederick L., *Europe on the Eve; the Crisis of Diplomacy.* New York, Knopf, 1939.

Sitwell, Sacheverell, *Roumanian Journey.* London, Batsford, 1938.
Taylor, Edmond, *The Fall of the Dynasties.* New York, Doubleday, 1963.
Tuchman, Barbara, *The Proud Tower.* New York, Macmillan, 1966.
Von der Hoven, Baroness Helena, *King Carol of Romania,* London, Hutchinson, 1940.

Name Index

Albert, future king of Belgium, 47
Albert, Prince ("Bertie"; George VI), 157
Albert Victor, Duke of Clarence, 18
Alexander II, Tsar, 3, 5, 13–14
Alexander III, death of, 57
Alexander Karageorgevich, King of Yugo-slavia, 176, 218, 235, 258; marriage to Mignon, 174–177; birth of Peter, 183–184; opinion of Marie, 250; assassinated, 257; funeral, 258
Alexander Obrenovich, King (Serbia), 174
Alexander, King (Greece), 168–169
Alexandra, Queen, 4, 18, 24, 159; death, 189
Alexandra, Tsarina (wife Nicholas II), 100, 101, 102, 135; disapproval of Ducky, 77
Alexandra (Sandra) sister of Marie, 10, 16, 264, 265, 273, 277; marriage, 58–59
Alexandra Victoria, 4
Alexis, Grand Duke, 13, 47
Alfonso, Infante, 159, 214–215
Alfred, Duke of Edinburgh (Affie), 3, 5–6, 10–11, 17, 24, 27, 157; marriage, 7; sent to Malta, 15; disapproves of Missy's engagement to Ferdinand, 42, 45; becomes Duke of Saxe-Coburg-Gotha, 58; death of son, Alfred, 69; death, 71
Alfred (brother of Marie), 4–5, 12, 69
Alonzo (son of Beatrice), 267
Anderson, Hans Christian, 11
Andrei (son of Mignon), 252
Angelescu, General, and Prince Carol, 190
Anne of Bourbon-Parma, Princess, 287
Anton of Habsburg-Lothringen, Archduke, marriage to Ileana, 236–238; Marie's visits to, 254; divorced by Ileana, 288
Antonescu, General Ion, 286
Antonia, Infanta of Portugal (mother of Ferdinand), 36, 42, 288
Astor, Gwendolyn, 72–74
Astor, John, 72, 79
Astor, John Jacob, 73
Astor, Nancy, 79, 159, 261–262, 280
Astor, Pauline, 76, 194; friendship with Marie, 72–75; King Carol I, 77–78
Astor, Waldorf, 72–79, 158, 180, 261, 280
Astor, William Waldorf, 72
Astors, 256; and Clivedon set, 266
Augusta, Queen of Prussia, 34
Averescu, General Alexander, 139, 195, 202, 213, 216; prime minister, 143; refusal to sign armistice, 145; replaced by Marghiloman, 145

Balfour, Arthur, 157
Ballard, General, 142
Ballif, Colonel, 113, 131, 136, 141
Barthou, Louis, 160, 257
Beatrice (Baby Bee; later, Infanta of Spain), 4, 66, 159, 265, 272, 284–285
Bergson, Henri, 157
Bernhard, General, 98
Berthelot, General, 131, 139, 144, 151

Bibesco, Princess Marthe, 83, 108, 112, 123, 131, 180, 189; companion to Marie, 81–82
Bismarck, Chancellor Otto von, 31; 117–118
Bolitho, Hector, 275
Boris, Grand Duke, 59
Boris, Tsar of Bulgaria, 177
Bourke, Captain Maurice, 17
Boyle, David, 203
Boyle, Joe (Klondike), 144, 149, 157, 158, 180, 187, 194; saves Romanian delegates from Bolsheviks, 147; and Marie, 146–148; death, 185–186
Bratianu, Elise, 86–87, 152
Bratianu, Ioan, 86; offers throne to Carol I, 29; concept of foreigner as king, 31
Bratianu, Ion (son of Ioan), 102, 114–115, 119, 120, 124, 134, 137, 150, 153, 159, 161, 182, 190, 196, 216–217, 218; political influence on Prince Carol, 95–96; as ruler, 116; use of Marie, 116–117, 118; resignation, 143; arrest, 148; declares war on Hungary, 165; resigns, 165–166; death, 219
Bratianu, Vintila, 219, 220, 226
Brusilov, General Aleksei, 122, 125
Busche, Herr von dem, 119–120
Buzdugan, Chief Justice George, 217, 226

Callimachi, Princess, 83
Cantacuzene, Jean, 136
Cantacuzino, Lieutenant Zizi, 73; romance with Marie, 66–68; exiled, 68
Carol I (formerly Karl Eitel, Prince of Hohenzollern-Sigmaringen), 50, 51, 52, 54, 63, 65, 66, 67, 76, 80, 222; ancestry, 27–28; character, 28–29, 36–37; accepts kingship, 31–32; proposal and marriage, 33–34; birth and death of daughter, 34; coronation, 35; and Ferdinand, 36, 37; reception by Queen Victoria, 44–45; dominates household, 55–56; and Marie, 57, 61, 90, 96, 105; exiles Cantacuzino, 68; ambivalence toward peasants, 82; approves of Barbu Stirbey, 86; influence on Prince Carol, 92–94; entertains Romanovs, 102–103; and Triple Alliance, 104; illness, 104; Council rejects proposal to side with Germany, 105; death, 108; reputation at death, 111–112; funeral, 113
Carol II, 69, 129, 131, 136, 141, 144, 148–149, 163, 169, 187, 189, 197, 213, 214–215, 240, 241, 245, 250, 252, 253, 254, 259, 263, 268, 270, 273, 275, 276, 277, 278, 280, 282, 283, 284–285; birth, 53–54; assists Marie in First Balkan War, 90; focus of conflict, 92; and Carmen Sylva, 92; and Barbu Stirbey, 93, 95; upbringing by Carol I, 93–94, 96; relationship with tutor, 93–95, 96; influence of Ion Bratianu, 95–96; goes to Potsdam, 97; and Olga of Russia, 98, 100–101; and Zizi Lambrino, 148, 149, 164, 170; confinement in Bistritza monastery, 149; marriage to Helen, 169, 170–171, 173; divorce of Helen, 181–184; renounces rights to throne, 190–191; at-

tempted coup, 220–221; return as Carol II, 228–231; persecution of Helen, 234; humiliation of Marie, 234–235, 237, 242; alienation from family, 235–236; role in Ileana's marriage, 236–238; Peles celebration and family reunion, 247–248; harassment and persecution of Marie, 253, 262, 263–264; relations with Marie, 269–271; exile of Nicolas, 272; declares self dictator, 278; against Iron Guard, 286; agreement with Hitler, 286; flees Romania, 286; marriage to Lupescu, 287; death, 288
Carp, Peter, 105, 115, 124
Carroll, Colonel John H., 203, 204, 206
Castellani, Dr. Aldo, 273
Catargiu, Lascar, 39
Charlotte of Saxe-Meiningen, Princess, 26
Chrissoveloni, Jean, 139
Churchill, Jennie, 10
Churchill, Winston, 14, 93, 158–159
Clemenceau, Georges, 153, 157, 159, 160; meets Marie, 156
Coanda, Colonel (later General and Prime Minister), 42–43, 150
Codreanu, Corneliu Zelea, 247, 248, 249, 252; assassination of, 286
Colette, 154
Collins, Frederick L., 177
Connaught, Prince Arthur, Duke of, 47
Constantine, King of Greece, 124, 168, 169; returned to throne, 170; second exile, 177; death, 183
Coolidge, Calvin, 199
Cristea, Patriarch Miron, 217, 226, 280
Cromwell, William Nelson, 201
Crowther, Miss (nurse), 252
Curzon, Lord, 158
Cust, Sir Charles, 157
Cuza, Alexander, 31
Cyril, Grand Duke of Russia, 59, 62, 77, 101, 136, 139, 143, 264
Czernin, Count Ottokar (Austrian minister), 119, 143; interview with Marie, 120

Daggett, Mabel Potter, 19, 171
Denney, Harold, 205, 206
Despina Doamna, Princess, 178
Disiscu, Madame, 180
Disraeli, 187
Dmitry, Grand Duke, murder of Rasputin, 135
Doletti, Jeanne Luci (see Jeanne, wife, Prince Nicolas)
Dollfuss, Chancellor Engelbert, assassinated, 255
Dubonik, General, 141
Duca, Jean, 95, 137, 171, 226, 248–249, 252; assassination, 249
Ducky (see Victoria Melita)
Dumaine, Jacques, 257, 258
Dumitrescu, Puiu, 233, 235, 245
Duse, Eleonora, 237

Edinburgh, Alfred, Duke of (see Alfred, Duke of Edinburgh)

Edward VII, 26, 77, as Prince of Wales, 6; favors George's marriage to Missy, 24; coronation, 71–72, 74;
Edward, Prince of Wales (David), 157–158
Edward VIII, 266–267
Edward, Prince (Eddy), 19, 23; death, 24
Eitel, Karl (see Carol I)
Elisabeth, Empress of Austria, 38
Elisabeth, Queen of Greece (Lisabetta), 57, 140, 141, 163, 176, 181, 184, 218, 230, 244, 280, 288; married to Crown Prince George of Greece, 167, 170; becomes Queen, 177
Elisabeth of Wied, Princess (see Carmen Sylva)
Elizabeth, Princess (later Queen Elizabeth II), 287
Ella, Grand Duchess Serge, 4, 13
Enescu, Georges, 121, 144
Eppinger, Professor Hans, 273, 275
Ernest, Duke of Saxe-Coburg-Gotha, 21–22, 43; death, 58
Ernest, Prince, Grand Duke of Hesse-Darmstadt, marriage to Ducky, 56; visit to Cotroceni, 61–62
Ernest, Prince of Hohenlohe-Langenburg, marriage to Sandra, 58–59

Falkenhayn, General Erich von, 125, 129; defeats Romanians, 129
Ferdinand, King of Romania (Nando), 24, 42, 43, 44, 45, 49, 51, 52, 58, 65, 67, 69, 70, 75–76, 78, 86, 106, 111, 113, 114, 116, 117, 127, 129, 131, 134, 138, 141, 143, 146, 149, 151, 153, 154, 163, 165, 166, 176, 189, 190, 191, 208, 213–214, 261, 283; proposal to Marie, 26; as heir-presumptive, 36–37; education under Carol I, 36–37; romance with Helene Vacarescu, 38–39; engagement to Marie, 40; wedding, 47–48; and coronation of Tsar Nicholas, 59; illness of, 65–66; and Astors, 75; and Prince Carol, 92, 101; and Schmidt, 96; accession, 108; proclaimed King, 112; and Carmen Sylva, 121; declares war on Austria, 123–124; denunciation by Wilhelm II, 124; and assassination plots, 141, 143; and armistice terms, 144; receives Marghiloman as Prime Minister, 145; and arrest of Bratianu, 148; dismissal of Marghiloman, 150; official tour, 167; coronation as King of Greater Romania, 178–179; death, 215–217; funeral, 218–219; codicil to will, 235
Filipescu, Nicu, 115
Foch, Marshal, 163, 179
Folliet, Miss (governess), 70, 93
Franz Ferdinand, Archduke, 103
Franz Joseph, Emperor, 49, 102, 103
Fräulein, 20–21
Frederick, Empress, 58, 61, 67; death, 71
Friedrich of Hohenzollern-Sigmaringen, 279
Fritsch, Dr. Alfred, 273, 274
Fuller, Loie, 194–195, 202, 205, 206–207

George V, King, 23, 24, 44, 70, 119, 157–158, 159, 213, 256; romance with Marie,

17–20; proposal to Marie, 24–26; marriage, 56; offer of refuge to Marie, 142; letter to Marie, 242–243; Silver Jubilee, 261; death, 263
George VI (Duke of York), 267
George II, King of Greece, 168, 181, 288; engaged to Lisabetta, 167; married, 170; becomes King, 177; exiled, 184
George Mikhailovich, Grand Duke, 24
Georgescu, Captain, 129
Georgin, Vlada, 257
Gracianu, Madame, 49
Green, Mary (nurse), 68, 92, 159, 184
Gunther, John, 175

Helen, Princess (Sitta), 168–169, 170, 171, 187–189, 218, 219, 222–223, 228–231, 232, 277; and Carol, 169, 170–171, 181–184, 234; exile, 238
Helene of Orleans, Princess, 23–24
Helferich, Fraülein, 20–21
Hill, Sam, 194–195, 205, 206–207
Hitler, 251, 266; Marie's opinion of, 255; invades Austria, 278; agreement with Carol, 286
Hohenzollern, Friedel, 98
Hoover, Herbert, 163

Ileana, Princess, 102, 128, 237–238, 130, 132, 140, 141, 147, 149, 154, 155, 157, 159, 162, 164, 166, 168, 170, 177, 189, 193, 196, 199, 203, 208, 218, 224–225, 235, 242, 249, 250, 254, 261, 263, 265, 268, 270, 272, 274, 275, 277–278, 281, 282, 288; birth, 89; fondness for Barbu Stirbey, 93; courtship and marriage, 236–238;
Irene, Princess, 168, 188

Jeanne (wife, Prince Nicolas), 259, 277; marriage, 241–242, exile, 272
Jonescu, Barbu, 220
Jorga, Nicolas, 272

Kalinderu, Ion, 91
Karl Anton, Prince, 27
Karl Eitel, Prince (see Carol I)
Karl, Prince, 28
Kent, Duke of, 282
Kerensky, 138; fall, 140

Lahovary, Simky, 177, 268
Lambrino, Jeanne Marie Valentine (Zizi), 173; affair with Prince Carol, 148, 149, 164, 166; death, 288
László, Sir Philip de, 263, 265
Lebrun, Albert, 258
Leopold, Prince, 36, 42, 43
Lexel of Pless, 225
Lisabetta (see Elisabeth, Queen of Greece)
Lloyd George, David, 153, 157, 159
Loti, Pierre, 39
Lupescu, Elena (Magda), 189, 197, 215, 252, 254, 263, 270, 285, 286, 288; and Carol's restoration, 228; return to Romania, 233–

234; influence of, 245–246; as Marie's enemy, 267; marriage to Carol, 287

Mackensen, Field Marshal August von, 119, 125, 127, 128, 129, 139, 140
Madge, Dr., 76, 77, 257
Mamulea, Dr., 96, 271, 272, 273, 274
Maniu, Juliu, 150, 166, 220, 226, 233; and Carol's return, 227–231; resignation, 234
Marghiloman, Alexander, 95, 115, 120, 124, 146; as Prime Minister, 145, 150
Marie, Queen of Romania (Missy), 61, 92, 106, 107, 112, 124, 138, 139, 145, 252, 254; ancestry, 3–4; childhood, 4–5, 9–14; and Romanov relatives, 13–14; girlhood at Malta, 15–20; romance with Prince George (later George V), 17–20; Ferdinand proposes, 26; meets Ferdinand's family, 42; meets King Carol I, 43; wedding, 47–48; in Bucharest, 50–53; birth of Prince Carol, 53–54; and King Carol, 55–56, 57; and Carmen Sylva, 56–57; birth of Elisabeth, 57; ill matched with Ferdinand, 58, 75–76; coronation of Tsar Nicholas, 59; love of riding, 59–60, 61; trip to Russia as turning point, 60; emergence into Romanian society, 63–65; romance with Cantacuzino, 66–68; birth of daughter Marie (Mignon), 70; friendship with Astors, 72–79; birth of Nicolas, 77; as society leader, 80–81; friendship with Barbu Stirbey, 84, 85–86, 88, 89; and Elise Bratianu, 86–87; and Buftea, 88–89; continued friendship with Nadeje Stirbey, 88–89; birth of Ileana, 89; birth of Mircea, 89; Carol as political confidant, 96, 97; view of Imperial Germany, 98–99; opposition to match of Prince Carol and Olga, 101; opinion of Carol, 104; and King Carol, 105; as pawn of Bratianu, 116–117; as pawn of Stirbey, 117; as negotiator, 118–119; interview with Von dem Busche, 119–120; interview with Czernin, 120; on joining Allies, 125; and Romanian reverses, 125; and hospital work, 125–126, 127; request for aid from Russia, 127; death of Mircea, 128–130; hazards of hospital work, 134–135; and Russian revolt, 135; appeal to America, 137; and Russian assassination plot, 141; and Romanian surrender, 142; and offer of refuge by George V, 142; and assassination plots, 141, 143; resistance to armistice terms, 144–146; and Joe Boyle, 146–148; concern for Prince Carol, 148, 149; homecoming, 150–151; as unofficial ambassador, 152–163; Clemenceau, 156; visits Paris, 154–157; opinion of Prince of Wales, 157–158; recognition as writer, 157; visits London, 157–159; revisits Paris, 159–163; and President Wilson, 160–162; and American aid, 163; official tour, 167; opinion of Mignon, 175–176; "Mother-in-Law of the Balkans," 164–177; coronation as Queen of Greater Romania, 178–179; as writer, 186–187, 223; and women's rights, 187; visits U.S., 193–209;

relationship with Helen, 232–234; and Carol, 231–235, 242, 244–245, 248; opinion of sons, 240–242; harassment by Carol, 253; opinion of Hitler, 255; and Versailles treaty, 255; and impending war, 255–256; visits England, 256–257; honored by Royal Literary Society, 260; persecution by Carol, 266; and abdication of Edward VIII, 267; relations with Carol, 269–271; illness, 271–280; interview with, 275; opinion of Carol, 275, 278; death, 280; funeral, 281–283; opinion of self, 283; last letter to her people, 284; burial of heart at Stella Maris, 284

Marie, Princess of Romania (Mignon), 70, 79, 140, 148, 157, 159, 163, 169, 170, 171, 184, 218, 225, 235, 242, 250–252, 254, 258, 266, 272, 273, 274, 278, 288; marriage to Alexander, 174–177; and birth of Peter, 184; widowed, 257

Marie Alexandrovna, Grand Duchess of Russia, 3, 5, 6, 8, 17, 41, 42, 46, 52, 57, 66, 101; marriage, 7; Victoria's objections to, 7–8; and her children, 9–10, 20–21; sent to Malta, 15; love of Coburg, 21–22; and proposed marriage of George and Missy, 24–26; approves Missy's engagement to Ferdinand, 41; attitude toward sex, 48; parting with Missy, 48–49; and birth of Prince Carol, 53–54; death, 169

Marie, Dowager Empress, 101, 121

Marie, Grand Duchess, 182

Marie-Ileana (Minola), 254

Marie Pavlovna, Grand Duchess, 101

Marina, Duchess of Kent, 168

Marlborough, Duchess of (Consuelo Vanderbilt), description of Marie, 73–74

Marr, Ida (governess, "Nimarr"), 170, 258

Martineau, Mrs., 171

Mary, Princess Royal, 157

Mary, Queen, 10, 157–158, 222, 256, 261; Marie's description, 185

May, Princess of Teck (later Queen Mary), 41; marriage, 56

Merz, Charles, 155, 187, 197

Michael, King of Romania, 174, 181, 218, 222, 229, 234, 259, 282, 287; king, 217; succession by Carol, 286–287

Michael, Grand Duke of Russia, 135

Michael the Brave, 29–30, 137, 178

Mignon (see Marie, Princess of Romania)

Mihalache (deputy), 228–229

Milne, Leila (governess), 152, 164, 170

Mircea, Prince of Romania, 89, 127–130, 137, 152, 265, 274

Mircea, son of Prince Carol and Zizi Lambrino, 166, 288

Missy (see Marie, Queen of Romania)

Morris, Ira Nelson, 203, 204

Mussolini, Benito, 237–238, 251, 266

Napoleon III, 31, 33

Neumann (servant), 65–66, 124

Nicholas II, Tsar, 14, 77, 98, 100, 119; accession, 57; coronation, 59; visits Romania, 102–103; and Triple Alliance, 104; request for aid by Marie, 127; abdication, 135; murder, 148

Nicolas, Prince of Romania (Nicky), 77, 102, 106–107, 128, 137, 140, 141, 159, 170, 196, 199, 217, 218–219, 226, 228, 229, 230, 232, 240, 259, 274, 277, 282, 288; marriage, 241–242; exile, 272

Nini (nurse), 112, 130, 131

Odobescu, Goe, 142

Olga, Grand Duchess of Russia, and Prince Carol, 100; refuses Carol, 102–103

Olga, Princess of Greece, 184

Orlando, Vittorio, 153

Paul, Prince, 184

Paul, Prince Regent, 282

Perticari, Helene, 98, 146

Peter I, King, 174, 177

Peter II, King, 184, 252, 257, 288

Philip of Flanders, 31

Pitcathly, Nana (nurse), 4, 11–12

Poincaré, Raymond, 157, 163

Ponsonby, Sir Henry, 8

Pope Leo XIII, 43

Precup, Major Vladimir, 228

Prezan, General, 139, 148

Proust, Marcel, 131

Pucci, Sister, 90, 91, 136

"Pumas" (Anton and Ileana), 254

Radu Negru, Prince (Rudolf the Black), 29

Rasputin, 100, 101; murder, 135

Rastrelli, 5

Romalo, Dr., 96, 141

Rothermere, Lord, 220

Saint-Aulaire, 134

Saratzeanu (regent), 226

Sazanov (foreign minister), 101, 102

Scalavi, Alexander, 244

Schmidt Herr (tutor), 93–95, 96, 222

Seton-Watson, R. W., 82

Sherwood, Robert, 208

Simpson, Wallis, 266, 267

Small, Lavinia, 223, 244, 248, 272

Sophie, Queen, 168, 169, 174, 183, 189

Stalin, Joseph, 284

Stefan, 254; birth, 243

Steinbach (servant), 131, 146

Stirbey, Prince Barbu, 81, 84, 85, 87–89, 91, 108, 124, 127, 132, 134, 135, 138, 141, 142, 145, 171, 177, 180, 182, 216, 223; with Marie, 83–86, 89, 117; Prince Carol's jealousy, 93, 95; and fall of Kerensky, 140; exiled, 233; death, 287

Stirbey, Princess Elise, 95

Stirbey, Princess Nadèje, 77, 81, 83, 84, 86, 88–89, 180

Störmer, Dr., 279, 281

Sylva, Carmen (Princess Elisabeth of Wied), 38–39, 46, 61, 66, 70, 87, 92, 96, 102, 105, 106, 107, 167, 172, 222; marries Carol I, 34;

birth and death of daughter, 34; role in Ferdinand's romance, 38–39; return from exile, 56–57; scandal-monger, 67–68; at Carol's deathbed, 111; death, 120–121

Titulescu (foreign minister), 255
Tisza (Hungarian Prime Minister), 119
Tomislav, 252

Vacarescu, Helene, 38–40, 64
Vacarescu, Radu, 64–65
Vacarescu, Theodore, 64
Vaida-Voeved, Alexander, 166
Vanderbilt, Consuelo (see Marlborough, Duchess of)
Venizelos (Greek Prime Minister), 168
Victoria, Queen, 9, 15, 58, 89; and Marie Alexandrovna, 6–8; at Windsor, 12; urges George V to marry, 23–24; favors George's marriage to Missy, 24, 26, 27; and Marie's engagement to Ferdinand, 40; sends English doctor, 53–54; as intermediary in Marie and Cantacuzino scandal, 68; death, 71
Victoria Melita, Princess of Coburg (Ducky), 4, 10, 16, 23, 24, 28–29, 41, 46, 52, 53, 61–62, 66, 235, 262; marriage, 56; divorce and death of daughter, 77; married, 101; and deprivation under Kerensky, 138; leaves Russia, 143; death, 264–265
Volpicka, Charles J., 115, 121
Vyshinsky, 287

Walker, James J., 198
Warnerkroze, Prof., 270, 281
Washburn, Major Stanley (war correspondent), 127, 203, 204, 206–207
Wied, Princess of, 46
Wilhelm II, Kaiser, 24, 26, 41, 47, 77, 99, 266; on Marie, 118; denunciation of Ferdinand, 124; flight, 150
Wilson, Edith Bolling, 161–162
Wilson, Woodrow, 153; and Marie, 160–162
Wittegenstein, Prince, 59
Woolf, Virginia, 256

York, Duke of (George VI), 179, 184

Zwiedineck, General, 250, 258, 262, 270, 274, 276–277, 282, 284, 288; love for Marie, 243–244

16 10